This

THE FIRST INDUSTRIAL REGION

Published in our
centenary year
≈ 2004 ∽
MANCHESTER
UNIVERSITY
PRESS

To my parents

The first
industrial region

North-west England, c.1700–60

JON STOBART

MANCHESTER UNIVERSITY PRESS
Manchester and New York

distributed exclusively in the USA by Palgrave

Copyright © Jon Stobart 2004

The right of Jon Stobart to be identified as the author of this work has been asserted by him in accordance with the Copyright, Designs and Patents Act 1988.

Published by Manchester University Press
Oxford Road, Manchester M13 9NR, UK
and Room 400, 175 Fifth Avenue, New York, NY 10010, USA
www.manchesteruniversitypress.co.uk

Distributed exclusively in the USA by
Palgrave, 175 Fifth Avenue, New York, NY 10010, USA

Distributed exclusively in Canada by
UBC Press, University of British Columbia, 2029 West Mall,
Vancouver, BC, Canada V6T 1Z2

British Library Cataloguing-in-Publication Data
A catalogue record for this book is available from the British Library

Library of Congress Cataloging-in-Publication Data applied for

ISBN   0 7190 6462 7   *hardback*

First published 2004

11   10   09   08   07   06   05   04   03   10   9   8   7   6   5   4   3   2   1

Typeset in Sabon
by Carnegie Publishing, Lancaster
Printed in Great Britain
by Bell & Bain Ltd, Glasgow

Contents

Figures

Tables

ix

Acknowledgements

Many people need to be thanked for helping me complete the research for and writing of this book. The staff in Cheshire and Chester Archives and Lancashire County Record Office were very patient in fetching thousands of probate records over a number of years – those itemised in the bibliography are the tip of a much bigger iceberg. Sections of the book have been given as seminar or conference papers and the constructive comments of participants helped to focus my ideas and correct my errors. A number of colleagues have kindly read draft chapters and my thanks go especially to Phil Dunham, Steve King and Alastair Owens. The excellent maps are the work of Stuart Gill and the quality of the final text owes much to the efforts of the staff at Manchester University Press, especially Sue Womersley. Finally, I would like to thank Jack Langton for introducing me to historical research and for his generous help and support over the years.

I

Introduction: shifting the economic development agenda

If Mrs Critchlow had been a philosopher, if she had known that geography had always made history, she would have given up her enterprise long ago.[1]

Britain's industrial revolution is popularly seen as a watershed in the transition to a modern industrial society. The abiding images are of steam engines and coal mines, of huge factories and machines; of Coketown, peopled by grey Lowryesque figures shuffling through dirty, polluted streets. In this picture, industrialisation occurred in the few decades either side of the turn of the nineteenth century and was driven by technological change and the creation of a massive new factory workforce. Sellar and Yeatman's caricature of the 'Industrial Revelation' as the discovery 'that women and children could work for twenty-five hours a day in factories without many of them dying or becoming excessively deformed' and that it 'would never have occurred but for the wave of great mechanical Inventors' contains just enough truth to be meaningful and ironic.[2]

Of course, professional historians know that this is all far too simplistic and that industrialisation was a long-drawn-out process with deep historical roots.[3] It was gradual and evolutionary – qualities which make it fit in with notions of natural progress.[4] It was, moreover, marked by strong continuities with earlier industrial or proto-industrial development and by slow and uneven growth in output and productivity.[5] In short, the industrial revolution was a time when 'less happened, less dramatically than was once thought'.[6] Indeed, this gradualist perspective has been reinforced by econometric analyses which dethrone the industrial revolution so completely that 'Hamlet is often performed without the Prince of Denmark'.[7] On top of this have come notions of dual economies which counterpoise a small technologically dynamic and progressive sector with a much larger 'laggard' traditional sector or, in Wrigley's terms, a mineral-based energy economy with one which was organic-based.[8] From these, it would seem to follow naturally that 'much of England in 1850 was not very strikingly different from that of 1750'.[9] But this misses the importance of geography as a cause as well as a consequence of historical change and highlights the way in which the theorising of the industrial revolution has suffered from over-historicisation and under-spatialisation.[10]

Although stability and continuity may have characterised many areas in the years of the industrial revolution, others underwent profound transformations. Even if the division between traditional and modern is accepted, and this is a notion strongly contested by Berg and Hudson in particular,[11] 'modern' industries were closely concentrated into particular parts of England, notably the north west, west Yorkshire, Midlands and south Wales.[12] This meant that these places at least experienced dramatic economic, social and spatial changes. Moreover, because of the strong links between modern and traditional industries, change was certainly more general than Musson implies not least as it 'spilled out' of the modernising areas. Even in the early eighteenth century, Defoe noted that 'New discoveries in metals, mines and minerals, new undertakings in trade, engines, manufactures … make England especially show a new and differing face in many places'.[13] And change through time was matched by contrasts over space. As Gregory argues, it is impossible to read Defoe's *Tour* without being struck by the 'profound regionalisation' of the country as certain trades or industries became so strongly associated with particular places that they were inseparable in economic terms and in the popular mind.[14] Thus we see the woollen industry in west Yorkshire and the West Country, cotton around Manchester, ironworking in the west Midlands and Sheffield, frame-work-knitting in rural Leicestershire and Nottinghamshire and earthenware manufacture in the Potteries.

Recognising the importance of the region is not to dethrone the industrial revolution, therefore, but rather serves to highlight the truly revolutionary nature of economic change during this period. Regional specialisations were well established by the early eighteenth century and were all the more remarkable because such 'marked geographical concentration of whole sectors of production had never been experienced before'.[15] They were also enduring and did much to shape the subsequent economic development of the country, becoming the cornerstones of Britain's world dominance of manufacturing in the middle decades of the nineteenth century. These industrial regions experienced the type of positive-feedback economies which underlie arguments for what we might call spatial path-dependence.[16] On the basis of initial advantages, additional benefits accrued which focused subsequent growth into the same areas: pools of skilled labour were formed, agglomerations of subsidiary trades appeared and a nexus of information flows focused onto these regions.[17] Economic change had a clear and important spatial dimension. Moreover, as the economic and commercial characteristics of different regions grew increasingly varied, the social experiences based on them also became more diverse. Regions developed distinctive culture or *mentalites* and they became social and cultural as well as physical, administrative and economic entities.[18] The regions of eighteenth-century England were not the organic *pays* envisaged by Vidal de la Blache: rather than being territorially bound and inward-looking, they were dynamic and defined by their relationship with other places as much as their internal characteristics.[19] The space economy of eighteenth-century England was thus marked by growing uniformity of character within regions and increasing fragmentation between them. Regions were much more than 'convenient box[es] into which masses of descriptive material is stuffed'.[20] They represented the spatial and functional scale at which many aspects of life operated in pre- and early-industrial England: they were the reality for most people and businesses.[21]

If regions command our attention because they were becoming increasingly differentiated from one another in terms of their economic and social character, then the inter- and intra-regional links which facilitated this specialisation must also be central to any spatially informed analysis of regional and national development. A growing awareness of the importance of this inter-connectedness lies behind arguments about contemporary globlisation and needs to inform historical analyses as well.[22] In the eighteenth century, spatial integration was effected primarily through transport systems, credit networks, trade and innumerable links between individuals. Innovations in transport networks, such as turnpikes, navigations and canals, and improvements in the services which ran along them – stage coaches, commercial carriers and the like – served to draw together both regional and national economies. The goods, people, capital and information which they carried were the lifeblood of economic growth and social and cultural development.[23] Indeed, particularly following Giddens, information has been increasingly emphasised in studies of modernisation.[24] Credit systems, meanwhile, provided capital for investment and helped to lubricate the flow of trade within regions and across the country,[25] stimulating growth and linking it to national and international economies. At one level trade meant mercantile activity in the great ports of Bristol, Liverpool, Newcastle, Hull and London which linked local production to overseas markets. Hull, for example, acted as the export centre for the Yorkshire woollen industry, minerals from the east Midlands and agricultural produce from across northern England as well as conducting extensive trade with much of Europe.[26] Trade also meant retailing and, as McKendrick argues, 'the prosperity of Lancashire cotton manufacturers, London brewers, Sheffield cutlers, Staffordshire potters, the toy makers of Birmingham – and the fortunes of the woollen, linen and silk industries – were based on sales to a mass market'.[27] This market was reached through the hundreds of retail markets and thousands of shops up and down the country, but was increasingly influenced by an emerging consumer society focused on London and the resort and leisure towns.[28]

Through transport, credit systems and trade, national and regional development was intimately tied to the service sector and its ability to both integrate
supplies and demands, and link spatially distinct production centres. In short,
geography mattered: it impacted upon the timing, pace and nature of growth.[29]
Just as 'new regional geographies' recognise the importance of the locality and
region in structuring then present-day economy and society, there is a growing
acknowledgement of their role in shaping historical development.[30] Indeed, it
is increasingly argued that economies past and present can only be understood
at a national or international level through regional analyses.[31] It is remarkable,
then, that most studies of economic development and especially the industrial
revolution tend to adopt 'spaceless models and the acceptance of containers
like nation-states as unproblematic definitions of economies'.[32] Those which
do adopt an explicitly regional approach often fail to provide a systematic
analysis of the spatial dimension of British economic development or do so in
the context of late eighteenth- and nineteenth-century industrialisation.[33] Given
the deep roots of industrial and urban growth, there is a clear need to explore
the geography of these processes in the early eighteenth century, not least
because this had a great bearing on subsequent processes and patterns of
development. In a sense, we have many of the pieces of the jigsaw and a pretty
good idea of what the final picture might look like, but seem reluctant to
explore what has shaped the individual pieces and, more importantly, how
they might be fitted together.

The aim of this book is not to piece together such a large puzzle, but to
explore some of the themes and approaches which could make such a task
possible and meaningful. This involves five closely related objectives. The first
is to explore the importance of early eighteenth-century processes of regional
formation and spatial integration and set these alongside later developments
in regionalisation established by Hudson and others. To achieve this, attention
is centred on north-west England in the period immediately preceding the
classic industrial revolution. Whilst it is possible to argue for both longer and
shorter temporal frameworks, the first half of the eighteenth century stands
out as it saw the establishment in the region of the developmental and spatial
matrix upon which subsequent factory-based industrialisation took place.[34]
Rather than simply telling the story of economic development in north-west
England – vitally important as it is to British industrialisation – the purpose
here is to respond positively to Hudson's call for theoretically-informed analyses of regional history.[35] The second objective, then, is to offer an integrated
analysis that seeks to link the detailed empirical evidence of local and regional
development with broader theoretical, historical and geographical concepts
and debates. This gives wider relevance and meaning to the former and
provides evidence with which to explore and test the latter. Third, the north

west is not treated as a case apart; rather, it is used as a methodological and historical exemplar. This approach offers new insights into processes of industrial and urban change, whilst the development seen in the region illustrates a range of processes shaping the national space economy. The north west, like the country as a whole, was marked by economic diversity and local specialisation, and its trade and transport systems developed rapidly in the eighteenth century to produce an internally and internationally integrated economy. The integration of social and spatial divisions of labour was central to regional formation and economic development during this period. These processes form the key themes of the book as a whole, since a better understanding of economic specialisation and spatial integration in one of the heartlands of the industrial revolution will shed welcome light on the nature of national economic development during the early stages of industrialisation. The fourth objective, then, is to explore thoroughly the relationship between specialisation and integration in a variety of key sectors and in the regional economy as a whole. This involves analysis of industrial location and the spatial structure of the regional economy. Within this, the role of the urban system is seen as being central: it helped to structure spatial divisions of labour and articulated internal and external spatial integration. The final objective is to build on this and provide a rounded picture of development in north-west England where industrial, trading, servicing and commercial leisure activities are treated as part of an holistic regional economy. Such an approach demands investigation of local development and the painting of a broader economic, social and cultural context.

To explore these themes, this book is loosely structured into three parts. The first establishes a clear and robust conceptual framework and a broad spatial and temporal context for the analysis. Chapter 2 introduces a range of theoretical perspectives on regional economic development, but argues that all tend to obscure the complexity of causal, operational and geographical aspects of industrialisation. In particular, they underplay the role of towns as key arenas for the production, distribution and consumption of goods, and as locations for the integrating functions which shaped and generated economic development. Only through the use of geographical models which link urban and regional structuring can we forge a new approach to development, one that recognises the mutually formative links between the urban system and the geography and growth of the regional economy. As a counterpoint to this theoretical basis for analysis, Chapter 3 explores economic development in the north west and in England as a whole as a spatially uneven process. Emphasis is placed on the close parallels that existed between region and nation in terms of geographical specialisation, the role of urban functions in integrating spatial divisions of labour and the shifting relationships between core and peripheral areas. North-west England is thus seen as an exemplar and instigator of wider processes of development.

The second part of the book explores three important sets of industries in greater detail, highlighting their growth and distribution, but also the ways in which local and regional specialisms were able to prosper through different systems of spatial integration. Chapter 4 focuses on textile industries as an example of advanced organic and proto-industrial development. Both concepts are critically appraised, especially in the light of the central role played by towns in the organisation and production as well as the finishing and marketing of cloth. It is argued that the dynamism and close integration of the hierarchically structured urban system in these textiles areas (focusing on Manchester as the principal export point) was vital in determining the pace and geography of growth in these industries. The differentiated nature of Britain's industrial regions is reflected in the development of an increasingly sophisticated mineral-based energy economy parallel to this organic textiles economy. Chapter 5 questions the overriding importance of resources as a locational constant in the development of these mineral industries. Rather, they displayed strong and often highly localised concentration, suggesting a measure of specialisation growth in addition to the more generally recognised 'power-growth' of centralised production in factories. The areal and hierarchical relationships of the textiles economy were replaced by point–point interaction between spatially discontiguous specialist centres. In Chapter 6, the perspective broadens to encompass a range of service industries. The growth-inducing potential of the tertiary sector is seen in the specialised and dynamic nature of urban service activities. They often formed important links with economic changes on the national or international stage or constituted the essential character of the urban economy, either in terms of long-distance trade or leisure activities. Service functions were also central to the integration of the regional economy. As such, the spatial and hierarchical structure of service provision (and the urban system more generally) was crucial in shaping the regional space economy. Liverpool, Manchester and Chester dominated service provision and so formed key locational constants around which a changing and growing urban system and regional economy was shaped. Interstitial secondary centres were defined by specialist trading functions as well as a quintessentially urban servicing role, suggesting the coexistence of hierarchical and point–point lines of spatial integration.

These processes of broader regional integration are brought into sharper focus in the final part of the book. Attention centres on the ways in which spatial interaction and integration both shaped and were shaped by the urban and transport systems. In Chapter 7, it is argued that, although transport is often seen as critical in shaping the overall structure of the urban system and in determining the potential for local, regional and national development, it was often responsive to rather than an initial stimulus of wider growth. Analysis of market areas, debt patterns, individual contact patterns and so on reveals a complex interaction system centred on Liverpool, Manchester and Chester. These were, in effect, gateway cities, drawing together the region and linking it to wider economic, social and cultural systems in the country as a whole. Here, and throughout the book, the analysis reveals the ways in which specialisation and integration were mutually formative processes which shaped regional development in the early eighteenth century and throughout the industrial revolution.

Notes

1 Bennett, *Old Wives' Tale*, p. 503.

2 Sellar and Yeatman, *1066 and All That*, pp. 100–1.

3 This scepticism began with Heaton, 'Industrial Revolution' and Clapham, *Economic History*. It was confirmed by Deane and Cole, *British Economic Growth*, and, more recently, Crafts, *British Economic Growth*.

4 David, 'Historical economics in the long-run', pp. 34–5.

5 Unwin, *Industrial Organisation*; Carus-Wilson, 'Industrial revolution'; Mendels, 'Proto-industrialization'; Crafts, *British Economic Growth*; Harley, 'British industrialisation'; Jackson, 'Economic growth'.

6 Cannadine, 'British history', p. 183.

7 Wrigley, *Continuity*, p. 2. Such studies include Lindert, 'English Occupations'; Feinstein and Pollard, *Studies in Capital Formation*; Harley, 'British industrialisation'. For critiques of this approach, see Berg and Hudson, 'Rehabilitating'; Greasley and Oxley, 'Rehabilitation sustained'.

8 See, for example: Mokyr, 'Industrial revolution'; Wrigley, *Continuity*.

9 Musson, *Growth of British Industry*, p. 149.

10 Soja, *Postmodern Geographies*, pp. 56–60, argues that this problem has characterised much theory.

11 Berg and Hudson, 'Rehabilitating'; Berg, *Age of Manufactures*, pp. 13–33.

12 Gregory, 'Geographies of industrialization', p. 352.

13 Defoe, *Tour through Britain*, quoted in Gregory, 'Geographies of industrialization', p. 351.

14 Gregory, 'Geographies of industrialization', p. 372.

15 Hudson, *Industrial Revolution*, p. 102.

16 Krugman, *Geography and Trade*. A broader view of path-dependence is found in Arthur, 'Competing technologies'. For a critique, see Leibowitz and Margolis, 'Path dependence'.

17 Krugman, *Geography and Trade*, pp. 36–54.

18 Langton, 'Industrial revolution'. For critiques of this thesis, see Freeman, 'Industrial revolution' and Gregory, 'The production of regions'.

19 Vidal de la Blache, *Principles of Human Geography*. For a review of recent conceptualisations of the region, see Stobart, 'Regions, localities and industrialisation', pp. 1,305–9.

20 Hudson, 'The regional perspective', p. 30.

21 Everitt, 'Country, county and town'.

22 See, *inter alia*, Knox and Agnew, *Geography of the World Economy*, especially chapters 6 and 7; Ogborn, 'Historical geographies of modernisation'; Daniels, 'Geography of the economy'.

23 Thrift, 'Transport and communication', pp. 458–9; Brayshay, Harrison and Chalkley, 'Knowledge, nationhood and governance'.

24 See Ogborn, *Spaces of Modernity*, pp. 17–22. See also Giddens, *Consequences of Modernity*.

25 Gregory, 'Geographies of industrialization', pp. 379–80; Zell, 'Credit in the woollen industry'.

26 Defoe, *Tour through Britain*, pp. 528–9.

27 McKendrick, 'Consumer revolution', p. 21.

28 Wrigley, 'London's importance'; Langford, *Polite and Commercial People*, pp. 59–122; Borsay, *Urban Renaissance, passim*; McInnes, 'Emergence of a leisure town'; Cox, *Complete Tradesman*, pp. 38–75.

29 See Scott and Storper, *Production, work, territory*; Dunford, *Regional Development*.

30 For analyses of present-day economic geographies, see Massey, *Spatial Divisions of Labour*; Storper, *Regional World*; Allen, Massey and Cochrane, *Rethinking the Region*; Scott, *Regions and the World Economy*. Key historical analyses include: Langton and Morris, *Atlas of Industrializing Britain*; Hudson, *Regions and Industries*; Gregory 'Geographies of industrialization'; Hudson, 'Regional and local history'.

31 Hudson, 'The regional perspective'; Krugman, *Geography and Trade*; Pollard, 'Economic development'.

32 Lee, 'Making Europe', p. 328.

33 Many of the chapters in Hudson, *Regions and Industries*, fall into the former category, whilst Gregory's 'Geographies of industrialization' tends to emphasise later periods, despite drawing its influence from Defoe's observations.

34 Stobart, 'Geography and industrialization'. The nature of the source material and the methodology adopted determine the precise dates for much of the analysis. Only from 1701 do the published indexes of wills record occupations in sufficient numbers to undertake the type of systematic, region-wide analysis attempted here (see Appendix 2). After 1760, listings of individual occupations and activities become increasingly inadequate as a marker of more general economic and social processes (see Chapter 3). That said, as somebody might die in their economic prime or long after they have ceased to be economically active, probate records reflect activities in the *circa* twenty-year period leading up to the date of death. This makes the study period effectively and approximately 1680–1760.

35 Hudson, 'The regional perspective', p. 18.

2

Economic development and the urban system

> The increase and riches of commercial and manufacturing towns, contributed to the improvement and cultivation of the countries to which they belonged ... they afforded a market for some part either of their rude or manufactured produce, and consequently gave some encouragement to the industry and improvement of all.[1]

When we remove ourselves from the rarefied atmosphere of econometric studies, we find that much of our present understanding of early industrialisation is derived from the work of classical economists of the eighteenth century, especially Adam Smith.[2] He argued that increased agricultural production and productivity provided the essential basis of sustainable urban and industrial growth. Agricultural surpluses were linked to urban markets, manufactures and services such that the 'natural progress' of economic development was from agriculture to manufacturing to overseas trade.[3] This type of development, Smith argued, was seen in the growing manufacturing areas of the Midlands and north of England where rural industries arose from regional agricultural surpluses. 'In this manner have grown up naturally, and as it were of their own accord, the manufactures of Leeds, Halifax, Sheffield, Birmingham and Wolverhampton. Such manufactures are the offspring of agriculture.'[4] In contrast, much European development reversed the relationship by 'planting' luxury manufacturing using imported raw materials. The result was 'the exploitation of the countryside by the town' and an industrial sector rendered unstable by the absence of a 'natural' agricultural underpinning.[5] Smithian development was quintessentially regional in its focus and operation. It was also organic in both character and resource base: agriculture and most early eighteenth-century industries were heavily dependent upon the land as a source of raw materials and energy.[6]

Whilst the fixed supply of land would limit growth in an organic economy, usually to a level some way below what was ecologically possible,[7] growth was still possible through increasing inputs of labour and capital or through a greater degree of specialisation bringing improved efficiency. The latter is often seen in terms of the social division of labour, but also occurred at a larger scale through the emergence of specialised industrial regions – effectively a broad spatial division of labour. The former generated increased agricultural production and efficiency and, it is argued, provided a vital foothold for the eighteenth-century growth of manufacturing industry.[8] This was effected via a number of channels. Alongside rising agricultural incomes came the growing market penetration of regional, local and family economies, particularly as women became increasingly engaged in wage-labour, which led to the commercialisation of rural as well as urban households.[9] Rural production and consumption both became increasingly market-oriented; in turn, this stimulated demand for the consumer goods and services of the towns, and formed a vital part of what de Vries has termed an 'industrious revolution'.[10] Both rural and urban commercialisation and industrialisation thus served to reinforce each other and generate sustained regional development.

Notwithstanding this, the key link between agricultural and industrial growth is often seen as the release of labour. This undoubtedly occurred at the aggregate level: rising productivity per unit of labour meant that the proportion of the workforce engaged in agriculture fell steadily while output continued to rise.[11] The obvious corollary of this is that progressively higher proportions of the population were engaged in non-agricultural occupations.[12] However, neither collectively nor individually did this necessarily mean industrial employment: growth in personal services, petty retailing and so on matched the expansion in manufacturing, and rural unemployment was widespread.[13] There is little evidence of widespread migration of 'surplus' labour from the commercialising agricultural areas of eastern and southern England to the burgeoning industrial areas of the Midlands and north. Quite apart from a mismatching of skills and strong sociocultural resistance to industry, migration was discouraged by the Settlement Laws and a poor relief system which was often operated to retain male labour on the land during slack seasons, ensuring an adequate harvest-time workforce.[14] Most of the labour 'freed' by agricultural improvement appears to have remained in the villages, supplementing family income by working in various by-employments which drew on female and slack-season labour. Hence we see the growth of lace-making, basket-weaving and straw-plaiting in several southern counties of England. However, these 'usually failed to achieve the firm base necessary for long-term success', perhaps as a result of comparative advantage which, Jones argues, produced specialist agricultural and industrial regions in the eighteenth and early nineteenth centuries.[15]

Theorising industrial change

Such arguments are integral to theories of proto-industrialisation which link commercial agricultural regions to those 'marked by the rapid growth of traditionally organised but market oriented, principally rural industry'.[16] Proto-industrial growth is generally seen as having been stimulated by the necessity for supplementary income due to under-employment on the land. As Jones and Mendels have both argued, this could arise from comparative advantage. Whilst agricultural improvement brought benefits to the light soil areas of southern and eastern England, for instance, the presence of heavier clay soils encouraged conversion to pastoral farming, especially in the Midlands. In turn, this created large numbers of seasonally and diurnally under- and unemployed people who looked to supplement their income and fill their time by turning to traditional rural handicrafts.[17] Thirsk and more recently Ogilvie have played down notions of comparative advantage, emphasising instead the importance of social institutions: rural industry was most likely to emerge where freeholds and tenants had strong property rights or where partible inheritance produced fragmented landholdings.[18] Proto-industries also emerged in areas of commercial arable farming where they grew in response to seasonal unemployment and, more specifically, female requirements for work as women became ever more marginalised from agriculture.[19]

These varied preconditions complicated the simple shift from independence to dependence seen by Kriedte, Medick and Schlumbohm as the inevitable result of capitalists gaining increasing control of the means of production.[20] The sequencing of the *Kaufsystem* of artisan or workshop production being gradually superseded by the *Verlagssystem* of putting-out, has more recently been rejected in favour of a multiplicity of coexisting and often competing systems. Putting-out dominated in the cotton trades of Lancashire, woollen production in the West Country and Yorkshire worsted industries as well as nail-making in south Yorkshire and the Black Country. In contrast, independent artisans remained central to the manufacture of woollens in Yorkshire well into the nineteenth century and the 'flexible specialisation' of the west Midlands metalworking trades was crucial in their eighteenth- and nineteenth-century growth.[21]

The diverse nature of proto-industrial regions was reflected in the marked variability of their subsequent development. Far from seeing it as a vital link between agriculture and 'full' industrialisation, most studies of proto-industrialisation in Britain have questioned its value and usefulness.[22] Coleman demonstrated that, of ten regions identified as 'runners in the proto-industrialization stakes', only Lancashire, west Yorkshire, the Vale of Trent and the west Midlands went on to experience industrialisation.[23] To these we might want to add the Ulster linen industries and various cloth-producing areas of Scotland.[24] Many others 'failed' and experienced de-industrialisation – for example, Essex, the West Country and East Anglia. In itself, this is unremarkable: Mendels himself stressed that 'whereas proto-industrialization preceded factory industrialization ... there was nothing unavoidable or automatic in the passage from phase one to the next'.[25] That said, the reasons for 'success' and 'failure' say much about the theory in general. Ultimately, the problem with proto-industrialisation as an economic theory has much to do with its implicit historicity and disregard of geography and particularity of regions. Its concerns are with change through time rather than the contrasts over space which had so struck Defoe in his tour. Variations in the social and institutional environment were important influences on the availability of capital; the level of regulation and competition; the type and flexibility of labour skills; and the development of diverse and complementary manufactures.[26] For Coleman, though, it was the geography of resource availability – specifically the presence of coal and iron – which was critical in determining the full industrialisation of a region. Development in areas without a tradition of proto-industrial manufacturing, notably south Wales and north-east England, served to underline his argument. The latter possessed a dynamic mineral economy based on local coal resources and the strong external ties of Newcastle, whilst the coal-based industry of the former 'suddenly emerged' in the late eighteenth century.[27] As Wrigley argues, it was the switch from an advanced organic to a mineral-based energy economy which held the key to sustained and accelerating economic growth in the eighteenth and nineteenth centuries.[28]

In Wrigley's conceptualisation of industrialisation, growth in an organic economy was ultimately limited by its dependence on land as a source of raw materials and energy. Proto-industries in their various forms were essentially extending or expanding production within this framework. Gains could be made through specialisation (individual or regional) and by increasing inputs of capital (through the putting-out system or through mortgages and loans to artisans), but most growth would be achieved by augmenting labour inputs. Within these labour-using industries, better technology allowed some additional productivity gains.[29] However, any concerted attempt to increase production year on year was likely to end in an energy crisis of the kind identified by Nef and Clapham in the seventeenth and eighteenth centuries.[30] In what can be seen as an overly deterministic argument, Wrigley suggests that by tapping into inorganic stocks of energy and thus reducing pressure on the land, a mineral-based energy economy released production from the limiting factor of land. Coal reserves dwarfed what it was practicable to produce from the land. Utilising them 'on a steadily increasing scale produced much the same effect as would have resulted from the addition of millions of acres of cultivable land to the landscape of England'.[31] For Wrigley, it was access to this coal and the increasing ability to use it as a source of energy and power in a wide variety of industrial processes which formed the key to industrialisation.[32] In particular, steam engines 'made possible the vast increase in individual productivity which was so striking a feature of the industrial revolution'.[33] Coal-powered machinery is therefore central to Wrigley's view of economic change as power growth in the mineral energy economy replaced the specialisation growth of organic economies.

Such arguments are persuasive, but are questionable in both developmental and spatial terms. It is easy to overlook the importance of increasing divisions of labour within and outside the steam-powered factory system. Equally, the changing geography of production associated with coal and steam power, whilst prominent at the local scale, can be overplayed at the regional level. In geographical terms, Wrigley argues that the organic economy, with its dependence on land, was essentially areal and diffuse, and most of its raw materials were locally available if in only limited quantities.[34] Economic growth was, in terms of natural resources at least, viable in most regions. As the mineral economy grew, however, development became ever more concentrated into areas with access to the 'new' raw materials so that coalfields or areas linked to them experienced most growth.[35] Such spatial concentration was reinforced by the development of bulk transport systems (principally canals) which made regional economies more cohesive and focused growth into these areas of cheap coal.[36] According to such arguments, the lack of (access to) coal would explain regional de-industrialisation as comparative advantage privileged growth in mineral-rich areas. However, 'the eclipse or success of many proto-industrial regions had mostly been assured before coal became a major locational influence as a source of power and had been precipitated by quite different factors' including social, political and cultural institutions, availability of capital and labour, and economic diversity.[37] Conversely, the presence of coal was not an assurance of general economic growth: development in south Wales failed to expand beyond coal and iron and into the engineering, chemicals and shipbuilding of the north east, and in north Wales coal production was unable to stimulate large-scale industrialisation of any sort.[38]

In themselves, then, Wrigley's arguments of an emerging mineral-energy economy seem insufficient as a basis for understanding the changing space economy of Britain in the industrial revolution. Coal may have been necessary to carry proto-industrial or even non-industrial regions into 'full' industrialisation, but was not sufficient in itself either to ensure this transition took place or to explain its geographical constitution.[39] As Krugman says of industrialisation in the United States, 'few would argue that natural resources explain more than a fraction of the observed unevenness of economic activity across space'.[40] Such natural determinism must be tempered by consideration of both sociocultural factors and the historio-geographical development of economies. Work by Ogilvie, Berg and Muldrew highlights the ways in which social institutions could influence access to resources, labour discipline, attitudes to entrepreneurship and credit networks.[41] It also echoes the recent 'cultural turn' in geography, a trend which, *inter alia*, emphasises that the economic is irretrievably embedded in the cultural and that cultural activities have a particular economic geography.[42] This broadening of perspective places individuals and localities within social and cultural as well as economic contexts. An important spatial context is provided by Massey's theorisation of space economy structured by 'layers of investment' laid down during previous production and consumption regimes.[43] In essence, she argues that present patterns of production and investment are shaped by an already established economic landscape. Following this argument, it is clear why the preceding traditions of craft and proto-industrial production were important in shaping the geographies of eighteenth- and early nineteenth-century industrialisation. So too were processes of spatial integration affected by expanding credit, information, transport and trading systems.[44] Ultimately, Pollard argues, sustained development was contingent on the establishment of a critical mass of inter-dependent industries, service trades, infrastructures and communications.[45] According to Myrdal, processes of cumulative causation would concentrate these into favoured locations and cemented them there through the creation of pools of skilled labour, the concentration of information flows and the agglomeration of subsidiary trades. Conversely, economically marginal areas experienced a downward spiral as labour, capital, innovation and entrepreneurship shifted into more dynamic localities.[46] The space economy is thus divided into core and peripheral areas which are functionally, spatially and hierarchically related to one another. For Krugman, though, cumulative causation involves secondary causal factors. They merely reinforce initial localisations which, he argues, were themselves 'historical accidents'.[47] Chance is an often under-emphasised factor in historical processes, but its emphasis here is unsatisfactory and illogical. It is difficult to see why geographical specialisms should originate by chance and then be cemented in space by consistently operating forces. More importantly, individuals and processes are located firmly within economic, social, cultural and spatial contexts which inform and mould their motivations, decisions and actions, and structure their operation.

The solution is often to look for certain 'constants' in the developing space economy. Amidst a vast array of location factors, Richardson identifies three such 'locational constants': resource sites, transport nodes and towns. These drew together the regional space and stimulated growth within it.[48] However, in early industrial development the 'constancy' of the first two of these is open to question: the nature of the resource base was changing through this period from organic to mineral-based and, since these two systems were expressed in entirely different patterns, the transport network also changed. In an organic economy, production and consumption are areal and diffuse. Many production locations are linked to an equally large number of consumption points by a dispersed transport network. In early-modern England, manufactured and agricultural goods were transported to numerous markets by a network of roads that was extensive, dense, and relatively lightly used.[49] A mineral-based economy, by contrast, depends on the mass and punctiform production of extremely heavy minerals and therefore requires a very different type of transport system. If coal were to be adopted, it had to be cheaply available to industry, and so a new transport network was essential; one designed to carry bulky raw materials along intensively used routes.[50] Canals (and canalised rivers) can be seen as a response to the demands of industry for a cheap supply of coal and other raw materials, and they grew as a complement to the existing and improving road network that still played an important part in the dispersal of goods to markets and in the growth of non-mineral based industries, such as textiles.[51] In the middle part of the eighteenth century, then, the space economy was being reconfigured around new resources and new forms of transport, and the 'constants' of resource base and transport nodes underwent fundamental changes in character, form and location.

What of towns? The central functions of the urban network remained largely unchanged through the eighteenth and nineteenth centuries. Towns remained the nodal points on the economic, social, communication and political lines which enmeshed both region and nation, making them foci of and instrumental in the process of spatial integration.[52] However, regarding them as locational constants is both problematic and limiting. On the one hand, urban growth was rapid and spatially uneven so that the network of towns changed considerably during the eighteenth century.[53] The towns themselves remained, by and large, constant in number and, of course, they were fixed in space; but the relative importance of different places changed fundamentally. On the other hand, regarding them only as inert and isolated points on the economic landscape is to ignore their essential active and relational role. As Lepetit argues, towns were not merely the concentration into a particular place of a specific group of production factors (although, as we have seen, even this attribute is often under-played in proto-industrialisation theory), they also acted as an important economic multiplier, creating favourable conditions for investment and growth. More importantly, they were agents in economic, social and cultural change rather than simply the arenas where such processes took place.[54] If we are to fully understand the importance of towns, the significance of the geographical structure of industrial development and the functional and spatial relationships between urban and economic growth, it is essential that we identify the main characteristics of the urban sector in the eighteenth century. In short, we must explore our urban history. In doing so, we must develop a relational perspective that 'emphasizes the idea of [towns and] cities as places of intersection between webs of social, cultural and technological flow'.[55]

Urban growth and urban functions

With the aid of two hundred years of hindsight, Britain's urban growth during the eighteenth and early nineteenth centuries appears modest in pace and patchy in coverage, especially before 1750.[56] In the context of wider European urbanisation, however, England especially experienced rapid and unprecedented growth.[57] From 1600 to 1800, 'the urban percentage in England quadrupled, scarcely changed in the rest of north-western Europe, and advanced rather modestly on the continent as a whole. The English experience appears to be unique';[58] all the more so if we regard growth rates of individual towns. The thirty-four large cities which doubled in size between 1600 and 1750 were spread throughout Europe. The largest number were in France (nine), but there were significant numbers in the British Isles (eight), Germany (four), the Low Countries (four) and Spain (three). This dispersal of growth was replaced in the second half of the eighteenth century by a focusing onto the British Isles which contained fifteen of the nineteen fastest growing cities; eleven were in England alone.[59] In contrast with the rest of Europe, much of this growth occurred in small towns: those with 5,000 to 10,000 inhabitants doubled in number in England, from fifteen in 1600 to thirty-one in 1750, but fell elsewhere in Europe from 372 to 331.[60]

Explanations for this growth draw heavily on Smith's ideas of 'natural' regional growth discussed above. Wrigley, in particular, has emphasised improved agricultural productivity and prosperity as an essential pre-condition for the urbanisation of England. Although this was an important enabling factor, what made the country unique in eighteenth-century Europe was industrial- and commercial-based growth.[61] Whilst some manufacturing activity had been lost to the countryside, and particular towns experienced a resultant downturn in their economic fortunes, any decline was more than matched by the growth of industrial towns, many of which 'had industrial specialisms which served, like the rural industrial areas, international markets'.[62] More generally, towns formed 'nurseries of skill' or acted as finishing or co-ordinating centres for rural manufacturing.[63] Indeed, many proto-industrial areas contained traditional urban-industrial centres (places like Leeds, Manchester and Birmingham) which prospered and grew within a context of rural industrialisation.[64] In this way, industrialisation and urbanisation were closely linked, with the latter being labelled as the dependent variable.[65] Industry is identified as having a profound and widespread impact on urban growth in a manner not previously seen: 'new' manufacturing towns outstripped their more established neighbours, which were often spectators in the industrialisation process (Table 2.1).

Table 2.1 *Growth of different categories of towns in the eighteenth century*

	Population totals (000s)			Percentage growth	
	1700	*1750*	*1801*	*1700–50*	*1750–1801*
England	5060	5770	8660	14	50
10 historic regional centres [a]	107	126	153	18	21
12 regional centres [A]	123	168	316	37	88
8 established ports [b]	81	128	190	58	48
11 ports [B]	94	168	308	79	83
4 'new' manufacturing towns [c]	27	70	262	159	274
8 manufacturing towns [C]	62	122	352	97	189

Sources: Wrigley, 'Urban growth', p. 49; Law, 'Urban population, pp. 22–6.
Notes: [a] Cambridge, Chester, Coventry, Exeter, Gloucester, Norwich, Salisbury, Shrewsbury, Worcester, York; [A] as [a] plus Birmingham, Manchester; [b] Bristol, Colchester, Great Yarmouth, Hull, Ipswich, King's Lynn, Newcastle, Southampton; [B] as [b] plus Liverpool, Sunderland, Whitehaven; [c] Birmingham, Leeds, Manchester, Sheffield; [C] as [c] plus Norwich, Oldham, Wigan, Wolverhampton.

Whilst these ideas contain much that is true – industrialisation was undoubtedly critical in the expansion of individual towns and the urbanisation of the country as a whole – there are several problems with such analysis. The first is the definition and composition of Wrigley's categories. In each, the adjective is as important as the noun: 'historic' centres were growing slowly, 'established' towns moderately and 'new' ones most rapidly. Indeed, in the last of these, the argument is almost tautological: towns are identified as 'new' because of their rapid growth; that they turn out to be growing more rapidly than other centres is thus scarcely surprising. A fairer and more accurate picture of the type of towns growing most quickly (and thus, by implication, of the causes of growth) would be gained by contrasting regional centres, ports and manufacturing towns. Thus, we could include Birmingham and Manchester (or Leeds and Sheffield for that matter) as regional centres, a procedure which means that such places were not necessarily growing slowly.[66] The slow-growing towns highlighted by Wrigley were often being superseded by expanding neighbours (for instance as Birmingham grew to eclipse Coventry and Worcester) and/or served functions which were not conducive to strong demographic growth. In places with pretensions to be resorts for the wealthy, for instance, industry and rapidly growing populations would have ill-served their image as sophisticated and exclusive urbane centres.[67]

Conversely, manufacturing towns were very varied in their pedigree and dynamism: Norwich, Wigan and Colchester were noted manufacturing towns, albeit 'old' and slow-growing ones, whilst Oldham, South Shields and Merthyr Tydfil could be regarded as genuinely new and rapidly expanding industrial towns.[68] A manufacturing function *per se* was clearly no guarantee of strong demographic growth, neither was it merely the 'age' of the town which determined its fortunes. Many of the manufacturing towns in relative or absolute decline in the eighteenth century had seen a reduction in the demand for their staple or competitors emerge elsewhere. Thus, Wigan's pewter industry shrank as fashion turned towards earthenware, whilst Norwich increasingly suffered from the expansion of textiles production in west Yorkshire.[69] Finally, in focusing only on established ports Wrigley excludes some of the most dynamic settlements of the eighteenth century. Whilst Bristol, Hull and Newcastle grew strongly, their threefold increases were overshadowed by Liverpool which increased about fifteenfold during the eighteenth century on the basis of its burgeoning trade with Ireland and the American colonies.[70] Lower down the hierarchy, the smaller ports around the East Anglian coast were growing only slowly, but the coal ports of Sunderland and Whitehaven grew rapidly.[71]

That industrialisation was not the only explanation for urban growth is increasingly widely recognised: agriculture, trade, transport and leisure were also important influences.[72] However, it should be remembered that towns were not the passive subjects of exogenous growth stimuli. Towns contained a variety of integrating functions which not only generated urban growth, but also engendered wider economic growth by drawing together local and regional specialisations. Transport, perhaps the most tangible element of these integration functions, was routinely centred on towns. It formed the dominant activity in certain towns, most notably the canal ports of the late eighteenth century and the railway towns of the mid-nineteenth century, and was also important in the development of numerous coaching towns.[73] Places such as Stamford and Stone prospered from their position on major thoroughfares, with links to London often proving crucial in generating traffic. Overall, towns formed the principal transport nodes with both infrastructure and services being closely mapped onto the spatial and hierarchical structure of the urban system. Even the emerging canal system tended to link together towns or, at least, connect certain towns with key resource sites.[74]

Integration was also affected through trading, service and information networks, and these again were focused onto towns. Towns were trading centres for local (rural) production and formed the link to national and international markets. The ports especially acted as collection and export points, a critical role given that more than more than half of Britain's cotton production (much of it from Lancashire) was exported and about 70 per cent of Yorkshire woollens and Birmingham and Wolverhampton hardwares was sold overseas.[75]

All three sets of industries were increasingly dependent on the colonies (and especially North America) as markets for their goods, whilst raw materials were being drawn in from across Europe and around the globe.[76] Under such circumstances, it was inevitable that rural producers became more dependent upon (urban) merchants for supplies and marketing services, because 'although production could be carried out in a worker's home, the worker could neither organise nor finance it'.[77] Overseas trading was a specialist role linking local to international economies, but all towns were linked to their hinterlands through market or retail activities. With household consumption as well as production being increasingly market-oriented, towns were vital in supplying the goods and services which facilitated this economic specialisation. As with manufacturing, the benefits of this growth were not spread evenly between towns: those which were well connected to transport networks and broader marketing systems (particularly those linked to London) experienced strongest growth.[78]

London also exerted a more general impetus for commercial expansion, through its demand for goods and services, its influence on commercial practices, facilities and attitudes, and its role in the growth and spread of consumerism in the eighteenth century.[79] These functions also diffused down through the hierarchy to smaller towns, and the urban system was especially important to the widespread diffusion of 'new patterns of consumption without which industrial growth would be impossible'.[80] From the Restoration, leisure and consumption gained a new centrality in the lives of many in the upper and middle ranks. Changing attitudes to wealth and material goods were linked to new forms of social activity to make many towns 'arenas of public consumption'.[81] Many towns, and especially the resorts, offered facilities for what Borsay calls 'civility and sociability' and grew in wealth from their ability to periodically attract a body of 'prime consumers'.[82] A growing leisure infrastructure of promenades, theatres, assembly rooms and so on was paralleled by the introduction or augmentation of amenities such as street lighting and paving, and the 'improvement' of the urban environment as building styles and materials shifted from the vernacular to an increasingly national standard of neo-classical architecture.[83] County towns, meanwhile, attracted a more permanent social elite of civil servants through their administrative functions (particularly the quarter sessions and assizes) as well as a large body of 'seasonal' visitors from the county as a whole, giving them an additional role as 'leisure towns'.[84] Such places served to integrate local and national economies and cultures, but rather than merely responding to outside influences, they helped to generate demand and redistribute wealth to productive sectors, encouraging national economic growth and maintaining the prosperity of many towns which were marginal to industrial development.[85]

Urban growth and the prosperity of towns and townspeople were clearly associated with a variety of new and resurgent urban functions. It was also associated with the emergence of increasingly specialised urban economies. Towns were differentiated not merely by size, but also by their economic, social and cultural activities and functions. This specialisation brought with it greater inter-dependence and interaction.[86] Notwithstanding Estabrook's recent arguments for the cultural separation of urban and rural, towns were intimately tied to their hinterlands, and it is possible to see 'town and country as part of an organic regional unit, interacting closely in a way which shaped the identity of each'.[87] However, towns also interacted with one another in an increasingly integrated system. Thus, as Lepetit argues, there is a need to progress from 'a bipolar analysis (town/country) to a multipolar analysis capable of accommodating a whole range of towns and their territories in a system of interrelations'.[88] To properly understand urban growth and change, he argues, it is necessary to explore the structure, interactions and dynamics of the urban system, not least because interaction within a city network could induce growth throughout the system.[89] Work by Berry and Horton, and Bourne and Simmons in North America; Rozman in China, Japan and Russia; and Robson, Pred, de Vries and Lepetit in Europe has emphasised the importance of networks or systems of cities.[90] They argue that the economic and social functions of towns are carried out in an inter-connected framework. This both determines the collective and individual role that cities can play in regional and national development and stimulates growth within towns. Indeed, Rozman goes so far as to argue that 'a mature urban system is a pre-modern achievement rather than a product of the industrial epoch. In his view, a certain very long term process of urban network creation is a necessary preparation for entry to the modern industrial world.'[91] In England, large-scale urbanisation may have followed industrialisation in the nineteenth century, but industrial growth was itself predicated upon a modern, integrated and dynamic urban system. This system was drawn together by the same integrating urban functions that linked specialist locations within the space economy and encouraged the formation of Pollard's 'critical mass', generating local and regional economic development.

To understand more fully the structuring and development of the economy of a *region*, it is helpful to conceptualise the region as an integrated system of towns together with their corresponding areas of influence. 'The urban system, in this broader sense, is still based on urban nodes, that is, on spatial concentrations of people and activities within the region or nation, but it also includes the relationships of the nodes to their surrounding areas and particularly the linkages among nodes.'[92] By taking this approach, regional economic growth becomes synonymous with the development of the urban system, and 'urban history, taken in the wider sense to connote the study of the function of the town within the economy as a whole, is therefore a strategic point of entry into the larger question of what stimulated growth or improvement in the past'.[93] The absence of this integrated approach from most economic and urban history, and the resulting need for a comparable and dynamic context for urban and economic development has been recognised since the 1970s.[94] Its continued absence from the mainstream of British analyses is all the more surprising given de Vries's seminal study of the European urban system as a whole.[95] A systematic and spatially sensitive approach would not only make urban history more sympathetic to the form and character of English urbanisation, but match far more closely the type of relationships outlined by theories of regional growth. The problem, though, is how to conceptualise the relationship between the evolving hierarchical and spatial structure of the urban system on the one hand, and the development and geography of the regional economy on the other.[96] Whilst economies and urban systems are ultimately social creations, the reality of the localised economic activities and spatial interactions which comprised these functioning systems formed tangible social, economic and spatial contexts for the lives and actions of individual people. In this way, urban systems and hierarchies were real and experienced, and not simply abstract concepts.[97] It is essential, therefore, to understand and to theorise how they were structured and how this related to and was significant for regional economic development. The following section explores various ways in which urban systems are conceptualised and what models of their hierarchical and spatial structure and functioning can tell us about their relationship with the wider economy.

Theorising urban systems

Any urban system may be arranged in some form of hierarchy since towns will inevitably differ in their demographic size or functional importance. What lies behind most of the interest shown in such hierarchies, however, is the conviction that regularity (that is, some form of relationship between rank and size) betokens the existence of an urban system.[98] Further, it is supposed that different types of system exhibit different forms of rank-size relationship. Four archetypes are identified which attempt to link the hierarchical structure of the urban system to its underlying socio-economic conditions.[99] In the first, a convex curve, often associated with pre-industrial economies, reflects a system dominated by small and medium-sized towns and low levels of integration. Subsequently (and generally coincidental with industrialisation), increased integration is seen as encouraging vigorously selective growth of certain larger centres and thus tends to eliminate the flat top of the rank-size curve.[100] The relationship described by the original convex curve might then be replaced by the second or 'rank-size distribution' but, more commonly, by what Jefferson termed the 'law of the primate city'.[101] A primate city can dominate a distribution which otherwise obeys the rank-size rule, in which case the rank-size curve is concave – the third archetype. Alternatively and fourthly, it can head a convex curve making the overall curve concave-convex.[102]

Rank-size analysis has been widely adopted in studies of urban systems to explore the urban-economy relationship.[103] Although useful up to a point, it is an essentially aspatial approach, collapsing regions or countries into spaceless unity. Towns become points on a graph or in a matrix rather than real places which interacted with one another over space. Like much economic analysis, then, the rank-size technique is set in a 'wonderland of no spatial dimensions'.[104] In this sense, it takes us little further than conventional urban histories in understanding the workings of urban systems; certainly it tells us nothing about the spatial inter-dependencies of towns and local economies. To gain insight into these, we need to be able to conceive the urban system in explicit spatial terms. Such an approach is offered by central place theory as elaborated by Christaller and refined by Lösch.[105] Both recognise the important reality that towns are linked and relate spatially and functionally to one another, yet they remain under-explored, if problematic, concepts in urban and economic history.

Christaller was interested in the distribution of service centres and argued that the size of a central place is effectively governed by demand from its hinterland. There are numerous smaller centres to serve the need for low order goods and services which are needed frequently and must, therefore, be available locally. Fewer larger centres are visited over greater distances more rarely for higher order goods and services which are more valuable and needed less often. The central places of a given order are arranged in a regular isometric lattice and the arrangement repeated for successively larger central places so that smaller hinterlands are nested within larger ones.[106] Different arrangements of this pattern, reflecting different sets of inter-relationships between centres can be achieved simply by altering the size and orientation of the original hexagonal net in relation to the settlement distribution. Nonetheless, 'Christaller's hierarchy consists of several fixed tiers in which all the places in a particular tier have the same size and function, and higher order places contain all the functions of the smaller central places.'[107] This gives a 'stepped' hierarchy in rank-size terms and allows no diversity amongst the central places of each tier and no variation in the relationship of one tier with the next.

In attempting to model the location of production, Lösch introduced a new flexibility into central place models by abandoning the fixed ratio between different orders of settlement. In his model, the sum of the minimal distances between places was itself minimised, and shipments and transport lines were also reduced to a minimum. By doing this, Lösch produced a pattern showing considerable variation between spatial sectors and with distance from the principal central place.[108] More importantly, the resulting hierarchy replaced the fixed tiers with an almost continuous sequence of centres. Also, settlements of the same size would not necessarily contain the same functions. Thus, larger central places need not always contain all the functions of smaller places and a degree of inter-dependence between the two is possible.[109]

There are numerous problems in applying these models to historical or present-day contexts. Basic assumptions of uniform plains and rational deci-sion-making are too simplistic and devalue the role of the individual in geographical or historical change.[110] Both models are based on an overly rigid hierarchy wherein each settlement has a fixed and prescribed functional and spatial position in relation to all others – a far cry from the increasing com-plexity of the urban specialisations and spatial divisions of labour noted earlier.[111] Most fundamentally, both are essentially static, being the supposed single state of equilibrium in a given set of circumstances. They therefore ignore the possibility of multiple equilibria and fail to accommodate historical evol-ution, apparently making them of limited value in studies of change and development within the urban system and the regional economy.[112] Even as representations of a steady state, towns and the urban system are viewed by central place theory as essentially responsive to exogenous stimuli. As has been emphasised already, eighteenth-century towns as well as present-day cities were active in generating change and growth in the broader economy, not least through the integrative functions which tied them to their hinterlands and to other towns.[113] It is necessary, then, to supplement such theories with more dynamic models.

Vance theorised that trade grows not from focusing a search for goods *inwards* onto certain locations, but with the *outward* projection of demand from consumption centres.[114] Demand leads to production and so it is demand from central places which stimulates production in hinterlands. Growth of the urban system or regional economy therefore comes from increased demand within the central places or, through them, from outside the region. Moreover, exchange of goods (wholesaling) allows a choice of locations for trade rather than the limited number determined by the producer. Trading functions thus release central places from spatially fixed hierarchies. Instead of the area-point or territorial relationship where production in the hinterland holds towns rigidly in space, Vance introduces the idea of 'gateway cities' which allow trading contacts between spatially removed places; that is, non-territorial or point–point interaction.[115] In central place theory, contact between towns is always restricted by the hierarchical relationships which exist, whether these are fixed (Christaller), or more flexible (Lösch). Vance abandons this notion, as one town can trade with any other in its own or another system, either directly or more usually through the 'gateway cities'. This obviously facilitates far greater variation in the choice of central place location and the location of urban growth, since the centres of trade no longer need to be situated within production locations. We thus have a model which seems accurately to reflect the potentially varied inter-town linkages which drew together specialised production, commercial and consumption centres in the eighteenth century. However, it is a theory which explicitly privileges trade over manufacturing and which obscures important spatial and operational connections between the urban system and the developing regional economy – not least those with rural industry. Such issues are addressed more directly in Simmon's model of long-term urban system development in North America. He posits the existence of four stages of development which applied to different places at different times from the sixteenth century to the present day. Of particular interest here are the middle two stages which he terms *Staple Export* and *Industrial Specialisation*. Whilst they relate to different economic regimes, both take an essentially relational view of towns, emphasising dynamic interaction over static production factors.

The staple-export model essentially describes the structure of an urban system within an advanced organic economy. Development is driven by external demand for staple products – Simmons suggests timber and cotton, but the products of rural manufacturing fit the model just as well – and is articulated through the hinterlands in which the raw materials or staples are actually produced.[116] This bottom-up growth means that towns interact with their hinterlands and their neighbours in the territorial-hierarchical relationships of central place theory. At one level, this portrays towns as passive actors in the development process, providing services to productive and dynamic hinterlands, but they can also be seen as generating growth through their provision of the vital links between local production and more distant markets.[117] Thus, growth might congregate around favoured production locations (in a Löschian manner) and/or around the Vancian 'gateway towns' with links to external markets. In regional terms this means that areas with outward-looking urban centres or those rich in resources will be those with the highest potential for growth. The industrial specialisation model suggests that growth is based on the agglomeration advantages which accrue as industrial production becomes increasingly concentrated in the towns.[118] It thus equates industrialisation with urbanisation, and matches the expansion of one with growth of the other. However, rather than link development only to the internal characteristics of the individual town or locality, the model emphasises the role of inter-dependence in generating local and regional growth.[119] High levels of specialisation lead to a correspondingly complex set of market linkages between towns as each centre needs to buy-in the goods and services which it does not itself produce. This complementarity and interdependence means that, whilst it is spatially localised, growth in one area will help to stimulate development elsewhere. In economic terms, what we see is network advantage as a real 'club good'.[120] In spatial terms, population and economic activity grow through agglomeration economies established around advantaged locations. Human and natural resources may be significant, but the importance of intra-regional trade means that patterns of development are highly sensitive to transport and business networks. However, since these increasingly focus on the larger towns, initial advantages are reinforced and growth stimuli concentrate in these privileged locations as they come to dominate information, technology and capital circulation systems.[121]

In place of the traditional emphasis on 'locational constants' of resources (from raw materials to skilled labour) and transport nodes, Simmons' models link the structure and development of urban and economic systems through the process of spatial integration. In this relational perspective, the links between places are as instrumental in generating growth as any of the intrinsic qualities of the places themselves. This spatial integration function is therefore critical to regional development and subsumes all the varied urban roles discussed above under three main headings: *Urban-rural integration*, that is, the co-ordination of rural production and the provision of goods and services to hinterland populations, as is seen in proto-industrialisation and staple product models; *External integration*: the linking of local production to distant markets and vice versa in long-distance trading relations, paralleled in Vance's gateway cities; *Internal system integration*: the inter-dependency of the various members of the urban system, each of which has a different and often specialised function. This specialism covers manufacturing, trading and servicing, and increases as agglomeration economies accrue.[122] The function and structure of the urban system can thus be related to regional development and to change within the network of towns themselves. Economic growth in a region is determined by the effective linking of supply and demand, and by the ability of the urban system to integrate the productive forces within the region and to disseminate innovations throughout the regional space as quickly as possible.[123] The nature and degree of integration which exists is therefore critical in determining the process and form of overall regional growth. This means that the urban system (directly or indirectly) influences economic growth within the region, but, because this influence is not evenly distributed between all centres in the system, certain towns will grow more than others and will, therefore, increasingly dominate the urban system and the region as a whole. The identity of these dominant towns is, in turn, strongly influenced by the strength of inter-town linkages and the spatial characteristics of the diffusion process.[124] Diffusion of information, ideas, capital and so on favours larger towns and those which are advantageously located *vis à vis* various locational constants.[125] Such places benefit from their location on the lines of flow of innovations and trade, and so progressively enhance their position both in the hierarchy and on communication networks. They become core centres within the regional economy.[126] Growth therefore accumulates in certain centres at the expense of others; large towns, those with strong external linkages, those on the transport nodes and those close to resource sites form the foci of economic and urban systems and their development.

Conclusions: ways forward

Established interpretations of early industrial growth in Britain emphasise continuity with pre-existing agricultural systems and the evolutionary nature of development. Both Adam Smith's notion of natural progress and proto-industrialisation theory present a view of development which is unified and progressive with a single end point. The (regional) economy moves from agriculture to rural industry to factory-based manufacturing, and any alternative development trajectories are seen as 'unnatural'. Within proto-industrial systems, however, commercial agriculture formed an alternative and complementary pathway to development. Moreover, the subsequent de-industrialisation of some proto-industrial regions underlines the fact that a number of different routes could be followed to a range of so-called 'final' situations. The possibility of multiple equilibria within economic development focuses attention on its spatial patterning, and the role of natural resources, sociocultural environments, transport infrastructure and so on in shaping this geographical structure. Although often downplayed in theories of regional growth, towns also played a central role in the economic structuring and development of regions in the eighteenth century. They were production and consumption centres (often forming nurseries of skill and centres of new consumerism), and were vital in the integration of regional and national economies through their servicing and trading functions which involved towns in close interaction with their hinterlands and with other towns. In effect, they formed an urban system.

The role of the urban system is often overlooked in urban and economic history. To provide a sound theoretical understanding of the part played by town in structuring and generating growth in the wider economy, it is necessary to look to modern geographical models. Unfortunately, the classic theories of settlement patterns are essentially static and do not easily admit the introduction of development economics. Taken together, though, they provide an invaluable theoretical framework into which empirical studies can be placed. Central place theory is useful in modelling spatial integration through service functions; Vance's notions of 'gateway cities' and their placement in the broader context of staple-export systems provide a matrix for analysing the influence of external trade; and ideas of industrial (and non-industrial) specialisation form an effective model of regional integration via internal trade. That said, it is not the intention here to slavishly apply these models to the reality of eighteenth-century England. Discrepancies between the two would be unsurprising and not, in themselves, very instructive. Rather, the aim is to investigate the spatial structure of the economic and urban systems of north-west England, firstly to assess the extent of geographical specialisation and the ways in which this shaped subsequent development in the region, and secondly to explore the role of the urban system in encouraging economic localisation and in generating growth through the integration of space economy.

Notes

1 Smith, *Wealth of Nations*, volume 1, p. 432.
2 For modern summaries of the ideas of Smith, Malthus and Ricardo, see Wrigley, 'Classical economists' and Berg, *Age of Manufactures*, especially chapter 3.
3 Berg, *Age of Manufactures*, pp. 58–9.
4 Smith, *Wealth of Nations*, volume 1, p. 409
5 Berg, *Age of Manufactures*, p. 59.
6 Wrigley, *Continuity*, p. 34.
7 Wrigley, *Continuity*, p. 19; Wrigley, 'Classical economists', p. 31.
8 Berg, *Age of Manufactures*, 77–97; Allen, 'Agriculture'; Hudson, *Industrial Revolution*, 64–97.
9 Hudson and King, 'Rural industrializing townships'; Hudson and King, 'Two textile townships'.
10 De Vries, 'The industrious revolution'.
11 Allen, 'Agriculture', pp. 110–19; Hudson, *Industrial Revolution*, pp. 66–8.
12 Wrigley, 'Urban growth', pp. 51–60.
13 Hudson, *Industrial Revolution*, pp. 78–81.
14 Boyer, 'The old poor law'.
15 Hudson, *Industrial Revolution*, p. 80; Jones, 'Environment, agriculture and industry', pp. 494–8; Coleman, 'Growth and decay'.
16 Mendels, 'Proto-industrialization', p. 241.
17 See Jones, 'Environment, agriculture and industry'; Mendels, 'Proto-industrialization'.
18 Thirsk, 'Industries', pp. 70–2 and 86–8; Ogilvie, 'Social institutions'. See also, Hey, *Rural Metalworkers*; Swain, *Industry*, pp. 35–51; Zell, *Industry in the Countryside*.
19 Hudson, 'Proto-industrialization in England', pp. 63–5; Vardi, *The Land and the Loom*. For a parallel argument in the London economy, see Green, *From Artisans to Paupers*.

20 Kriedte, Medick and Schlumbohm, *Industrialization before Industrialization.*
21 Wadsworth and Mann, *Cotton Trade*, pp. 78–91; Mann, *Cloth Industry*, pp. 1–36 and 89–119; Gregory, *Regional Transformation*, pp. 80–138; Hudson, *Industrial Capital*, pp. 53–104; Hey, *Rural Metalworkers*, pp. 42–9; Berg, 'Factories.'
22 See, for example, Coleman, 'Proto-industrialization'; Berg, *Age of Manufactures*, pp. 70–6; Hudson, 'Proto-industrialization in England', pp. 58–61; Timmins, *Made in Lancashire*, pp. 61–82; Burt, 'Metal mining industries'.
23 Coleman, 'Proto-industrialization', pp. 441 and 443. See also King and Timmins, *Industrial Revolution*, pp. 39–49.
24 Clarkson, 'Environment and dynamic of pre-factory industry'; Whyte, 'Proto-industrialisation in Scotland'.
25 Mendels, 'Proto-industrialization', p. 246.
26 Ogilvie, 'Social institutions'; Hudson, *Industrial Capital*, pp. 105–208; Randall, 'Work, culture and resistance'; Berg, *Age of Manufactures*, pp. 255–79; Rowlands, *Masters and Men,* pp. 125–46.
27 Evans, 'Two paths', p. 210.
28 Coleman, 'Proto-industrialization'; Wrigley, *Continuity.*
29 Gregory, 'Geographies of industrialization', p. 361; Wrigley, *Continuity*, p. 51.
30 Nef, *British Coal Industry*, volume 1, p. 161; Clapham, *Economic History*, volume 2, p. 78.
31 Wrigley, *Continuity*, p. 57.
32 Wrigley, 'Classical economists', p. 33.
33 Wrigley, 'Raw materials, p. 12.
34 See Wrigley, 'Raw materials'.
35 Langton, 'Urban growth', pp. 455–6.
36 Wrigley, 'Raw materials', pp. 6–10; Turnbull, 'Canals'.
37 Hudson, *Industrial Revolution*, p. 113. See also Berg, *Age of Manufactures*, pp. 98–115.
38 Evans, 'Two paths'.
39 Gregory, 'Geographies of industrialization', p. 374.
40 Krugman, *Development*, p. 36.
41 Ogilvie, 'Social institutions'; Berg, *Age of Manufactures*, pp. 179–80; Muldrew, *Economy of Obligation*, especially pp. 123–57.
42 See Peet, 'Cultural production of economic forms'; Crang, 'Cultural turns and the (re)constitution of economic geography'; Scott, 'Capitalism, cities and the production of symbolic forms'.
43 Massey, *Spatial Divisions of Labour*, pp. 117–19 and 196–215; Gregory, 'Areal differentiation and post-modern geography'.
44 Berg, *Age of Manufactures*, pp. 169–88; Gregory, 'Geographies of industrialization', pp. 377–84.
45 Pollard, *Peaceful Conquest*, p. 39.
46 For a useful summary of these ideas, see Dicken and Lloyd, *Location in Space*, pp. 239–52 and 384–91.
47 Krugman, *Geography and Trade*, p. 35.
48 Richardson, *Regional Growth Theory*, pp. 172–3; Hayter, *Industrial Location*, pp. 83–110.
49 Aldcroft and Freeman, *Transport in the Industrial Revolution*, pp. 22–4; Chartres and Turnbull, 'Road transport'.

50 Wrigley, *Continuity*, pp. 68–97. Coal cost about 1 shilling per ton to transport by road (doubling the price within 5–8 miles of the pithead); by canal it cost only 3 pence per mile (the price doubling in 20–30 miles).

51 In certain instances (for example the Liverpool–Prescot road), turnpikes were also a response to the demand for improved transport routes for coal – Albert, *Turnpike Road System*, p. 46.

52 Berg, Hudson and Sonenscher, *Manufacture in Town and Country*, pp. 26–8.

53 Langton, 'Urban growth', pp. 465–86; Langton, 'Town growth', pp. 15–17 and 23–30.

54 Lepetit, *Urban System*, pp. 81–93.

55 Allen, Massey and Pryke, *Unsettling Cities*, p. 9.

56 Williamson, 'Coping with city growth', pp. 333–4.

57 De Vries, *European Urbanization*, pp. 158–67

58 Wrigley, 'Urban growth', p. 64.

59 De Vries, *European Urbanization*, pp. 158–67.

60 Wrigley, 'Urban growth', p. 66. See also, Clark, *Small Towns*, pp. 1–21.

61 Wrigley, 'Urban growth', pp. 51–60; Langton, 'Urban growth', pp. 479–81.

62 Langton, 'Industry and towns', p. 185.

63 Everitt, 'Country, county and town'; Trinder, 'Industrialising towns'; Ellis, *Georgian Town*, pp. 47–65.

64 Berg, Hudson and Sonescher, *Manufacture in Town and Country*, p. 27.

65 This interpretation of urbanisation is most clearly seen in Daunton, 'Towns and economic growth', pp. 249–50, but the orthodoxy runs deep and has re-emerged, in modified form, in *inter alia*, Wrigley, 'Urban growth' and more recently Langton, 'Urban growth'.

66 Borsay, *Urban Renaissance*, pp. 16–37; Ellis, 'Regional and county centres', pp. 673–84.

67 Arguments of this sort were commonly used to promote an image of certain towns as being free from what were increasingly seen as the detrimental impacts of industrialisation – Sweet, *Urban Histories*, pp. 125–41.

68 See, Corfield, 'A provincial capital'; Sharpe, 'De-industrialization and re-industrialization'; Gurr and Hunt, *Oldham*.

69 Hatcher and Barker, *British Pewter*, p. 285; McKendrick, 'Consumer revolution', pp. 10–12; Lloyd-Prichard, 'Decline of Norwich', pp. 373–5; Wilson, 'Yorkshire cloth industry', pp. 231–7.

70 Clemens, 'Rise of Liverpool'.

71 Corfield, *English Towns*, pp. 34–44; Jackson, 'Ports', pp. 705–14.

72 Stobart, 'A regional approach to urban growth'.

73 Porteous, *Canal Ports, passim*; Kellet, *Impact of Railways*, pp. 3, 137, 159 and 347.

74 Pawson, *Transport and Economy*, pp. 15–62; Porteous, *Canal Ports*, pp. 38–53.

75 The home market was also increasingly sophisticated, but formed the smaller part of the market for these goods: Hudson, 'Proto-industrialization in England', p. 53.

76 Mathias, *First Industrial Nation*, p. 88; Darity, 'British industry and the West Indies plantations'; Smith, 'Market for manufactures'.

77 Langton, 'Industry and towns', p. 183; Gregory, 'Geographies of industrialization', pp. 353–9.

78 Noble, 'Regional urban system'; Wrigley, 'London's importance'; Ellis, *Georgian Town*, pp. 40–3.

79 Wrigley, 'London's importance'. For the emergence of a consumer society, see Hudson, *Industrial Revolution*, pp. 173–80; Fine and Leopold, *World of Consumption*, pp. 63–72; Glennie, 'Consumption within historical studies'; and King and Timmins, *Industrial Revolution*, pp. 150–64.

80 Daunton, 'Towns and economic growth' p. 250.

81 Towner, *Recreation and Tourism*. For the growing literature on leisure and consumption, see, *inter alia*, Weatherill, *Consumer Behaviour and Material Culture*; Borsay, *Urban Renaissance*; Brewer and Porter, *World of Goods*.

82 Borsay, *Urban Renaissance*; Sweet, *English Town*, pp. 219–56; Ellis, *Georgian Town*, pp. 79–82.

83 Jones and Falkus, 'Urban improvement'; Borsay, *Urban Renaissance*, pp. 39–113; Borsay, 'Rise of the promenade'; Borsay, 'The London connection'; Ogborn, *Spaces of Modernity*, pp. 75–115.

84 McInnes, 'Shrewsbury'; Stobart, 'Shopping streets'.

85 Borsay, *Urban Renaissance*, pp. 323–67.

86 Clark, 'Small towns in England', p. 120.

87 Borsay, *Eighteenth Century Town*, p. 83; Estabrook, *Urbane and Rustic England*, *passim*.

88 Lepetit, *Urban System*, p. 97.

89 Capello, 'City network paradigm'.

90 See Berry and Horton, *Geographical Perspectives on Urban Systems*; Bourne and Simmons, *Systems of Cities*; Rozman, 'Urban networks'; Robson, *Urban Growth*; Pred, *City Systems*; de Vries, *European Urbanization*; Lepetit, *Urban System*.

91 De Vries, *European Urbanization*, p. 10.

92 Simmons, 'Urban system', p. 61.

93 Wrigley, 'Parasite or stimulus', p. 309.

94 Clark, *Early Modern Town*, p. 23.

95 De Vries, *European Urbanization*. A small number of studies of nineteenth-century urbanisation have attempted an urban systems approach – see, for example, Robson, *Urban Growth*; Carter, 'Towns and urban systems'.

96 Richardson, *Regional Growth Theory*, pp. 75–6.

97 The idea and structure of hierarchies of towns was evidently very important to the people of Newcastle-upon-Tyne. When the first census demonstrated that their town was relatively small in comparison with the burgeoning industrial centres, they demanded a recount.

98 Robson, *Urban Growth*, p. 34.

99 For a discussion of the early development of these ideas, see Robson, *Urban Growth*, p. 20 and Lepetit, *Urban System*, pp. 181–2.

100 De Vries, *European Urbanization* pp. 95–120; Johnson, 'Rank-size convexity'; Smith, 'Urban Primacy'.

101 Zipf, *National Unity and Disunity*; Jefferson, 'The primate city'. See also, Smith 'Urban primacy'; Kowalewski, 'Primate regional systems'.

102 Lepetit, *Urban System*, p. 185; de Vries, *European Urbanization*, pp. 113 and 119.

103 For example, see Robson, *Urban Growth*; de Vries, *European Urbanization*; Lepetit, *Urban System*.

104 Walter Isard, quoted in Krugman, *Development*, p. 33. See also Massey, *Spatial Divisions of Labour*, p. 45.

105 Christaller, *Central Places in Southern Germany*; Lösch, *The Economics of Location*. See also, Haggett, *Geography*, pp. 287–92; Beavon, *Central Place Theory*, *passim*; Carter, *Urban Geography*, pp. 25–98.
106 Haggett, *Geography*, p. 287.
107 Haggett, *Geography*, p. 292.
108 For a fuller discussion, see Beavon, *Central Place Theory*, pp. 80–105.
109 Pred, *City Systems*, p. 19.
110 Lepetit, *Urban System*, p. 180; Pred, *City Systems*, p. 18; Carter, *Urban Geography*, pp. 61–98.
111 Camagni, 'From city hierarchy to city networks'.
112 Richardson, *Regional Growth Theory*, p. 76; Lepetit, *Urban System*, p. 180; Robson, *Urban Growth*, p. 27.
113 Capello, 'City network paradigm', pp. 1925–31.
114 Vance, *Merchant's World*, p. 8.
115 Vance, *Merchant's World*, especially chapter 1.
116 Simmons, 'Urban system', p. 63.
117 See Berg, Hudson and Sonenscher, *Manufacture in Town and Country*, pp. 25–8.
118 This echoes Marshallian explanations for the localistation of industry – see Krugman, *Geography and Trade*, pp. 35–54.
119 Simmons, 'Urban system', p. 67.
120 Capello, 'City network paradigm', p. 1925.
121 Pred, *City Systems*, pp. 78–92; Richardson, *Regional Growth Theory*, pp. 73–4.
122 Richardson, *Regional Growth Theory*, pp. 175–96. See also Capello, 'City network paradigm'.
123 Richardson, *Regional Growth Theory*, pp. 135–8; Robson, *Urban Growth*, pp. 131–86.
124 Robson, *Urban Growth*, p. 140; Berry and Horton, *Geographic Perspectives on Urban Systems*, p. 87.
125 Pred, *City Systems*, pp. 21–2 and 78–92; Robson, *Urban Growth*, p. 210.
126 Dicken and Lloyd, *Location in Space*, pp. 386–7.

3

Uneven development: geographical specialisation and inter-dependency

New discoveries in metals, mines and minerals, new undertakings in trade, engines and manufactures ... make England especially show a new and different face in many places.[1]

If England was, to use Peter Mathias's phrase, the 'First Industrial Nation', then north-west England can lay strong claim to be the first industrial region. There are many English regions with a longer industrial history, some of which led in terms of certain key technologies and others which experienced more rapid growth: woollen production was strongly established in East Anglia and the West Country by Tudor times when Lancashire was still 'an obscure, remote, insular and backward corner of England'; Coalbrookdale spawned many advances in the production and use of iron, and south Wales underwent explosive industrial and urban development in the early nineteenth century.[2] The north west, though, possessed a unique combination of industries, many of which were in the vanguard of technological and organisational developments (including the use of coal and the move to factory-based production) and were being traded throughout the country and the world.[3] At the forefront of eighteenth-century growth was cotton, but the region also contained extensive iron-producing and -working industries; the country's most productive saltfield; important supplies of high-grade coal; copper, brass and pewter industries; and notable agricultural specialities. These specialisms were drawn together by a growing network of turnpike roads and the first and most highly integrated canal system in the country. They also depended on an urban system which developed from a scattering of small towns in 1600 to include, in Liverpool and Manchester, two of the largest towns in England by 1750.

In effect, the north west was achieving Pollard's critical mass of interdependent industries in the first half of the eighteenth century. The foundations were being laid for its emergence as a core region of industrial Britain. As such, north-west England not only forms a region of considerable interest in its own right and a useful comparison to studies of neighbouring regions, but can also provide insights into wider national processes of specialisation and integration.

For each of these potentialities to be realised, though, it is vital that the object of study is the region as a whole. Walton's emphasis on south and especially south-east Lancashire as the 'cradle of the world's first industrial revolution' undoubtedly holds much truth – it is certainly reflected in Timmins's study of industrialisation in the county.[4] However, in privileging cotton and factory production, we risk underplaying significant specialisms outside this area (the salt and silk industries of Cheshire, the coal-based heavy industries of Merseyside, Chester and Preston as social and leisure towns, and the overarching importance of agriculture) and the importance of spatial interdependence and integration in generating development. By effectively collapsing the production of the north west onto one part of the region, the influence and impact of the geography of economic activity is lost. The region considered here must be more broadly defined to encompass the varied economic, social and cultural development of the area. Defining and delimiting such a region is problematical, however, since its boundaries undoubtedly changed through time and varied considerably between different economic and social activities.[5] Certainly, it is unwise simply to assume that the administrative and economic north west were one and the same – manufacturing, trade and commerce were no respecters of county boundaries. That said, Cheshire and the southern half of Lancashire taken together appear to have formed a reasonably coherent economic entity and, as will be seen later, an area of considerable interactive integrity. They defined what Paasi refers to as the 'territorial shape' of the region.[6] The actual boundaries are formed to the west, south and east by county borders and to the north by the River Ribble. To this area Preston is added as it had strong links with the rural parishes of Leyland to the south as well as Amounderness to the north. The various specialist districts of the region were often interdependent and were certainly linked by substantial flows of goods, people, information and capital. In short, it was a real and functioning region.

In this chapter, economic and urban development in the north west is set alongside that of England as a whole. This provides a context for the subsequent discussion of regional development and, more importantly, serves to highlight the parallel developments taking place in region and nation, thus underlining the usefulness of north-west England as an exemplar of wider processes. Three aspects are emphasised: first the early establishment and persistence of geographical specialisation; second the importance of towns in integrating these spatial divisions of labour; and third the geographically uneven growth that resulted from these processes. In effect, the chapter introduces many of the ideas, structures and geographies discussed in more detail in succeeding chapters. It begins, though, by comparing the pace and structure of national and regional development in the eighteenth century.

Contexts and parallels: national and regional development in the eighteenth century

Urban growth offers a valuable insight into broader processes of economic, social and cultural change, and can be usefully employed as a proxy for local or national development. The rapid urbanisation of eighteenth-century England outlined in Table 3.1 was exceptional in a European context, but the impact on individual towns was very variable.[7] Many places experienced unprecedented expansion; some grew more modestly; and others – often very small or marginal places – had 'disappeared from the urban map' by the nineteenth century.[8] But such decay was exceptional: Clark suggests that absolute decline occurred in just 17 out of 582 small towns.[9] Nonetheless, selective growth made the eighteenth century 'one of the most mutable periods in English urban history' and transformed the hierarchy and geography of the country.[10] The top five towns (after London) in 1670 were Norwich, Bristol, Newcastle, Exeter and York. They had dominated England's urban system since the late middle ages and the overall structure of the urban hierarchy had changed little since then. Indeed, Table 3.2 shows that it was substantially the same towns occupied the top twenty positions in the urban hierarchy between 1600 and 1670.[11] Whilst the problems of estimating population totals for the seventeenth century must colour our analysis somewhat, the picture of stability is remarkable. That said, the changes to come in the late seventeenth and eighteenth centuries were clearly presaged. Manchester, Birmingham and Leeds all had populations of around 4,000 and ranked somewhere between twenty and thirty.[12] Such places were the rising stars of urban England. By 1750 towns of long-established importance in the urban hierarchy were being eclipsed by these burgeoning centres. Exeter and York are the most widely noted casualties, but Colchester, King's Lynn, Cambridge, Canterbury, Salisbury, Oxford and Shrewsbury all lost their places in the top twenty. Fifty years later the transformation was virtually complete: of the leading five towns in 1801 only Bristol remained from 130 years previously and the top twenty contained thirteen 'new' centres, including Bolton, Portsmouth and Bath. In contrast with Robson's argument for stability at the top of the urban hierarchy,[13] Norwich had fallen from second place in 1670 to tenth by 1801, York from fourth to twenty-fifth and Exeter from sixth to twentieth. They were replaced by Manchester, Birmingham and Leeds. Most striking was the rise of Liverpool, which rose something in excess of 200 places from a small town of around 1,300 people in the 1660s to the third largest urban centre in England by 1801. Change in the nineteenth century was less dramatic: the top ten towns remained the same through to 1831 (their relative positions being remarkably constant) and even by 1891 there were only three additions to the top ten – Bradford, Nottingham and Hull.[14]

Table 3.1 *Population estimates for England and north-west England*

		c.1664	c.1775	Growth 1664–1775 (%)
England and Wales	Total	5,050,000[a]	7,400,000[c]	46.5
	Urban	780,000[b]	1,875,705[c]	140.5
	Rural	4,270,000	5,524,295	29.4
North west[d]	Total	200,000	495,000	147.5
	Urban	41,506	142,969	244.4
	Rural	158,494	352,031	122.1

Sources: [a] Corfield, 'Urban development', p. 241; [b] calculated from Corfield, *English Towns*, p. 8 and Wrigley, 'Urban growth', p. 45; [c] Law, 'Urban population', p. 22; [d] Stobart, 'Eighteenth-century revolution?', p. 36.

Table 3.2 *The English urban hierarchy, 1600–1801 (populations in 000s)*

c. 1600		c.1670		c.1750		1801	
London	55	London	475	London	675	London	959
Norwich	15	Norwich	20	Bristol	50	Manchester	89
York	12	Bristol	20	Norwich	36	Liverpool	83
Bristol	12	York	12	Newcastle	29	Birmingham	74
Newcastle	10	Newcastle	12	Birmingham	24	Bristol	60
Exeter	9	Exeter	10	Liverpool	22	Leeds	53
Plymouth	8	Great Yarmouth	9	Manchester	18	Sheffield	46
Salisbury	6	Colchester	8	Leeds	16	Plymouth	43
King's Lynn	6	Chester	8	Exeter	16	Newcastle	42
Gloucester	6	Ipswich	8	Plymouth	15	Norwich	36
Chester	6	Plymouth	8	Chester	13	Portsmouth	33
Coventry	6	Worcester	8	Coventry	13	Bath	33
Hull	6	Coventry	7	Nottingham	12	Hull	30
Colchester	5	King's Lynn	7	Sheffield	12	Nottingham	29
Great Yarmouth	5	Canterbury	6	Ipswich	12	Sunderland	26
Ipswich	5	Cambridge	6	York	12	Stoke	23
Cambridge	5	Hull	6	Chatham	10	Chatham	23
Worcester	5	Salisbury	6	Great Yarmouth	10	Wolverhampton	21
Canterbury	5	Oxford	6	Portsmouth	10	Bolton	17
Oxford	5	Shrewsbury	6	Sunderland	10	Exeter	17

Sources: Wrigley 'Urban growth', p. 42; Langton, 'Urban growth', pp. 473–4.

Whilst English urban growth was rapid, it was outpaced by that of the north west (Table 3.1).[15] In 1664, the total population of the region was about 200,000 of which 41,506 (21 per cent) was urban, but only Chester exceeded the 5,000 threshold of urban status set by Wrigley.[16] By the 1770s, the overall population had more than doubled to around 495,000; the urban total amounted to 142,969 or 29 per cent, and seven towns had more than 5,000 inhabitants. In contrast with Wadsworth and Mann's observation that 'the increase in the population of Lancashire was not so much an urban increase as a thickening of the population over the countryside',[17] the north west was urbanising and the urban system was, demographically speaking, far more important at the end of the eighteenth century than it had been at the start. Although no towns in the north west experienced absolute decline in the eighteenth century, overall expansion of the urban population masks some striking variations in growth rates.[18] Nantwich grew by only 18 per cent and four other towns added less than half to their 1660s populations, whereas seven towns grew more than fourfold and Liverpool by a remarkable 2,603 per cent (Table 3.3). In all, just fourteen of the thirty towns grew faster than the overall regional average.

Such variability is unsurprising, and Johnson and Robson both argue that increased integration within an urban system would lead to the preferential growth of a small number of the larger towns,[19] causing the rank-size hierarchy to move from convexity to something approaching Zipf's rank-size rule. Whilst there is some evidence that the smallest towns in the north west were growing relatively slowly, the most notable feature of the regional and national hierarchies is the growth seen in all sizes of towns (Figure 3.1). In both, though, this stability is illusory: many centres, both large and small, moved significantly up or down the hierarchy. Just as Manchester, Birmingham and Sheffield climbed the national hierarchy, we see the regional rise of towns such as Liverpool, Ormskirk and Leigh; equally, the relative decline of Exeter, York and Norwich is mirrored in the north west by the fall of Nantwich and Congleton. Within the region's urban hierarchy, only Manchester, Bolton and Northwich occupied the same position in the 1770s as they had done one hundred years previously.

Of course, both changes in rank and percentage growth rates can be some-what misleading, since large numbers could be added in absolute terms without a concomitant change in rank or significant proportional growth. Nonetheless, these findings stand in apparent contrast to Robson's suggestion of minimum rank changes and maximum growth rates in the largest centres. The evidence points instead to selective growth in a maturing urban system of the type highlighted for the country as a whole by Corfield, Daunton and more recently Langton.[20] That said, there was a broad distinction between the upper and lower halves of the urban hierarchy of north-west England. Although a

Table 3.3 *The urban hierarchy of north-west England*

1664		c.1775		Percentage growth			
Chester	(7,817)	Liverpool	(34,407)	Liverpool	(2,603)		
Manchester	(3,690)	Manchester	(22,481)	Manchester	(509)		
Nantwich	(2,826)	Chester	(14,713)	Warrington	(354)		
Macclesfield	(2,628)	Warrington	(8,100)	Rochdale	(349)		
Wigan	(2,133)	Macclesfield	(6,000)	Blackburn	(327)		
Congleton	(1,939)	Preston	(5,500)	Leigh	(316)		
Preston	(1,890)	Wigan	(5,000)	Ormskirk	(288)	urban mean	(244)
Warrington	(1,786)	Stockport	(4,600)	Stockport	(232)		
Bolton	(1,615)	Bolton	(4,568)	Prescot	(215)		
Bury	(1,539)	Blackburn	(4,500)	Colne	(225)		
Stockport	(1,386)	Rochdale	(4,000)	Preston	(191)		
Liverpool	(1,273)	Nantwich	(3,325)	Haslingden	(185)		
Blackburn	(1,053)	Colne	(2,880)	Bolton	(183)		
Rochdale	(891)	Congleton	(2,375)	Northwich	(148)	regional mean	(148)
Colne	(886)	Bury	(2,090)	Burnley	(134)		
Knutsford	(881)	Leigh	(2,000)	Wigan	(134)		
Sandbach	(697)	Ormskirk	(1,900)	Macclesfield	(128)	rural mean	(122)
Chorley	(670)	Knutsford	(1,767)	Sandbach	(108)		
Northwich	(653)	Northwich	(1,620)	Chorley	(101)		
Middlewich	(630)	Haslingden	(1,500)	Knutsford	(101)		
Clitheroe	(607)	Sandbach	(1,477)	Newton	(90)		
Altrincham	(594)	Chorley	(1,350)	Chester	(88)		
Haslingden	(526)	Middlewich	(1,131)	Middlewich	(80)		
Malpas	(499)	Altrincham	(1,029)	Altrincham	(73)		
Ormskirk	(490)	Prescot	(993)	Frodsham	(54)		
Leigh	(481)	Burnley	(874)	Clitheroe	(37)		
Newton	(396)	Clitheroe	(833)	Bury	(36)		
Burnley	(373)	Newton	(751)	Malpas	(36)		
Frodsham	(342)	Malpas	(678)	Congleton	(22)		
Prescot	(315)	Frodsham	(527)	Nantwich	(18)		

Source: Stobart, 'Eighteenth-century revolution?', p. 36 and p. 40. See also Appendix 1.
Note: There were many places with populations in excess of the smaller urban centres, but which were certainly not recognised as towns in 1664: urban status was not merely a product of demographic size.

Figure 3.1 *Rank-size distributions: England and the north west,*
1660–c.1750

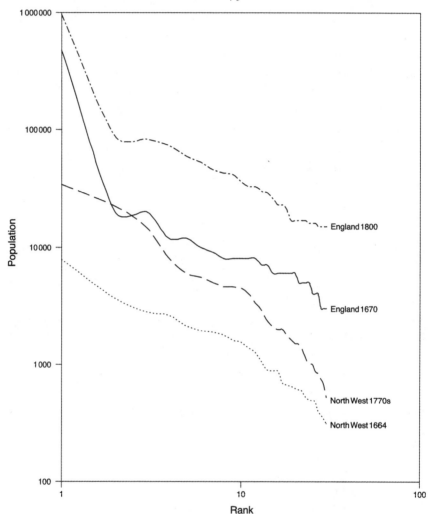

Source: Wrigley 'Urban growth'; Langton, 'Urban growth'; Stobart, 'Eighteenth-century revolution?'

similarly large amount of movement in rank order occurred within each half of the hierarchy, aggregate growth rates were very different, averaging 273 per cent and 126 per cent respectively. Even here, though, support for Robson's thesis is equivocal: the 'fast-growers' are not concentrated at the top of the hierarchy, but spread throughout the upper half. As Wrigley observed, *some* of the larger centres rather than necessarily the largest ones were growing most rapidly – generally those with a specialist function. In the north west, these were epitomised by Rochdale, Warrington and Blackburn; on a national scale, equivalents were found in towns such as Sheffield, Manchester and Hull. Thus, in both region and nation, urban growth was taking place at an unprecedented level and led to profound restructuring of the regional and national hierarchies. Such development was linked to wider economic transformation which involved the expansion of industrial and commercial activity and the emergence of new production systems.

Recent estimates suggest that growth in industrial output was more modest than once thought. In particular, the marked surge in growth recorded by Deane and Cole for the last few decades of the eighteenth century has been ironed out to a considerable degree by Crafts' revisions.[21] Indeed, the accepted wisdom now is that industrial output grew relatively slowly before the 1830s and that agriculture probably grew as strongly as manufacturing.[22] That said, individual industries followed very different growth trajectories, with the timing and geography of growth varying considerably. Cotton and iron enjoyed progressively stronger growth up to 1800 before the pace slackened slightly in the early nineteenth century; silk and especially linen experienced a marked decline in growth between 1780 and 1800, but then grew rapidly in the next thirty years; only coal production saw no downturns in its growth rate, rising steadily at first and more rapidly after 1760. Much of this development was associated with the growing export market for their products and, again with cotton in particular, overseas supplies of raw materials.[23] By 1800 cotton (35.4 per cent), woollens (22.1 per cent) and metals (15.2 per cent) accounted for nearly three-quarters of British exports, and the increasing concentration of these key industries into the north west, west Yorkshire, and south Yorkshire and the west Midlands inevitably meant that these regions in particular were heavily dependent on overseas markets.[24]

Growth in production and trade was naturally reflected in the composition of the workforce (Table 3.4). Agriculture had begun its slow decline as an employer of men (and particularly women): even if all labourers are assigned to agriculture as Crafts suggests, the proportion of the male population engaged in agriculture fell from 37.1 per cent in 1688 to 29.3 per cent in 1811.[25] The corresponding growth in manufacturing employment was slow during the eighteenth century, but more rapid in the early nineteenth century. This appears to suggest only gradual expansion of rural industries, but it is possible that these aggregate occupation counts underplay the growth in manufacturing. They certainly mask its regional concentration. Viewing all labourers as part of the agricultural workforce becomes increasingly problematical as time went on, so that the decline in agriculture and rise of manufacturing and building might be more pronounced than has been suggested. Also, considerable amounts of manufacturing work are undoubtedly hidden by the part-time and gendered nature of much proto-industrial employment in the eighteenth century.[26] As Berg argues, the male bias of employment data remains a perennial problem of analyses of eighteenth-century industrialisation.[27]

Table 3.4 *Male occupations in England and Wales, 1688–1811*

	1688		1740		1811	
	Total	%	Total	%	Total	%
Agriculture	241,373	20.0	386,976	26.6	315,616	14.1
Building	77,232	6.4	122,529	8.4	240,442	10.7
Manufacturing / Mining	194,856	16.1	258,765	17.8	480,618	21.5
Labourers	206,933	17.1	175,240	12.1	340,710	15.2
Services [a]	200,928	16.6	230,992	15.9	382,093	17.1
Other [b]	286,314	23.7	279,282	19.2	480,098	21.4
Total	1,207,636		1,453,784		2,239,577	

Source: Lindert, 'English occupations', pp. 702–4.
Notes: Titled and Poor are omitted; [a] Commerce, Professions and Other Services; [b] Army, Maritime, Servants and Apprentices.

The same trends appear in north-west England (Table 3.5). Probate records from 1701 to 1760 offer a spatially comprehensive if socially selective picture of male employment in the region. Women were rarely afforded an occupational title in the records and so are, regrettably, largely excluded from the present analysis, although their activity in textile manufacturing has been accommodated to some degree. Despite these problems, which are discussed in detail in Appendix 2, the broad geography, structure and organisation of the economy remains clear. There was a clear decline in agricultural employment (especially after 1740), but it appears that the 'slack' was taken up across the board rather than moving *en masse* into manufacturing. Indeed, transport (4.7–9.5 per cent) and dealing (8.2–10.3 per cent) grew as strongly as manufacturing (32.6–34.4 per cent) – a salutary reminder not to ignore developments elsewhere in the economy whilst searching for growth in industrial employment.[28] Notwithstanding this, it is probable that change was more profound amongst the sections of the population who did not leave probate records: those engaged in proletarianised industries, dual occupations, and women and children. Certainly, the problem of under-counting individuals involved in manufacturing becomes increasingly severe through the eighteenth century; not only was more of the manufacturing sector becoming proletarianised, but the growing scale of capitalist organisation makes it increasingly difficult to equate one individual with one unit of production. In 1700 a glassmaker, brewer or even cloth manufacturer would, in all likelihood, have been one man working for and even by himself. By 1750, however, these individuals were equally likely to be employed by another person or employing many other people and operating as part of a large industrial unit such as the ironworks at Haigh which employed 400 people and cost £40,000.[29] Probate data perhaps exaggerate the degree of economic stability, but there was little sign of a dramatic surge in secondary industrial employment during this lead-up to the industrial revolution. Instead, we have a region sustaining what were already quite high levels of manufacturing and commercial employment and moving increasingly towards export-oriented activities and capitalist industries.

Table 3.5. *Male occupations in north-west England, 1701–60*

	Total		1701–20		1721–40		1741–60	
	Number	%	Number	%	Number	%	Number	%
Agriculture	9796	36.5	3030	39.0	3945	40.9	2821	30.1
Mining	52	0.2	12	0.2	20	0.2	20	0.2
Building	772	2.9	246	3.2	260	2.7	266	2.8
Manufacture	8830	32.9	2537	32.6	3065	31.8	3228	34.4
Textiles	6312	23.5						
Metals and shipbuilding	602	2.3						
Leather, wood, etc.	789	2.9						
Dress and shoes	714	2.7						
Food and drink	413	1.5						
Labourers	78	0.3	19	0.2	22	0.2	37	0.4
Transport	1617	6.0	363	4.7	361	3.7	893	9.5
Dealing	2491	9.3	634	8.2	895	9.3	962	10.3
Textiles	340	1.3						
Food and drink	1072	4.0						
Other	1077	4.0						
Public and prof.	973	3.6	277	3.6	344	3.6	352	3.8
Dom. service	108	0.4	24	0.3	40	0.4	44	0.5
Gentry	2086	7.8	637	8.2	701	7.3	748	8.0

Source: Probate records, 1701–60.

The level of manufacturing employment in north-west England was much higher than that in the country as a whole: 33 per cent compared to about 22 per cent. Even allowing for differences in the method used to calculate Lindert's and the present figures,[30] it is clear that the north west was already characterised by exceptionally high levels of industrial development in the early eighteenth century. Within this, the importance of textiles as a growth pole of regional development is evident: it may have accounted for as much as two-thirds of manufacturing employment (Table 3.5).[31] However, given the likely under-counting of the proletarianised workforce in mining, large-scale metalworks and so on, it is clear that early eighteenth-century development in the north west took place across a broad front, incorporating coal and salt mining, metalworking and shipbuilding and a range of locally-oriented craft industries as well as textile production. Taken together, these gave the region the critical mass needed for rapid industrialisation in the late eighteenth and nineteenth centuries. At the national scale, it was growth in a similar combination of industries which generated the overall impetus for a more widespread industrial revolution. The development seen in north-west England thus presaged indus-trialisation in the country as a whole. It also offers interesting parallels in terms of economic structuring, especially with the dynamic relationship between a key growth pole and a wide variety of other industries. The social division of labour which this involved was evident at both the regional and national scale; it was matched by a spatial division of labour that resulted in marked local and regional geographical specialisation. It is to this growing specialisation that the discussion turns next.

Geographical specialisation and industrial development

According to Hudson, 'there was something unique about the process of regional specialisation taking place in the late eighteenth century and in the first half of the nineteenth'. Thus, she argues, 'the industrial revolution created regions different in kind to those existing now and also to those earlier'.[32] For Hudson, regions are important because they were the vehicles of industriali-sation, but the concentration of particular industries into particular regions was already established in the early eighteenth century, before the classic industrial revolution. Defoe noted the metalware trades of the west Midlands and south Yorkshire, cotton manufacture in south-east Lancashire, the pro-duction of woollens in the West Country, west Yorkshire and Norfolk, framework knitting in the east Midlands, Newcastle's coal trade and the myriad manufactures of London. He also commented on local specialities such as Stilton cheeses, Stourport glass and the Monmouth cups made at Bewdley.[33] The regional concentrations especially played an important part in bringing about wider industrialisation. They helped to generate pools of skilled labour, networks of credit, capital and information, and improved transport systems and their existence encouraged technological change and entrepreneurial ac-tivity.[34] The differential use of technologies and varied organisational systems which distinguished these regions during the industrial revolution were also apparent in the early eighteenth century.[35] Within textile manufacturing, putting-out systems characterised Lancashire cotton production, the woollen industry of the West Country and the manufacture of worsteds in west Yorkshire; the West Riding woollen industry was the seat of independent artisans; and silk production in Cheshire and Derbyshire was centred on large proto-factories. Similar variations characterised textile industries elsewhere in Europe.[36] Although marked by internal variations, metalworking in the west Midlands was often characterised by artisan-organised production, whereas putting-out systems predominated in south Yorkshire.[37] Overlain on these home-based or workshop systems was the centralised production seen in mining and metal-processing, in cloth-printing and earthenware manufacture.[38]

Such differences depended on a range of factors, including skill levels, access to capital and credit, the location of markets and supplies, and the 'institutions and social structures within industries and communities'.[39] In turn, these early-established systems of production had a considerable influence over subsequent developments of organisational structure. Putting-out systems most readily transformed to centralised factory production, although the relationship was by no means axiomatic. Artisan-organised production was sometimes overtaken by similar centralised manufacture, but a measure of independence was often maintained, for example in the co-operative mills of the West Riding.[40] In the metal trades, small independent workshops remained the norm throughout the nineteenth century in networks of 'flexible specialisation' which closely resemble the flexible production systems characteristic of post-Fordism.[41] Even in larger units internal contracting was common.[42] Continuities of this type are by no means the historical lock-in of path-dependency: a number of alternative production systems often coexisted and interacted within one sector and region, as for example in the factory and sweating systems seen in nineteenth-century framework knitting in Nottinghamshire.[43] They were, though, important in shaping the nature, geography and pace of subsequent development.

Specialisation was also marked within regions, as is clear from analysis of the space economy of north-west England where various branches of manufacture had distinctive geographies and systems of organisation. A broad distinction can be drawn between the centre and east of the region where manufacturing was a significant element of the economy of town and country, and the western parts of the region which were predominantly agricultural areas (Figure 3.2). Within the manufacturing districts, south-east Lancashire and north-east Cheshire were dominated by textiles, which accounted for around three-quarters of manufacturers, and formed the centre of Wadsworth and Mann's rural textiles economy. Local specialisation varied from woollens and worsteds in the east, through fustians and checks to linen further west in a pattern which is now well recognised (see Chapter 4). An outlier of this

Figure 3.2 *Geographical specialisation in north-west England, 1701–60*

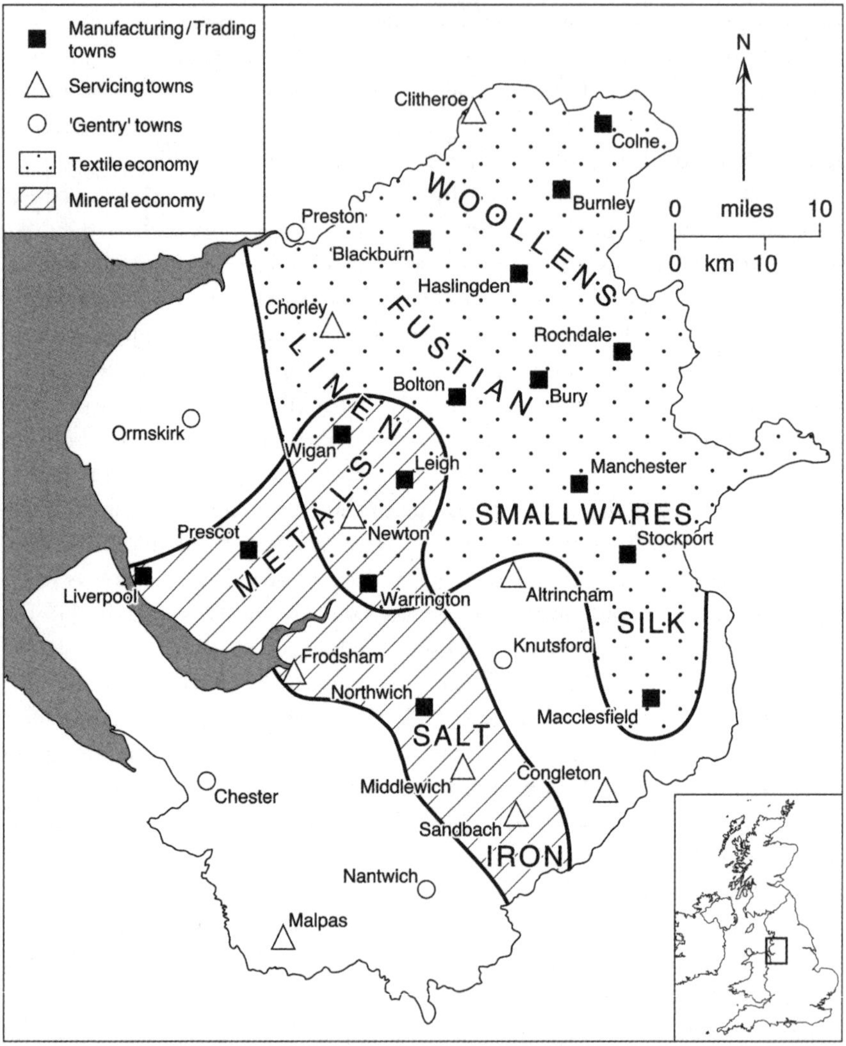

Source: Probate records, 1701–60.

district was the silk industry centred on Macclesfield, but extending to Stockport and Congleton in the mid eighteenth century.[44] In the centre and south of Lancashire, textiles were complemented by metal-working, especially around Wigan and Leigh where nail-, lock- and hinge-making were widespread. Brass and pewter industries were found in Wigan itself and, in Warrington, there were copper- and glass-works, pin-making workshops and an extensive linen trade. To the south, the *wich* towns of central Cheshire formed the focus of the county's salt industry, and to the west lay Liverpool with its port functions and growing range of mineral-based and port-related industries (see Chapter 5).

Of the thirty towns in the north west, as many as sixteen can be identified as manufacturing centres. As well as providing locally-oriented servicing functions, these places were engaged in producing specialist goods for export from the region (Figure 3.2). The rest were generally characterised by more local activities, chiefly providing goods and services for their hinterlands although, as Trinder notes in a wider context, many county and market towns also developed specialist industries.[45] In Chester, for example, shipbuilding remained significant, at least until the end of the century. A conservative estimate suggests that 61 ships (a total of 8,144 tons) were built between 1775 and 1786, including twenty-two for Liverpool, seven for London and six for Whitehaven. A further 75 were finished before 1800 when terminal decline set in.[46] Long before then, however, Chester had emerged as a leisure town and a centre for high order consumer-oriented crafts such as clockmaking, tobacco-and snuff-making, and silverware.[47] It was central to the growth of consumerism and leisure in north-west England and developed social and cultural infrastructure accordingly (see Chapter 6). Similarly, Nantwich had lost its significance in salt production around the turn of the eighteenth century, but (as in many small county towns) was gaining a reputation as a minor social centre and for its food processing and leather industries.[48] Preston too was an important social centre. As Defoe noted 'here's no manufacture; the town is full of attorneys, proctors and notaries ... [and] a great deal of good company', but the town also had its share of clockmakers, upholsterers and goldsmiths.[49] The transformation of Preston to a textiles town came later and was a product of the spread of power looms and watermills.[50] Elsewhere, Congleton had important leather industries, but these were gradually eclipsed by the (ultimately unsuccessful) establishment there of copper-works in 1763 and, more importantly, the construction of one of the largest silk mills in the region in 1755. This signalled the rise of Congleton as an significant textiles town – an important process, but one which only began to take hold in the 1780s, well after the end of the period considered here.[51] Similarly, in the 1760s, coal-based development took off around Prescot and St Helens following the completion of the Sankey Brook navigation in 1757, swamping the previous specialised tool- and watchmaking industries.[52] Twenty years later the opening of Arkwright's mill at Birkacre near Chorley in 1777 signalled the start of rapid growth in the town.[53]

Local specialised production was thus widespread in early eighteenth-century Lancashire and Cheshire, but overall, two specialist sub-regional industrial economies can be identified: textiles manufacture concentrated in south-east Lancashire and centred principally, but not exclusively, on Manchester, and mineral-based production in central and south-west Lancashire and central Cheshire, with its principal fulcrum in Liverpool. Commercial agriculture was important across the region, but dominated much of Cheshire and west Lancashire and formed a third broad economic unit in the region. As will be seen, these specialisms formed the basis of the industrial geography of north-west England during the industrial revolution. Indeed, their development and interaction was instrumental in the industrialisation of the region. To an extent, this was a product of the emerging agglomeration economies especially within the manufacturing districts, but much also depended on the development of integrating systems and functions which drew together these productive localities and linked them to the wider economy. In the north west, as elsewhere, these functions were focused on towns.

Towns and the integration of spatial divisions of labour

Spatial integration was achieved through many different channels, but especially via the servicing and trading activities of towns and the information, credit and capital networks and transport systems which focused on them. Services and trading were the quintessential roles of a town and, with the growth of rural manufacturing in the seventeenth and eighteenth centuries and the emergence of industrial villages in the nineteenth, they often formed the defining criteria for urban status. The nexus of market, shops, professional services and administrative functions is all too easily overlooked as analysis concentrates on the growing specialisms of eighteenth-century towns. However, these formed the basis of urban economies up and down the country. Indeed, 'the small market towns were ... the predominant components of the urban network'.[54] The servicing activities of these places had long been important in integrating the economy of town and country, and they were vital in facilitating the growing specialisation and commercialisation of households. That said, not all market towns prospered and, with improved transport and marketing systems, the larger, more accessible and better-provisioned towns tended to erode the market areas of their smaller neighbours. Chartres estimates that the number of markets in England and Wales fell from 874 in 1690 to 728 by 1792, although many of those lost were marginal rural or semi-rural markets which had, in some cases, existed more in name than terms of actual trading activity.[55]

Alongside this general servicing role, certain towns also served to integrate local, regional and national economies through more specific trading or cultural functions. The county towns and especially the resorts linked consumers in small towns and villages to fashions from London and the Continent, and introduced new leisure and consumption patterns.[56] Such places formed important meeting places for the rural and emerging urban gentry thus drawing together town and country and also tied local society and culture to national standards and trends. This is not to imply that provincial towns were in thrall of London; there was critical comment as well as acquiescence.[57] Nonetheless, they linked the 'surplus' wealth generated by agricultural, industrial or commercial growth to new social and cultural attitudes and novel consumer goods and leisure practices.[58] At the same time, inland and overseas trade was growing inexorably. The ports in particular played a key role in linking local production and requirements for raw materials to overseas markets and supplies. Growth was almost universal, but Liverpool, Hull and Sunderland expanded their trade most rapidly[59] – a reflection of the industrial development of their hinterlands as well as their growing links with overseas trading partners. Certain inland towns also emerged as important commercial centres, acting as collecting and marketing centres for the production of their hinterlands and urban neighbours. Birmingham, Manchester, Leeds, Sheffield and Newcastle, for example, were vital in financing and co-ordinating manufacturing in their hinterlands, and in integrating such production with wider supplies and demands.[60] These places came to dominate local manufacturing systems and symbolise these to the outside world. 'Not all Manchester fustians ... Norwich stuffs, Sheffield knives, or Birmingham "toys", were actually made in the towns; but their reputation was already stamped upon their local industries'.[61]

All these functions were being carried out by the towns of north-west England. Whilst the rural areas were dominated by agriculture, textile manufacturing or metal working, towns had more complex economies (Table 3.6). Urban manufactures were diverse, including significant numbers in the leather and clothing industries and in food and drink processing – the type of manufactures which linked towns with the daily needs of their hinterlands.[62] Towns also dominated service and dealing activities: they contained over two-thirds of professionals and public servants, a similar proportion of food and drink retailers (all of whom were important to local integration) and nearly three-quarters of the merchants and other traders who provided extra-regional commercial linkages. The general servicing role was epitomised by small market towns such as Sandbach, Chorley and Ormskirk, whereas mercantile activity was concentrated into particular places: Rochdale, Colne, Bolton, Warrington and especially Liverpool and Manchester. The former was the most rapidly developing port in the early eighteenth century and the latter formed the commercial centre for the textiles trade and contained nearly as many dealers as manufacturers according to the probate records. As is discussed in detail in Chapter 7, the integrating functions of these places encouraged wider economic development as they drew together local production into regional and national economic systems. Attitudes to leisure and consumption were also influenced by key centres with Chester and Preston especially linking local wealth and county society to new fashions, novel purchasing practices and a growing range of consumer goods.

Table 3.6 *Male occupations in north-west England, 1701–60: urban and rural specialisation*

	Urban		Rural	
	Number	%	Number	%
Agriculture	1244	12.7	8552	50.2
Mining	14	0.1	38	0.2
Building	432	4.4	340	2.1
Manufacture	3070	31.4	5760	33.7
Textiles	1598	16.3	4714	27.6
Shipbuilding	116	1.2	13	0.1
Metal and machinery	231	2.4	242	1.4
Household	135	1.4	54	0.3
Leather and wood	342	3.5	258	1.5
Dress and shoes	368	3.8	346	2.0
Food and drink	280	2.9	133	0.8
Labourers	37	0.4	41	0.2
Transport	1403	14.4	214	1.3
Dealing	1837	18.9	654	3.8
Textiles	293	3.6	47	0.3
Luxury	740	7.4	252	1.4
Food and drink	728	7.5	347	2.0
Other	76	0.8	8	0.1
Public and prof.	669	6.9	304	1.8
Dom. service	69	0.7	39	0.2
Gentry	979	10.0	1107	6.5

Source: Probate records, 1701–60.

Information was vital to both local production and the effective integration of the economy.[63] Its core was undoubtedly London which, as well as being the centre for fashions, was also the focus of informal and official mail services. The coaches carried price lists, orders and invoices, samples and patterns, banknotes and bills, as well as newspapers and of course letters. They provided commerce across the country with current market information and often the means to act on it, and were thus crucial to the integration of the national space economy.[64] Particularly important in this respect were newspapers. These contained reports of current affairs (political intrigues, wars, treaties and so on) which, given the expansion of the world economy, had an increasing bearing on trade, prices and the availability and terms of capital and credit. They also carried a growing number of advertisements for products, tradesmen and recreational events and thus informed both consumption and leisure practices.[65] Although strongly influenced by London, the provincial press grew considerably in the eighteenth century, both in the number of publications (150 newspapers had appeared in fifty towns by 1750) and in finding its own distinctive voice.[66] The towns of the north west were closely linked to London fashions, not least through the activities of individual tradesmen who visited the metropolis for the latest fabrics, furnishings and trinkets (see Chapter 6). They were also quick to advertise this to an eager public in the growing number of local newspapers.[67] The first newspaper in the north west appeared in Liverpool in 1712 and was followed in Manchester (1719) and Chester (1727). All these ventures were short-lived and it was not until the 1730s that regular publications were firmly established in each town.[68] Links to national information networks were also strong, initially by carriers and coaches, but increasingly via the London and cross-post mail coaches. By the 1790s, only a handful of towns were not connected to the mail service (see Chapter 7).

National credit and capital systems were focused onto the metropolis, with London banks often acting as the reservoirs and principal channels for inter-regional flows of capital.[69] This reinforced the position of the metropolis as the centre of control in the spatial and hierarchical division of labour within Britain as a whole. Intra-regional credit systems were provided by attorneys and after 1750 by country banks located in a growing number of provincial towns.[70] The most important function of these individuals and institutions was to supply short-term loans to local businesses (at the same time providing investment opportunities for those with surplus capital), but this local integration was counterbalanced by links to London where many bills of exchange accepted locally were discounted. Thus, at the start of the eighteenth century, Daniel Peck was discounting bills through a number of London merchants, especially Thomas and Michael Carbonnell.[71] The relatively slow spread of banks in the north west reflects the effectiveness of credit and capital linkages provided through personal business contacts and by attorneys rather than any lack of commercial activity in the region.[72] However, Neal's suggestion that the 'success of these older forms of intermediary and instrument ... can, perhaps, be attributed to the dominance of the cotton trade'[73] fails to acknowledge the diversity of industrial and commercial activity and its varied needs and demands for capital. Moreover, there were banks in Chester, Manchester, Liverpool, Preston and Stockport by the 1770s. Fortunes were mixed, but, whilst the Stockport bank failed soon after its establishment, those at Chester and Manchester had some of the most extensive branch networks in the country by the 1830s.[74]

Ultimately, of course, spatial integration was dependent upon the movement of goods, people, ideas and capital. This, in turn, relied on transport systems, particularly turnpike roads and canals. The former had their origin on the Great North Road in 1663, but growth of the network began in earnest only in 1696 before becoming a 'mania' after 1750.[75] The 22,000 miles of road which had been turnpiked by 1772 enmeshed England and Wales in a web which offered considerably improved transport routes and journey times, the latter being enhanced by the introduction of stagecoaches in the late seventeenth century.[76] Naturally, the improved road network and the services which ran along it were centred on towns. London, at the centre of the national space economy, was already the clear focus of the turnpike system in 1720 and it retained that position over the following century. Other towns formed local and regional foci: Bristol and Exeter in the south west; Shrewsbury in the Welsh marches; Hereford, Worcester and later Birmingham in the west Midlands; Leicester in the east Midlands; Leeds in west Yorkshire and Manchester in the north west.[77] A similar list of towns was also prominent in coach and carrier networks. Many ran to and from London, but others plied a more local or 'cross-country' trade, reflecting the geographical cores of national and regional economies.[78]

The same improvements were seen in the north west, usually in response to rising levels of traffic in textiles and minerals, but also reflecting important routes to London.[79] Thus, 'in 1725 the improvement-minded Liverpool merchants obtained an act for the road to Prescot. The desire for cheaper coal transport was the paramount consideration both here and on the road from Warrington through Wigan to Preston, turnpiked in 1727.'[80] Further south, the carriage of pig- and bar iron was responsible for the turnpiking of the road from Lawton to Cranage, linking the furnaces in the former to the slitting mill in the latter, and both to Staffordshire's coalfield. In eastern Lancashire, meanwhile, pressure from the merchant community resulted in several cross-Pennine routes being turnpiked in the 1730s.[81] These included a trust on the road leading from Manchester through Stockport to Saltersbrook and hence to Doncaster and Hull (1732), and two important wool routes; one from Manchester to Austerlands (and hence to Huddersfield and Wakefield) and the other from Rochdale to Halifax and Elland (1735). These improvements were felt to be necessary because:

> the Towns of Manchester and Stockport are very large, and considerable Trading Towns, and send weekly great Quantities of Goods, Merchandizes, and Manufactures to Doncaster, in the County of York; which are carried from thence by Water

Figure 3.3 *The transport infrastructure of north-west England, c.1780*

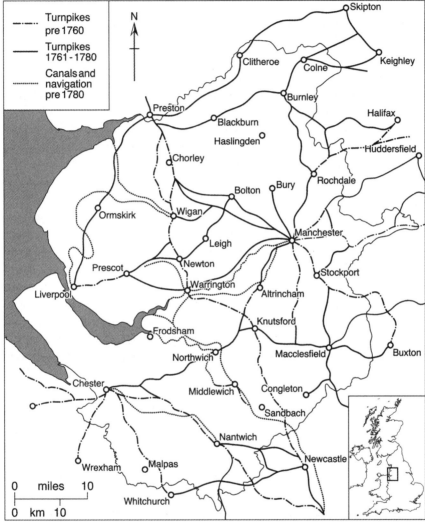

Source: Albert, *Turnpike Road System*; Pawson, *Transport and Economy*; Hadfield and Biddle, *Canals of North-west England.*

to Hull, in order to be shipped to London, and foreign Parts; and bring back considerable Quantities of Flax, Yarn and other Commodities, which are manufactured in the said Towns of Manchester and Stockport.[82]

The results of this activity are illustrated in Figure 3.3, which shows that three broad groups of turnpikes existed by 1750: one linking the main towns of west and central Lancashire; a second connecting the textiles centres of eastern Lancashire with their counterparts in west Yorkshire, and a third joining the principal towns of southern Cheshire.[83] Over the next thirty years, these separate units were effectively united to provide a more integrated if still somewhat unbalanced transport system, but the impetus for improvement remained the same. Thus, several branches were added from Prescot to the Warrington–Preston road; linkages to the Cheshire salt towns were enhanced; and improvements made to roads into east Lancashire on the cross-Pennine routes and from the centre of the county.

Navigations and canals also rose to prominence in the English space economy during the eighteenth century. Again, these had early antecedents in terms of the Exeter Canal (1564–66) and numerous navigation schemes, but extensive canal building is generally seen as dating from the opening of the Bridgewater Canal in 1761. Development over the following fifty years was undertaken to enhance the supply of raw materials (as with the Bridgewater and Staffordshire and Worcestershire canals); to improve linkages between areas of production and regional entrepôts (Trent and Mersey and Aire and Calder canals); or to directly or indirectly link together river systems (Oxford, and Kent and Avon) – sometimes all three. By 1790 a skeletal national network was in place, although most canal traffic was local and the canals themselves were concentrated into the Midlands and north.[84] The net effect was to promote greater regional integration rather than unify the regions into a single economic system. They were an important stimulus to local and regional development and were vital in the growth of Wrigley's mineral-based energy economy, as is clear from development within north-west England.[85]

Navigation schemes in Lancashire and Cheshire began with the dredging of the Mersey as far as Warrington, the first stage of a more ambitious project to improve the river system all the way to Manchester. The stretch to Warrington was completed in 1701, largely at the behest and expense of Thomas Patten (a Warrington merchant), but the link to Manchester had to wait another thirty-five years.[86] This second stage was 'overwhelmingly a Manchester project', and greatly eased the movement of textiles out of the town.[87] In the interim, the Weaver navigation was completed, as far as Northwich by 1732 and to Winsford by the following year.[88] The river thus linked the saltfields of northern Cheshire with supplies of coal from southern Lancashire and (via Liverpool) with the growing Irish, American and north European markets. Meanwhile, the Douglas navigation was completed to link the coalfield around Wigan to the Ribble estuary and hence by sea to Liverpool. The Sankey Brook navigation was the culmination of these early navigation schemes in the north west. This was needed to ease the fuel crisis being felt in the south-west corner of Lancashire (and particularly Liverpool) as increasing amounts of coal were carried south along the Weaver. It was authorised in 1755 and, upon completion two years later (mainly thanks to Liverpool money), linked the coal pits around what was to become St Helens to the Mersey and hence to Liverpool or the Cheshire salt industry. In reality, the Sankey Brook was a dead-water canal, and was quickly followed by other canals. The Bridgewater was financed and built by the Duke of Bridgewater, initially to link his mines at Worsley with Manchester (the principal market), but a later extension (1773) provided an alternative to the still meandering Mersey. The Leeds–Liverpool Canal (1774) was largely paid for by Liverpool and Bradford men keen to improve access to the central Lancashire coalfield. The Trent and Mersey (1777) linked Liverpool and the Mersey to the potteries of north Staffordshire, and the initially unsuccessful Chester Canal (1780) ran from Chester to Nantwich – a route which afforded no obvious traffic as it failed to secure a connection with the Trent and Mersey Canal.[89] Many of these navigations and canals (and those which followed in the 1790s and early nineteenth century) focused on Liverpool and made it 'the best-connected port in England' by 1800.[90]

Towns thus formed the foci of growing transport, credit and information networks. This, coupled with their economic, social and cultural complexity, made the urban system central to the integration of local and regional divisions of labour. These twin processes of specialisation and integration in turn shaped the geography of economic and urban growth in the eighteenth century.

Geographies of uneven development: cores and peripheries

The regions experiencing industrial development in the eighteenth century are familiar enough: the north west, west and south Yorkshire, the west and east Midlands, the north east, south Wales and perhaps the West Country. These were emerging as core economic areas, enjoying increased capital investment in industry as well as higher productivity and wages, and they increasingly overshadowed development elsewhere.[91] In contrast, other regions experiencing industrial stagnation or in the last throws of decline – for example, East Anglia (although Suffolk was suffering more problems than Norfolk) and the Weald – were becoming peripheral to national economic growth.[92] The timing and pace of change varied considerably, with large-scale development coming later in the east Midlands than in the west; the west Yorkshire wool textiles industries growing more strongly than those in East Anglia and the West Country; and the long-drawn-out decline of the Weald contrasting with explosive growth in south Wales. Beyond these broad distinctions, systematic analysis of differential regional growth is more difficult. Many of the growing regions lay on coalfields and comparisons of the growth of output confirm the general

Figure 3.4 *Change in counties' rank order of wealth, 1693–1843*

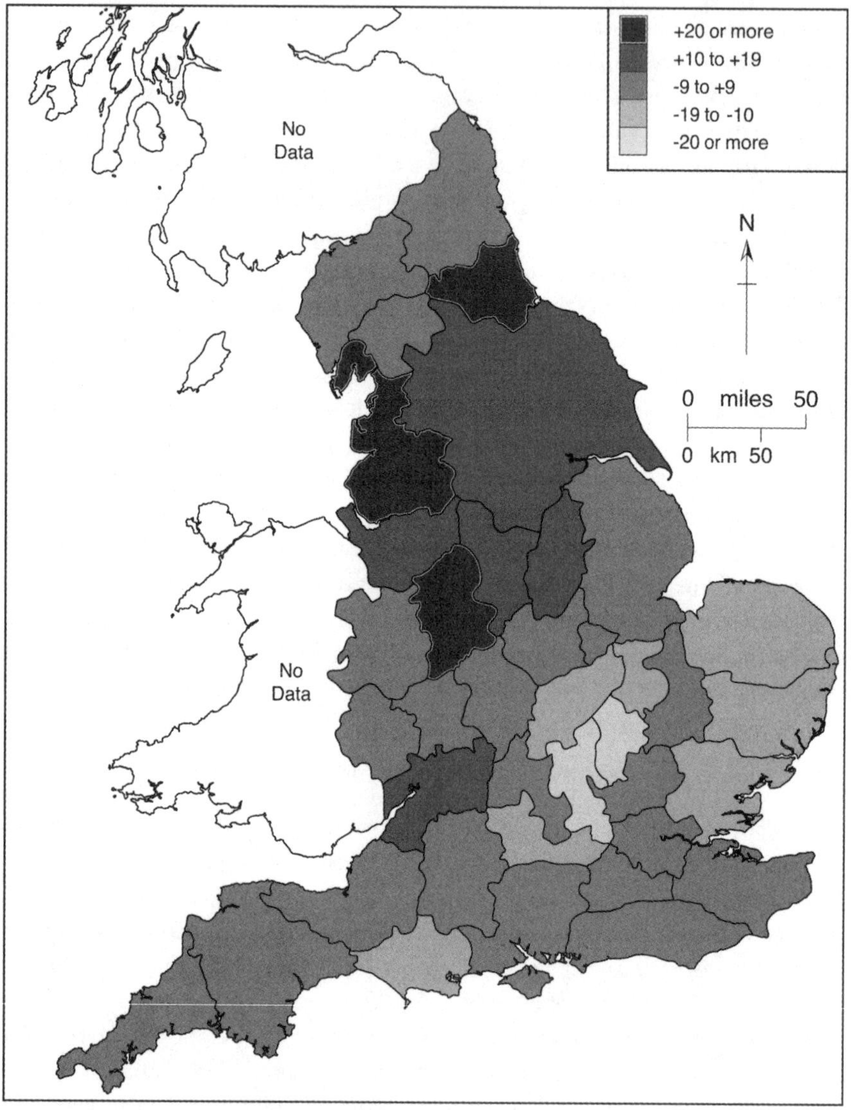

Source: Buckatzch, 'Geographical distribution of wealth'.

impressions of regional development (Table 3.7).[93] The west Midlands, York-shire and especially the north east led coal production in 1700 and each grew steadily over the next 130 years. More rapid growth occurred elsewhere, however, and eroded the dominant position of the north east. The Lancashire coal industry expanded most strongly in the early eighteenth century and its share of national output had grown fourfold by 1775. Growth accelerated in south Wales after 1750 and in the east Midlands from the 1770s, expansion in the former being more significant in national terms.

And yet coal was only one aspect of economic development and was more significant in the industrialisation of metalworking regions than those concerned with textiles production. A more general if somewhat blunt measure of the strength of a regional economy can be taken using the changing wealth of individual counties between 1693 and 1843.[94] Although there are dangers in over-interpreting these data, they paint a striking picture of regional growth and decline during the long eighteenth century (Figure 3.4). There is a stark contrast between the rising wealth of the industrialising counties of the Midlands and north, and the relative decline of those in the south and east of England. Lancashire rose by far the greatest number of places (33) to rank second in 1843; it was followed by Staffordshire (25), Durham (23) and Cheshire (19). Of the southern counties, only Gloucestershire – seat of the West Country woollen industry – moved up, whilst the home counties and those in East Anglia fell by an average of about 12 places. Wealth was increasingly generated by industry and commerce, and these were clearly concentrated into the counties of the Midlands and north – the emergent core regions of the national economy. The long eighteenth century thus witnessed a restructuring of core and periphery within the national space economy. Whilst London remained at the core of economic, social and cultural activity, the relative strength of regions fundamentally shifted with power increasingly located in the north and west rather than the south and east of the country.

Table 3.7 *Estimated output of coal in England, 1700–1830*

Mining region	Output (000s tons)					Percentage growth			
	1700	1750	1775	1800	1830	1700–50	1750–75	1775–1800	1800–30
Lancashire	80	350	900	1,400	4,000	337	157	56	186
South Wales	80	140	650	1,700	4,400	75	364	162	159
South west	150	180	250	445	800	20	39	78	80
East Midlands	75	140	250	750	1,700	87	79	200	127
West Midlands	510	820	1,400	2,550	5,600	61	71	82	120
Yorkshire	300	500	850	1,100	2,800	67	70	29	155
North east	1,290	1,955	2,990	4,450	6,915	52	53	49	55

Source: Flinn, *British Coal*, volume 2, p. 26.

The same processes of spatial reorganisation are apparent from urban growth rates (see Table 3.2).[95] Around 1670, only six of the top twenty towns were in the north and the west Midlands, and none were what might be termed 'industrial towns'. By 1750, the pattern was changing: nine of the biggest towns were in these industrialising regions, including Manchester, Birmingham, Leeds and Sheffield as well as the established regional centres and ports. In 1801, the north-south balance was reversed and the national urban hierarchy was dominated by the burgeoning towns of the North. Furthermore, three-quarters of the forty-three 'new' towns identified by Langton for the period 1670 to 1801 were in the north west, west Yorkshire or the west Midlands. This relationship between economic and urban growth should not necessarily be seen as one of uni-directional cause and effect. Undoubtedly, many of the new towns to emerge during the eighteenth century were directly linked to industry. Langton suggests that fourteen were textiles towns, seven were engaged in coal and iron production and six in mining and the manufacture of pottery or glass.[96] Moreover, the great northern towns (Manchester, Leeds, Sheffield and the like) are generally seen as the product of industrialisation. However, as was previously argued, these towns and others were also crucial in generating the right conditions for local, regional and national economic development, not least through their commercial and their integrating functions. Notwithstanding the availability of coal and other resources over wide areas of the industrialising regions, it is notable that urban development often clustered around a major town. This is seen in the groupings of Newcastle, Tynemouth and South Shields; Manchester, Salford, Oldham, Ashton-under-Lyne and Stockport; and Birmingham, Walsall, Wolverhampton, Wednesbury and West Bromwich. More widely, the relatively strong growth of so-called 'non-industrial' towns within industrialising regions contrasts with the slower growth of such places elsewhere. Chester, for example, more than doubled its population between 1670 and 1801 whereas York and Salisbury grew by less than 40 per cent. Likewise, Liverpool's meteoric rise contrasts with the more gradual growth of Bristol. This is not to imply that endogenous factors were unimportant in the relative fortunes of these towns, but their local economic and urban context was clearly influential.

Within an emerging core economy such as that of north-west England, development was also geographically uneven. In 1664 the larger towns were concentrated into Cheshire and central and south-east Lancashire, whereas north-east and south-west Lancashire contained only relatively small urban settlements. By the 1770s the balance had swung towards these latter areas and, most notably, away from southern Cheshire: a fundamental shift in core and peripheral status within the regional urban system. Stockport moved up the hierarchy and Northwich maintained its position, but other Cheshire towns fell by an average of 3.7 places. In Lancashire, the pattern was more complex with neighbouring settlements experiencing very different fortunes: several small textiles towns (Leigh, Colne, Burnley, Blackburn and Haslingden) grew rapidly and rose up the hierarchy, whereas some of their neighbours (Clitheroe,

Figure 3.5 *Urban growth in north-west England, 1664–1780*

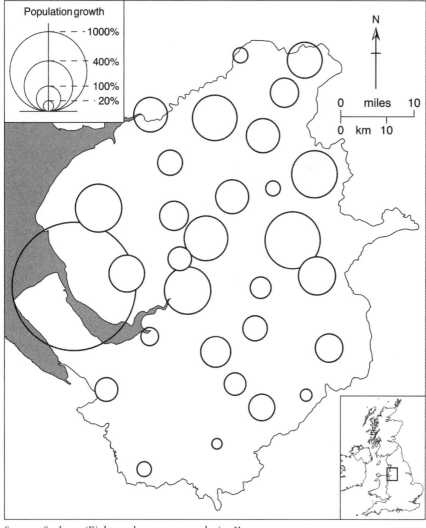

Source: Stobart, 'Eighteenth-century revolution?'

Wigan and Bury) fell slightly. Overall, though, the shift in urban locus north and eastwards was clear: only two of the top ten towns were in southern Cheshire; central and south-eastern Lancashire contained four (Manchester being prominent amongst them); the north had two, and Liverpool stood out on the western edge of the region. These trends are confirmed by the geography of the percentage growth rates (Figure 3.5). South and west Cheshire towns expanded slowly, and only Northwich and Stockport experienced growth above the regional average. The Lancashire towns enjoyed much stronger growth, with seven growing more than the urban average for the region, and a further five exceeding the overall regional average. Chester's long-standing domination of the region was being challenged and superseded by Liverpool and Manchester – new core areas in the north west. Liverpool's growth was greater than that of Manchester up to the 1770s, but, as Wadsworth and Mann suggest, it was 'growth of an isolated centre of population compared with that of the central point of a thickening industrial belt'.[97] The clustering of growth which was both cause and effect of economic localisation was apparent in the north west and the country as a whole. However, the fall-out of this localised development was felt more widely, both in terms of general demographic growth and prosperity, and in the changing form of the regional economic and urban structure.

Conclusions: specialisation and integration

In its economic and urban growth, north-west England can be seen as both microcosm of and an engine for wider development processes. The region as a whole experienced strong urban growth and saw the emergence or strengthening of a range of key activities in the early eighteenth century, arguably achieving Pollard's 'critical mass' of industries, services and communications. Whilst it remained the largest employer of men through to the mid-eighteenth century at least, agriculture was being replaced by manufacturing as the major economic activity and the principal form of employment, in part as rural industry became increasingly widespread. Within this, urban economies remained buoyant as towns provided key manufacturing and service functions. Indeed, urban growth in north-west England outpaced that seen elsewhere in the country and the level of industrial development and specialisation at least matched other specialised regions such as west Yorkshire and the west Midlands.[98]

At the same time, Langton's observation that 'single holistic national economic and urban systems did not exist in Britain in this period, and quite often different processes were operating at different levels' can also be applied to individual regions such as the north west.[99] In short, development was often localised and specialised. At a national scale, regions were increasingly specialised both in product and production systems – a process which depended as much on effective intra- and extra-regional integration as local availability of human and natural resources. This integration was effected through service and trading functions, and through credit and communication networks, all of which were largely focused on towns. The changing patterns of urban growth during the eighteenth century were therefore a stimulus for as well as a response to this regional economic development. Within north-west England, local specialisation was pronounced. Textiles production was concentrated into east and central Lancashire and was organised along proto-industrial lines, with manufacturing being characteristically rural and generally fast-growing towns acting as servicing and trading centres for their manufacturing hinterlands, as well as production centres in their own right. The mineral-based industries of central and south-west Lancashire and central Cheshire displayed greater internal variation with putting-out, centralised production and artisan workshops often existing side by side. The agricultural economy of much of Cheshire and west Lancashire was characterised by slower growth and an urban network which provided services for its hinterland. Throughout the region, though, towns were vital in articulating these spatial divisions of labour.[100] As Hudson argues for west Yorkshire, 'it was the towns which were instrumental in forging extra-local ties and those national and international commercial relationships which created the specialised industrial region out its diverse parts'.[101]

The product of this heightened specialisation and integration was a shift in core-periphery relationships in both national and regional economies. This transformation invites one or other (or both) of two broad conclusions, which, in turn, have important implications for the economic growth of the region and nation. First, the growth of the certain (new) towns might have been dependent upon different bases and economic functions from that their (older) neighbours. If this was the case, attention should redirected away from the forces which were used to explain the preferential growth of larger towns; that is, away from Robson's ideas about the role of hierarchical diffusion or Myrdal's notions of cumulative causation.[102] Instead, we should look towards other growth-inducing factors, such as production opportunities, specialisation, spatial integration and transport nodality. Second, the organisation of the urban system and the space economy were being rearranged around these emerging centres as core-periphery relationships changed at the national and regional level. This process shifts attention away from analysis of location factors and towards the relational nature of economic development. Two possible scenarios arise here. At one level, there must have been a shift in the loci *within* one organisational system; the centres of the diffusion process must have changed as new towns grew and became the diffusion centres for (new sets of) information, innovations, capital and so on. Meanwhile, at a second level, the organisational system itself must have been changing as new forces came into play.[103] As well as the economy and the urban system being structured by the hierarchical relations inherent in processes of diffusion, it was also being shaped by the same sets of forces responsible for the individual growth of these 'newer' settlements. Thus, as the urban system helped to shape transport systems, production opportunities and access to new raw materials, these factors began to play a greater role in structuring the urban system. What might be happening during this period of economic and hierarchical change is a fundamental transformation in the structure and functioning of the urban system. This is important in understanding the internal structuration and dynamics of regional growth, and demands closer investigation of the economic characteristics and functions of the region and its urban system. It also demands that we view these developments not in spatial isolation from one another, but as part of a relational system. This approach is attempted over the next three chapters.

Notes

1 Defoe, *Tour through Britain*, quoted in Gregory, 'Geographies of industrialization', p. 372.
2 Walton, *Lancashire*, p. 7; Trinder, *Industrial Revolution in Shropshire*; Evans, 'Two paths'.
3 See Timmins, *Made in Lancashire*, pp. 11–34.
4 Walton, *Lancashire*, p. 3. Part 1 of Timmins, *Made in Lancashire*, is largely concerned with textiles.
5 See Hudson, 'Regional and local history', pp. 7–8.
6 Paasi, 'Deconstructing regions', pp. 243–5. See also Stobart, 'Regions, localities and industrialisation', pp. 1306–8.
7 Langton, 'Urban growth', pp. 465–86.
8 Clark, 'Small towns in England', p. 119.
9 Clark 'Small towns in England', pp. 108–10.
10 Corfield, *English Towns*, p. 11; Wrigley, 'Urban growth', p. 42.
11 Wrigley, 'Urban growth', p. 43; Corfield, 'Urban development'.
12 Wrigley suggests 1670 totals of c.6,000 for each of these towns, 'Urban growth', p. 43. However, in every case these seem too high. Manchester (even with Salford) scarcely exceeded 5,000, Birmingham around 4,500 and Leeds a similar amount. See Stobart, 'Eighteenth-century revolution?', p. 40, and Chalklin, *Provincial Towns*, pp. 22–3 and 33.
13 The larger size differences between high-ranking towns make changes in rank less likely, even if considerable growth occurs. Furthermore, high-ranking towns have little chance to move up the hierarchy; Robson, *Urban Growth*, p. 40.
14 Lawton and Pooley, *Britain 1740–1950*, p. 92.
15 For a full discussion of these population estimates, see Appendix 1.
16 Towns are defined as those places identified as 'market towns' by Blome, *Britannia*; Adams, *Index Villaris*; Cox, *Magna Britannia*.
17 Wadsworth and Mann *Cotton Trade*, p. 311.
18 Across the country, fourteen small towns and a handful of larger centres lost population during the 1700s. See Clark, 'Small towns in England', p. 110.
19 Johnson, 'Rank-size convexity'; Robson, *Urban Growth*, pp. 214–28. See Lepetit, *Urban System*, pp. 181–5 for a critique of these ideas.
20 Corfield, *English Towns*; Daunton, 'Towns and economic growth'; Langton, 'Urban growth'.

21 Deane and Cole, *British Economic Growth*, pp. 78 and 166; Crafts, *British Economic Growth*, p. 23. See also Jackson, 'Economic growth'.

22 Crafts, 'Industrial Revolution'.

23 See, *inter alia*, Mathias, *First Industrial Nation*, pp. 84–97; Hudson, *Industrial Revolution*, pp. 181–92; Engerman, 'Overseas trade'.

24 Mathias, *First Industrial Nation*, p. 88; Hudson, 'Proto-industrialization in England', p. 53.

25 Crafts, *British Economic Growth*, p. 14.

26 This argument cuts both ways, since industrial employees may well have been engaged in part-time agricultural pursuits either during harvest or on smallholdings. Crafts, *British Economic Growth*, p. 14.

27 Berg, 'Women's work'.

28 Berg and Hudson, 'Rehabilitating', p. 32.

29 Langton, *Geographical Change*, p. 178.

30 Lindert's figures (Table 3.4) do not include the multiplier for spinners (Appendix 2). As the probate records under-emphasise proletarianised industries, the proportion of the workforce omitted from the two estimates may not be dissimiliar. The national figures assume that as many as one-third of labourers were working in manufacturing and so are possibly over-estimates.

31 For discussion of growth pole theory, see Richardson, *Regional and Urban Economics*, chapter 7.

32 Hudson, *Industrial Revolution*, pp. 101 and 102. See also Hudson, 'Regional and local history', pp. 8–14.

33 Defoe, *Tour through Britain*, pp. 370 and 424.

34 See Gregory, 'Geographies of industrialization', pp. 372–5; Wadsworth and Mann, *Cotton Trade*, pp. 324–39; Hudson, *Industrial Capital*, pp. 105–208; Langton, 'Liverpool'; Hudson and King, 'Two textile townships', pp. 706–17.

35 Berg, *Age of Manufactures*, pp. 208–79.

36 Wadsworth and Mann, *Cotton Trade*, pp. 78–91; Hudson, *Industrial Capital*, pp. 30–40; Mager, 'Proto-industrialization'; Freudenberger, *Industrialization of a Central European City*, pp. 26–80.

37 Rowlands, *Masters and Men*, pp. 78–109 and 147–68; Hey, *Rural Metalworkers*, *passim*.

38 Berg, 'Factories', pp. 128–9; Weatherill, *Pottery Trade*, pp. 59–75.

39 Berg, 'Factories', p. 129. These same factors are seen as important to industrial location today – see Hayter, *Industrial Location*, pp. 83–110.

40 Hudson, *Industrial Capital*, pp. 76–81.

41 See Bryson and Henry, 'Global production system', pp. 360–2; Dicken, *Global Shift*, pp. 165–8.

42 Berg, 'Factories', p. 136; Clapham, *Economic History*, volume 1, p. 176.

43 Berg, 'Factories', p. 135. See also Ellis, "The stocking country".

44 See Corry, *Macclesfield*, pp. 193–7.

45 Trinder, 'Industrialising towns', pp. 823–7.

46 Craig, 'Trade and shipping'.

47 Kennett, *Georgian Chester*, pp. 15–19. For Chester's growth as a leisure town, see Stobart, 'Shopping streets'.

48 Trinder, 'Industrialising towns'; Platt, *Nantwich*, pp. 10–13; Aikin, *Country round Manchester*, p. 407.

49 Defoe, *Tour through Britain*, p. 548.
50 Chaloner, 'Salt in Cheshire'; Phillips and Smith, *Lancashire and Cheshire*, pp. 96–8.
51 Corry, *Macclesfield*, pp. 193–5; Stephens, *Congleton*, pp. 138–9 and 154.
52 Langton, *Geographical Change*, pp. 136–45; Bailey and Barker, 'Watchmaking'; Barker and Harris, *Merseyside Town*, pp. 75–130.
53 Phillips and Smith, *Lancashire and Cheshire*, p. 96.
54 Corfield, *English Towns*, p. 17. See also Clark, 'Small towns in England'; Ellis, *Georgian Town*, pp. 41–2.
55 Chartres, 'Marketing of agricultural produce', pp. 409–20; Chalklin, *Rise of the English Town*, pp. 1–12.
56 Wrigley, 'London's importance'; Glennie and Thrift, 'Urbanism and modern consumption'.
57 Borsay, *Urban Renaissance, passim*; Sweet, *Urban Histories*, pp. 238–41 and 252–6; Sweet, *English Town*, pp. 257–66.
58 Glennie and Thrift, 'Urbanism and modern consumption', pp. 429–30; Stobart, 'County, town and country'.
59 Corfield, *English Towns*, p. 40.
60 See Berg, 'Commerce and creativity', p. 196; Wadsworth and Mann, *Cotton Trade*, pp. 71–96; Gregory, *Regional Transformation*, pp. 111–21; Hey, *Rural Metalworkers*, pp. 42–9; Cromar, 'Coal industry on Tyneside'.
61 Corfield, *English Towns*, p. 22.
62 Trinder, 'Industrialising towns', pp. 805–8 and 823–7.
63 Gregory, 'Geographies of industrialization', pp. 377–81; Ogborn, *Spaces of Modernity*, pp. 7–8 and 203–10.
64 See Gregory, 'The friction of distance?'.
65 Borsay, *Urban Renaissance*, pp. 130–1. For the development of advertising, see McKendrick, 'The art of eighteenth-century advertising'.
66 Borsay, *Urban Renaissance*, p. 129; Gregory, 'Geographies of industrialization', p. 381; Sweet, *Urban Histories*, pp. 252–6.
67 Mitchell, 'Urban retailing', pp. 275–7; Stobart, 'Shopping streets', p. 11.
68 Muir, *Liverpool*, p. 187; Bruton, *Manchester and Salford*, p. 144; Kennett, *Georgian Chester*, p. 39.
69 Pressnell, *Country Banking*, pp. 105–15; Black, 'Money, information and space'.
70 Hudson, *Industrial Capital*, pp. 211–27; Anderson, 'Early capital market'; Neal, 'Finance of business', pp. 167–9.
71 Neal, 'Finance of business', p. 168; Cheshire and Chester Archives (CCA), CR 352/1 Letter Book of Daniel Peck.
72 Anderson, 'Early capital market'.
73 Neal 'Finance of business', p. 168.
74 Gregory, 'Geographies of industrialization', figure 13.11.
75 Pawson, *Transport and Economy*, pp. 341–60.
76 See Chartres and Turnbull, 'Road transport'.
77 Pawson, *Transport and Economy*, pp. 137–40 and 151.
78 Turnbull, 'Provincial road carrying'; Chartres and Turnbull, 'Road transport', pp. 80–94.
79 Only the routes are examined here, services will be explored in more detail in Chapter 7.

80 Albert, *Turnpike Road System*, pp. 46–7. The Liverpool–Prescot road was linked to the Warrington–Preston road at Newton shortly afterwards.

81 Pawson, *Transport and Economy*, p. 143; Albert, *Turnpike Road System*, p. 47.

82 Journals of the House of Commons (1735) 23: 575, quoted in Pawson, *Transport and Economy*, p. 143.

83 The Chester–Newcastle road was turnpiked in 1744 linking the city to London. There is contradictory evidence as to the date of the turnpiking of the Chester–Whitchurch route; Albert suggests that the turnpike stretched only as far as Barnhill (about 6 six miles south of Chester) before being extended to Chester in 1760, whereas Pawson implies that Chester was linked to this turnpike as early as 1706.

84 Turnbull, 'Canals', pp. 540–5.

85 Wrigley, 'Raw materials', pp. 6–10.

86 The link to Warrington was authorised in 1694 but was not finally completed until 1701. See Parkinson, *Port of Liverpool*, p. 77.

87 Walton, *Lancashire*, p. 71. The support (and money) coming from Manchester suggests that the merchants and manufacturers of the town had much to gain from this link.

88 This scheme was also a long time in reaching the production stage, with seven bids being made before the interests of the Liverpool merchants and south Lancashire colliers finally overcame the opposition of Staffordshire miners and road hauliers in 1720. Work was then further delayed by internal wrangling amongst the Cheshire brine-men.

89 Walton, *Lancashire*, p. 73; Langton, *Geographical Change*, pp. 169–74; Kennett, *Georgian Chester*, p. 18.

90 Langton, 'Liverpool', p. 7.

91 For an excellent overview of these processes, see King and Timmins, *Industrial Revolution*, pp. 33–66.

92 See the various contributions in Hudson, *Regions and Industries*, and Stobart and Lane, *Urban and Industrial Change*.

93 Langton, 'Urban growth', pp. 465–86.

94 Buckatzch, 'Geographical distribution of wealth'.

95 Corfield, *English Towns*, pp. 12–14; Langton, 'Urban growth', maps 14.1–14.5.

96 Langton, 'Urban growth', p. 466.

97 Wadsworth and Mann, *Cotton Trade*, p. 312.

98 Gregory, 'Geographies of industrialization', p. 352; Lawton and Pooley, *Britain 1740–1950*, pp. 57–89; Hudson, *Industrial Revolution*, pp. 115–32.

99 Langton, 'Urban growth', p. 489.

100 Berg, Hudson and Sonenscher, *Manufacture in Town and Country*, pp. 26–8.

101 Hudson, 'Capital and credit', p. 71.

102 See Robson, *Urban Growth*; Myrdal, *Economic Theory*.

103 Stobart, 'Eighteenth-century revolution?', pp. 44–7. See also Langton, 'Urban growth', pp. 486–90; Kenny, 'Lancashire cotton industry', p. 6.

4

An advanced organic economy: the textile industries

> It is true, that the increase of the manufacture may be by its extending itself farther
> in the country, and so more hands may be employed in the county without any
> increase in the town. But I answer that though this is possible, yet as the town
> and parish of Manchester is the centre of the manufacture, the increase of that
> manufacture would certainly increase there first.[1]

North-west England and its textile industries lie at the heart of popular and
academic constructions of the industrial revolution. Whilst the latter have
been greatly modified over the last two decades in both temporal and sectoral
terms, the cotton industry especially retains its position in the vanguard of
British industrialisation.[2] Cotton manufacturing grew rapidly from the late
eighteenth century and took a leading role in wider industrial, economic and
social modernisation,[3] although this dramatic development is increasingly
seen as arising from much deeper-rooted processes. Empirical and theoretical
analyses alike portray textiles industries as moving steadily from a network
of relatively independent and often rural-based artisans (*Kaufsystem*) in the
seventeenth century, through an increasingly complex and centralised system
of putting-out (*Verlags-system*), to a workshop-then factory-and machine-
dominated industry by the early nineteenth century.[4] The relative importance
to this transition of technological change, the supply of capital, labour and
raw materials, transport improvements and consumer demand (both domestic
and overseas) have been discussed in detail elsewhere and little can be added
to such debates here.[5] However, the systems of manufacture and pace of change
varied greatly from place to place, often in accordance with local social and
institutional differences and variations in product and process.[6] Such variations
are important for the long-term development of the north-west region and yet
they remain under-emphasised in many studies.

It was awareness of this variability that prompted Mager to generate his
typology of proto-industry.[7] In it he identified limited centralisation and
capitalisation in linen production which 'remained archaic' in organisational
terms, especially in comparison with cotton and worsted manufacture where

putting-out systems were highly developed from an early stage. The cotton industry also saw the earliest development of machine spinning initially operating within the broader putting-out systems. Mager's analysis covers much of western Europe and inevitably tends to gloss over important differences seen within single industries and particular places. For example, the organisation of the West Country woollen industry was very different from that of west Yorkshire; and the systems of production seen within the latter ranged from the independent artisan entrepreneurs of the Leeds-Wakefield broadcloth area to the putting-out system of the kersey (later worsteds) districts around Halifax.[8] This highlights the significance of geographical and organisational variation within textile production and emphasises the importance of such factors in the long-term development of these industries: they were both a reflection of previous growth and a strong factor in determining subsequent areas of specialisation and expansion.[9] Given this, it is unfortunate that neither this idea of path-dependency, nor Mager's typology have been fully explored in the British context. More worryingly, most studies of textile production in north-west England fail even to consider the detailed geography of textile manufacture beyond the broad outlines of production areas. Much more attention is paid to the 'post-industrial revolution' patterns, the (spatial) inter-relationships between key individuals and groups, and the growing role of technical innovations.[10] Only recently has Timmins's work given us anything like a comprehensive analysis of the space economy of textile manufacturing in the north west, but even he fails to discuss in any depth the patterns or importance of the changing geography of production.[11] In order to fully understand the structure of this growth pole of the regional economy, we need to know more about the early geographical configuration of these manufactures and the nature of spatial interactions within the regional production and marketing processes. In other words, a broader geographical framework than has hitherto been constructed is necessary to assess the significance of early concentrations and specialisations for subsequent growth and development of the industry. Such a framework has two dimensions: specialisation by product and specialisation by process. These are examined in turn to assess the geographical and hierarchical structure of this set of growing industries. More specifically, three key questions are addressed. First, to what extent should the various textile industries of north-west England be seen as distinct and separate production systems? Second, what role did towns play in these industries: were they as marginal as classic proto-industrialisation theory and recent work by Timmins would have us believe? Third, how did the network of towns serve to structure the textile space economy?

Geographical specialisation: a case of unintegrated production?

We begin by examining the basic geography of textile production in the north west. The analysis highlights the early establishment and long-term persistence of clear local specialisms and underlines the very different economic and demographic regimes that characterised linen, woollen, fustian and silk producing districts. It also requires us to consider their broader integration: should they be seen as separate and independent local economies or as part of a single integrated textile economy?

Of the four main cloth types manufactured in eighteenth-century Lancashire and Cheshire, linen was the most common, accounting for 43 per cent of textile workers appearing in the probate records once spinners are taken into account (see Appendix 2). Initially an indigenous manufacture, flax was increasingly imported from Ireland and northern Europe to supply what was overwhelmingly a rural-based industry (Table 4.1). Workers 'normally learned to weave on their fathers' looms and set up on their own when they married, preferably on a holding with some land,'[12] although the economic importance of this landholding seems to have varied significantly across the region. Woollen cloths, including coarse kerseys and bays, finer serges, worsteds and also felt, formed the second largest group, with 29 per cent of textiles workers. Several types of woollens were indigenous to the region, but the introduction of 'newer' cloths, especially worsteds, increased dependency on supplies of wool from Yorkshire, the Midlands and even south-west England.[13] The relatively higher proportion of woollen manufacturers found in towns in part reflects the under-counting of rural woollen manufacture in the upland districts of Whalley, Bury and Rochdale parishes where the interaction between manufacturing and agriculture was probably closest.[14] Added to this was the urban predominance in felt-making: thirty-three of the forty-seven felt-makers recorded in the probate records were located in towns, including fourteen in Chester and seven in Manchester. Fustians (20 per cent) formed the third main textiles group. The term 'fustian' was variously used to refer to linen and wool or linen and cotton mixes, and even pure cotton fabrics. Generally, though, it indicated cloths with a linen warp and cotton weft – a technique which was introduced to the north west in the early seventeenth century and thereafter grew strongly, drawing on the traditional skills of linen and woollen weavers in the region.[15] Much more than its parent industries, fustian production was heavily dependent upon supplies of raw materials from overseas. Cotton initially came from the eastern Mediterranean via the Levant Company of London, but the eighteenth century saw growing supplies arriving from America and the West Indies.[16] Production, though, was primarily rural, if less closely linked to agricultural occupations than that of linen or woollen cloths. Silk and smallwares manufacture, which made up the remainder of textiles production in the north west, were rather different. Silk production was also dependent upon raw materials from overseas, but spinning especially moved to factory production much earlier. The first silk-weaving factory in the region opened in Preston in 1704, and powered spinning mills were established in Stockport (1732), Macclesfield (1743) and Congleton (1755), often using technology originally developed in Italy.[17] Small-wares, using the expensive Dutch looms (introduced via London some time before 1683) were the provenance of artisan workers, again located close to and usually within towns.[18]

Table 4.1 *Textile occupations in north-west England 1701–60: urban and rural specialisation by cloth type*

Cloth type	Rural		Urban		Total
	Number	*%*	*Number*	*%*	
Linen	1137	84.8	204	15.2	1341
Woollen	594	64.2	331	35.8	925
Fustian	463	71.9	181	28.1	644
Silk	8	11.3	63	88.7	71
Smallwares	33	20.9	125	79.1	158
Unknown	2479	78.1	694	21.9	3173
Total	4714	74.7	1598	25.3	6312

Source: Probate records, 1701–60.
Note: Figures include a multiplier for spinners (see Appendix 2).

The different characteristics of these various branches of textiles production were reflected in divergent geographies and interactions which, like those in west Yorkshire, appear to have been linked to the nature of the cloth and the agricultural and social characteristics of the locale.[19] In effect, the textiles economy formed a mosaic of specialist districts which were, by and large, geographically distinct from one another. This reflected a complex sectoral-spatial division of labour and implies the development of separate systems of production. To what extent was this the case?[20]

Silk production was probably the most spatially concentrated textile and certainly the most specialised in the region. There were silk weavers in Manchester, Preston, Ormskirk, Nantwich and Chester, but the industry was most prominent in Macclesfield, with lesser concentrations in Stockport and later in Congleton.[21] Unfortunately, these important industries are poorly represented in the probate records. The making of silk buttons, which originated in Macclesfield around the mid-sixteenth century, was organised as a cottage industry by the town's chapmen.[22] One such individual was Samuel Thornicroft whose probate inventory, proved in 1710, listed £105 12s 6d in shop goods,

Figure 4.1 *Specialisation in textile production in north-west England,*
1701–60

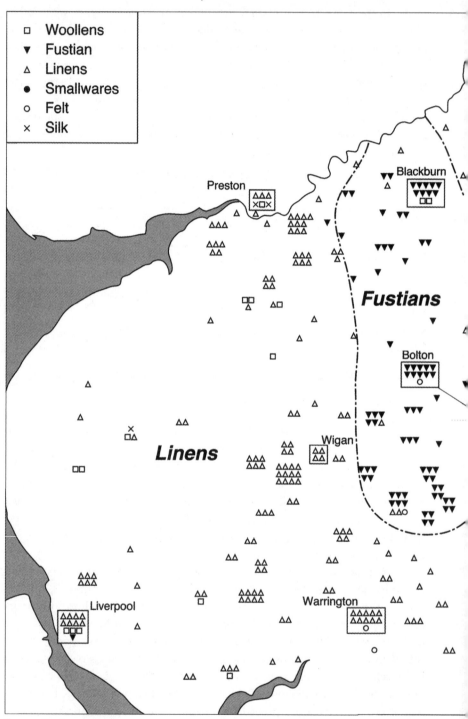

Source: Probate records, 1701–60.

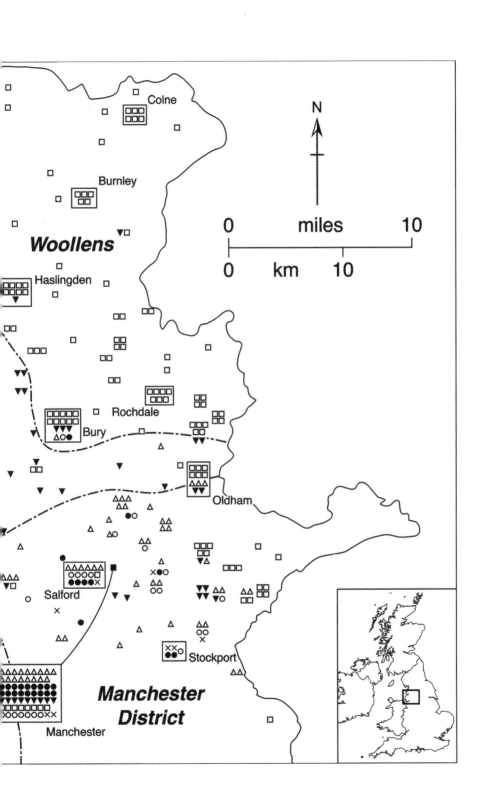

Colne

N

Burnley

Woollens

miles   10

km   10

Haslingden

Rochdale

Bury

Oldham

Salford

Stockport

Manchester District

Manchester

buttons, mohair and silk, and £120 19s 10d owing in trade-related debts. Similarly, on his death in 1729, Richard Worthington had £591 7s 6d owing to him as well as £227 11s 1½d worth of buttons, silk and mohair in his warehouse and £46 12s 10d of similar goods in the hands of his 'outworkers'. Such men were clearly prosperous, but their occupation titles give only a limited indication of their activities. Conversely, their employees were often very poor and were frequently women or children, who left few clues of their vital economic function in this hugely important industry.[23] Of silk spinning or throwing we have more clues. By 1761, there were seven large silk mills in Macclesfield employing 2,470 men and women, and a further twelve smaller mills with around 1,000 workers between them. Four years later, an estimated 12,000–15,000 people in Macclesfield and the surrounding villages were employed in working up the waste from these mills. This was the peak of the eighteenth-century silk industry: recession hit in the 1780s and several mill owners were bankrupt.[24] Such huge numbers find but a pale reflection in the probate records (perhaps not surprising in such a heavily proletarianised industry), but the concentration of throwsters and twisters into Macclesfield is notable: from a regional total of thirteen such individuals, Macclesfield contained nine, Stockport two, and Preston and Rudheath one each.

As Wadsworth and Mann suggested, linens were dominant in the lowland areas of central and western Lancashire, with the concentrations around Warrington, Wigan and Preston being prominent in a broad band of activity running through the three towns (Figure 4.1).[25] Warrington especially stands out. In 1673, Blome noted its 'considerable market' for linen cloths, a feature still apparent fifty years later when Defoe suggested that £500 of linen was sold there each week 'all made in the neighbourhood of the place'.[26] Within the 'linen' area, 168 out of 192 textiles workers appearing in the probate records with a specified cloth type were involved in the manufacture of linen cloths (Table 4.2). It formed the main non-agricultural activity in most townships and employed around one quarter of the male population in Walton-le-Dale and Penwortham in the 1720s.[27] Equally, central Lancashire dominated linen production in the region, accounting for over two-thirds of linen workers. Notwithstanding the widespread nature and local importance of linen manufacture, western and central Lancashire was, above all, a productive agricultural area. These lowlands were characterised by arable and mixed farming or market gardening, and by a relatively prosperous resident gentry willing to invest in agricultural improvement.[28] Similar circumstances in the lowlands of west Yorkshire were, Hudson argues, instrumental in sustaining the small independent clothiers and the dynamic woollen industry which they personified.[29] In the linen district, however, textiles production generally formed a 'supplement to primarily agricultural domestic economies, rather than the main prop of a rural proletariat'.[30] When industry did become dominant in the local economy in the late eighteenth and early nineteenth century, it took the form of factory-based cotton production in Preston, Chorley and Wigan, and coal-based industries around Wigan and in south-west Lancashire.[31] In the early eighteenth century, however, the linen districts formed a spatially coherent system characterised by particular agricultural-industrial relationships.

Table 4.2 *Occupational specialisation in textile production in north-west England (cloth type), 1701–60*

Cloth type		Linen district		Woollen district		Fustian district		Manchester district		Total
		Total	%	Total	%	Total	%	Total	%	
Linen	total	168	87.5	1	1.1	16	11.8	61	36.7	246
	%	68.3		0.4		6.5		24.8		100.0
Woollen	total	14	7.3	85	89.5	13	9.6	29	17.5	141
	%	9.9		60.3		9.2		20.6		100.0
Fustian	total	5	2.6	7	7.4	105	77.2	19	11.4	136
	%	3.7		5.1		77.2		14.0		100.0
Smallwares	total	0	0.0	1	1.1	0	0.0	29	17.5	30
	%	0.0		3.3		0.0		96.7		100.0
Felt	total	2	1.0	1	1.1	2	1.5	21	12.7	26
	%	7.7		3.8		7.7		80.8		100.0
Silk	total	3	1.6	0	0.0	0	0.0	7	4.2	10
	%	30.0		0.0		0.0		70.0		100.0
Total		192	100.0	95	100.2	136	100.1	166	100.0	

Source: Probate records, 1701–60.
Notes: Does not include the multiplier for spinners; includes only the area marked on Figure 4.1.

The majority of woollen textile manufacture was concentrated into, and pre-eminent within, the Pennine uplands in the east of the region where it accounted for almost 90 per cent of textile workers (see Table 4.2). There were notable concentrations in north-east Lancashire, Rossendale and the hills and valleys north and east of Bury and Rochdale.[32] These areas were characterised by marginal and subsistence agriculture similar in potential and practice to that of the neighbouring districts of west Yorkshire. Most families appear to have combined manufacturing with cattle or sheep raising and possibly a little arable farming in the form of oats, but they almost invariably did so on very small plots of land.[33] Irrespective of local variations in inheritance customs, holdings in these areas were increasingly sub-divided in the seventeenth and eighteenth centuries. This was partly a result of the piecemeal enclosure of wastes and the sale of the resulting plots, and partly due to the growing practice of sub-letting small parcels of land – a practice also common in west Yorkshire. As a consesequence, land was held in plots too small to form genuinely economic enterprise and there was a growing reliance on textile production to sustain household incomes.[34] As early as the start of the seventeenth century, around 70 per cent of those leaving probate inventories in north-east Lancashire owned at least one piece of cloth-making equipment. In Rossendale a similar proportion was recorded for the late seventeenth century at a time when less than 40 per cent of male occupations in the parish records were textiles-related. This indicates the extent to which textile production was hidden by the wide spread of so-called dual occupations in east Lancashire. It also shows the growing importance of the woollen industry by the early eighteenth century. Textile-related occupations of men rose to half the parish register entries in southern Rossendale and Haslingden by the 1720s and to two-thirds by the 1740s. In Saddleworth, the figures were even higher: 76 per cent in 1720 and 88 per cent by 1760.[35] The production of woollen cloths grew here as a result of inadequate agricultural incomes, but displaced agriculture around the turn of the eighteenth century as the principal livelihood of a growing proportion of households. As with the linen district to the west, these woollen textile areas were geographically distinct and coherent.

One clear exception to this spatial concentration of woollen textile manufacturing was felt-making. Apart from concentrations of rural workers around Stockport and Manchester, this was principally found in the larger towns and especially Chester (Figure 4.2). Such a pattern reflects the distribution of hat-making in the region which, after being introduced to Chester in 1550, gradually spread eastwards and became strongly established in the greater Manchester area. Burgeoning growth there overshadowed the more traditionally organised Chester trade which was in terminal decline by the 1750s. In the late eighteenth and early nineteenth centuries, hat-making in and around Stockport and Manchester was increasingly drawn into national networks of production and employed 5,606 people by 1851.[36] By that time, south-east Lancashire was largely dominated by the cotton industry, but this felt- and hat-making district formed another specialist local economy.

Cotton was probably first used in the north west in the production of fustians, established by 1630 in the country between Bolton and Blackburn and around Oldham. By the early eighteenth century other forms of cotton-linen mixes (notably checks) and pure cotton cloths were being produced in these areas.[37] The broadly defined fustian district formed the final major geographical area of specialist production in the north west, spatially intermediate to the first two districts.[38] Cotton-based cloths accounted for three out of every four textile workers in this area, with specialisation being particularly pronounced around Bolton which acted as a significant regional centre for their manufacture and

Figure 4.2 *Felt- and hat-making in north-west England, 1550–1800*

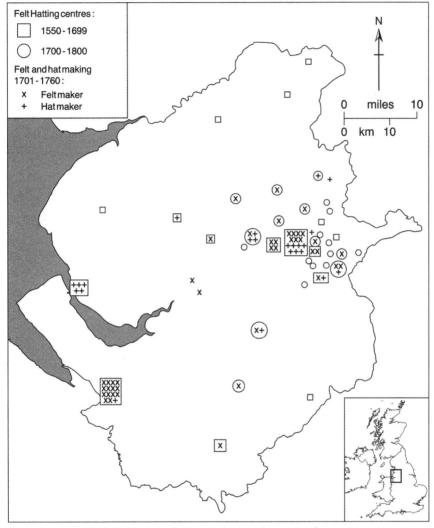

Source: Smith, 'English felt and silk hat trades'; probate records, 1701–60.

marketing. Cloth-making accounted for about half the males registering births in Oldham and Denton in the 1720s and in Radcliffe by the 1740s. Middleton was even more dominated by textiles, with figures of 60 per cent in the early 1730s and 70 per cent in the middle of the century.[39] Whilst these proportions reflect those seen in the woollen and linen districts, manufacturing had penetrated these 'cotton' townships far more completely as it had in the Blackburn area.[40]

The fustian districts were characterised by specialised production and were increasingly dominated by full-time textile manufacturing. From here, fustians also diffused into the Manchester district, notably to the east and south of Manchester in Ashton-under-Lyne, Denton, Hulme and Chorlton Row as well as in the town itself (Figure 4.1). This added another layer to an already complex local economy wherein the region's different textile economies over-lapped with one another. As Timmins notes, Manchester was the region's leading production area for linens and this, in turn, formed the most common cloth type in the district (see Table 4.2). Coarse woollens were also produced in some quantity as was felt. But it was the manufacture of smallwares which distinguished this district from other parts of the textile-producing areas. Smallwares involved thread- and button-making, but principally comprised tape- and ribbon-weaving, trades which used the 'new' Dutch looms.[41] Of the thirty makers of smallwares appearing within the textile districts (Figure 4.1), twenty-nine were located within the Manchester district and there were twenty in Manchester alone. Throughout the fustian and Manchester districts, but especially in Manchester parish itself, textile production increasingly formed the mainstay of local and household economies. Landholdings were very small by the eighteenth century and even the larger plots were probably too small to be economic agricultural units. Most were more in the nature of allotments, supplying the needs of the immediate household only.[42] Walton's conclusion that 'landless or almost landless cottagers, dependent entirely on manufactur-ing, were growing in numbers rapidly by mid-century' seems evident, as does its implication for general demographic growth.[43] Importantly, then, this most dynamic area was characterised by a growing concentration onto textile manufacturing, but also by a diversity of products and processes.

In broad terms, textile production in the north west appears to conform with Mager's typology. There were coherent and specialised production areas based on a spatial division of labour by cloth type. Each area was characterised by its own demographic and economic regime and by its own growth trajec-tory. And yet it would be wrong to see these districts as entirely separate from one another: they clearly overlapped both spatially and operationally in and around Manchester (a point discussed in detail below) and their geography and make-up were far from static.[44] Whilst the broad outline of these specialist districts was generally constant, there was significant expansion of the area dominated by the production of fustians. In the first twenty years of the eighteenth century, fustians were quite closely concentrated in a corridor running from Blackburn in the north to Leigh in the south. Subsequent growth was centred initially around Blackburn, but then in the Bury and Oldham areas. By the middle of the eighteenth century, the area of fustian manufacture was almost 25 per cent larger than it had been in 1700, growth occurring chiefly at the expense of woollen production.[45] Of more telling significance for the regional economy as a whole, fustians now formed a significant element of textile manufacturing in Manchester itself. No fustian workers were recorded in the probate records in the town before 1720, but fustians accounted for 30 per cent of known textiles workers by the 1740s and 1750s and a further 22 per cent were engaged in smallwares manufacture – some of whom undoubtedly were using cotton as well as linen yarns.

Over a longer time period, we can see the eventual subsuming of all these districts within an expansive factory-based cotton industry. However, the focus and spatial patterning of the textiles industry in the region which was to persist for the next 70, arguably the next 170, years was firmly established by the middle of the eighteenth century.[46] The organisation of production and sometimes the type of cloth being manufactured in particular places may have changed through time, but its broad geography survived the advent of mechanisation, factories and coal. Localisation of the textiles trades was clearly much more than a reflection of resource availability.[47] Manchester was central to the cotton industry, and production grew most strongly in urban and rural settlements within a twenty-five mile radius. Samuel Crompton's 1811 census shows cotton-spinning from Warrington to Halifax, but about two-thirds lay within the fustian and Manchester districts identified above.[48] Similarly, the cotton and fustian manufacturers listed in Pigot and Dean's 1815 directory as attending the Manchester market came from as far afield as Halifax, Colne and Preston, but around three-quarters were from the nascent cotton districts of south-east Lancashire.[49] As late as 1921, when cotton production had spread throughout eastern and central Lancashire and north-east Cheshire, 55 per cent of the region's 539,743 textiles workers (around 90 per cent of whom were working with cotton) lay within this same area.[50] As both Kenny and Timmins have argued, then, the geography of textiles production in north-west England was established early and retained its basic structures despite profound changes in the technology and organisation of the manufacturing process. Naturally, the switch to water and later steam power affected the location of cotton and other textile manufacture, but these changes were to the detailed distribution of production units rather than the regional or even sub-regional patterns. Gregory has argued that these 'primary contours' had been marked out long before the introduction of steam by 'the matrix of domestic production and the availability of water power'.[51] The evidence here suggests that the first of these may have been the critical factor. But this is problematical. Recognising the importance of preceding patterns and systems of production falls some way short of understanding why the geography of the previous *modus operandi* was so significant in shaping the space economy of industrialising Britain. We need to explore more fully the geography and structure of the 'domestic system': its internal organisation and external integration.

Proto-industrial production? The role of towns and country

The proto-industrialisation model posits a basic spatial division of labour, with towns performing a fairly uniform set of activities *vis à vis* their hinterlands. According to the model, rural manufacturers and urban dealers experienced a locally symbiotic relationship, with links out of the locality being co-ordinated through the hierarchy of towns. In more nuanced interpretations, they are also seen as having a key role in the finishing stages of production.[52] This range of functions was apparent in the Yorkshire woollen and worsted industries, where towns were the principal locations of trading activity, the foci of vital commercial and credit networks and important centres for the capital-intensive finishing trades.[53] Notwithstanding such findings, doubts continue about the nature of urban involvement in proto-industrial production systems, especially in the context of north-west England. Timmins, in particular, has argued that the role of towns remains uncertain and has been misinterpreted and/or over-played.[54] What little evidence there is, he suggests, points towards widespread rural participation in the organisation of production; a surprising lack of urban service occupations; and a correspondingly heavy involvement of towns in all stages of production. In short, there was little to distinguish town and country: certainly the divide was far less in seventeenth- and eighteenth-century Lanca-shire than classic proto-industrial theory would suggest. These arguments, though, are based on very limited evidence. In order to gain a fuller picture of the spatial and organisational structure of the textiles industries, it is necessary to examine the location and activities of both finishing and dealing. A prepon-derance of such trades in towns would suggest a strong and distinctive urban role in proto-industrial systems. Equally, if spatial concentrations in the fin-ishing and marketing functions were apparent, then it could be argued that certain elements of the urban system or particular sub-regions were acting as co-ordinating centres for the region as a whole. Such 'industrial specialisation' would result in forms of interaction which would break down the regular territorial-hierarchical interaction of traditional proto-industrial development into less rigid links between specialist centres. They would also serve to inte-grate further the geographical specialisations discussed above. This section examines in detail the role of towns in textile production and marketing.

Table 4.3 confirms that, despite problems of under-counting, spinning and weaving were predominantly rural activities whereas towns were pre-eminent in the finishing trades. Already, then, there is evidence to suggest a more distinctive role for towns than Timmins allows. However, whilst this urban-rural dichotomy is valid, it is rather superficial. As is apparent from Figure 4.3, certain towns dominated the finishing industries (Manchester was most notable) and rural involvement in these key processes was closely concentrated

Figure 4.3 *Textile-finishing industries in north-west England, 1701–60*

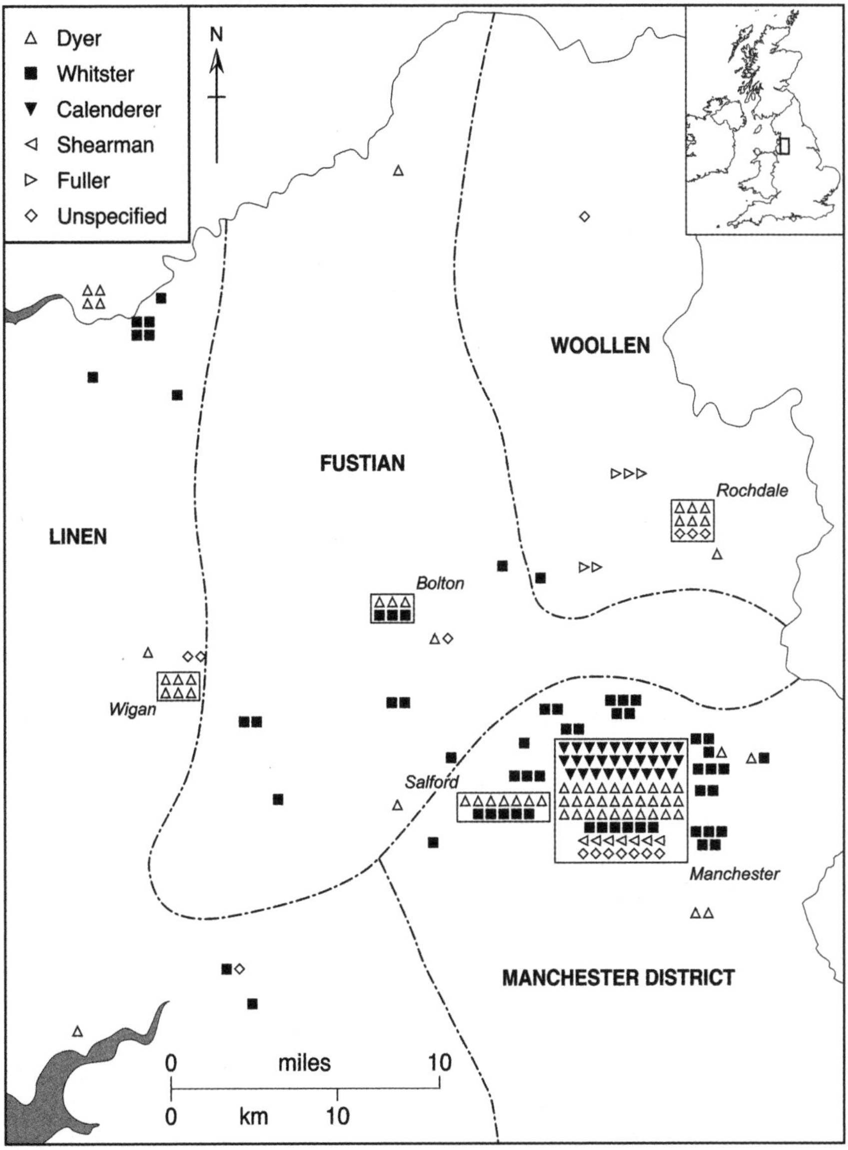

Source: probate records, 1701–60.

into the Manchester area. Across Lancashire as a whole, finishing comprised only one in twelve of rural textiles occupations appearing in the probate records, but around Manchester the figure rose to about one in three. Salford accounted for some of these and so they were, effectively, urban, but there

Figure 4.4 *Crofters and whitsters in the Manchester area, c.1773*

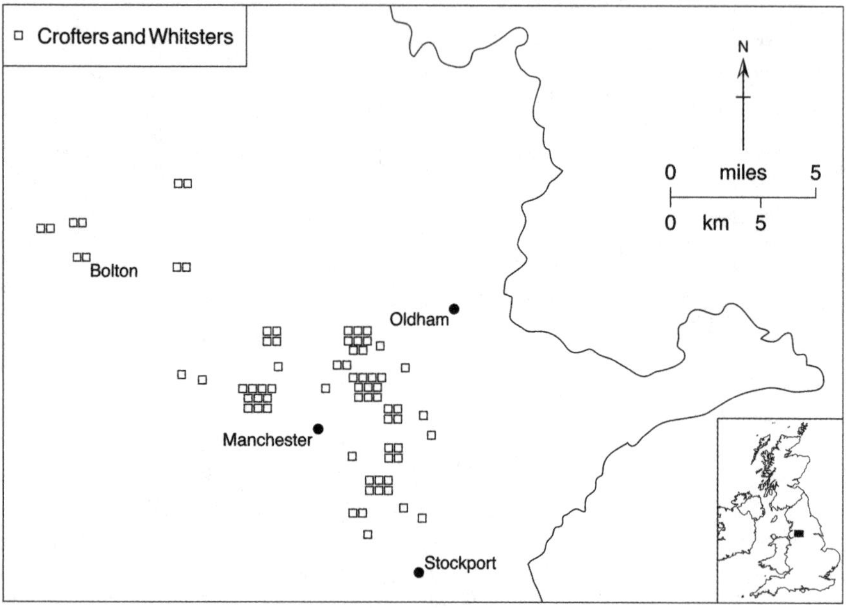

Source: Raffald, *Directory of Manchester and Salford.*

were numerous others located in a broad arc north and east of the town. Given the more even distribution of textile production established above, the concentration of over half of the region's cloth finishing processes suggests that this area was acting as a collecting and finishing area for textiles produced outside the locality. Certainly, it is difficult to explain such a distribution merely in terms of the finishing trades' need for large areas of land and good supplies of pure water.[55] There were many other parts of Lancashire with such resources and competition for water supplies in and around Manchester was increasingly intense. Far more critical in shaping the geography of these activities was Manchester's position at the centre of the region's textiles trade, hinted at above. It was customary for the merchants to receive cloth 'in the grey' from weavers and arrange the bleaching, dyeing or printing according to their customers' requirements.[56] The strong incentive for spatial clustering which this implies is confirmed in the geographical 'lock-in' of whitsters and crofters around Manchester. Moston bleachers were central to the linen trade of the Manchester district in the sixteenth and seventeenth centuries and these same areas are still apparent in both Aikin's description and trade directories from the late-eighteenth century.[57] In particular, Raffald's 1773 directory of Manchester includes a listing of rural crofters and whitsters whose location matches closely the distribution of textiles finishers in the probate records (compare Figures 4.3 and 4.4).

Table 4.3 *Textile occupations in north-west England, 1701–60: rural and urban specialisation by stage of production*

	Spinning		Weaving		Finishing		Other		Total	
	Total	%	Total	%	Total	%	Total	%	Total	%
Rural	3790	77.2	758	77.2	78	37.7	88	41.3	4714	74.7
Urban	1120	22.8	224	22.8	129	62.3	125	58.7	1598	25.3
Total	4910		982		207		213		6312	

Source: Probate records, 1701–60.
Note: Rural spinning is probably under-emphasised here because spinners are allocated to town and country per weaver. It is likely that many urban weavers were supplied by rural spinners: Wadsworth and Mann, *Cotton Trade*, pp. 82–3.

To the north of this area, Wigan, Bolton and especially Rochdale also stand out as significant if secondary finishing centres, particularly for dyeing (Figure 4.3). These activities, in turn, comprised an important element of textiles production in these towns. Even allowing for the multiplier for spinners, finishing industries accounted for about 17 per cent of textile workers in Wigan, 15 per cent in Rochdale and 7 per cent in Bolton, suggesting that they were acting as small- or medium-scale finishing centres for each of the three specialist textiles districts. Certainly, Rochdale was the established finishing centre for the woollen districts throughout the eighteenth century and Bolton, with fustians merchants and extensive warehousing, was important in the fustians trade until the 1750s at least.[58] The status of Wigan is less clear: Warrington was more closely associated with the linen trade, but had very few cloth finishers listed in the probate records; the only other concentration of such activities was found in the rural townships south of Preston.

In fact, it seems that much of the finishing of linens took place in and around Manchester, and the town formed the principal centre of finishing trades for the whole region. It was the location of more than one-third of finishing trades in the north west and its textile production was largely dominated by these activities. Of course, being high-skill and capital-intensive enterprises, finishing trades are much more likely to have featured in the probate records than the generally more modest spinning and weaving occupations, thus exaggerating their importance within Manchester's textile economy. The 4,674 looms reported in Manchester parish in 1751 are poorly reflected in the totals identified in the probate records: sixty-two cloth weavers, makers or workers in the town and seventy-two in the rural townships.[59] Nonetheless, the concentration of seventy-eight finishers into Manchester alone remains remarkable and represents around half of the textiles workforce recorded in the probates. More significantly, perhaps, Manchester included finishing trades which related to each of the cloth types produced in the region. There were calenderers, cloth dressers, dyers, fustian dyers, fustian shearers, hot pressers, inkle calenderers, linen dyers, shearers, whitsters and woollen dyers. Manchester finishing trades clearly received cloth from a very productive hinterland and from the region as a whole, including north-east Cheshire and central Lancashire. There was thus a hierarchical-spatial division of labour, with Manchester forming the key centre of control in the textile space economy, effectively integrating specialised production systems throughout the north west.

Part of the explanation for this clustering of finishing processes was the close relationship which existed between the various trades. 'Much of the dyeing was done in Manchester, and it was customary for the dyer to send on the goods to the calenderer', almost invariably located in the town.[60] The arrangement between Samuel Heaward, a maker and dealer in various cloths 'commonly called Manchester Wares', and Edward Gibson, a Manchester calenderer, appears typical. Between May 1728 and December 1731, Heaward sent twenty-five different sorts of cotton and linen goods worth £640 to Gibson, who kept the finished goods in his Manchester warehouse before they were inspected by Heaward and sold on to Manchester linen drapers or London merchants, often by Gibson himself.[61] This type of relationship was clearly common amongst manufacturers located in south-east Lancashire and beyond. Some had their own warehouses in Manchester, but even so the operational and geographical links to the calenderers remained strong. Raffald's list of 'Country Tradesmen with Warehouses in Manchester' highlights a strong concentration of fustian manufacturers in a broad band from Oldham through Bury to Leigh, with the largest number residing in Bolton (Figure 4.5). Check manufacturers, meanwhile, were found principally within Manchester parish – mostly in the townships east and north of the town.[62] Within Manchester, the 'warehouses' of these rural manufacturers and dealers were sometimes at the same address as the calenderers with whom they dealt, in which case they probably had one or more rooms in the warehouses of the latter. Without fail, though, they were clustered into the same streets and courts around the Market Place (Figure 4.6). This close linking of rural manufacturers with Manchester finishers was the 'fact on which the growing tendency of the town to monopolise the marketing functions of the trade was largely based'. Indeed, by the late eighteenth century, 'most of the production of the country manufacturers passed through Manchester'.[63] Its trade grew strongly, sometimes (as in Bolton) at the expense of other towns. It was pre-eminent as the finishing and marketing centre for various textiles, but particularly the burgeoning cotton trade. More generally, there was a distinctive urban role in textile manufacturing. Whilst

Figure 4.5 *Fustian and check manufacturers in the Manchester area,* *c.1773*

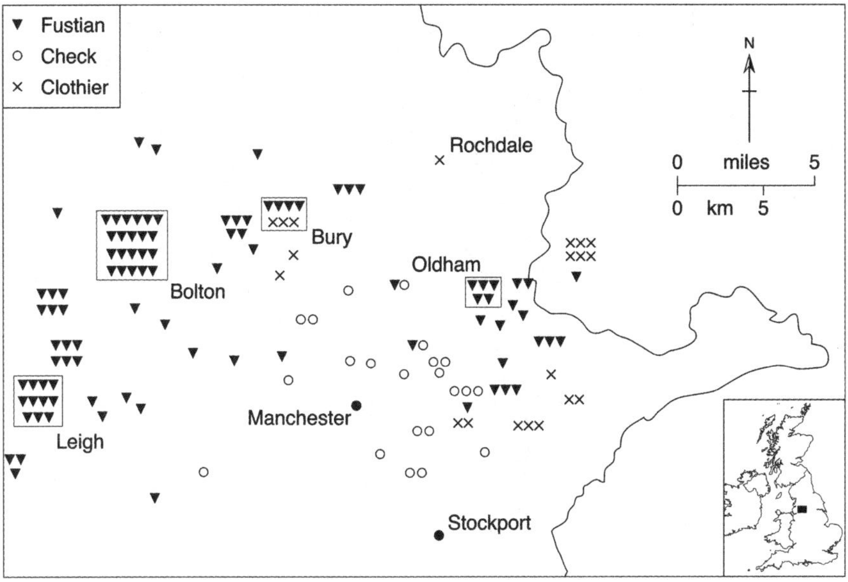

Source: Raffald, *Directory of Manchester and Salford.*

most towns specialised in the same cloth types as their hinterlands, they were characterised by more capital-intensive and centralised activities.

Towns were pre-eminent in dealing as well as in finishing processes. The extent of this domination is not easy to gauge, however, because of the difficulty in precisely defining and identifying textile dealers. This problem has two dimensions. The first involves the multiple roles played by key individuals in the textile trades. We have already seen that calenderers operated as agents, selling on commission, and that certain fullers in the woollen industry appear to have done the same.[64] Clothiers too were often dealers and 'capitalists' as well as manufacturers. Indeed, in west Yorkshire, the term could cover anything from a country weaver to substantial urban (or rural) merchants controlling a large network of producers.[65] Chapmen, whilst later seen as general and often itinerant dealers, were intimately involved in textile dealing and even manufacturing in early eighteenth-century Lancashire and Cheshire. This is readily apparent from several inventories which included looms and cloth put out to weavers. That of James Beck of Manchester included £503 6s 7d of 'goods in ye warehouse and homes'; John Antrobus of Manchester had £4 9s 3¾d of cloth 'in ye weavers hands' and £37 10s of yarn being spun; Roger Key of Bolton owned three pairs of looms, and Thomas Smalley of Blackburn

Figure 4.6 *Warehouses of fustian and check manufacturers in Manchester, c.1773*

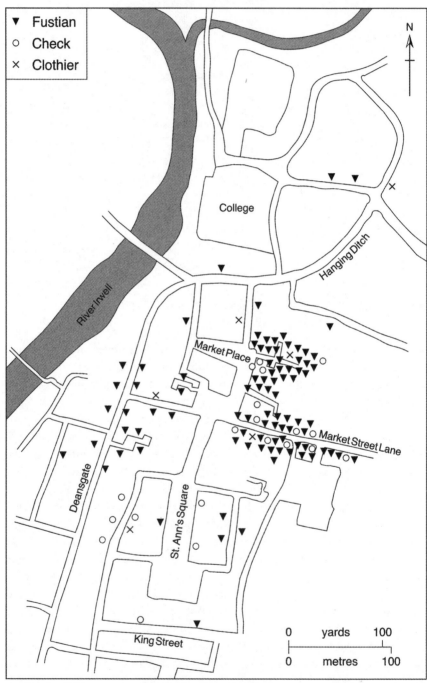

Source: Raffald, *Directory of Manchester and Salford.*

had cloth, yarn, looms, reeds, cards and weights in his inventory. Similarly, John Sherwin, an alderman and chapman from Macclesfield, had £15 10s 0d of goods in button-makers' hands, £825 17s 11d in goods and debts in travellers' hands and at London, and a further £233 4s 9d in desperate debts. In Stockport, Thomas Gilbody, a chapman and button-maker, had £33 6s worth of buttons left in the country, £47 of button in his warehouse and £83 13s 6d of credit in his button-making book. But he also had about £100 of stock in his 'grocer shopp'. Clearly, such men were not necessarily dedicated textile dealers, but such activities often formed a large part of their trade, as they did at a more modest scale for the itinerant petty chapmen who did much to supply the rural poor especially with textiles and clothing.[66] The second problem arises from the difficulty in distinguishing wholesale and retail activity. Again, many individuals would be involved in both forms of trade, although such tendencies varied considerably from place to place. Thus a linen draper in Manchester was undoubtedly a very different type of tradesman from one in Chester or Nantwich for example. He was probably a merchant as much as, or perhaps rather than, a shopkeeper. The analysis offered here, then, makes no systematic attempt to differentiate the two forms of dealing, but it does distinguish various 'types' of activity, as well as those involving different cloths.

Table 4.4 *Textile dealing occupations in north-west England, 1701–60: urban and rural specialisation*

	Town			Country			Total
	Total	%	Cumulative %	Total	%	Cumulative %	
Mercers and drapers	209	87.4	87.4	30	12.6	12.6	239
Chapmen	267	59.9	69.5	179	40.1	30.5	446
Clothiers	25	25.0	63.8	75	75.0	36.2	100
Total	501			284			785

Source: Probate records, 1701–60.
Note: Includes only the area marked on Figure 4.1.

Textile dealing in its strictest sense was dominated by urban tradesmen who outnumbered their rural counterparts by about five to one (Table 4.4). These were often the high status drapers and mercers with large premises, a number of apprentices and extensive stock and credit networks.[67] The chapmen, more varied in their status and more catholic in their activities, were still predominantly urban, but the balance was more even. That said, the inclusion of Macclesfield's thirty-three chapmen (omitted from Table 4.4 because the town lies outside the main area of textile production) would re-emphasise urban domination. Clothiers were essentially rural; those towns which contained

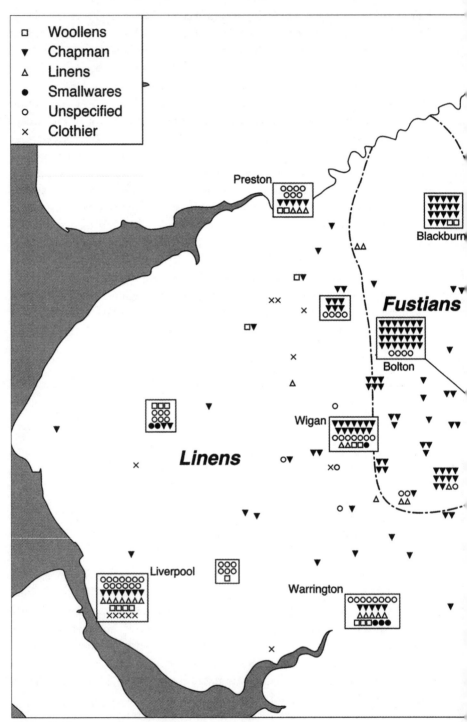

Figure 4.7 *Textile dealing, 1701–60*

Source: Probate records, 1701–60.

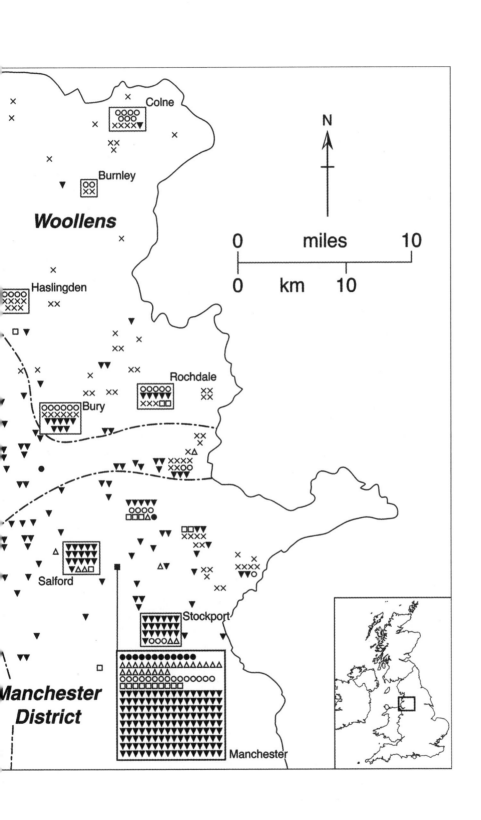

meaningful numbers of such traders – Haslingden, Colne and Burnley – were themselves generally small. Both clothiers and chapmen were concentrated into particular areas, suggesting not only a strong relationship between these activities and certain cloth types, but also that rather different structures obtained in the textiles industries of different places. Clothiers were found principally in the woollen districts of the eastern uplands, and chapmen were predominantly located in the fustian-producing areas and in Manchester district; both were largely absent from the western linen-making areas (Figure 4.7). This distribution suggests that the urban-rural relationship in terms of dealing activities varied from district to district.

The east Lancashire woollen trades had much in common with the worsted industries in west Yorkshire to which they were linked.[68] Rural activities were not restricted to manufacturing, but it was urban tradesmen who carried on the bulk of cloth dealing in terms of shops, markets and fairs.[69] Owens noted that the fairs at Bury, Clitheroe, Colne, Haslingden and Rochdale all specialised in coarse or woollen cloth.[70] Moreover, there appears to have been a loosely structured hierarchy within the woollen towns. The markets at Haslingden and Bury were 'small' or of 'no great account'; those at Burnley and Colne were deemed 'good', whilst at Rochdale and Manchester they were 'very considerable'.[71] Colne was the traditional centre of the woollen trade in north-east Lancashire, whilst Rochdale marketed much of the production from Rossendale and Hundersfield in the seventeenth and early eighteenth centuries.[72] Unsurprisingly, then, these towns contained significant numbers of textiles dealers (including clothiers and chapmen). What is also apparent, though, is the growing cluster of clothiers around and especially in Haslingden. This underlines Tupling's argument that Rossendale clothiers were becoming more numerous and more prominent in the organisation of woollen production in the area. They supervised all the manufacturing stages, and were active in passing semi-finished goods from one worker to another. Less evident in the probate records, but clear from local parish records, was the emergence of wool staplers and chapmen as significant dealers in Rossendale. Combined with the clothiers, these tradesmen served to diminish the day-to-day involvement of Rochdale merchants in the Rossendale woollen trade.[73] Such developments suggest the appearance of a proto-industrial system in this area, and Schwarz, in highlighting the declining wealth and growing population as important parts of the increased dependence on textiles production seen in north-east Lancashire, indicates a similar regime farther north.[74] This was the organic 'bottom-up' growth of classic proto-industrialisation, with rural spinners and weavers far exceeding their urban counterparts in terms of numbers, and prompting *local* urban development of dealing functions.[75] Indeed, tracing the growth of rural woollen production back to its agricultural origins links this development to Smith's ideas of 'natural progress'. Having said that, the arrangement of textile dealing in the woollen district remained complex and internally differentiated. Whilst substantial clothiers in Rossendale increasingly traded directly with London, Rochdale maintained its centrality for the smaller producers and probably enhanced its role in the late eighteenth century: a resurgence at once signalled and reinforced by the construction of a cloth hall in 1792.[76] Further north, cloth-making in and around Colne remained firmly linked to that of the West Riding and much of the dealing took place via Halifax.[77] At the same time, Manchester retained significant links with woollen production in Bury, Saddleworth and Stalybridge from whence manufacturers regularly visited Manchester's woollen hall. Such links were strengthened and extended, of course, as fustian and later cotton production began to penetrate these areas from the mid-eighteenth century.[78] What distinguished the woollen trade for much of our period, though, was the involvement of both rural and urban manufacturers in dealing activities – a feature characteristic of west Yorkshire, but less common in the other textiles areas of north-west England.

In the linen district to the west, rural activity was largely confined to spinning and weaving; dealing functions being dominated by the urban system. Most towns were essentially dealing centres and, in terms of textiles, were generally dominated by local retailing rather than merchanting activities. Ormskirk, Prescot, Liverpool and Preston were marginal to cloth production and marketing in both geographical and functional terms. They contained relatively large numbers of mercers and drapers serving the town and hinterland populations, but these were central place activities: few tradesmen were involved in linking production to distant supplies and markets. Once the canal network began to emerge and grow from the 1760s onwards, Liverpool became increasingly important in the regional supply of raw materials (especially cotton) and the export of finished goods.[79] However, its early eighteenth-century development was based on completely different trades (see Chapter 5). At this time, then, both Liverpool and its neighbours to the north were, so far as the textile industries were concerned, little more than Christallerian central places. Moreover, there was 'no built-in tendency to specialisation in textiles or other manufactures for distant markets'; as such, 'there were parts of the proto-industrial jigsaw ... but not enough resulted to justify the label'.[80] The concentration of dyers in Wigan does not seem to have been matched by an extensive system of merchanting based in the town. Only around Warrington was linen production linked to wider markets by the local urban centre as Defoe was quick to note.[81] This no doubt reflects the importance of local and regional consumption of the linen cloths produced, but also the increasing penetration of the area by Manchester merchants.

In the northern part of the fustian district, there was a similar lack of rural dealing activity. Here, though, Blackburn was central to the production and marketing of textiles. There were significant numbers of fustian weavers and makers in the town; the surrounding fields were 'whitened with the materials lying to bleach', and there was a strong concentration of chapmen who were important in linking local production to the markets in Manchester and even London.[82] In this way, the fustian and check trades resembled that in woollens: the merchants in Blackburn and also those in Leigh generally acted as feeders to the larger markets in Bolton and Manchester, although some independence was evident.[83] In the early decades of the eighteenth century Bolton was the focus of much of the south Lancashire fustians trade, as well as an important manufacturing centre in its own right. As Cox noted in 1731, 'this town is the Staple Place for Fustians, which ... are brought to this Market and Fair from all Parts of the Country'.[84] It was to Bolton that the Manchester chapmen travelled to purchase fustians 'in the grey' before finishing and selling them on to London merchants. It was the Bolton tradesmen who controlled the market and built warehouses to store the cloth and present it for sale – paralleling the activities of the Rochdale clothiers and the organisers of the worsted trade in west Yorkshire.[85] However, as noted above, the growing importance of Manchester as the centre of the finishing processes led to the gradual erosion of Bolton's commercial vitality. By the 1750s the warehouses were increasingly being deserted or demolished as most of the production of 'country' manufacturers (including Bolton itself) by then passed through the Tuesday, Thursday and Saturday markets at Manchester.[86]

The commercial importance of Manchester thus grew in a similar way to that of Leeds. Despite notable differences in the precise mechanisms which underlay their dominance – the pre-eminence of Leeds owed much to the fierce defence and promotion of its two cloth halls – both formed the principal focus of textiles production and marketing in their respective regions. Moreover, both occupied positions towards the edge of the main textiles manufacturing areas but drew in goods from and extended capital, credit and information to places up to twenty-five miles distant.[87] Manchester's influence spread across the whole region and incorporated an even greater variety of cloths than were seen in Leeds. The Yorkshire town faced significant competition from the cloth halls in Bradford, Halifax, Huddersfield and Wakefield. The result, as Gregory demonstrates, was the partial partitioning of market areas between the various towns: Leeds dominated the broadcloth trade, Huddersfield specialised in narrowcloths, and Bradford and Halifax were mainly dedicated to worsteds and fancy goods.[88] These functional divisions reflected spatial patterns of production so that marketing was, to an extent at least, geographically partitioned between these four towns. In the north west, such geographical sub-divisions were present and, indeed, were probably still more localised, with

separate marketing systems focused on Colne, Rochdale, Bolton and Warrington and, to a lesser extent, Bury, Rossendale and Blackburn. However, whilst
each sub-system had considerable autonomy in the form of links to national
markets (usually through London), all were drawn into Manchester's commercial sphere of influence.[89] In the mid-seventeenth century the town was already
being described as 'the very London of these parts, the liver that sends blood
into all the countries thereabouts'.[90] In other words, it was the centre of control
in a complex spatial-hierarchical division of labour. By the early eighteenth
century Manchester clearly dominated the region's trade in textiles. The probate records list forty-nine mercers and drapers and a growing body of chapmen:
thirty-four appear between 1701 and 1720, forty-four from 1721 to 1740 and
sixty-four from 1741 to 1760. In all, the probate records list some 206 textile
dealers in the town, more than twice the number in Bolton, Rochdale, Colne
and Warrington combined. In contrast to Timmins' characterisation of mid-
seventeenth-century Manchester as a manufacturing town, it was clearly a
major commercial centre by the early eighteenth century.[91]

This underlines two key characteristics of the regional textile economy. The
first is that towns played a distinctive role, acting as finishing and marketing
centres, although in both they faced significant if variable competition from
rural manufacturers and tradesman. Urban involvement itself was uneven: as
Walton argues, at the geographical heart of textiles production towns were
central to the production process; towards the spatial margins of production,
the towns themselves were more marginal to local manufacturing patterns.[92]
The second is that urban finishing and dealing were hierarchically structured.
This suggests that commercial linkages especially were structured in accordance
with the staple-export model. Demand and supplies were transmitted up and
down the hierarchy, from Manchester (and ultimately London and the world
market) via sub-regional centres to generally rural producers. Such hierarchical
interaction by no means precluded direct linkages from the sub-systems to
external markets (woollens, smallwares and especially fustians and checks were
dependent upon the export market [93]), but there is limited evidence of, and little
apparent need for, interaction *between* the different textiles districts. To what
extent, though, were these trading interactions reflected in the geography and
structure of industrial organisation; is there evidence, for instance, of extensive
urban-based putting-out systems in the north west?

Urban networks and the structure of the textile space economy

Proto-industrialisation theory, especially in its neo-Marxist reworkings, places
great emphasis on the move from independence to dependence amongst
workers as organisational structures shifted from *Kauf-* to *Verlags*-systems.

Producers were effectively proletarianised as they were drawn into extensive putting-out systems. The construction of centralised workshops and factories meant that they were concentrated into one place, but the fundamental capitalist-worker relationship had already been established. In reality, these different 'ideal' types of system tended to coexist because of the diverse nature of cloths and their production techniques; different local agricultural and landholding practices; social and institutional structures and so on.[94] The woollen trade in the West Country and worsted production in the West Riding were characterised by a putting-out system focused on substantial merchant-manufacturers and drawing in large numbers of dependent clothiers, weavers and spinners. By contrast, the clothiers of the west Yorkshire woollen industry retained their independence despite the increasing mechanisation of production in the eighteenth century and were only drawn into centralised capitalistic systems with the spread of factory production in the mid-nineteenth century. Even then, this was often via co-operative mills.[95] And, of course, centralised capital-intensive units (in the form of fulling-mills, dyeing and bleaching works, for example) were an essential part of each system. The different branches of textile production in the north west were similarly varied in their organisation and all were experiencing change during the first half of the eighteenth century. Perhaps more than elsewhere in the country, though, towns were important in the organisational structure of each type of cloth. This role is explored further in this section.

Perhaps the most centralised form of textile manufacture was seen in the silk industry. In Macclesfield, and also in Stockport, the prosperous chapmen and factory owners extended the twisting and throwing of silk into the country, often employing women and children as well as men. Indeed, by the middle of the eighteenth century, there was a complex wage structure covering these different categories of workers. Men were paid 7s per week (1s more than agricultural labourers in the area), women received 3s 6d and children (usually employed on three-year contracts) got 6d in their first year, 9d in the second and 1s in the third.[96] With a whole family thus employed, household incomes could rise by as much as 50 per cent. The silk trade was unusual in its organisation, however. In place of domestic outworking, throwing was increasingly organised into centralised 'throwing houses', often to prevent theft of what was a valuable raw material. These formed important precursors of the silk mills which appeared in Macclesfield from the 1740s and in Stockport even earlier, and constituted the most direct control over of the 'domestic' workforce organised through an urban-based putting-out system.[97]

Other than the significant manufacture of sail-cloth centred on Warrington and drawing in outworkers in the town and surrounding countryside, such systems were much less developed in the linen districts.[98] The fustian, check and smallwares trades were, by the early eighteenth century, characterised by a highly centralised and hierarchical system of putting-out. Indeed, the production of smallwares increasingly required substantial capital investment in new looms, and was centralised into workshops and even a water-powered factory before 1760. More generally, the limited and intermittent supply of cotton and its fluctuating price had already isolated producers from supplies of the raw material in the seventeenth century. However, so long as his credit remained good, the producer was rarely tied to one particular supplier and the Bolton fustian market (effectively the equivalent of the Yorkshire cloth halls) guaranteed some independence for most weavers. Towards the end of the seventeenth century, the Manchester linen drapers and merchants became more directly involved in the organisation of production, partly as a response to the lengthening lines of supply and credit, and partly to ensure closer control over the type and quality of cloth produced.[99] As a result, they played an increasingly important part in determining the work-patterns of the individual rural workers as 'many of the smaller independent manufacturers ... were gradually drawn into dependence on putters-out and became, effectively, employees operating on a piece-rate wage'.[100] Raw materials, finished and semi-finished goods, capital and credit, market information, and power and influence thus passed up and down the urban hierarchy, ultimately centring on Manchester and its textile merchants (Figure 4.8).

The putting-out sometimes involved raw materials or yarn being put to dependent spinners or weavers, a relatively simple set of territorial linkages. Alternatively it could be done via an intermediate class of tradesmen: the 'country manufacturers' appearing in Figures 4.5 and 4.8. These men worked on commission for the Manchester merchant, putting-out cotton and yarn and collecting yarn and cloth, but they also made fustians on their own account.[101] This produced more complex territorial-hierarchical interactions which were complicated still further because the cloth had to be sent to finishers before returning to the merchant for distribution to London dealers (often via agents), local retailers or the itinerant 'Manchester Men' who supplied fairs, markets and retailers throughout the north of England.[102] This web of relationships was bound together by credit networks (see Figure 4.8). As in other putting-out systems, these networks were centred on key individuals: clothiers in the Kent woollen trade, merchant-manufacturers in west Yorkshire and, in the north west, the Manchester merchants.[103]

The larger 'country manufacturers' worked independently of the Manchester merchants and dealt direct with London merchants. In most cases, however, they operated at a fairly modest scale from rural settlements or, more usually, one of the smaller towns. Joseph Hampson, a chapman from Leigh, may be typical of this type of tradesman. He was involved in weaving and dealing, but

Figure 4.8 *The cotton-linen putting-out system*

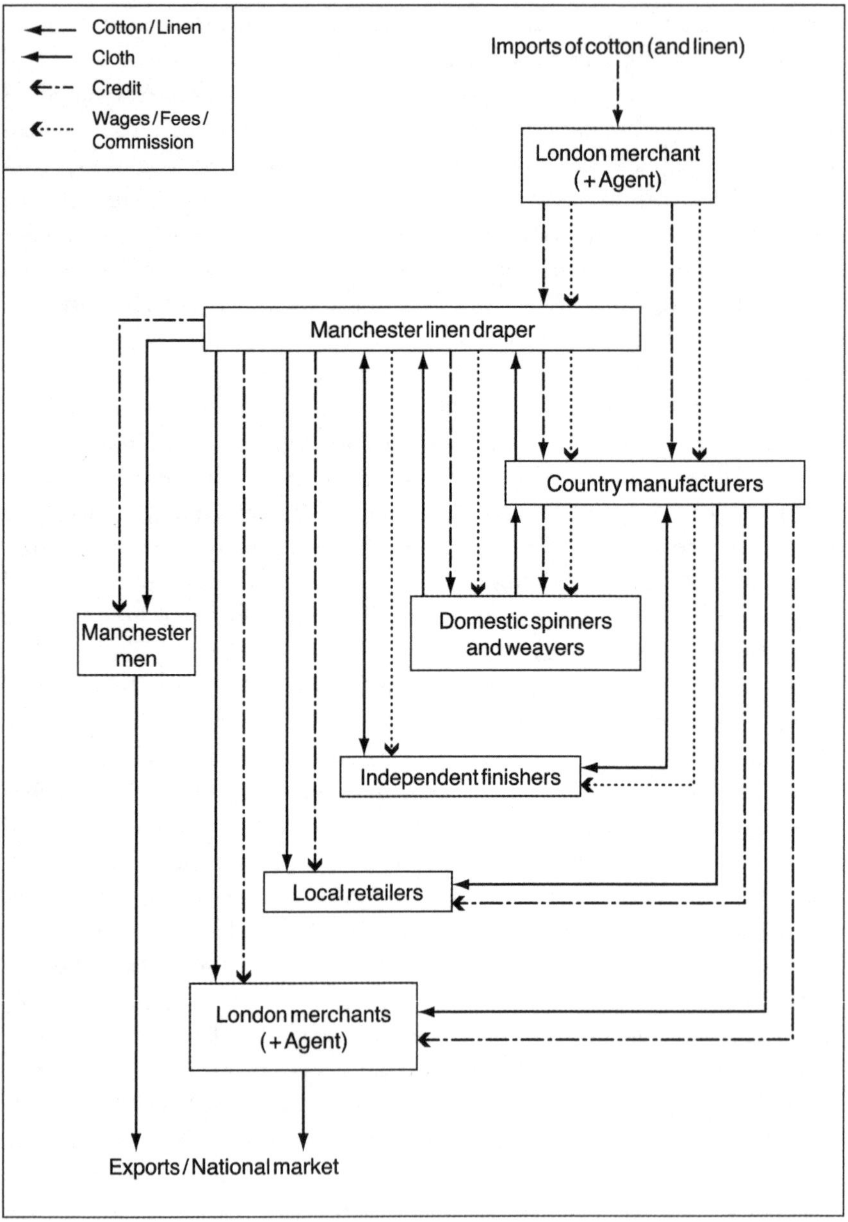

Source: Wadsworth and Mann, *Cotton Trade*, pp. 78–96.

also in putting-out work to both spinners and weavers. His single pair of looms was clearly insufficient to use the £31 2s 6d worth of yarn, wool, weft and twist which appear in his inventory. Equally, it seems unlikely that he could have produced the £163 12s 6d of cleans, stripes, fustians and pillows. Certainly, he had £8 13s 5d of warp and weft in the hands of eight weavers and £2 1s 5d of weft being spun by an unspecified number of individuals. This mixture of activities was repeated in Blackburn by Thomas Smalley who owned cards, reeds, weights, warping woofs and gigs; he had wool, yarn and weft to the value of £40 19s 4½d and various cloths worth £40 5s 8d, and was owed £2 5s for white yarn out with spinners. However, the relatively modest scale of his operations is indicated by the fact that he had only a half-share in a horse. At a rather larger scale, James Beck of Manchester had £503 6s 7d of 'goods in ye warehouse and homes', whilst Richard Lathom, a Wigan chapman, had £1,432 3s 6½d in his home and warehouse, owned £124 5s 6d of yarn which was out at weavers and was owed £386 2s in trade debts. It is not clear where these men obtained their cotton, but it may well have come from a Manchester linen draper such as Joseph Jolley whose probate inventory tells us much about the hierarchical organisation and gendered nature of textile production. On his death, Jolley left £431 17s 3d of goods in his warehouse and a further £548 9s 6d in the weighhouse. There was also £272 15s 6d of 'yarn at croft' in the hands of eight men and £178 15s 6d of yarn being woven by forty men and two women, illustrating the male domination of these activities.[104] In contrast, £15 10s 6d of 'yarn at winding' was being worked by ten women and just three men. Added to these amounts were £5 3s 7d (113 lb) of cotton at spinning and £8 13s 4d of yarn at dyeing, giving a grand total of £1,461 5s 2d in yarn and cloth and a production network involving well over sixty individuals. In addition, Jolly was owed £1,145 4s by seventy-four people, whilst he had accrued twenty-eight debts totalling £1,043 5s. The nature of these debts was less clear, but they were generally for larger amounts and included a number in excess of £100. In all, the inventory of Joseph Jolley included £1,524 3s 5d of debts owed by or credit-extended to 137 people. Unfortunately, it is impossible to trace the location of many of Jolley's contacts, but it is apparent that such dealers formed the apex of a complex putting-out and mercantile hierarchy similar in many ways to that found in the Yorkshire worsted industry.[105] This was centred on Manchester and structured by links out into the local countryside and down the regional urban hierarchy.

The woollen industry also became more centralised during the eighteenth century, but the clothiers retained far more independence than their counterparts in the fustian and cotton-linen trades. This was due to the relative ease of access to supplies of wool (producers with good credit could obtain wool from staplers in Rochdale, Colne and Rossendale) and to the more open market offered by the Manchester, Rochdale and Halifax cloth halls.[106] In effect, it was more difficult for merchants to dominate or monopolise the trade – a situation closer to that in west Yorkshire than in the West Country.[107] That said, the putting-out of wool and yarn was extensive and increasingly organised along similar lines to those seen in the fustian and cotton trade, albeit with a greater emphasis on the independent 'country manufacturers' or clothiers. Similar patterns of interaction were evident as a result. Thus, we see men like John Wareing, a Bury merchant who kept a wholesale wool book which included debts of £1,024 11s 2¾d owed by twenty-eight individuals for wool advanced to them or woollen textiles sent for sale. Wareing would probably have sent the cloth to Manchester to be dyed and perhaps to be sold, but he also did some trade direct with London merchants. A similar spatial-hierarchical division of labour existed between Colne and Halifax, although the former, like Bury, had its own market.[108] In Rossendale, the emergence of staplers, clothiers and chapmen in and around Haslingden formed an important intermediate tier between the local spinners and weavers, and the Rochdale merchants. Attempts to develop a market centre for the Rossendale bays at Newchurch around 1746 were ultimately unsuccessful, but it is apparent that the Haslingden traders in particular played an important part in the organisation of the developing putting-out system in the area.[109] They included clothiers like James Heyworth of Haslingden who was owed a total of £37 2s 4½d for thirteen pieces of cloth in the hands of six weavers, and James Anderton (active in the 1760s and 1770s) who purchased wool, gave it out to be carded, spun and woven, put out the cloth to be finished and then sold it to a dealer.[110] This dealer was increasingly likely to be a local chapman, but he would still tend to sell the cloth on to one of the merchants in Rochdale (or possibly Manchester), who would organise its shipment to and sale in London or elsewhere. Goods thus moved from countryside to Haslingden and thence to Rochdale and London – the classic territorial-hierarchical interaction seen within a staple-export system.[111]

Two things are clear from this. First, in contrast with Timmins's argument, the whole urban system was important to the operation of the textile industries of north-west England. Towns were the locations of significant levels of production, but more particularly they were pre-eminent in the specialist finishing processes and in the marketing of the cloth produced in the surrounding countryside and the town itself. Those most closely involved in the textile industries were amongst the fastest growing centres in the region (see Figure 3.5). Blackburn, Bolton, Leigh, Manchester and Stockport all grew faster than the population of the region as a whole and more than quadrupled their combined populations. By contrast, in the linen district, with its weakly developed commercial structures, and the woollen district, where significant amounts of trading by-passed the towns, urban growth was more subdued and variable.[112] Clearly, both the type of rural textiles manufacture and the links which existed between countryside and town were important in stimulating urban growth and in structuring local and regional economies. This links to the second point: that the urban network was significant in structuring the spatial organisation of production. This was most apparent in the way that Manchester dominated the textiles industries. The large overall number of individuals involved in the textile industries, the concentration of specialist operations, and its pivotal role in the putting-out system,[113] all reflected the extent to which this town formed the hub of cloth production in the north west. The merchants of the town undoubtedly short-circuited some local rural-urban interactions by linking directly with rural and urban producers throughout the region. Thus we see the declining importance of the Bolton middlemen in the second quarter of the eighteenth century; Manchester's continued significance as a market centre for woollens limiting the development of dealing (and perhaps growth) in Bury; and the lack of any indigenous organising centre within the linen district in western Lancashire.[114]

Conclusions: textile production and industrial organisation

The existence of four spatially distinct sub-economies within the textiles industries of early eighteenth-century north-west England is confirmed by the analysis presented here. They correspond broadly with Mager's typology of proto-industry,[115] but, whilst their overall geography showed remarkable stability throughout the eighteenth and nineteenth centuries, all experienced considerable change in organisational terms even in the early eighteenth century. This undermines some of the distinctions which Mager draws between the structures of each type of system. Woollens and linens were becoming increasingly capitalised and centralised, the latter most frequently as cotton-linens penetrated the traditional linen-producing areas.[116] More importantly, although geographically distinct, they were far from being functionally isolated from one another, as their production as well as their products were brought together through the activities of merchants in various towns, most notably Manchester.

Rural activity in all textiles areas was characterised by spinning and weaving, and this, added to the numerical dominance of rural manufacturing in all sub-regions, provides strong evidence for the type of 'bottom-up' growth suggested by proto-industrial theory. In spatial terms, this meant that areal production was fed into local urban centres and thence up the hierarchy and out of the region: a spatial-hierarchical division of labour. That said, the distinctive and important integrative function played by the urban system was clear from its centrality to finishing processes, the marketing of textiles and putting-out systems. The network of towns drew together production from surrounding rural areas into an economic system based around a staple export – cloth.[117] However, since different cloth types were characterised by different supplies, demands and production processes, local and sub-regional specialisations cut across the proto-industrial inter-dependencies and undermined any uniformity in the relationship between town and country. The particular functions of the two varied from place to place, and the balance of urban and rural economic power shifted accordingly. Classic proto-industrialisation and its peculiar spatial interactions and relations were most evident in eastern and especially south-eastern Lancashire, where towns functioned in a symbiotic relationship with their hinterlands. Bolton and Rochdale acted as co-ordinating and controlling centres for rural production, but were overshadowed by the concentration of manufacturing and commercial activities in Manchester which sat at the apex of a set of territorial-hierarchical interactions. This underlines Walton's assertion that 'the cotton-using manufactures of south-east Lancashire exhibited all the characteristics required by proto-industrial theory, and to the fullest extent'.[118]

The operational and spatial structuring of these putting-out systems must form part of the reason for the marked geographical stability of the region's textiles industries through the eighteenth and nineteenth centuries. These structures were important in the reasoning behind and location of early factories which were often constructed to centralise production as much as introduce powered machinery.[119] The urban system, with its predominance in capital-intensive finishing industries, its commercial infrastructures and networks, and its expanding and increasingly sophisticated systems of capital and credit, formed a stable framework around which changing spatial divisions of labour were arranged. As Gregory argues, changing resource sites and transport systems served to modify the detail, but the overall geography of the textiles industries and the spatial structure and focus of their organisation altered far less. Nineteenth-century Manchester was still the focus of activity: 'like an industrious spider, [it] is placed in the centre of the web, and sends forth roads and railways towards its auxiliaries ... which serve as outposts to the grand centre of industry'.[120] Already established as the key centre of control by the mid-seventeenth century, this position was progressively strengthened through subsequent generations of industrial development.

As the urban system did so much to shape the textiles economy, it might be possible to see the industries of the countryside as extensions of urban economic activity into rural areas. This was apparent in geographical terms in Blackburn Hundred where industry was clearly concentrated around the towns.[121] It can also be seen in the increasingly close control exerted over rural production by

Figure 4.9 *Spatial structure of the textile industries*

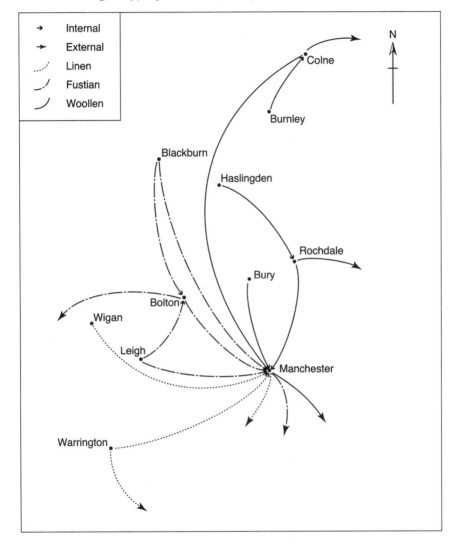

Manchester traders, sometimes through 'country manufacturers' such as the Bolton fustian-makers. In this way, production was *of* but not necessarily *in* the towns. Given this, a region-wide system of industrial specialisation (both in manufacturing and trading functions) can be suggested without undermining local proto-industrial relationships between town and country. Manchester, though, was the centre of a regional rather than merely local textile economy: it played a crucial part in the co-ordination of rural production throughout

Lancashire and north-east Cheshire (through finishing and putting-out), and was also vital in linking production in each of the textiles sub-economies of the north west with markets outside the region, both directly and through sub-regional centres such as Bolton and Rochdale. Moreover, there is little evidence of the direct growth-inducing interaction between specialist centres *within* the region of the type seen in Simmons's industrial specialisation model and theorised as a 'club good' by the city network paradigm.[122] The resultant structure appears to be a complex hybrid of local proto-industrial relationships, sub-regional cells of industrial specialisation and regional integration effected through the urban system and focused on Manchester (Figure 4.9) Indeed, the parallels between Manchester and London are strong, with each forming the centre around which the economy was organised and through which much business was transacted. Manchester replicated London's capacity for stimulating, generating and shaping national economic growth within the textile districts of north-west England. However, like England as a whole, the north west was not one single economy: the region's mineral-based economic system had a distinct spatial focus and a very different geography.

Notes

1 Defoe, *Tour through Britain*, p. 545.
2 See, for example, Hawke, 'Reinterpretations of the Industrial Revolution'; Berg, *Age of Manufactures*, pp. 13–33; Timmins, *Made in Lancashire*, pp. 85–93.
3 Von Tunzelman, 'Technological and organizational change'; Berg, *Age of Manufactures*, pp. 234–54; Mokyr, 'Technological change'.
4 For a critique of this type of overview, see Berg, *Age of Manufactures*, pp. 208–34.
5 Wadsworth and Mann, *Cotton Trade, passim*; Schwarz, 'North-east Lancashire', pp. 53–9; Hadfield and Biddle, *Canals of North-West England*, pp. 19–29; Lemire, *Fashion's Favourite*, especially pp. 12–42 and 86–9; Timmins, *Made in Lancashire*, pp. 35–60.
6 See Hudson, *Industrial Capital*, pp. 61–70; Wadsworth and Mann, *Cotton Trade*, pp. 29–53 and 314–23; Gregory, *Regional Transformation*, pp. 38–59; Hudson and King, 'Two textile townships', pp. 706–17.
7 Mager, 'Proto-industrialization', pp. 189–97.
8 Gregory, *Regional Transformation*, pp. 38–59; Hudson, *Industrial Capital*, pp. 25–41. See also Mann, *Cloth Industry* and Heaton, *Yorkshire Woollen and Worsted Industries*.
9 Stobart, 'Geography and industrialization', pp. 691–2. For more general discussion of these points, see Massey, *Spatial Divisions of Labour*; Dunford, *Regional Development*.
10 Walton, 'Proto-industrialisation'; Kenny, 'Lancashire cotton industry'; Wadsworth and Mann, *Cotton Trade*; Laxton, 'Textiles'; Timmins, *Made in Lancashire*, pp. 40–3. The absence of spatial analyses is also notable in national surveys of textiles industries.
11 Timmins, *Made in Lancashire*, pp. 11–19, 85–98 and 178–89.

12 Phillips and Smith, *Lancashire and Cheshire*, p. 90.

13 Walton, 'Proto-industrialisation', p. 51.

14 Swain, *Industry*, pp. 35–51; Wadsworth and Mann, *Cotton Trade*, pp. 317–18; Schwarz, 'North-east Lancashire', pp. 66–72.

15 Wadsworth and Mann, *Cotton Trade*, pp. 23–5.

16 Phillips and Smith, *Lancashire and Cheshire*, p. 90.

17 Corry, *Macclesfield*, pp. 63–70 and 193–5; Wadsworth and Mann, *Cotton Trade*, p. 107; Phillips and Smith, *Lancashire and Cheshire*, p. 91; Unwin, *Samuel Oldknow*, chapter 2.

18 See Wadsworth and Mann, *Cotton Trade*, pp. 98–106.

19 See Hudson, *Industrial Capital*, pp. 61–104; Hudson and King, 'Two textile townships'; pp. 706–17; Caunce, 'Complexity'.

20 See Dicken and Lloyd, *Location in Space*, p. 386.

21 Hodson, *Cheshire*, pp. 149–52.

22 Wadsworth and Mann, *Cotton Trade*, pp. 98–106; Spufford, *Great Reclothing*, especially pp. 43–4.

23 Hodson, *Cheshire*, p. 151.

24 Davies, *Macclesfield*, pp. 122–8; Corry, *Macclesfield*, pp. 63–70; Hodson, *Cheshire*, p. 149.

25 Wadsworth and Mann, *Cotton Trade*, pp. 23–5; Walton, 'Proto-industrialisation', pp. 45–7; Timmins, *Made in Lancashire*, pp. 13–16.

26 Blome, *Britannia*, p. 133; Defoe, *Tour through Britain*, p. 544.

27 Wadsworth and Mann, *Cotton Trade*, p. 314.

28 Walton, 'Proto-industrialisation', *passim*; Walton, *Lancashire*, pp. 74–6; Aikin, *Country round Manchester*, p. 306.

29 Hudson, *Industrial Capital*, pp. 64–5. The most important agricultural areas lay to the east of Leeds and especially in the East Riding.

30 Walton, 'Proto-industrialisation', p. 48. See also Timmins, *Made in Lancashire*, pp. 14–16.

31 Timmins, *Made in Lancashire*, pp. 85–108; Langton, *Geographical Change*, pp. 176–81.

32 See Swain, *Industry*, pp. 203–3; Tupling, *Rossendale*, chapter 6; Wadsworth, 'Rochdale woollen trade'; Gray, *History of Bury*, chapter 1; Timmins, *Made in Lancashire*, pp. 11–14. The production of woollen cloth also took place in many towns including Chester, Knutsford and Preston.

33 Walton, 'Proto-industrialisation', p. 55; Tupling, *Rossendale*, pp. 164–6; Swain, *Industry*, pp. 35–51.

34 Tupling, *Rossendale*, pp. 76–95; Swain, *Industry*, pp. 70–89; Walton, 'Proto-industrialisation', p. 54.

35 Swain, *Industry*, p. 128; Walton, 'Proto-industrialisation', pp. 54–6.

36 For details of this industry, see Smith, 'English felt and silk hat trades'.

37 Timmins, *Made in Lancashire*, pp. 16–19; Wadsworth and Mann, *Cotton Trade*, pp. 25 and 111–16.

38 The origin of fustians as a woollen-linen mix may hold the key to their location. See Wadsworth and Mann, *Cotton Trade*, map and note on p. 24, and pp. 317–27; Aikin, *Country round Manchester*, p. 23, and Kenny, 'Lancashire cotton industry', pp. 9–11. Significantly, the 'minority' cloth appearing in the fustian district changed from linen in the south and west to woollens in the north and east.

39 Wadsworth and Mann, *Cotton Trade*, pp. 29–53, 78–96 and 324–5.

40 Schwarz, 'North-east Lancashire', p. 66.

41 Wadsworth and Mann, *Cotton Trade*, pp. 98–106.

42 Chapman, *Lancashire Cotton Industry*, p. 10.

43 Walton, 'Proto-industrialisation', p. 61. Like Wadsworth and Mann, he places emphasis on rural rather than urban growth, despite the rapid expansion of Manchester, Bolton, Leigh and Blackburn.

44 Stobart, 'Textile industries', figure 2.

45 The reasons for the growth of fustian and cotton manufacture are complex, but it is clear that the expanding overseas markets for the finished cloths and its relatively privileged position within the intricate regulatory system which governed textiles production were vital to its success; Wadsworth and Mann, *Cotton Trade*, pp. 91–6 and pp. 248–50; Edwards, *British Cotton Trade*, chapters 9 and 10.

46 See Kenny, 'Lancashire cotton industry'; Timmins, *Made in Lancashire*, pp. 11–19, 85–98 and 178–89; Laxton, 'Textiles', pp. 108–9.

47 Krugman, *Development*, p. 36. See also Timmins, *Made in Lancashire*, pp. 35–60 and 125–54.

48 Daniels, 'Crompton's Census'.

49 Pigot and Dean, *Manchester and Salford Directory*.

50 Phillips and Smith, *Lancashire and Cheshire*, pp. 256–9.

51 Gregory, 'Geographies of industrialization', p. 374.

52 Mendels, 'Proto-industrialization', pp. 77–9; Berg, Hudson and Sonenscher, *Manufacture in Town and Country*, pp. 25–8; Hudson, 'Proto-industrialization in England', pp. 53–4; Freudenberger, *Industrialization of a Central European City*, pp. 55–80.

53 Gregory, *Regional Transformation*, pp. 111–20; Hudson, *Industrial Capital*, especially pp. 31–3 and 156–60.

54 Timmins, *Made in Lancashire*, pp. 71–4. See also Daunton, *Progress and Poverty*, pp. 161–9.

55 Kenny, 'Lancashire cotton industry', p. 9; Phillips and Smith, *Lancashire and Cheshire*, p. 96; Timmins, *Made in Lancashire*, p. 63.

56 Chapman, *Lancashire Cotton Industry*, p. 10.

57 Aikin, *Country round Manchester*, pp. 163–6 and 244.

58 Wadsworth, 'Rochdale woollen trade', p. 93; Wadsworth and Mann, *Cotton Trade*, p. 55.

59 Wadsworth and Mann, *Cotton Trade*, pp. 326–7.

60 All twenty-nine of the calenderers appearing in the probate records were located in Manchester. Wadsworth and Mann, *Cotton Trade*, pp. 253.

61 Wadsworth and Mann, *Cotton Trade*, pp. 253.

62 Raffald, *Directory of Manchester and Salford*. See also Aikin, *Country round Manchester*, p. 158.

63 Wadsworth and Mann, *Cotton Trade*, p. 252.

64 Wadsworth and Mann, *Cotton Trade*, p. 48.

65 Gregory, *Regional Transformation*, pp. 92–4.

66 Spufford, *Great Reclothing*, *passim*; Styles, 'Clothing the North'.

67 Cox, *Complete Tradesman*, pp. 38–75; Wadsworth and Mann, *Cotton Trade*, pp. 72–8.

68 Gregory, *Regional Transformation*, pp. 111–20; Hudson, *Industrial Capital*, pp. 156–60.

69 Tupling, *Rossendale*, p. 166 and pp. 176–7.

70 Owens, *Book of Fairs*.

71 Blome, *Britannia*, pp. 133.

72 Swain, *Industry*, pp. 123 and 146; Walton, 'Proto-industrialisation', pp. 54–5; Wadsworth and Mann, *Cotton Trade*, pp. 39–46.

73 Tupling, *Rossendale*, pp. 181–3 and 186. See also King, 'Rossendale', chapters 10–12.

74 Schwarz, 'North-east Lancashire'.

75 Tupling, *Rossendale*, pp. 181–91; Swain, *Industry*, pp. 199–204.

76 Wadsworth and Mann, *Cotton Trade*, pp. 43–5 and 88; Tupling, *Rossendale*, pp. 190–1.

77 Swain, *Industry*, p. 146; Gregory, *Regional Transformation*, p. 118.

78 Wadsworth and Mann, *Cotton Trade*, pp. 71–96 and 278; Tupling, *Rossendale*, pp. 203–4; Aikin, *Country round Manchester*, p. 276 and 279.

79 Hyde, *Liverpool*, pp. 25–39.

80 Walton, 'Proto-industrialisation', p. 50.

81 Defoe, *Tour through Britain*, p. 544. Kirkham formed the centre of a similar putting-out system: Walton, 'Proto-industrialisation', pp. 47–8.

82 Aikin, *Country round Manchester*, p. 270.

83 Wadsworth and Mann, *Cotton Trade*, pp. 78–87.

84 Cox, *Magna Britannia*.

85 Baines, *County of Lancaster*, volume 1, p. 534.

86 Wadsworth and Mann, *Cotton Trade*, p. 252; Aikin, *Country round Manchester*, pp. 158 and 263.

87 Gregory, *Regional Transformation*, pp. 112–19; Lloyd-Jones and Lewis, 'Economic structure of "Cottonopolis"', p. 82; Hudson, *Industrial Capital*, p. 28 and *passim*.

88 Gregory, *Regional Transformation*, pp. 115–17.

89 The exception to this was silk. Centred on Macclesfield, this formed a largely independent system of marketing. See Davies, *Macclesfield*, pp. 122–6.

90 Letter by Arthur Trevor to the Marquis of Ormonde, 21 December 1642 – quoted in Baines, *Liverpool*, p. 302.

91 Timmins, *Made in Lancashire*, pp. 73–4.

92 Walton, 'Proto-industrialisation', pp. 59–63.

93 Wadsworth and Mann, *Cotton Trade*, pp. 224–40; Walton, 'Proto-industrialisation', pp. 51 and 61.

94 Ogilvie, 'Social institutions'; Hudson, 'Proto-industrialization in England', pp. 63–5; Caunce, 'Complexity'.

95 Mann, *Cloth Industry*, pp. 63–119; Hudson, *Industrial Capital*, pp. 25–48; Gregory, *Regional Transformation*, pp. 121–38 and 186–220.

96 Davies, *Macclesfield*, pp. 122–6.

97 Unwin, *Samuel Oldknow and the Arkwrights*, chapter 2; Davies, *Macclesfield*, p. 124.

98 Walton, 'Proto-industrialisation', p. 48; Wadsworth and Mann, *Cotton Trade*, pp. 284–303.

99 The growth of fustian and check exports meant that there was more need to gear

production towards the often changing demands of overseas markets, especially those in Africa and North America. Wadsworth and Mann, *Cotton Trade*, pp. 36–8 and 124–8.

100   Walton, 'Proto-industrialisation', p. 62.

101   Wadsworth and Mann, *Cotton Trade*, p. 82; Timmins, *Made in Lancashire*, p. 72.

102   Styles, 'Clothing the North'; Timmins, *Made in Lancashire*, p. 54.

103   Zell, 'Credit in the woollen industry'; Hudson, 'Capital and credit', pp. 84–93; Wadsworth and Mann, *Cotton Trade*, pp. 91–2.

104   Amounts owed by each weaver varied from £1 2s to £11.

105   Heaton, *Yorkshire Woollen and Worsted Industries*, pp. 296–7; Hudson, *Industrial Capital, passim*.

106   Wadsworth and Mann, *Cotton Trade*, p. 278; Wadsworth, 'Rochdale Woollen Trade'.

107   Gregory, *Regional Transformation*, pp. 26–38. See also Zell, 'Credit in the woollen industry', pp. 669–76.

108   See Heaton, *Yorkshire Woollen and Worsted Industries*, p. 381.

109   Tupling, *Rossendale*, pp. 183 and 188.

110   Tupling, *Rossendale*, p. 188.

111   Simmons, 'Urban system', p. 63. See also Dicken and Lloyd, *Location in Space*, pp. 386–7.

112   Wadsworth and Mann, *Cotton Trade*, pp. 28–9; Walton, 'Proto-industrialisation', p. 48; Tupling, *Rossendale*, pp. 180–91.

113   Thomas Smith, an administrator of the estate of a Manchester chapman called David Jackson was described as 'putter-out of goods'.

114   Wadsworth and Mann, *Cotton Trade*, pp. 250–73; Tupling, *Rossendale*, p. 177.

115   Mager, 'Proto-industrialization', pp. 188–97.

116   Kenny, 'Lancashire cotton industry', pp. 6–11.

117   The extent to which urban capital penetrated rural production areas is crucial and, notwithstanding Wadsworth and Mann's work on this area (*Cotton Trade*, pp. 78–96 and pp. 241–50), requires fuller and more systematic enquiry if it is to be properly mapped and understood.

118   Walton, 'Proto-industrialisation', p. 63.

119   Wadsworth and Mann, *Cotton Trade*, pp. 97–108 and 284–308. See also Berg, *Age of Manufactures*, pp. 229–34.

120   Faucher, *Manchester in 1844*, p. 15.

121   Schwarz, 'North-east Lancashire', p. 77.

122   Simmons, 'Urban system', p. 68; Capello, 'City network paradigm', p. 1,925.

5

A mineral-based energy economy: coal-using industries

> The most valuable mineral production of Lancashire is coal, the great plenty of which has been a considerable encouragement to the settlement of manufactures in the county.[1]

The complex putting-out systems which characterised many branches of the textiles industries by the second half of the eighteenth century (and especially those which incorporated cotton production) are portrayed by Wrigley as the climax of an organic economy. Before the widespread adoption of steam engines in the early nineteenth century, textiles growth involved a deepening division of labour, broadening markets and ultimately the uptake of water power. In effect, it was 'exploiting old lines of development with a new intensity rather than striking out in a radically different direction'.[2] For Wrigley, this new direction was the use of coal to provide heat and, most especially, mechanical energy.[3] The steam engine, along with innumerable innovations and improvements to machine-based production, provided the key to the successful application of mechanical energy. Newcomen engines were probably first introduced to the north west at Whiston in 1729.[4] They became more widespread through the middle decades of the eighteenth century, increasingly replacing soughs, water wheels and horse gins as pits became deeper and capital investment grew.[5] By the 1780s, steam power was being used to return water over the water wheels which powered spinning mills and, ten years later, it was becoming dominant in the cotton-spinning districts, especially around Manchester itself.[6] Notwithstanding the close links which existed between factory spinning (in a mineral-based energy economy) and handloom weaving (still part of the organic economy), the growing application of steam power was clearly critical in generating huge leaps in productivity seen in cotton production in the late eighteenth and early nineteenth centuries.[7]

Whilst any wholesale switch to mechanical energy was a long way distant, the early eighteenth century did see a widespread use of coal to provide heat energy. It is possible to distinguish two distinct aspects to this energy economy which differed in both spatial and operational terms. The first consisted of a range of industries which required fuel to heat equipment or for stoving purposes. These included leather tanning, salt-, sugar- and soap-boiling, brewing and distilling, bleaching and dyeing textiles, printing cottons and fustians, and hot-pressing woollens, and were spread across the region.[8] Coal was easily substituted for wood as an energy source in these processes since there was no direct contact between fuel and material and no chance of undesired chemical interaction.[9] Its uptake was thus a matter of cost and availability rather than technical feasibility. The second aspect was the spatial clustering of coal-using industries in south-west Lancashire. These included several of the trades identified above, but were characterised by the so-called 'furnace' industries including iron, non-ferrous metals, glass and pottery.[10] Here, the adoption of coal could be more problematical because impurities from the fuel could react with the product. The use of coal was thus influenced by technological as much as economic factors, although it is clear from these industries' spatial concentration that the availability of cheap and/or good-quality coal was crucial.[11]

This chapter considers both of these aspects of coal-based industrialisation in the region and explores a number of ways in which the geography and organisation of production might be understood. It opens with a consideration of coal and transport nodes as locational constants and then examines the links between the organic and mineral-based economies, chiefly in terms of salt and iron production; but the main focus is on the growing cluster of coal-using industries in south-west Lancashire. Of central concern is the spatial structure of this nascent mineral-based economy. This is explored in terms of: first, key location factors, agglomeration economies and the localisation of production; second, the systems for organising production (putting-out and centralisation); and third, the integration of these spatial divisions of labour through the urban network.[12] Unfortunately, several of the these industries are poorly represented in the probate records: coal, salt and iron especially were heavily proletarianised and characterised by part-time working, whilst the owners were often gentlemen or merchants.[13] Moreover, the highly differentiated nature of these industries necessitates a different approach from that of the last chapter, one that considers them in turn before attempting to make any generalisation about the mineral economy as a whole.

Coal production in north-west England

Coal is not a ubiquitous raw material; even within coal measures, output is focused at the pitheads, making production punctiform in nature.[14] Since the movement of coal over anything other than very short distances added greatly to its cost and reduced its attraction as a fuel source, use was often

Figure 5.1 *Coal and salt resources and production in north-west England, c.1750*

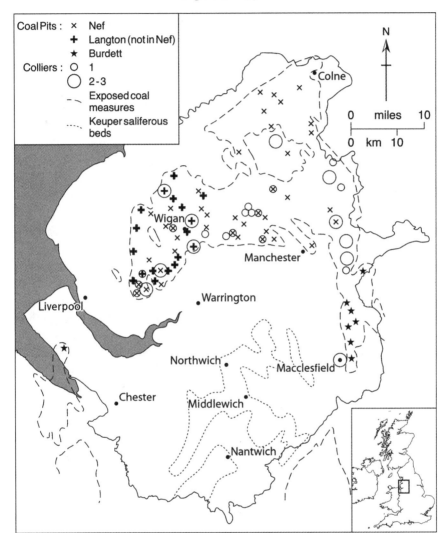

Source: Nef, *British Coal Industry*, volume 1; Langton, *Geographical Change*; Burdett, *Survey of County of Chester*.

similarly concentrated. Coal could cost up to one shilling per mile to move by road, with the result that it could double in price within 5–8 miles of the pit. Water transport was significantly cheaper, reducing transport costs to well under a quarter, but coal still became increasingly expensive further away from the pit.[15] As Mokyr has argued, price was not necessarily the key to the

uptake of coal in given sectors or processes, but it was often critical in determining *where* it might be used.[16] Coal-using industries tended to congregate
in areas of cheap coal which effectively meant the pits themselves or places
linked to them by bulk transport systems, be they coastal shipping (so significant to the prosperity of the coal industry in north-east England), turnpikes or
inland navigations.[17] For these reasons, coal is often seen as a key locational
constant.

In the north west, coal measures covered much of southern and eastern
Lancashire and parts of eastern Cheshire. There was also coal at Parkgate and
Neston (part of the north-east Wales coalfield), whilst rich seams lay just
outside the region in north Staffordshire. The collieries there 'were said to have
the greatest thickness of workable seams in Britain' and had been sending coal
overland to Cheshire's salt-boilers since the early seventeenth century.[18] From
the seventeenth century, pits in north Wales were also supplying Cheshire,
probably more for use in domestic hearths in Chester than industry.[19] Within
Cheshire itself, coal was being extracted from several pits around Macclesfield,
but these were of minor significance compared to their counterparts in Lancashire, at least partly because of the lack of demand for coal in the immediate
area.[20] In Lancashire, Nef identified four different areas of activity (Figure 5.1).
The first and probably the smallest was in the forests of Pendle and Trawden.
Coal had been mined here from the thirteenth century and Swain suggests that,
whilst production in the dozen or so pits of the area was marked by seasonal
variations, mining formed an important and profitable activity.[21] Further south
was a cluster of pits around Manchester, particularly to the west of the town.
Indeed, 'the Bridgewater mines at Worsley were only the most famous of
several major operations, and small-scale working was widespread'.[22] The final
two groupings were those around Wigan and in the Prescot-St Helens area.
These were probably the most important coal-mining areas in the region, with
production in the two combined rising from 28,000 tons in the 1690s to 199,000
tons by 1760, or from about one-third to one-half of the output of the north
west.[23] Within these two areas, the focus of production shifted during the
period, chiefly in response to changing demand and transport patterns (Table
5.1). Activity was initially greatest in the central area, but with the turnpiking
of the Liverpool–Prescot road in 1726, the south-western zone grew most
strongly, before it too was overtaken by the southern zone as the latter responded to the extension of the turnpike to the Warrington–Preston road
(1753), and the opening of the Sankey Brook Canal in 1757 (see Figure 3.3).[24]
Much of this latter growth in output came from the development by John
Mackay of mines at Ravenhead and Thatto Heath which were producing
40,000 tons per annum by the 1770s, making Mackay one of the largest coal
producers in Britain.[25]

Table 5.1 *Geographical change in coal production in south-west Lancashire*

Coal district	Output	1690s	early 1720s	late 1730s	1760
Centre (Wigan)	tons	10,500	13,400	13,200	29,000
	share	38%	30%	19%	15%
South (St Helens)	tons	5,700	16,600	5,800	115,000
	share	20%	37%	8%	58%
South West (Prescot)	tons	6,900	7,500	39,800	55,000
	share	25%	17%	58%	28%
North + West	tons	4,900	8,000	10,100	–
	share	18%	17%	15%	–
Total		28,000	45,500	68,900	199,000

Source: Langton, *Geographical Change*, pp. 93 and 154.

The way in which transport improvements changed the geography of coal production within south-west Lancashire again calls into question the status of resource sites as locational constants within regional economic development.[26] The location of the resources was certainly constant, but changing accessibility made them more or less important as the foci of coal production and, as will be shown later, coal-based development. Only in the Worsley areas does transport innovation appear to have confirmed the geography of production and here largely because the Duke of Bridgewater owned the mines and built his canal to serve them. Conversely, innovations in the transport system served to reinforce Liverpool's position as the principal market for coal in the north west.[27] Indeed, many of the improvements were sponsored by Liverpool merchants and reflected their growing centrality in the organisation of the coal trade and coal mining itself. Liverpool men were the principal backers of the Weaver and Sankey navigations and the Leeds–Liverpool Canal, and were prominent amongst outside investors in collieries around Prescot and St Helens.[28] This investment brought increasingly large amounts of coal to the Liverpool market (about 350,000 tons a year were being hauled to the port by the 1790s – over half the output of the south-west Lancashire coalfield) and made it the pivotal point for coal and other exports from this mineral-based economy.[29]

More generally, transport improvements made coal from this area increasingly competitively priced within the region and in the wider national market.[30] By the 1770s, according to Arthur Young, coal probably cost less in Liverpool than in coalfield towns such as Leeds, Wakefield and even Newcastle itself, and similar prices obtained throughout Lancashire coalfields, at least in the immediate vicinity of the collieries.[31] The essential geography of the mineral economy was thus established in a climate of increasingly reliable and cheap supplies of coal. It was a geography which, notwithstanding the rise and fall of Liverpool as a manufacturing centre, remained in place throughout the nineteenth-century growth of heavy industry.

Linking organic and mineral economies: salt and iron production

It is logical to suppose that the localised production of and access to coal supplies would profoundly influence the geography and development of coal-using industries as production became concentrated around pitheads and key transport infrastructure. However, many of these industries had existed for centuries, drawing on organic sources of energy and power. The question arises then of how the (often gradual) switch to coal-based production served to restructure these industries. This is explored through an examination of salt and iron production in the north west.

For centuries salt was manufactured in Cheshire by the evaporation of brine from lead-lined pans using wood as fuel.[32] Nantwich was the principal salt town in the sixteenth century, containing twice as many salt houses as Middle-wich and Northwich combined. By the early seventeenth century, however, shortages of timber were encouraging the uptake of coal brought overland from north Staffordshire and southern Lancashire. This shift from organic to mineral energy supplies promoted technical changes in production methods (larger and more heat-resistant iron pans replacing the old lead pans) and the geographical restructuring of output. Isolated from coal supplies and plagued by more restrictive practices, Nantwich declined, whilst production in Northwich grew apace, being linked from an early date to supplies of coal from the St Helens area (Table 5.2). Nationally, though, production was dominated by coastal salt works and especially those of the north east which operated on a huge scale (one works employed 1,000 men) and benefited from good supplies of cheap coal – much of it the waste not suitable for shipping to London.[33]

The discovery of rock salt at Marbury near Northwich in 1670 was thus doubly significant. Locally, it cemented the close relationship between Lanca-shire coal and Cheshire salt, linking salt production into an emergent regional mineral-based economy; nationally, it projected Cheshire salt into international markets with Liverpool as its major commercial outlet and principal source of inward investment. But its effect on the geography of production was complex and changing. Initial exploitation took the form of three refineries on the Mersey (Figure 5.2). These enjoyed the advantage of cheaper fuel due to lower transport costs: coal which cost about 3s per ton at the pithead was 5s 6d at Dungeon and 16s 8d at Northwich.[34] Further migration away from the saltfield was halted in 1702 by an Act of Parliament which restricted refining to within

Table 5.2 *Salt production in Cheshire and Lancashire (tons)*

	1682	*1770s*	*c.1795*
Northwich	15,878	31,862 (+ 37,787 rock)	55,086 (+ 49,382 rock)
Winsford	(2 pans)	3,680	18,838
Middlewich	5,590	c.10,000	4,000
Nantwich	5,460	c.4,500	60
Liverpool			3,000
Frodsham		c.7,000	3,000
Dungeon			2,500
Lawton			1,500
Total	26,928	c.57,042	87,984

Sources: Barker, 'Lancashire Coal', p. 84; Calvert, *Salt in Cheshire*, pp. 622–3 and 770–8; Aikin, *Country round Manchester*, pp. 429–30.

ten miles of the salt mines and focused development (somewhat artificially) onto Northwich. That said, both white and rock salt were sent to Liverpool. Much of the former came from central Cheshire (Table 5.2), often from small-scale refiners like James Parratt of Middlewich whose inventory includes £30 3s 6d of salt, two pans worth £38 10s and debts of £17 9s 8d owed by an unspecified number of Liverpool merchants. Some of the rock salt arriving in Liverpool was refined in the port's own salt works, but most was exported unrefined, giving Liverpool a reputation as a salt port and undermining New-castle's dominance in the trade.[35] However, Liverpool's position as the centre of the control of this salt trade was not unchallenged. At the start of the eighteenth century, Daniel Peck was trading in white salt refined at Flint as well as rock salt from Northwich.[36]

Whilst legislation made resource locations critical to the geography of pro-duction, the link between coal and salt was further reinforced by transport innovations: a process which began with the completion of the Weaver navi-gation in 1732. The project was sponsored by Liverpool merchants anxious to enhance supplies of salt for the export market and, from its opening, it carried mostly salt and coal.[37] The volumes of both grew steadily and accounted for 86–96 per cent of cargoes from 1759 to 1795.[38] The navigation prompted considerable growth in salt production at Northwich and Winsford which, in turn, helped to stimulate growth in output from the collieries around St Helens, Prescot and Whiston. The reliance on overland transport from the pits to the Mersey made supplies costly and uncertain, but again Liverpool interests took the initiative: the corporation ordered a survey of the Sankey Brook and money was supplied in significant part from the owners of the Dungeon and Liverpool saltworks. Thus, 'although the Sankey Canal may be said to have been in

Figure 5.2 *Major mineral works built before 1760*

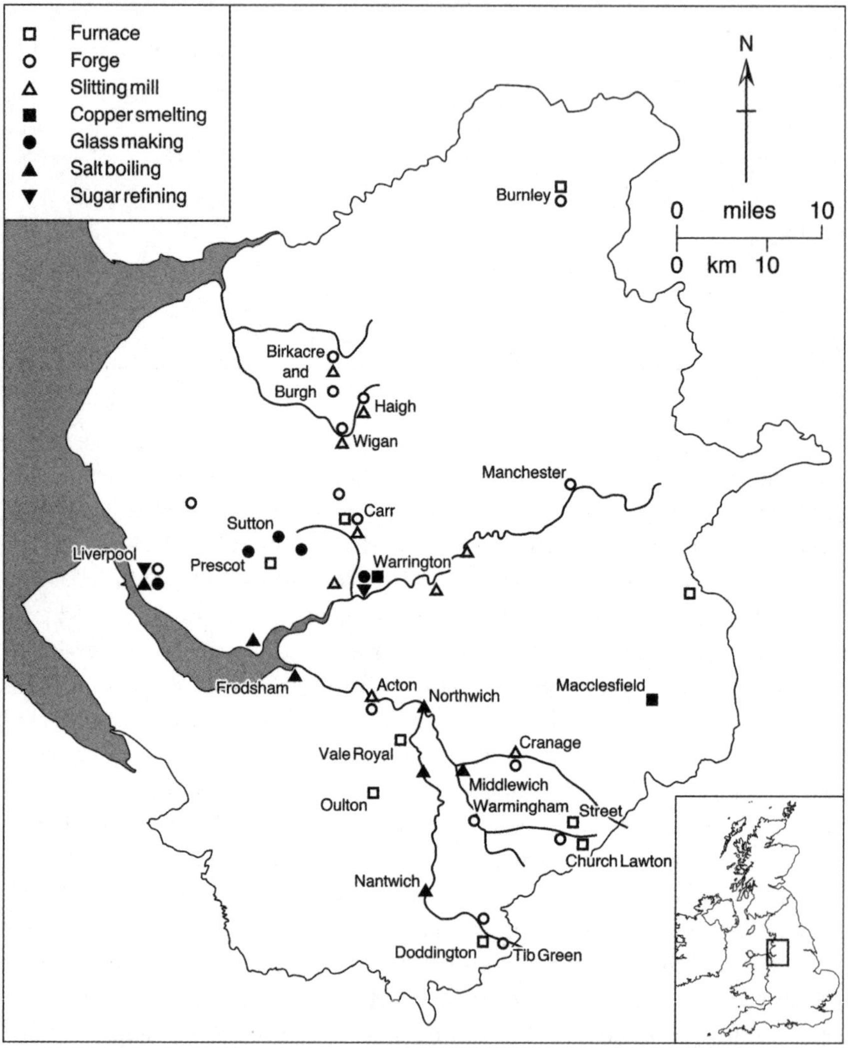

Source: Langton, *Geographical Change*; Langton, 'Liverpool'; Wallwork, 'Mid-Cheshire salt'; Awty, 'Charcoal ironmasters'; Barker, 'Lancashire coal'; King, 'Vale Royal'; Johnson, 'Foley partnerships'.

general a Liverpool venture, it was, in particular, a salt makers' creation'. The net effect of these two navigations was to create a triangular trade between Liverpool, the St Helens coalfield and the Cheshire saltworks.[39] From the start of the eighteenth century, the link between salt and coal was firmly established and the essential geography of the salt industry in place. So too were the links which encouraged the early nineteenth-century growth of chemicals manufacturing along the Northwich–St Helens axis, including the Brunner-Mond vinculum at Winnington and the numerous alkali works at Widnes and Runcorn.[40] As in the north east, then, coal and salt production preceded and were instrumental in determining the growth and location of nationally important chemicals industries.[41]

Iron smelting in the north west 'symbolised the new industrial economy which grew after the completion of the canals into the coalfields'.[42] This was, in effect, Wrigley's mineral-based energy economy, to which iron was so important. However, this was an industry undergoing profound changes across the country in terms of its fuel supply and geography: the search for new supplies of wood carried production away from its traditional centre in the Weald and eventually to the coke-fired furnaces of Shropshire and south Wales. The north west was very much a part of these broader changes. Iron production began with the establishment of a refining forge at Tib Green on the Staffordshire border in 1619 (Figure 5.2) – a development which might best be seen as an extension of the Staffordshire iron industry which had been supplying Lancashire nailers since the sixteenth century.[43] Growth accelerated from the 1650s, initially in southern Cheshire, but later in the centre of the county and, particularly from the 1720s, in southern Lancashire.

Table 5.3 *Urban and rural distribution of coal-using works in north-west England, 1701–60*

	Urban	Rural
Furnaces	0	9
Forges	2	11
Slitting mills	1	9
Copper-works	2	0
Glass-works	4	2
Salt refineries	5	2
Sugar refineries	2	0
Total	16	33

Sources: Awty, 'Charcoal ironmasters'; King 'Vale Royal'; Langton, *Geographical Change*, pp. 94–100 and 176–81.

Resource sites were important in determining the location of furnaces, forges and slitting mills in the north west, but it was generally sources of power, rather than iron, which were critical.[44] Before the conversion of Carr Mill to coke-fired production in 1759, all the furnaces burned charcoal and were located towards reliable supplies of wood, often defined in terms of large landowners willing to sell timber, and always outside towns (Table 5.3).

Ironstone was brought from Staffordshire and most furnaces also drew on supplies of haematite from Furness and Cumberland to produce blended pig-iron.[45] Forges and slitting mills could use either charcoal or coking-coal and their location reflects the need to preserve supplies of timber (being situated some distance from both furnaces and towns) or the availability of appropriate coal (Figure 5.2).[46] More important in determining the specific location of these refineries, especially on the Lancashire coalfield, was water. Power, provided by streams like the Yarrow, Douglas and Sankey, was needed for the hammers and bellows in the forges, and the cutters and rollers in the slitting mills. Subsequently, water transport confirmed the locational advantages of some of these, but undermined others. By 1757, the Carr, Haigh and Wigan ironworks had good access to either the Sankey or Douglas navigations, but those on the Yarrow were about six miles from the Douglas – a factor which was influential in their decline and eventual closure in 1775.[47]

The geography of iron production in the north west thus reflected its ties to both the organic and mineral-based economies of the region. The shift from the former to the latter was a long-drawn-out process. As late as 1750, the charcoal-fired forge at Warmingham had an annual output of about 300 tons, making it one of the largest in the country.[48] However, change was inexorable. Within the north west, this meant a re-orientation towards the coke-fired forges and slitting mills of southern Lancashire; nationally, it meant a decline in the region's importance in iron production as growth shifted to the Midlands and south Wales, and later the north east.[49] Nonetheless, the Haigh ironworks and the associated collieries formed the nucleus of the vast Wigan Coal and Iron Company, established in 1865 as the largest joint-stock company in the world.

Coal was also increasingly important to the textile-finishing industries, particularly bleaching and dyeing, but, in contrast with salt and iron production, it did little to change the industrial geography of the district. Rather, the spatial concentration of the finishing processes in and around Manchester was reinforced by the ability to meet the rising demand for coal *in situ*. As growth outstripped traditional sources of coal to the east and north of the town, increasing amounts of coal were hauled overland from Worsley and Clifton.[50] Again, demand stimulated transport improvements, first with the navigation of the Mersey as far as Manchester (1736) and later with the construction of the Duke of Bridgewater's canal (1761).[51] Importantly, the link took coal to Manchester rather than drawing industry onto the coalfield. This underlines the fact that, in the eighteenth century at least, textile production remained first and foremost an organic economy; it also connects to Gregory's argument that the broader geography of textile production – established through domestic and proto-industrial systems – remained in place despite the subsequent growth of coal-powered factory production.[52] Where widespread use of coal encouraged a fuller conversion to a mineral-based economy, the geographical reorganisation of industry was more profound. This was seen in iron and especially salt production, but was most deeply felt in the growing nexus of metal, glass and processing industries organised around Liverpool.

The spatial structure of a mineral-based economy: specialisation and localisation

Notwithstanding the importance of the salt and textiles industries, the major concentration of coal-using industry in the north west was undoubtedly found in south-west Lancashire. Like the corresponding textiles district, this area formed a microcosm of industrial diversity and possessed the critical mass needed for sustained economic development.[53] Within this, geographical specialisation was pronounced and divisions of labour were highly localised, towns and their hinterlands often being engaged in completely different forms of manufacture. Many of the ironworkers, like the forges and slitting mills which supplied them, were rural, whilst non-ferrous metals were urban; pottery- and watchmaking were more evenly split as was malting, but brewing, distilling and refining were essentially urban trades (Tables 5.3 and 5.4). More particularly, the pewterers and braziers of Wigan contrasted sharply with the ironworkers of the town's hinterland, and Liverpool stood at some distance from rural coal-using industries of any sort (Figure 5.3). This section explores the detailed differentiation which characterised this nascent mineral-based economy. Attention focuses on the marked spatial divisions of labour and on the role of locally available mineral resources in creating and nurturing these industrial specialisms.

In terms of ironworking, blacksmiths formed the most widespread trade, although the extent to which they used coal in their smithies undoubtedly depended on its cost in comparison to charcoal. They were dependent on local customers and so their distribution was broadly commensurate with that of population. More significant were the clusters of specialised ironworking which bespoke local or sub-regional economic growth. Nail-making had been important in southern Cheshire in the late seventeenth century, but was less significant by the eighteenth century, as Cheshire ironworking (particularly at Warmingham and, after 1702, Street) increasingly specialised in the production of salt pans.[54] More apparent from the probate records is the concentration of nail-making in the countryside around Wigan (Figure 5.3), particularly in Chowbent which contained about one-third of the nailers listed. Even these numbers are understated, however: Tupling suggests that about 100 nailers were enumerated in Upholland chapelry between 1699 and 1739,[55] and there was a notable cluster of hinge- and lock-makers in Ashton-in-Makerfield. In Warrington pin-making

Figure 5.3 *Geographical specialisation in the mineral energy economy,*
1701–60

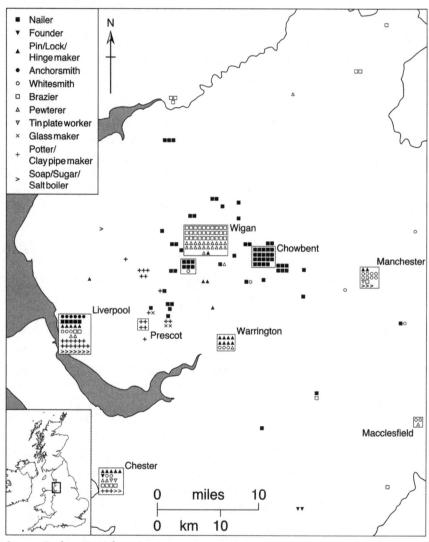

Source: Probate records, 1701–60.

was developing steadily through the eighteenth century and there was a growing number of anchor-smiths in Liverpool.

The various branches of metalworking in south-west Lancashire were of
considerably less national importance than the cutlers, scythe-makers and
nailers of Sheffield or the nailers, lock- and hinge-smiths, scythe-makers,
lorimers, toymakers and so forth of the west Midlands.[56] Nonetheless, they

were a significant element of the regional economy and certain trades, notably toolmaking, had established a national reputation by the late seventeenth century.[57] Many trades appear to have reached their peak in the 1720s (half the nailers listed in the probate records for 1701–60 appear in that decade – Figure 5.3), but the more important long-term trend was, as Langton argues, their increasing orientation towards Liverpool.[58] That said, ironworking took place elsewhere in the region: Bury formed a minor centre of nail-making; there were pin-makers, locksmiths and whitesmiths in Manchester, and a significant concentration of cutlers in Chester. Above all, though, ironworking was a dispersed and rural occupation – even without blacksmiths, nearly two-thirds were found outside towns. This dispersal may reflect easy access to coal throughout these areas, iron being acquired from a variety of local and more distant sources. However, as we shall see, the complex geography also related to the systems of putting-out through which production was organised.

Table 5.4 *Urban and rural distribution of coal-using trades in north-west England, 1701–60*

	Urban	Rural
Blacksmiths	67	147
Nailers	10	59
Hinge-, lock- and anchor-smiths	22	4
Whitesmiths	24	6
Watch- and watch part makers	27	15
Pewterers	29	3
Braziers	45	0
Potters and pipe-makers	23	13
Brewers and distillers	81	1
Maltsters	81	42
Total	409	290

Source: Probate records, 1701–60.

A dispersal of workers was also found in the watchmaking trades of the Liverpool and Prescot area (Figure 5.4). This network of specialised craftsmen had its origins in the seventeenth century when an extensive trade with London was established by two families from Toxteth Park – an origin which helps to explain the continued importance of rural manufacturing (Table 5.4). From there, production expanded across south-west Lancashire, drawing on and enhancing traditional toolmaking skills.[59] The extent to which these watch-makers were using coal in their workshops is impossible to determine, but they were a growing part of the mineral economy of the region, more than trebling

Figure 5.4 *Watchmaking in south-west Lancashire, 1701–60*

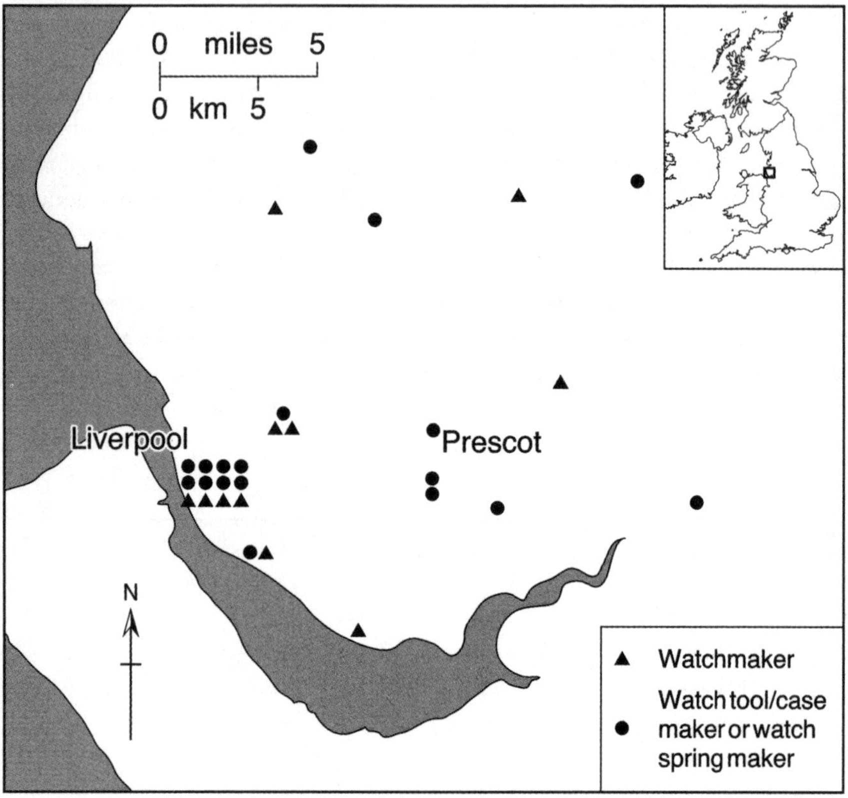

Source: Probate records, 1701–60.

in number during the study period. Significantly, this growth took place within the spatial parameters of seventeenth-century production, a geographical concentration which persisted into the late eighteenth and nineteenth centuries. The *Universal British Directory* (*UBD*) lists forty-eight watchmakers in Liverpool and thirteen in Prescot, but only three in Warrington and two each in Ormskirk and Wigan.[60] Both metalworking in general and watch- and toolmaking in particular were important in providing the basic skills, as well as the business networks and spatial distributions, of the engineering industries which emerged in southern Lancashire towards the end of the eighteenth century.[61] Once more, this illustrates the geographical and operational importance of early-established industries in shaping the subsequent development of the region – a form of spatial path dependence.

A clustering of trades which was still more marked, if less resilient, was that of pewter and brass working in Wigan. Again, these industries were well established by the seventeenth century, when bells from Wigan were sent throughout northern England and the town was second only to London as a centre of pewter manufacturing.[62] The probate records show that thirty of the forty-five braziers and twenty-one of the thirty-two pewterers recorded in the north west worked in Wigan, whilst Chester – its nearest rival and itself a noted centre for the manufacture of brass tableware – recorded just two pewterers and four braziers.[63] Crude pewterware could be made relatively easily and it is clear from several probate inventories that a number of rural nailers were also making brass and pewter goods. Typical were Christopher Mann from Tyldesley, whose inventory included £1 worth of pewter and brass, and Henry Tarbocke of Parr, who had 27 lb of pewter, 8 lb of pan brass and 15 lb of pot brass together valued at £1 10s 9d. Wigan dominated these trades, however, and they, in turn, formed the major industrial speciality of the town, accounting for about 16 per cent of its workforce according to probate evidence. The decline in Wigan brass- and pewter-making from their zenith around the turn of the eighteenth century is well established, but is not reflected in falling numbers in the probate records.[64] In part this stability is illusory. The town's brass- and pewter-makers were becoming wealthier as they increased the scale of their operations in the early eighteenth century and so a higher proportion would have left wills.[65] However, after a noticeable drop in the 1730s, numbers in both trades were apparently rising again in the 1740s and especially the 1750s.[66] Moreover, this growth was largely restricted to Wigan, so that the town's share of pewterers grew from 55 per cent in 1701–20 to 90 per cent by 1741–60. The demand for pewter may have been declining through the eighteenth century in the face of competition from the more fashionable china and earthenware,[67] but this seems to have affected other towns more than Wigan, whose non-ferrous metal trades prospered into the second half of the eighteenth century. That said, the relatively modest growth of Wigan (134 per cent between 1664 and c.1775) contrasts with the rapid expansion of Warrington (354 per cent) and Prescot (215 per cent), and suggest that the town's principal industries were less potent forces from growth than the smelting, refining and trading activities industries of its neighbours. When renewed growth came to Wigan in the late eighteenth century, it was generated by iron, not brass and pewter.[68] Nonetheless, Wigan remained a testament to the 'complexity of the industrial geography of "pre-industrial" England',[69] and its industries represented major elements in the region's mineral economy. Both the brass and pewter industries were using coal by the mid-seventeenth century; indeed, the presence of good-quality coal does much to explain the concentration into Wigan of such specialised production.[70] If cannel coal formed a key locational factor, it was undoubtedly strengthened by agglomeration economies that accrued as the brass and pewter manufacturers of Wigan drew on an established skill base within the town and developed close links with other industries in the local area, most notably the copper smelter established at Warrington in 1719 (see Figure 5.2).

As with iron smelting, the copper-works relied on imports of ore and were drawn to Warrington because of the availability of local coal and the improved river access afforded by the 1701 navigation of the Mersey.[71] Resources and transport were key location factors, but were far from geographically fixed. Charles Roe's copper-works at Macclesfield opened in 1758 with the expectation of using local coal and copper ore from mines at Alderley Edge, but from the outset imports of ore were needed, initially from Coniston and, after 1765, from Roe's hugely profitable mines at Parys Mountain in Anglesey.[72] Transport requirements thus changed and, despite extensive lobbying for a canal (which finally came in 1831), Macclesfield's attraction as a location for copper smelting was in decline. The Anglesey copper reserves, coupled with growing demand in Liverpool, made the Mersey the obvious location for the copper indus-try.[73] Roe established a works at Liverpool in 1767, but, as at Bristol which declined as a centre of copper production with the growth of Swansea,[74] these were soon overshadowed by copper-works at Garswood (1772) and Ravenhead (1780) – the latter quickly accounting for one-sixth of national output.[75] These were situated to take advantage of the good supplies of local coal and the access afforded by the Sankey navigation. The locational advantages (coal and water transport) which brought smelting to Warrington at the start of the eighteenth century were reinforcing the distribution of the copper industry eighty years later, but the preferred location had shifted twice in the meantime, first to ore reserves and then towards the market. Simple geographical lock-in and reading-off apparent 'natural' or resource advantages are clearly simplistic as explanations for the location and operation of these activities: access to markets, capital and information was also vitally important.

Similar arguments can be made for glass-making. This was also located at 'points of raw material extraction and at waterside markets' which often meant towns (Figure 5.2 and Table 5.3).[76] Initial development took place in Warring-ton and in Sutton around 1695, but was quickly followed by the erection of smelters at Prescot, Thatto Heath (in Sutton) and Liverpool. Later growth was concentrated at the head of the Sankey Brook, with the construction of the massive British Plate Glass Manufactory in 1773 and a smaller works nearby in 1782.[77] St Helens grew around the glass- and copper-works and the collieries to become one of the first genuinely new towns of the industrial revolution. All the early glass-works prospered at least through to the 1740s, but those in Liverpool, with the best access to markets, formed the largest centres of manu-facture up to the 1770s. That said, the coalfield works had crucial long-term advantages. Glass-making required enormous quantities of coal. Langton estimates that, by 1740, more than 6,000 tons per annum were supplied to the glassworks by pits at Prescot and Thatto Heath.[78] It was this ready supply of energy at a price increasingly lower than that pertaining in Liverpool, combined with the external economies of scale deriving from specialised local production systems which held the key to the ultimate success of the St. Helens glass industry.[79] Again, this situation was closely paralleled in Bristol where glass-making was moving out of the city in the 1780s to exploit cheap coal around Nailsea.[80]

Much the same was true of the pottery industry, although here the geographical shifts in production were far greater. Local clays had been used to produce coarse earthenware around Prescot for many years and small quantities were being exported from Liverpool by 1667.[81] Production spread to Liverpool which, by the mid-eighteenth century, had become the main centre of pottery manufacture in the north west. It contained thirteen of the eighteen potters and clay pipe makers listed in the probate records for 1741–60 (Figure 5.3) and had several large-scale pot-works by the third quarter of the eighteenth century.[82] There were at least seven china-works and upwards of twelve earthenware manufactories, mostly located on the eastern side of town away from the docks (Figure 5.5). These factories prospered during the 1770s and 1780s: not only did they enjoy access to good supplies of cheap coal, they could also tap into supplies of flints and Cornish china clay being carried to the north Staffordshire Potteries along the Trent and Mersey Canal. Furthermore, they had good access to regional and national markets, and to up-to-date market information in what was becoming an increasingly fashion-led trade.[83] Links to the burgeoning and dynamic earthenware, stoneware and porcelain manufactories of the Potteries were strong in terms of both personal and business contacts. For example, William Reid (a Liverpool china-maker) was in partnership with John Baddeley of Shelton from 1756; at the same time, he received large shipments of earthenware from John Wedgwood of Burslem.[84] Later, in 1801–11, J. B. Wood of Burslem sent crates of his wares to a number of Liverpool merchants, including over twenty to John Dunbibin who had operated his own pot-works in Liverpool in the 1770s and 1780s.[85] As with other manufactures, though, Liverpool's domination and dynamism did not outlast the eighteenth century: Reid's porcelain business ended in bankruptcy as early as 1761, but a more general decline was discernable by the 1790s and all the china works were closed by 1806. Ultimately, the Liverpool earthenware and china-makers were unable to compete with the specialised production in the potteries of north Staffordshire to which went many of Liverpool's skilled potters.[86]

This ebb and flow from Liverpool did not greatly affect its traditional coal-using processing industries of sugar refining, distilling and brewing which

Figure 5.5 *China and earthenware manufacturing in Liverpool in the mid-eighteenth century*

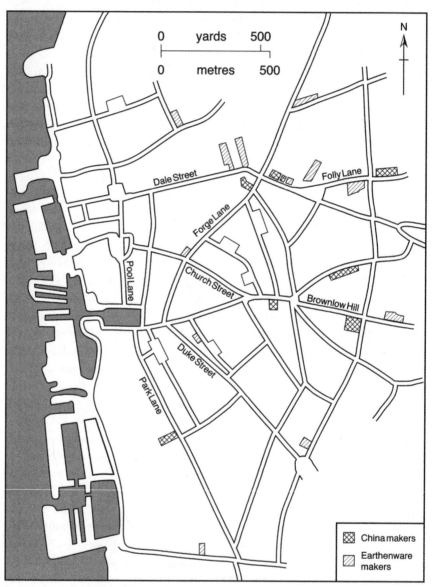

Source: Boney, *Liverpool Porcelain*.

increasingly used coal as an energy source. The first of these was closely related to Liverpool's colonial trade and imports of sugar grew rapidly from 35 tons per annum in the late 1660s to 580 tons at the turn of the century, about 5,000 in the 1740s and 8,250 by 1770.[87] The first refinery opened in the 1660s and, despite competition from a Warrington refinery and from sugar boilers in Chester (Figures 5.2 and 5.3), the port continued to dominate throughout the eighteenth century and beyond. Of the six sugar bakers and boilers listed in the probate records, five were found in Liverpool and by the 1760s there were at least eight sugar houses in the port with a combined output of 6,000 hogsheads per annum in the 1780s – figures which probably compare with Bristol's twenty refineries at the end of the century.[88] Distilling was similarly concentrated into the ports of Liverpool and Chester, but, as the latter's shipping trade declined through the eighteenth century, Liverpool increasingly dominated.[89] Both sugar refining and distilling were capital-intensive industries reliant on materials imported into the region: their domination by port towns is there unsurprising. Although brewing was rather more widespread, the seventy-one brewers listed in the probate records were located in just seven places, making this an urban trade (Table 5.4). Chester (with twenty-four brewers) and Liverpool (thirty-eight) again overshadowed output from other centres. Indeed, by the 1780s, Liverpool had thirty-nine public breweries, sixty-nine brewers of table beer and a large porter brewery.[90] Despite this, output was inadequate and increasing amounts of ale had to be imported, as was much of the malt used by Liverpool brewers. Malting was a widespread activity and was practised in both towns and villages, at least fifty-five settlements in all. Unsurprisingly, activity appears to have been concentrated into Cheshire and western Lancashire where most barley was grown, Chester, with twenty-seven maltsters, being the main centre of production.[91]

Overall, the coal-using industries in south-west Lancashire emerged during the late seventeenth and early eighteenth centuries as a major component of the economy of north-west England: one which was very different in nature from the textile economy to the east of the county. It was based on a variety of mineral resources – many of which were imported into the region – but was at least partly structured around local availability of, or access to, coal. These points of supply and demand were, of course, increasingly linked by intensively used transport corridors: turnpiked roads, canalised rivers and dead-cut canals (see Chapter 3). In short, it was developing into a classic mineral-energy based economy: the supply of energy being critical to industrial growth that was spatially structured around coal and key transport infrastructure. That said, neither the constitution nor the geography of this sub-regional economy was fixed. Brass and pewter manufacture in Wigan and ironworking in the surrounding hamlets were increasingly overshadowed by the large-scale smelters, potteries and refineries of the Mersey corridor. Moreover, the initial advantages of local resources were often superseded by the benefits of improved transport, agglomeration economies and better access to key markets. This suggests that, as production spread across the south-west Lancashire coalfield in the eighteenth century, it was links to Liverpool, and the wider supplies and demands to which the port gave access, that were vital to local economic growth.

This brings us back to the broader question of the spatial and organisational structure of this mineral-based economy. Production was both specialised and localised, implying that the notions of economic localisation and industrial specialisation may be useful in understanding its operation. However, there are problems here. Many of the industries were scattered across the district: nail-making especially was dispersed through dozens of hamlets and villages, but glass, copper and pottery production and the ironworks were also far from being concentrated in any single place (see Figures 5.2 and 5.3). Furthermore, in Simmons's model it is inter-linkages between specialist production centres (in the form of supplies and demands) that form the principal cause of regional economic growth: the system is not necessarily closed, but the growth impetus is internal.[92] Within the north west, the coal-using industries appear to have interacted only sporadically or tangentially: local ironworks supplied the nailers; the copper smelters provided for the needs of the braziers; and all were linked and positively fed back to coal production. However, there is little evidence of systematic and endemic inter-connections between the various specialist economies. More importantly, it was external demand which drove production in each of these industries and, indeed, accounted for a significant amount of coal production itself.[93] Many of these exports were channelled through Liverpool, suggesting that a highly diversified export model with Liverpool as the principal core area may be more appropriate than one of industrial specialisation. In order to understand fully these structures and the impact they had on the development of the coal-using industries of north-west England, it is necessary to explore the internal organisation and external linkages of this sub-regional space economy.

The organisation of production: centralisation, putting-out and the urban network

Within a mineral-based energy economy, the growing importance of coal not only has an increasing bearing on the location of industry, it also encourages a growth in the scale of production and changes in its organisational structure.[94] This would classically involve the emergence of centralised and proletarianised manufactories financed and controlled by industrial capital. However, at best this simple model is the end product of long processes of change; at worst it obscures a large range of diverse organisational systems within a mineral economy, from the centralised factory to the small workshop.[95] Such diversity is well illustrated in the coal-based industries of the north west. This final section examines the various production systems and, in particular, explores the role of the urban network in both integrating local specialisms and linking them to wider supplies and demands.

The changing relationship between workers and coal owners or coalmasters, and the transformation which occurred in the control and running of collieries has been discussed in detail by Langton.[96] Little needs to be added here, except to note the gradual shift away from gentry-run operations and the concomitant rise in the influence of Liverpool and, to a lesser extent, London and Cheshire interests in the collieries of south-west Lancashire.[97] Liverpool money flowed into salt refining in Cheshire, but, as Langton argues, it is easy to exaggerate the importance of this flow of funds since most investment went into transport infrastructure.[98] Moreover, whilst they were increasingly central in the operation and control of coal and salt production in the north west, the Liverpool merchants could never match the power of the Newcastle coal owners. The market which they controlled was far less important than the lucrative London trade and even within the region they never effected anything like the monopolistic control over the supply of coal achieved through the vend.[99] Indeed, such a monopoly was impossible given the multiplicity of coalmasters in south-west Lancashire and the constant presence of the Duke of Bridgewater who could, it was argued, undercut other suppliers in Liverpool and more than once threatened to do so.[100] The presence of alternative markets for coal within the coalfield itself (both for domestic and industrial use) gave the coalmasters a range of options when selling. In reality, the growing involvement of Liverpool merchants in the production of coal (and salt) arose from the need to secure adequate supplies rather than achieve the sort of market domination seen on Tyneside.[101] That said, Liverpool did benefit greatly from its role as the centre of control for this mineral-based economy. Its link with the region's coal industry was closer to that between Bristol and southern Glamorgan, but the spatial proximity of Liverpool and its hinterland contrasts sharply with Bristol's removal from the south Wales coalfields which formed its major area of investment.[102] This undoubtedly had an impact on the relative fortunes of the two ports in the nineteenth century: although production drifted away from Liverpool, the commerce created by industrialisation in its expanding hinterland assured the port's continued prosperity.

Closer parallels may be found within the north west. In many ways the Liverpool merchants occupied a similar position to the Manchester linen drapers: originally engaged in selling the products of industry, they became increasingly involved in controlling and financing production. Equally, the spatial and structural relationships between manufacturers and these controlling merchants bears comparison. Notwithstanding the punctiform nature of coal and salt production and the channelling of goods along bulk transport routes, the essential territorial-hierarchical relationships remain. Packhorses and increasingly wagonways linked the production of scattered pits to the turnpike or canal by which the coal travelled to Liverpool.[103] Thus, as in the north east and later in south Wales, technological advances in terms of proto-railways were needed to realise the full potential of water transport systems.[104] In this sense, the mineral-based economy of the north west, like that elsewhere, was inducing positive feedback in the form of increased demand for iron rails, wagons and so on, but was doing so to link quasi-areal production to key lines of access and transport nodes, principally Liverpool.[105]

This was not proto-industry: at least not in its traditional conception. The coal and salt industries showed a degree of centralisation and capitalisation considerably greater than that seen in pre-factory textile production. Individual pits could be purchased for as little as £40 in the mid-eighteenth century and the pans for salt boiling were to be had for about £20 in the 1710s, but ever-larger amounts of capital were required for coal pits and for salt mines and refineries to remain profitable. Both were also characterised by early proletarianisation of a workforce which had few opportunities for independent economic activity within coal or salt production and a declining tendency for income generation from secondary or seasonal employment.[106] That said, coal and salt were staple products, and Liverpool interests largely controlled both exports and much of the internal flow of these commodities. The Liverpool merchants thus short-circuited many urban hierarchical linkages in a similar manner to their Manchester counterparts. As with the linen drapers, though, the merchants' domination was by no means complete: coal was sold in towns and villages throughout the region, whilst unknown quantities of salt were still being sent out along the old saltways as well as being exported through Chester by men such as Daniel Peck. In January 1704, for example, he sent 765 bushels of white salt to Dublin and lost an unspecified amount when a ship bound for Lisbon was taken by the enemy fleet. In the following months he sent 4,009 bushels in three separate shipments to Rotterdam.[107]

In many ways, this complex overlaying of spatial economic systems was repeated in iron smelting and refining. Despite the persistence of numerous small ironworks, considerable financial resources were generally needed to purchase raw materials, but more especially for ongoing investment in the fixed capital of ironworks.[108] The furnace at Church Lawton, for example, was supplied with an initial purchase of £3,000 worth of timber in 1658, whilst the stock at Haigh Mill was £2,277 in 1666 and an estimated £40,000 a century later.[109] In the seventeenth century, these huge amounts of money were drawn together by large-scale partnerships often involving landowners and almost always extending over several counties.[110] To a considerable extent, such large-scale capitalism operated independently of local economic and urban systems: it was structured by patterns of inter-personal contacts, often through the extended family or ties of religion. Catholic landowners, notably Sir Roger Bradshaigh, were central to development of coal and iron around Wigan. They drew on contacts with other Catholics in the region and beyond, creating a marriage of industry and religion which forms an interesting counterpoint to the more famous non-conformist domination of south-east Lancashire.[111] These, and many other locally controlled and integrated business ventures became more prominent as the larger national partnerships of ironmasters broke up in the early eighteenth century. There was a growing tendency for close vertical integration in the ownership and production of coal and iron. For example, in the 1750s and 1760s, the Chadwicks owned forges in Birkacre, Burgh and Bottlingwood, and slitting mills at Birkacre and Scholes (near Wigan); they supplied both from their own pits at Burgh and Birkacre and at Bottlingwood. Whilst the pig-iron was brought in from outside, this was also organised by the Chadwicks themselves.[112]

This same vertical integration characterised the copper- and glass-works of Merseyside and later St Helens. All three coalfield glasshouses were linked to specific collieries in the early eighteenth century – ensuring a reliable and discounted supply of coal – and similar arrangements were also established by the Ravenhead glass-works in the 1770s.[113] This was 'modern' industrial capitalism in the making, with centralised and capital-intensive production, a proletarianised workforce and strong vertical linkages. It was also strongly linked with world and especially colonial economies. For example, large amounts of investment capital were generated in Liverpool by the slave trade; the Earl of Balcarres spent large amounts of money earned whilst governor of Jamaica on developing his mines and ironworks at Haigh, and the East India Company was an important investor in the Ravenhead copper-works.[114] The future organisation of much of British industry was presaged in the heavy industries of south-west Lancashire.[115] Moreover, unlike south Wales, where Bristol merchants were central to investment in iron and copper smelting, capital was raised by and often provided from the personal fortunes of the entrepreneurs within the industrial enterprises and was spatially fixed in the production locations.[116]

For links to the market, the ironworks of Lancashire and Cheshire, like their counterparts in the west Midlands, were reliant on merchants, particularly ironmongers.[117] It is difficult to quantify precisely those engaged in iron dealing as a range of occupations appears to have been involved. In south Yorkshire chapmen were amongst the principal iron dealers, but, although some in the north west were engaged in buying and selling metals, a survey of inventories shows that most, even around Chowbent, were textile rather than iron dealers.[118] In contrast, Joseph Titley, who was one of the main Warrington iron dealers, styled himself as grocer on his will. All these trades, and particularly that of

ironmonger, were predominantly urban, Chester and Warrington being the
principal centres (Table 5.5). Certainly the main buyers of bar iron from
Cranage, Warmingham and Bodfari in Wales in the seventeenth century were
ironmongers from these towns, plus a handful from Sandbach, Knutsford and
Nantwich.[119]

Table 5.5 *Location of ironmongers in north-west England,*
1701–60

	1701–20	*1721–40*	*1741–60*	*Total*
Chester	15	7	8	30
Warrington	3	3	1	7
Liverpool	0	2	4	6
Nantwich	0	3	1	4
Knutsford	1	1	1	3
Preston	1	0	2	3
Sandbach	2	1	0	3
Manchester	0	1	1	2
Northwich	2	0	0	2
Leigh	1	0	0	1
Macclesfield	1	0	0	1
Ormskirk	0	1	0	1
Stockport	0	0	1	1
Wigan	1	0	0	1
Total	27	19	19	65

Source: Probate records, 1701–60.

Prominent amongst the customers of these ironmongers were rural ironworkers, most notably those of south-west Lancashire. These workers were
generally organised through putting-out systems centred on key centres in the
urban system. The urban ironmongers acted as intermediaries between the
ironmasters and the manufacturers; they also merchanted the finished goods
throughout the country, often via factors or London wholesalers.[120] Most
important in this respect were the Warrington ironmongers, through whom
bar and rod iron from the forges in Cheshire and north Wales reached nailers
in south Lancashire. Increasingly, these dealers, like their counterparts in the
west Midlands, were involved in the production processes as well. Some, like
Joseph Titley, purchased slitting mills, thus assuring their own supply of iron;
most were engaged in putting-out materials to workers in the surrounding
countryside.[121] This could involve supplying iron on credit to independent or
semi–independent workers, the cost of the iron being offset against the value

of the finished goods; it might also involve paying piece-rate wages to effectively dependent employees. It is likely that this was the type of business run by John Bulling, a Warrington ironmonger whose probate inventory includes £173 10s 10½d in book debts and £260 9s 4d in 'ready coin'. Iron was also put-out by master nailers with their own (semi-)dependent workforce. One such individual was Nicholas Withington, a Chowbent nailer whose inventory contained debts of at least £38 12s 4d owing from upwards of fifteen workmen. Many of these would have been other nailers in the village – men like John Hatton and Richard Chow who were worth just £7 15s and £8 16s 2d respectively – but Withington probably supplied nailers in the surrounding villages as well. His goods and stock-in-trade (valued at £69 5s 3d) were far greater than the £4 15s 4d of smithy goods owned by George Taylor of Atherton or the £3 11s 1d of goods and equipment in the shop and smithy of Francis Roby of Billinge. It is impossible to tell whether Withington was working on his own account or as an agent for an ironmonger, but it is clear that manufacturers were increasingly involved in dealing as well as putting-out iron.[122] Withington himself was owed £111 6s 9d in book debts, including £12 13s 1d from Wales and £4 5s from Liverpool, and had £64 14s 4d of goods at Chester, Skipton and Liverpool. This indicates an extensive trading network for a single manufacturer in a small Lancashire village and highlights the importance of these three towns as gateways to the north Wales, Irish, northern England and colonial markets.[123]

The importance of these manufacturer-dealers made the putting-out of iron more like that of the west Yorkshire woollen industry, with its master clothiers, than that of the nascent cotton trade which overlapped spatially with the metalworking districts.[124] There are also parallels to be drawn with the 'country manufacturers' who organised the local putting-out for Manchester linen drapers (see Chapter 4). The similarity with west Yorkshire was strengthened by the marked and continuing independence of the workforce. Nailers remained tied into a dual economy more closely and perhaps longer than the textile workers of south-east Lancashire. Rowlands suggests that many smiths in the west Midlands had secondary sources of income (usually agriculture) and that, at least through to the 1750s, their annual work patterns were determined by ploughing and harvesting rather than demand for their iron-work.[125] Many nailers in south-west Lancashire had agricultural as well as industrial stock. Indeed, it was often of considerably greater value: Samuel Morris of Tyldesley had £7 of corn and hay and £8 of livestock, but just £4 14s in his shop and warehouse; Francis Roby had £16 16s of agricultural goods compared with £3 11s 1d in his smithy and shop. As in Yorkshire, such holdings undoubtedly gave security for the purchase of equipment and the acquisition of credit. Certainly, workers with good credit could obtain iron from a variety of sources, thus maintaining some independence. Moreover, Rowlands' suggestion that the higher-skill tradesmen, such as scythe- and toolmakers, bought directly from the Worcestershire forges finds its echo in the direct supply of iron from the Colnbridge forge in Yorkshire to nailers in Chowbent.[126] The Lancashire nailers even became involved in supplying their own rod iron when a group of Chowbent nailers set up in partnership with a local ironmaster and a Liverpool merchant to run Carr forge and Sankey slitting mill between 1775 and 1783 – a process echoing the co-operative mills of west Yorkshire.[127]

As in the west Midlands and south Yorkshire (and, indeed, the west Yorkshire woollen trade) there does not seem to have been any systematic move to dependency amongst the workforce before the growth of centralised workshops and factories in the late eighteenth and early nineteenth centuries.[128] Proletarianisation was a sectorally, spatially and temporally differentiated process. In many ironworking trades, it was associated with changing locations and systems of production, but in the non-ferrous trades of Wigan in particular, it occurred within traditional frameworks. The decline in the number of braziers and pewterers disguises a distinct shift from artisanal to proletarianised and quasi-factory production as craftsmen employed more non-apprenticed workers.[129] Alongside this was the growing tendency to specialisation: individuals and workshops concentrating on one or two rather than carrying out all the stages of production themselves. Thus Robert Banks had equipment for casting and a shop where he sold pewterware, but no means of finishing the items he cast, whereas Laurence Marsden had tools for turning, but no raw materials or finished goods. This Smithian division of labour parallels developments in the fustian and cotton trades, and, as with these, there is evidence that organisation was becoming more centralised. Peter Latham, a bell-founder, owned equipment worth £40 6s and £645 6s 7d of stock-in-trade being used in a separate location by Ambrose Jolley.[130] This nascent proletarianisation was important in an industry supposedly in terminal decline, but was cut short by the development of factory-based textile production, iron foundries and collieries in late eighteenth-century Wigan. In this way, these non-ferrous metal trades suffered a similar fate to that of the woollen industry of east Lancashire.

Arrangements of this type complicate any attempt to interpret the basic structure of the workshop and putting-out systems. Simple territorial linkages were undoubtedly operating and the presence of master manufacturers operating (in part) as agents replicates the territorial-hierarchical arrangement of the cotton trade. However, the considerable and persistent independence of producers and their ability to access raw materials and markets served to cut across these linkages. Equally, the growing overlap between the activities of manufacturers and dealers, which in many ways paralleled developments in the west

Figure 5.6 *Business contacts of Peter Stubbs*

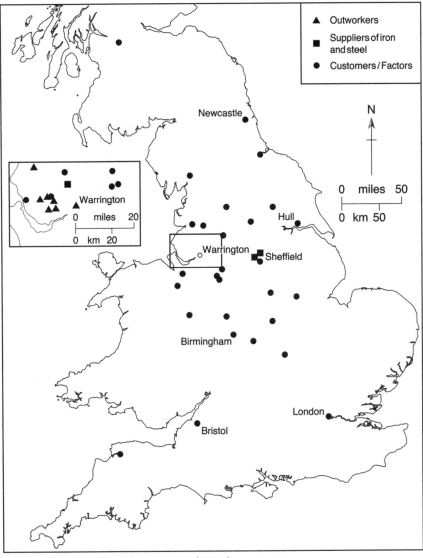

Source: Ashton, *Eighteenth-Century Industrialist.*

Midlands, brought a further element of vertical integration (production and sales) often missing from textile trades at this time. It also brought important market information and the possibility of flexible specialisation to workshop manufactures.[131] Specialisation was thus matched by integration, both at a local and regional level. Whilst production remained largely rural in the first half of the eighteenth century, its organisation was increasingly dependent upon complex systems of supply and demand that were focused onto towns.

The complexity of urban-centred production can be illustrated by brief reference to a single manufacturer-dealer: Peter Stubbs, a file-maker from Warrington who, although he was active later in the eighteenth century, was typical of many mid-century tradesmen.[132] Stubbs initially worked as an independent craftsman, making tools for several merchants within south-west Lancashire, but by 1788 he was putting-out iron to about twenty local workers (Figure 5.6). Some of these did regular work whilst others were employed more sporadically, but none appears to have been wholly dependent upon Stubbs for orders before he began to centralise production in his Warrington workshops in the 1790s. By this time he was moving away from putting-out and towards direct employment on fixed wages. This move from employed to employer was matched by a growing involvement in dealing activities. Stubbs began by obtaining his materials from local ironmongers, but by the late 1780s was placing orders directly with Sheffield and later Rotherham steel factors. Equally, having initially used factors in Ashton-in-Makerfield, Wigan, Leeds and Skipton, Stubbs became more involved in merchanting his own wares. By the 1790s he was supplying his tools to shops, fairs and manufacturers throughout the country (Figure 5.6) and, via Liverpool and London, overseas as well. Over a twenty-five year period, Peter Stubbs built up a complex web of interactions linking the supply of raw materials, production itself and dealing operations. Like textile production, the system was focused onto an urban merchant-manufacturer, but unlike textiles, it was encapsulated within a single firm from a relatively early date.

Conclusions: the structure of a mineral-based energy economy

In Wrigley's conception of a mineral-based energy economy, positive feedback generates ongoing growth in a system dominated by the movement of large amounts of goods along bulk transport systems running between centralised and punctiform production locations.[133] In spatial and interaction terms, this equates with Simmons's industrial specialisation model, but finds only a partial reflection in the mineral economy of eighteenth-century Lancashire and Cheshire. This comprised highly developed spatial and social divisions of labour which created a series of specialised and localised industries where centralised production and putting-out systems existed side by side. It was a loose confederation of spatially and functionally overlapping systems whose internal structures were divergent and whose inter-linkages were often limited to their shared dependence on coal. Links were closest between coal and salt: both were centralised and proletarianised, and increasingly focused on the port and capital supplies of Liverpool. Nonetheless, they were, in Simmons' terms, staple exports as much as industrial specialisations, and their development and geography through much of the eighteenth century and beyond was determined by extra-local and extra-regional demand as much as positive interactions within the sub-regional mineral economy. The coal-manufacturing link was also very close in the iron, copper and glass industries. It was cemented both by the location of individual works and the vertical integration of coal production and iron smelting, the result being centralised and large-scale production plants generating intense traffic particularly along the emerging navigation and canal network. Here, then, was industrial specialisation, except that there was little positive feedback of demand from one industry to another: much demand was again external. Conversely, there was no single staple and no single gateway to wider markets. Liverpool formed the principal external link, but trade also passed through Warrington and Chester, and many works had their own links to the national economy. Coal was also essential to the metal trades of south-west Lancashire, but here production was organised along proto-industrial lines. Manufacture was often domestic and rural, and was brought together in a series of territorial interactions by the activities of ironmongers and master manufacturers. These same men largely exported the finished goods. That said, the lack of any single clearly defined centre meant that the developed hierarchical systems of the textile industries were replaced by more loosely structured interactions often based around key individuals.

With a mineral-based economy, what drew together the various production systems and structured the mineral economy as a whole were natural resources and transport systems. However, as coal was to be had throughout much of south-west Lancashire and beyond (Figure 5.1),[134] it was, as Turnbull argues, transport which played the larger part in structuring this coal-using economy. New transport infrastructure favoured different locations at different times – firstly the Prescot area, then St Helens and Worsley and later Wigan – so that, whilst it was always important, its geographical dimensions and consequences changed through the course of the eighteenth century.[135] The one constant was the focus of these networks onto towns, especially Liverpool but also Warrington, Wigan, Northwich and Chester. Liverpool and Warrington were the 'fastest developing industrial locations ... where navigable water approached closest to the coalfield'.[136] By the 1750s Liverpool was emerging as the major industrial centre within the mineral economy and, like Manchester in the textile districts and London nationally, it formed a focus and stimulus of growth. It was the centre of control in a highly complex spatial-hierarchical division of labour.[137] The town contained a similar range of processing industries to those seen in Bristol, but like Newcastle, it also had salt refineries, ironworks and a significant trade in both salt and coal. What distinguished Liverpool from both

Figure 5.7 *Spatial structure of the mineral energy economy*

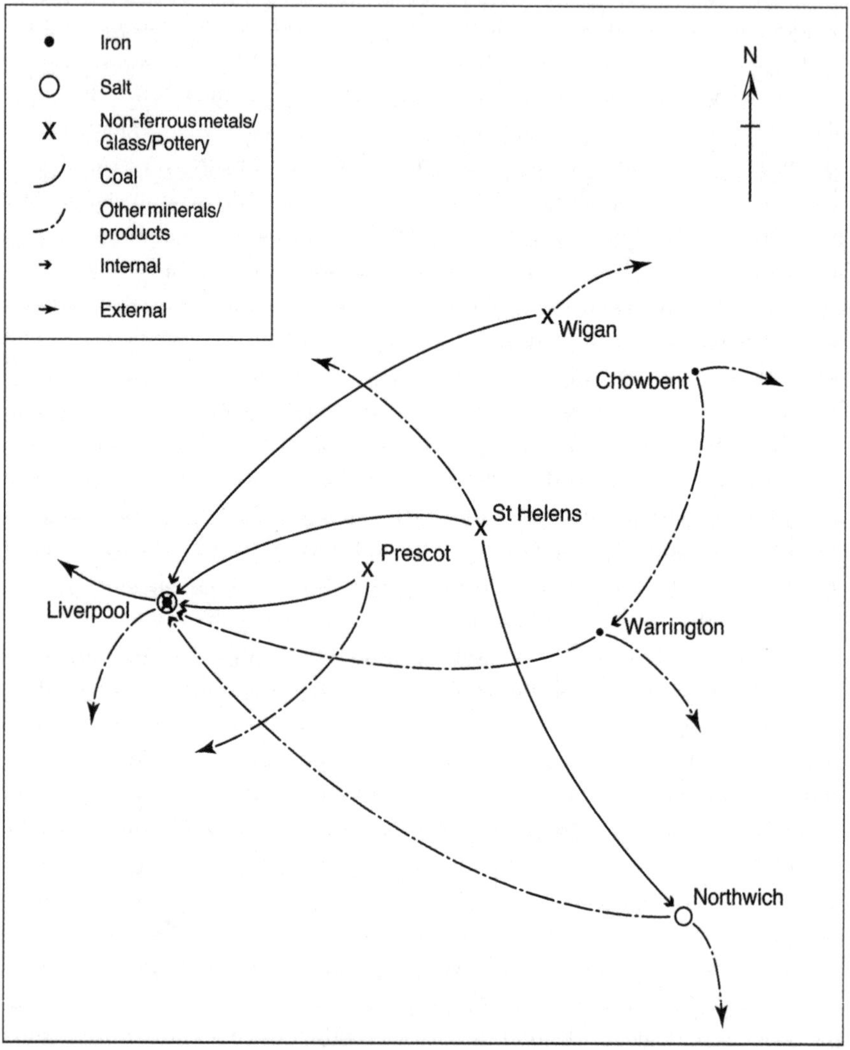

these were the growing links which existed between the port and a hinterland which was itself experiencing strong industrialisation. In effect, it presaged by several decades the emergence of the Newcastle-centred coal, iron and chemicals nexus.[138] This was true not merely in terms of the diversity of mineral-based economic development, but also in the way in which this was subsequently dispersed across the coalfield: in the north west this dispersion was occasioned by canals, in the north east the railways were responsible. Critical here is Turnbull's argument that 'canals could be constructed to exploit potential opportunities, linking places at will by deliberate, rational economic calculation' so that 'bulk transport could be brought favourable manufacturing sites instead of a forced movement in the opposite direction'.[139] The transport improvements which initially favoured Liverpool by generating a cornucopia of resources increasingly undermined that position as external economies of scale and cheaper more reliable supplies of coal were to be found in specialised production centres.[140] As Walton says, 'the initiatives of mid-century were to provide the basis for a new heavy industrial economy in the classic "Industrial Revolution" years, although ultimately this lucrative harvest was reaped in St Helens, Warrington and the surrounding area rather than Liverpool itself'. However, his caveat is important in that 'the growth of large-scale, capital-intensive industry in the area, in symbiotic relationship with the coalfield and fuelled by investment from Liverpool ... was beginning in earnest by the 1760s'.[141] Production may have drifted elsewhere, but, through its port function and inward investment, Liverpool remained important in the wider integration of the mineral economy and that of the north west as a whole.

This was an industrial system in the process of formation and its spatial and organisational structure were in flux throughout the eighteenth century. Increasingly, mineral-based industries were characterised by vertical integration of fuel supply, manufacture and marketing. This concentrated economic activity onto key locations, principally urban-based but – most obviously in the case of St Helens – resource/transport nodes. Intensified and localised specialisation reflected a deepening spatial division of labour which was structured by the flows of goods and capital both through the district and to and from external markets. In production terms, Liverpool's position changed considerably through the eighteenth century, but it remained the key to these flows and thus to the emergent mineral-based economy (Figure 5.7). The parallels with south-east Lancashire are strong, local independence being overlain with the wider role of a core centre in stimulating and shaping economic growth. And, as in the textile districts, trading as much as manufacturing activity served to structure the space economy.

Notes

1 Aikin, Country round *Manchester*, p. 21.
2 Wrigley, 'Raw materials', p. 13.
3 Wrigley, *Continuity*, pp. 78–9.
4 The engine noted by Blundell in 1719 was probably water-powered: Langton, *Geographical Change*, p. 110.
5 Langton, *Geographical Change*, *passim*; Langton, 'Sir Roger Bradshaigh'.
6 Timmins, *Made in Lancashire*, pp. 85–96; Phillips and Smith, *Lancashire and Cheshire*, pp. 170 and 186.

7 See Wrigley, 'Raw materials' pp. 12–14; Timmins, *Made in Lancashire*, pp. 125–32 and 165–71.
8 Tann, 'Fuel saving', p. 149.
9 Wrigley, *Continuity*, pp. 77–8.
10 Tann, 'Fuel saving', p. 149.
11 Wrigley, *Continuity*, p. 78; Mokyr, 'Technological change', pp. 25–7; Langton, *Geographical Change*, pp. 96–100 and 176–81. For a more general discussion, see Hyde, *Technological Change*.
12 Krugman, *Geography and Trade*, pp. 35–54; Simmons, 'Urban system'; Capello, 'City network paradigm'.
13 Langton, *Geographical Change*, pp. 113–15 and 120–8; Barker, 'Lancashire coal', pp. 83 and 96–7.
14 Gregory, 'Geographies of industrialization', p. 364. See Langton, *Geographical Change*; Flinn, *British Coal*, volume 2; Nef, *British Coal Industry*, volume 1 for discussions of labour, capital and output.
15 Turnbull, 'Canals', pp. 547–8.
16 Mokyr, 'Technological change', p. 25.
17 Wrigley, 'Raw materials', pp. 6–11; Turnbull, 'Canals', pp. 545–52; Gregory, 'Geographies of industrialization', pp. 364–6 and especially figure 13.6.
18 Flinn, *British Coal*, volume 2, p. 16; Crosby, *Cheshire*, p. 70; Phillips and Smith, *Lancashire and Cheshire*, pp. 51–2.
19 Nef, *British Coal Industry*, volume 1, p. 56.
20 The pit at Fernilee in Derbyshire was of more significance, but none of these undertakings was very considerable; Nef, *British Coal Industry*, volume 1, p. 61.
21 Swain, *Industry*, pp. 163–80.
22 Walton, *Lancashire*, p. 73.
23 Langton, *Geographical Change*, pp. 93 and 154; table 2.6.
24 See Turnbull, 'Canals', pp. 551–2 for a summary of these ideas.
25 Langton, 'John Mackay'.
26 Richardson, *Regional Growth Theory*, pp. 172–3.
27 Walton, *Lancashire*, p. 73; Langton, *Geographical Change*, pp. 165–73.
28 Langton, *Geographical Change*, pp. 127, 221–4 and 165; Hodson, *Cheshire*, p. 141; Barker, 'Lancashire coal', p. 97.
29 Langton, 'Liverpool', pp. 14 and 17.
30 Turnbull, 'Canals', pp. 547–52.
31 Young, *Tour through the North of England*, volume 3, pp. 280–3; Aikin, *Country round Manchester*, pp. 205 and 237.
32 Wallwork, 'Mid-Cheshire salt', p. 171.
33 Barker, 'Lancashire coal', p. 84; Chaloner, 'Salt in Cheshire', pp. 63–5.
34 Chaloner, 'Salt in Cheshire', p. 67; Barker 'Lancashire coal', pp. 86 and 92–9.
35 Aikin, *Country round Manchester*, p. 429; Barker, 'Lancashire coal', p. 92; Walton, *Lancashire*, p. 68.
36 CCA, CR 352/1 Letter Book of Daniel Peck.
37 Barker, 'Lancashire coal', pp. 90–3; Chaloner, 'Salt in Cheshire', p. 68.
38 Willan, *Navigation of the Weaver*, pp. 208–28.
39 Barker, 'Lancashire coal', pp. 93–4; Wallwork, 'Mid-Cheshire salt', p. 172; Barker, 'Lancashire Coal', p. 94.
40 See Barker and Harris, *Merseyside Town*, pp. 223–39.

41 Warren, 'Chemicals'.
42 Langton, *Geographical Change*, p. 179.
43 Awty, 'Charcoal ironmasters', pp. 72–3.
44 Langton, *Geographical Change*, p. 178.
45 King, 'Vale Royal', p. 3; Awty, 'Charcoal ironmasters', pp. 74–7; Langton, *Geographical Change*, pp. 97–8 and 177–9.
46 Langton, *Geographical Change*, pp. 98 and 178.
47 Langton, *Geographical Change*, pp. 177–9.
48 Hodson, *Cheshire*, p. 143.
49 Hyde, *Technological Change*, 53–68; Scrivenor, *Iron Trade*, p. 87; Riden, 'Iron and steel'.
50 Phillips and Smith, *Lancashire and Cheshire*, p. 48; Nef, *British Coal Industry*, volume 1, p. 64; Walton, *Lancashire*, p. 73.
51 Malet, *Bridgewater*, pp. 32 and 80–2.
52 Gregory, 'Geographies of industrialization', p. 374.
53 Pollard, *Peaceful Conquest*, p. 39.
54 Awty, 'Charcoal ironmasters', p. 76.
55 Tupling, 'Early metal trades', p. 21.
56 See Hey, *Rural Metalworkers*; Rowlands, *Masters and Men*.
57 Bailey and Barker, 'Watchmaking', pp. 6–7.
58 Langton, *Geographical Change*, p. 97.
59 Bailey and Barker, 'Watchmaking', pp. 3–6.
60 *UBD*, volume 3, pp. 635–730; volume 4, pp. 177–9, 247–9 and 755–61.
61 Tupling, 'Early metal trades', *passim*.
62 Langton, *Geographical Change*, p. 53.
63 Kennet, *Georgian Chester*, p. 19
64 Langton, *Geographical Change*, pp. 176–7; Moran, 'Pewtermaking in Wigan', pp. 6–7.
65 Moran, 'Pewtermaking in Wigan', pp. 9–11.
66 Firm conclusions are difficult because of the small numbers involved. Also, as there is a definite, but indeterminate lag between the period in which a tradesman was active and when he died, it is impossible to tie this increase into actual production.
67 McKendrick, 'Consumer revolution', p. 10; Hatcher and Barker, *British Pewter*, p. 285.
68 Stobart, 'Eighteenth-century revolution?', p. 40.
69 Langton, *Geographical Change*, p. 52.
70 Hatcher and Barker, *British Pewter*, p. 221; Shelley, 'Wigan and Liverpool pewterers'; Langton, *Geographical Change*, p. 54.
71 Sprunt, 'Old Warrington trades'.
72 Davies, *Macclesfield*, pp. 115–20; Phillips and Smith, *Lancashire and Cheshire*, p. 101.
73 Langton, *Geographical Change*, p. 180; Hatcher and Barker, *British Pewter*, pp. 75–89.
74 Jones, *Modern Wales*, pp. 20–2.
75 Langton, *Geographical Change*, p. 180. Barker and Harris, *Merseyside Town*, pp. 75–89. The Liverpool works closed in 1794 – Langton, 'Liverpool' p. 17.
76 Langton, *Geographical Change*, p. 99.

77 Barker and Harris, *Merseyside Town*, pp. 12, 108–9 and 112–19.

78 Langton, *Geographical Change*, p. 99.

79 The quality of coal was also significant: the copper-works obtained good coal from the Ravenhead Main Delf seam and the glass-works drew on supplies from Rushy Park – Langton, *Geographical Change*, pp. 179–80; Langton, 'Liverpool', pp. 19–20.

80 Betty, *Wessex from AD 1000*, p. 193.

81 Barker and Harris, *Merseyside Town*, p. 129; Picton, *Memorials of Liverpool*, volume 1, p. 131.

82 Langton, 'Liverpool', p. 17; Hyde, *Liverpool*, pp. 19–20; Mallet, 'John Baddeley', p. 128.

83 Blake, 'Wedgwood and the porcelain trade', pp. 93–4; McKendrick, 'Josiah Wedgwood'; Weatherill, 'Middlemen in the English pottery trade'.

84 Mallet, 'John Baddeley', pp. 124–33; Weatherill, *Pottery Trade*, p. 88. John Wedgwood's Crate Book is transcribed in full in Mountford, 'Thomas Wedgwood'.

85 Stoke on Trent Archives, D4842/14/3/25 Crate Book of J. B. Wood; Boney, *Liverpool Porcelain*, p. 22.

86 Blake, 'The porcelain trade', p. 93; Boney, *Liverpool Porcelain*, p. 23; Finer and Savage, *Josiah Wedgwood*, p. 75.

87 Clemens, 'Rise of Liverpool', p. 212; Hyde, *Liverpool*, pp. 26 and 34.

88 *Gore's Liverpool Directory*, 1766; Langton, 'Liverpool', p. 15; Minchinton, 'Bristol', p. 77.

89 Kennet, *Georgian Chester*, pp. 17–19.

90 Langton, 'Liverpool', p. 15.

91 Phillips and Smith, *Lancashire and Cheshire*, p. 79; Aikin, *Country round Manchester*, pp. 18–21, 314–30 and 403–74; Crosby, *Cheshire*, p. 63.

92 Simmons, 'Urban system', pp. 67–8.

93 Langton, *Geographical Change*, pp. 100–1 and 166.

94 Wrigley, *Continuity*, p. 81.

95 Berg, *Age of Manufactures*, pp. 72–6 and 203–5.

96 Langton, *Geographical Change*, pp. 67–78, 113–28 and 194–224.

97 There is little eighteenth-century evidence of miners leasing collieries themselves, as happened in the east Midlands and the Forest of Dean. See Berg, 'Factories', p. 141; Langton, 'Proletarianization in the industrial revolution'.

98 Langton, 'Liverpool', p. 18.

99 Evans, 'Two paths', p. 207; Cromar, 'Coal industry on Tyneside'.

100 Langton, *Geographical Change*, p. 172.

101 The contrast is clear from Barker, 'Lancashire coal' and Cromar, 'Coal industry on Tyneside'.

102 See Evans, 'Two paths', p. 210; Minchinton, 'Bristol', pp. 81–4.

103 Langton, *Geographical Change*, pp. 143, 193 and 230.

104 Evans, 'Two paths', p. 211; Freeman, 'Transport'.

105 Wrigley, *Continuity*, pp. 29–30 and 46–7.

106 Langton, *Geographical Change*, pp. 113–23 and 194–216; Flinn, *British Coal*, volume 2, pp. 190–205 and 329–411; Langton, 'Proletarianization in the industrial revolution'.

107 See Crump, 'Saltways from the Cheshire Wiches'; CCA, CR 352/1 Letter Book of Daniel Peck.

108 Berg, 'Factories', p. 141.
109 Awty, 'Charcoal ironmasters', pp. 74 and 83; Langton, *Geographical Change*, p. 178.
110 See Johnson, 'Foley Partnerships'; King, 'Vale Royal'; Awty, 'Charcoal ironmasters'.
111 See Langton, 'Lancashire Catholicism', pp. 90–1; Walton, *Lancashire*, pp. 91–5.
112 King, 'Vale Royal', p. 4; Langton, *Geographical Change*, pp. 178–81; Awty 'Charcoal ironmasters', p. 105.
113 Langton, *Geographical Change*, pp. 99 and 181.
114 Hyde, *Liverpool*, pp. 31–6; Langton, *Geographical Change*, p. 219; Barker and Harris, *Merseyside Town*, p. 113.
115 Barker and Harris, *Merseyside Town*, p. 340.
116 Minchinton, 'Bristol', pp. 83–4.
117 Awty, 'Charcoal ironmasters', pp. 93–4; Rowlands, *Masters and Men*, pp. 54–62.
118 Hey, *Rural Metalworkers*, pp. 42–3.
119 Awty, 'Charcoal ironmasters', p. 94.
120 See, for example, Rowlands, *Masters and Men*, pp. 54–62.
121 Awty, 'Charcoal ironmasters', pp. 93–4 and 106–7; Rowlands, *Masters and Men*, p. 60.
122 Rowlands, *Masters and Men*, pp. 150–3.
123 Ashton, *Eighteenth-Century Industrialist*, pp. 52 and 59; Barker and Harris, *Merseyside Town*, p. 124.
124 See Gregory, *Regional Transformation*, pp. 121–38; Hudson, *Industrial Capital*, pp. 25–48. Similar arrangements were found in watchmaking: Bailey and Barker, 'Watchmaking'.
125 Rowlands, *Masters and Men*, pp. 80 and 156–8; Wadsworth and Mann, *Cotton Trade*, pp. 314–23.
126 Rowlands, *Masters and Men*, p. 67; Awty, 'Charcoal ironmasters', p. 102.
127 Barker and Harris, *Merseyside Town*, p. 126.
128 Rowlands, *Masters and Men*, 78–84 and 155–66; Gregory, *Regional Transformation*, pp. 121–38 and 186–220.
129 Moran, 'Pewtermaking in Wigan', pp. 9 and 11.
130 For more discussion of these points, see Moran, 'Pewtermaking in Wigan', pp. 15–20.
131 Berg, 'Factories', pp. 136–7.
132 Ashton, *Eighteenth-Century Industrialist*.
133 Wrigley, 'Raw materials', pp. 6–11; Wrigley, *Continuity*, pp. 68–97.
134 Langton, *Geographical Change*, p. 250 shows the dispersed nature of coal mining in the eighteenth century.
135 Turnbull, 'Canals', pp. 550–1.
136 Langton, *Geographical Change*, p. 100
137 See Dicken and Lloyd, *Location in Space*, p. 386.
138 See Langton, 'Liverpool', pp. 3–15; Evans, 'Two paths', pp. 211–14.
139 Turnbull, 'Canals', pp. 539–40.
140 Langton, 'Liverpool', pp. 15 and 18.
141 Walton, *Lancashire*, p. 74.

6

The service sector and urban hierarchies

Now I pray you, what is a commercial nation, but a collection of commercial towns? [1]

In studies of industrialisation, the significance of the service sector is often underplayed, attention focusing instead on changes in manufacturing.[2] For example, two recent collections of essays on the economic and industrial history of Britain contain six general surveys, five discussing social and demographic aspects, three on government and politics, three on technology, as well as contributions on *inter alia* agriculture, industrial organisation, women and even sex. Out of a total of twenty-five essays, there are just two on trade and one on industrial finance. None examine the service sector more generally or the specific role of transport, retailing or professional services.[3] And yet, even narrowly defined, the service sector employed between one-fifth growing to one-third of the workforce through the eighteenth and early nineteenth centuries (see Table 3.4), and contributed an increasing amount to the national economy.[4] Service industries were vital to both domestic and international trade; the commercialisation of household and local economies; and the emergence of consumerism.[5] Too often, though, such changes are obscured by more general and ultimately rather sterile discussions of supply and demand driven growth. These focus on the extent to which either consumer-led demand or exports formed autonomous stimuli for industrial growth.[6] Unsurprisingly, the general conclusion seems to be that it was the positive interaction between these new or growing sources of demand and a modernising industrial base which prompted sustained economic development.[7]

If the role of the service sector in economic development is to be more fully appreciated, it is necessary to fix these general ideas more closely into the regional space economy. To achieve this, four distinct dimensions of the service economy are highlighted. First is the broadening and deepening of consumption occurring in the eighteenth century as market exchange became increasingly important in the everyday lives of individual households. Broadening consumption involved the economic specialisation and commercialisation of family economies which, in practice, meant that a growing number of individuals were reliant on retail outlets to provide for their basic needs.[8] In effect, de Vries's 'industrious revolution' had as much to do with commerce as industry. At the same time, the middling sorts especially were consuming luxury and semi-luxury goods in ever-greater quantities, thus deepening consumption. These changes were reflected in and stimulated by a growing range and number of specialised service providers and shopkeepers. Where was this growing range of services located and how did it relate to manufacturing activity?

Such questions link to the second dimension examined here: that of spatial divisions of labour within the service economy. A useful distinction can be drawn between services which are non-tradeable and simply follow the geographical distribution of the goods-producing population and those which can be traded and which may, as with manufacturing, become concentrated into specialist locations or towns.[9] Focusing on tradeable services draws our attention to the role of urban merchants in linking local products to wider national or international markets. In general terms this leads us to the relationship between external demand and regional economic growth. More specifically it emphasises the gateway function of the ports, especially those, like Liverpool, with expanding colonial trade. Such places formed the focus of significant economic growth and, as Simmons and Vance argue, did much to structure how and where growth stimuli were transmitted.[10] The third dimension builds on the idea of specialisation, but centres on the inter-relationship between emerging leisure and consumerism and the urban service sector. Growth in consumption and an increasingly leisure-oriented 'middling sort' stimulated the development of resort towns, some of which (Bath and Brighton for example) were amongst the fastest growing towns of the eighteenth and early nineteenth centuries.[11] It also added considerably to the prosperity of many county towns such as Chester and Preston. Conversely, towns in general and the resorts in particular helped to create and communicate new patterns of consumption which stimulated the home market for manufactured goods.[12]

Last, and tying all of these together, is the way in which trade between individuals and between places helped to structure the geography and operation of the regional economy. We have already seen that urban merchants were often crucial to industrial organisation (especially putting-out systems), but they were also central to the spatial and hierarchical structure of the urban system itself. Two possibilities arise here. In one, broadly concomitant with staple export or Christallerian systems, demand from rural hinterlands stimulates the provision of services in a centre. This promotes a territorial rural-urban relationship with growth of the town being dependent upon expanding rural demand for central place services fuelled by population increase, expanding rural production or increased rural specialisation. The dependencies between towns would be governed by hierarchical relationships which were uniform throughout the region. In the other, industrial specialisation and its associated need for longer-distance trading between production centres encourages urban growth based not only on local manufacturing, but also on the activities involved in this exchange of goods with distant centres. The stimulus for growth thus comes from within the urban system (or through it from more distant demand), and depends as much on urban merchants looking for trading opportunities as on the presence of industrial production.[13] In these cases, the rural-urban and inter-urban relationships are much less rigidly structured, being governed more by the supply of and demand for the local speciality and the accessibility of the centre than by hierarchical patterns of interaction.

Consumption, services and access to the world of goods

The growth and spread of consumption in eighteenth-century England was linked to expansion in the number and range of shops and professionals and the goods and services they provided. Mui and Mui estimate that, in 1759, there was one shop for every forty-two people, a figure which suggests wide and local access to a growing world of goods.[14] Evidence from the probate records suggests that the importance of service industries to the economy of the north west increased during the eighteenth century.[15] Excluding transport and domestic service, the service sector grew from 11.7 per cent to 14.1 per cent of the region's workforce. Unsurprisingly, this growth and the overall distribution of service industries were dominated by the urban sector (Table 6.1). Towns contained almost three-quarters of all service sector tradesmen listed in the probate records. They were especially dominant in higher status activities such as medicine and law, hairdressing and arts, and luxury dealing. The urban service sector was not merely more numerous, it was also more sophisticated and varied. Towns contained a total of fifty-one different dealing and fifty-four public service or professional occupations; the surrounding villages had scarcely half that number – twenty-eight and twenty respectively – and were dominated by the more common trades such as chapmen, innkeepers and clerks. Whilst Estabrook argues for a strong separation of urban and rural society at this time, the evidence here points to close interaction and interchange (see also Chapter 7).[16] It was the towns that facilitated growing specialisation and commercialisation of household economies, and gave access to an expanding range of goods. They contained both a range of services providing for needs, wants and desires which could not be met within the household itself and the merchants who linked local production to more distant markets.

Table 6.1 The urban–rural balance in the service industries of north-west England, 1701–60

| | Rural | | | | | | | | Urban | | | | | | | |
| | 1701–20 | | 1721–40 | | 1741–60 | | Total | | 1701–20 | | 1721–40 | | 1741–60 | | Total | |
	Total	%	Total	%	Total	%	Total	%	Total	%	Total	%	Total	%	Total	%
Service total	91	33	109	32	103	29	303	31	186	67	234	68	249	71	669	69
Government	46	39	59	44	61	43	166	42	71	61	74	56	82	57	227	58
Education and religion	33	55	37	46	29	46	99	49	27	45	43	54	34	54	104	51
Medicine and law	11	15	12	13	13	11	36	13	64	85	80	87	105	89	249	87
Hairdressing and arts	1	4	1	3	0	0	2	2	24	96	37	97	28	100	89	98
Dealing total	145	23	246	28	262	27	653	26	490	77	649	72	700	73	1839	74
General	55	25	88	29	97	27	240	27	166	75	215	71	265	73	646	73
Hardware	5	13	4	11	3	10	12	11	33	87	33	89	28	90	94	89
Textiles	17	14	16	14	14	13	47	14	107	86	98	86	90	87	295	86
Food and drink	66	29	136	33	144	33	346	32	163	71	273	67	292	67	728	68
Luxury	2	9	2	6	4	14	8	10	21	91	30	94	25	86	76	90
Total	236	26	355	29	365	28	956	28	676	74	883	71	949	72	2508	72

Source: Probate records, 1701–60.

This basic picture contains much truth, but it is clear that the situation was by no means straightforward or unchanging. Studies of the development of retailing usually suggest that the more profound changes took place from the mid-nineteenth century onwards with the emergence of department stores, multiples, product advertising and so on.[17] However, recent work has shown that the eighteenth century saw important changes in the nature and practices of shopping; in the intra-urban, regional and national geography of retailing, and in the organisation and regulation of professional services.[18] It is inappropriate to cover all these here, but two have particular significance for the present discussion. The first is the relationship between the commercialisation of the rural economy and the development of retailing in the countryside. The second is the expansion in the range, specialisation and sophistication of urban services as they responded to internal and external demand, not least from increasingly discerning 'middling sort' consumers.[19]

It is clear from studies of probate inventories that villagers had access to new consumer goods. Indeed, many rural households were as innovative in their consumption as their urban counterparts. Some of the goods consumed came from fairs or itinerant salesmen, but the majority were supplied by a growing number and range of urban shopkeepers.[20] Certainly, there is little evidence of a dramatic transformation in rural retailing. Occupations listed in the probate records suggests that there was little overall change in the urban-rural distribution of services (Table 6.1): the urban share of dealing fell slightly (77–73 per cent), whilst its domination of public and professional services grew a little (67–71 per cent). However, this apparent stability masks considerable growth in absolute terms in both town and country. By the middle of the eighteenth century, there were 81 per cent more dealers in the countryside than had been the case in 1700. This growth included a considerable expansion of general dealers (mostly chapmen), many of whom were undoubtedly involved in linking local textile production to wider markets (see Chapter 4). More numerous, though, were rural food and drink retailers who more than doubled in number, and accounted for two in every five rural service providers by the 1750s. In contrast, there was very little growth in the number of public and professional services or more specialised dealers in rural settlements. Throughout the period, just a handful of individuals were engaged in medicine, the law, high order personal services such as hairdressing or specialist textile retailing. The more common schoolmasters, clerics and clerks grew slightly in number, but declined in their relative importance in the rural economy. Although the service sector grew in the countryside, then, it remained dominated by low order functions with essentially local clienteles. Some rural retailers held extensive stock: for example, the probate inventory of Richard Smith of Bunbury listed £88 2s 8½d of goods in the shop and Thomas Kent of Church

Hulme had £87 17s 4d of cloth, haberdashery and groceries. More typical were Joseph Heald and Thomas Booth with stock worth between £4 and £5. These rural tradesmen provided for the immediate needs of the villagers rather than bringing them into contact with a new range of goods and services or new forms of consumption. Such functions were largely the preserve of professionals and shopkeepers towns.[21]

Although the number of urban dealers and professionals grew fairly modestly during the first half of the eighteenth century, the range and sophistication of many urban service trades was considerably enhanced.[22] The number of dealing trades rose from thirty-one in the first two decades of the eighteenth-century to forty-two by the 1740s and 1750s; at the same time, public and professional services increased from thirty-two to forty-three trades. Such trends continued through the century. Gore's 1766 directory records sixty-three different service occupations in Liverpool alone and by 1782 there were sixty-eight in Chester, including electricians, architects, bankers and dancing masters.[23] This had much to do with the growing specialisation of individual tradesmen. In medicine, for instance, we see the steady decline of the generalist apothecary as medical men restyled themselves as druggists, surgeons or physicians. Meanwhile, merchants became increasingly common as wholesale and trading activities were gradually separating from retail functions. Their numbers grew between 1701–20 and 1741–60 from 62 to 122, with the rise being especially prominent in Liverpool and Manchester where 'merchant' appears to have been replacing 'draper' as the title for those engaged in textile trades.

These specialist tradesmen were able to supply a sophisticated and fashion-able range of goods and services, thus serving to deepen as well as broaden consumption in both town and country. Apothecaries, for example, sold a growing range of remedies, many of which they prepared themselves from a remarkable range of ingredients. In Knutsford, John England's inventory listed 195 items, whilst his contemporary Thomas Gyles of Nantwich had 282 sep-arate items in his shop including vitriol, senna, fenugreek, borax, alumina, euphorbia and laudanum. Such diversity was, in part at least, possible because of the low cost of such materials: Gyles' shop goods were valued at £28 6s 7d in total, of which over £8 was comprised of scales and weights, bottles and vials, mortars and drawers. But variety was also the product of complex supply chains linking shops in north-west England to supplies from across the world. Thomas Moreton's grocery shop in Chester truly represented a window onto the world of goods. He had Valencia and Jordan almonds, brandy from France, tobacco (probably from the American colonies), Jamaican pepper, sugar and molasses, and coriander, cloves, cinnamon, and aniseed from south-east Asia. Mercers had perhaps the most extensive range of stock, with many selling not only cloth, but also haberdashery, finished or semi-finished items of clothing and groceries.[24] Zachariah Shelley sold hooping cane, stay tape and stockings from his Congleton shop; in Stockport, Richard Upton had stockings, petticoats and breeches, and James Rathbone of Macclesfield had cravats, handkerchiefs, girdling, fans, stockings, cloth and leather gloves and even a sable muff. He also sold oils and Hungary waters, hair powder and even books, whilst Shelley offered a range of groceries, including pitch, alum, soap, wormwood, tobacco, sugar, brandy, ginger, cloves, mace, pepper, coriander, carraway seeds and raisins. Together, these groceries comprised 10 per cent of his stock. What is more striking, however, is the variety and quantity of cloth carried by these tradesmen. Shelley had £408 6s 4¼d worth of textiles including tammies, shalloons, tansies, serges, worsteds, flannels, fustians, checks, canvas, calicoes, crêpes, silks, lace and mohair. Rathbone's stock was equally varied, but characterised by greater proportions of finer cloths such as printed calicoes, muslins, ribbon, silks, velvets and especially lace. Upton, meanwhile, specialised more in woollen cloths, but also carried mohair, silk and gold and silver threads.

Table 6.2 *Stock-in-trade of Robert Wilkinson of Nantwich, tailor*

Bodices	11	1.4.6
Women's gowns	4	1.2.6
Petticoats	16	2.10.0
Men's riding coats	4	1.8.0
Men's coats	39	11.15.0
Men's waistcoats	26	3.5.0
Men's breeches	25	2.18.0
Boys' coats	9	1.4.0
Boys' waistcoats	10	0.14.0
Boys' breeches	10	0.13.0
Men's frocks	5	0.14.0
Children's coats	4	0.9.0
	163	27.17.0

Source: CCA, WS 1721, Robert Wilkinson of Nantwich.

The huge range of cloths available to the consumer was drawn on by the region's tailors who were increasingly oriented towards providing specialised and fashionable clothing. Some of this was ready-made – Robert Wilkinson of Nantwich having 163 items of men's, women's and children's clothing in his inventory (see Table 6.2) – but most was made to order. Here fashion became all-important: Richard Ormes advertised that he made 'Josephs, Jackets and Ridinghabets of all sorts, after the best and neatest fashion, as in London'.[25]

As Borsay has argued, the link to London was increasingly important, especially in Chester's high status retailers. Thus, George Lowe, a Chester silversmith, held cutlery, watches, jewellery, snuffboxes, tea urns and 'an extensive range of the most fashionable items' purchased in Birmingham, Sheffield and London.[26] Similarly, George French had a shop on Eastgate Street in Chester 'where all Persons may be served with Goods of any kind whatsoever in the Toyshop Business, intirely new, from London'.[27] Retailers in smaller towns were also tied to London supplies and fashions: in Nantwich, Samuel Garnett's inventory included £119 7s 11d of mercery goods to be returned to London.

Overall, there is some indication of the spread of dealing if not professional service activity into rural areas during the eighteenth century. Rural demand was important in the (re-)emergence of markets at Tarporley and Neston in the second half of the eighteenth-century,[28] but the majority of any additional spending deriving from an increasingly specialised and/or prosperous rural economy was focused onto the existing network of towns. Here it combined with growing urban-based consumption to produce a florescence of shops, goods and services. Both rural and urban development were thus feeding through to the urban service sector in the type of bottom-up growth described in Christallerian central place systems (see Chapter 2). In other words, the growing number, range and sophistication of urban services was a response to rural as well as urban demands.[29] Conversely, and notwithstanding Estabrook's arguments with regard to the social and cultural gulf between Bristol and its rural hinterland, by stocking and advertising new, exotic and fashionable goods, urban tradesmen were vital in projecting novel consumption patterns into towns and the surrounding countryside, making the economic interchange a two-way process.[30] As in west Yorkshire, towns also housed the vast majority of goldsmiths, scrivenors, attornies and merchants who formed the embryonic banking system for the region; accepting deposits of cash for safe-keeping and linking supplies of money to demands for capital investment by arranging personal loans.[31]

What does this tell us about the structure of the urban system of north-west England? Urban merchants were the key to trading as well as servicing in the region so that towns formed the commercial gateways for local or regional industrial and agricultural specialities. They linked these to the national and international markets which were increasingly important to the industries of the north west and the country as a whole.[32] This suggests that the interactions within the urban system would be a combination of territorial-hierarchical servicing linkages (or, in the case of supplying novel goods and projecting new consumption patterns, hierarchical-territorial) and point–point trading links. This complexity arose partly from the multiplicity of functions carried out in a single town and partly from the development of detailed spatial divisions of labour within the service sector. It is to these specialisations that we turn to next.

Specialisation: tradable services and trading towns

The geographical distribution of tertiary activities is influenced by the nature of both the service and the place in which it might be provided. Non-tradeable services tend to follow the distribution of population, whereas those which can be traded may become concentrated into certain places privileged by their geographical location, resource base, or position within the urban system. Importantly, the location of both types of services can serve to structure that urban system, as we shall see later. The distribution of rural services in north-west England reflected both of these processes. Public and professional services were dispersed throughout the region, generally in accordance with population distribution: rather more were found in the densely populated areas in southern Lancashire and west Cheshire than in the upland areas to the east of the region. More specifically, and for obvious reasons, villages at the centre of parishes were the most common locations for clerics, clerks and schools. The tendency for the sparsely populated uplands of east Lancashire to be poorly served by such functions is thus strengthened, since they were also characterised by very large parishes. The more even distribution of food and drink dealing reinforces this last point. Such activities were clearly very localised and even small villages contained an innkeeper or a butcher, the former being found in over 150 settlements throughout the north west. Being situated on a major road, especially those to London, appears to have encouraged additional development, as at Tarporley, Tarvin, Church Hulme and Walton-le-Dale. Tarporley was fairly typical. It was noted for its 'situation on the thoroughfare to Chester' and formed a stage for London coaches; probate evidence from the early eighteenth century indicates the presence of a surgeon, grocer, writing master and mercer, as well as a number of clergymen, innkeepers, butchers, shoemakers and tailors. By 1783, the village contained twenty-one service providers including six shopkeepers, two surgeons, two butchers, two bakers, a cheesefactor, a shoemaker and four innkeepers.[33] In the early eighteenth century, however, there were few such notable concentrations, retailers being found in sixty-seven villages in Cheshire – twice the number of settlements in which shop tax was paid in 1785.[34] The clear exception to this general dispersal was the concentration of chapmen in south-east Lancashire. They were closely associated with textile manufacturing in the area and were instrumental in linking local production either with urban merchants or directly to extra-regional markets (see Chapter 4). Even in these specialist trading areas, the location of rural services appears to have been affected relatively little by towns, despite the obvious competition which they would present to dealers especially. In several instances, villages in the immediate neighbourhood of towns were thriving, if minor service centres. This was seen in Newbold Astbury next to Congleton, Walton near Liverpool, Standish by Wigan and Lachford south of Warrington. Only in Neston does development seem to have been spurred by the *lack* of towns in the area, the Wirral being an urban desert until the growth of Ellesmere Port and Birkenhead in the nineteenth century.[35]

Unsurprisingly, the urban sector displayed a considerably higher degree of specialisation, with tradeable services being localised in key towns.[36] However, as Lepetit suggests, specialist functions did not necessarily match up with particular towns, so that several functions were overlain upon one another in a single town.[37] Despite this, it is possible to make a broad distinction between those towns with a large proportion of their service sector accounted for by trading activities and those where more locally-oriented functions were predominant. In the trading towns, general, hardware and textile dealing accounted for over 40 per cent and often more than half of the service sector. These towns were concentrated into the textile manufacturing districts in the east of the region and, as discussed in Chapter 4, were heavily involved in the organisation of textile production and the marketing of the finished cloth. As such they had strong links with their immediate hinterlands and with other trading towns in the area. These contacts were often hierarchically structured, with key towns (Colne, Rochdale, Bolton and especially Manchester) acting as gateway towns for specialised local production. Most striking was the massive concentration of drapers, chapmen and merchants in Manchester. These made the town central to regional textile manufacture, but also marked it out as a specialised regional trading centre. Spatial and hierarchical divisions of labour thus characterised the manufacturing and service aspects of the regional economy, and they served to structure the geography and operation of both.

Liverpool also stood out as a specialist service centre, its trading activities linking into regional production systems and outwards to national and international economies. Up to the 1660s, Liverpool's trade was largely limited to Ireland (salt, coal, copper and a variety of manufactures were shipped out; hides, flax, iron and linens were brought back) and a small number of ships sailing to Bordeaux and Bilbao.[38] It grew over the next hundred years to become the second largest port in the country, after London. Trade with the West Indies and the American colonies expanded rapidly, with imports of sugar and tobacco increasing by about 250 per cent and 760 per cent respectively between c.1700 and the 1740s (Table 6.3). From this date profits were further enhanced as Liverpool merchants became more involved in the slave trade. Exports of salt and coal also grew rapidly and formed what Langton sees as the centre of Liverpool's vortex of trade.[39] The port was thus the focus of two forms of triangular trade, one linking it with West Africa and the American colonies and the other tying it to central Cheshire and southern Lancashire. Both were highly profitable and crucial in Liverpool's development, but so too was the growing range of manufactured goods which passed through the port. For example, by the 1760s, Liverpool was second only to London as an entrepot for the pottery and porcelain trades: John Wedgwood of Burslem was regularly sending crates of earthenware to Liverpool merchants from the late 1750s and, in the last quarter of the eighteenth century, Josiah Wedgwood dispatched an almost constant stream of wares from his Etruria factory along the Trent and Mersey Canal to Liverpool.[40]

Table 6.3 *Exports of salt and coal, and imports of tobacco and sugar from Liverpool*

	Coal (ooo tons)	Salt (ooo bushels)	Tobacco (million lb)	Sugar (ooo cwt)
1660s	4.4	6.0	0.0	0.7
1680s	0.2	30.0	0.7	5.7
c.1700	–	300.0	1.8	11.6
1720s	2.6	428.0	2.1	29.6
1740s	1.3 [a]	–	6.1	100.0
c.1770	c.10.0	–	–	–

Sources: Clemens, 'Rise of Liverpool', p. 211; Langton, *Geographical Change*, pp. 53, 100–1 and 166.
Note: [a] Includes exports from Mostyn.

Liverpool was increasingly the centre of overseas trade in the north west. Its trade grew about seventeenfold by volume between 1709 and 1790, whilst that of Chester, the north west's former head port, was in relative then absolute decline. In the late seventeenth and early eighteenth centuries, Chester merchants such as Daniel Peck and Mattthew Anderton were engaged in sending Welsh lead and coal and Cheshire salt and cheese to Portugal, Holland and especially Ireland. As the century progressed, trade was increasingly restricted to Irish and coastal traffic.[41] These changes in fortune are reflected in the number of mariners appearing in the probate records between 1701–20 and 1741–60. In Liverpool they grew from 244 to 738; in Chester they went from eleven to sixteen.[42] More significantly, Liverpool outpaced all of its provincial rivals: trade in Hull increased about ten times and that in Bristol about three times in the eighteenth century.[43] By the 1740s, Liverpool was shipping a greater volume of goods than its southern rival, although in terms of value, Bristol held sway until later in the century. Direct competition between the two ports was probably limited, however, Defoe suggesting that:

The people of Liverpoole seem to have a different scene of commerce to act on from the city of Bristol, which to me is a particular advantage of both, namely, that though they rival one another in their appearances [and] in their number of shipping ... yet they need not interfere with one another's business, but either of them seem to have room enough to extend their trade ... without clashing with one another.[44]

Liverpool, though, was capturing a greater share of the increased coastal and overseas trade of the eighteenth century. It was expanding its links with the Baltic (a process in which the export of salt was crucial[45]) and strengthening ties with North America, the West Indies and Ireland. In 1709, Thomas Johnson shipped 8,084 bushels of salt and a variety of manufactures including nails, pipes, haberdashery and bridles to Virginia, the ship returning with 383,000 lb of tobacco. He imported sugar, indigo and wood from the West Indies, exporting a similar range of manufactures, and also traded with Ireland, bringing in linen yarn and cloth, soap and hides and sending out salt, nails, haberdashery, leather goods and so on.[46] Similarly, the probate inventory of Richard Houghton noted £130 2s of goods shipped to the York River, £241 2s sent to the Potomac River and shares (from one-eighth to eleven twenty-fourths) in seven ships worth a total of £1,021 10s 6¼d. He also had money owing to him from Montserrat, Jamaica, St Christopher, Antigua and Barbados (a total of £531 5s 0½d); Virginia (£25 0s 7¾d); Rotterdam and Stockholm (£543 12s 5d), and Cork, Dublin, Kinsale and Drogheda (£1,524 8s 3d). Liverpool merchants were also increasing their involvement in the river and later canal trade in the north west (see Chapter 5) whilst the corporation was both willing and able to invest considerable sums in the development of dock facilities.[47] When it was completed in 1715, Liverpool's was not only the first commercial wet dock in England, it was also conveniently located near the centre of the town and an immediate success – a fine testament to what could be achieved within oligarchical corporations.[48] This contrasted sharply with attempts to improve facilities in Bristol where successive dock schemes suffered from poor siting and a general lack of urgency and enthusiasm from the Council and the Society of Merchant Venturers.[49]

As a port, Liverpool grew strongly throughout the eighteenth century and increasingly enjoyed three crucial advantages over its southern rival. First was the commercial dynamism of the corporation, symbolised by the ongoing investment in and improvement of dock facilities. Second was the diverse economic base and strong industrial growth of a hinterland that stretched throughout the north west and beyond, incorporating textiles, minerals, agricultural and earthenware production amongst many others. Third were the constantly improved and increasingly effective communication systems, many of them funded at least in part from Liverpool, which linked the port to this developing hinterland.[50] It is telling that the Birmingham canal system linked the town to the Trent and Mersey Canal and thence to Liverpool rather than the Severn and to Bristol. These links meant that 'Liverpool was not built on a pontoon anchored out in the Irish Sea, penetrated by nothing but Atlantic shipping and influences emanating from it'.[51] Rather, it was an integral and important part of the wider commercial economy and infrastructure of north-west England. Moreover, its specialist trading activities provided external linkages and helped to structure regional integration. Rural and urban produc-tion locations and other specialist centres within the regional service economy were linked to the port for access to supplies and markets, new commodities (most notably tobacco and sugar), information and capital. This returns our attention to the service sector of the urban system more generally. The trading towns, and particularly Liverpool and Manchester, undoubtedly enjoyed the lion's share of extra-regional commerce of the north west, but other towns also had specialised service economies which often defined their overall char-acter. Such places form the focus of attention in the next section which relates specialisation of service function to the spread of consumerism and the emer-gence of a culture economy, especially in the gentry or leisure towns.

Specialisation: leisure and consumerism

The rise of towns as arenas of public consumption rested on both the presence of a growing range of services and the creation of specific and specialised social and cultural infrastructure.[52] In combination, these could serve to attract large numbers of wealthy visitors or residents who, in turn, stimulated demand for the goods and services of local craftsmen and traders. Moreover, they encour-aged a greater awareness of national (and particularly metropolitan) fashions and tastes amongst provincial traders. The diversity of urban services has already been noted. Social and cultural facilities reinforced these in particular places to create what McInnes has termed leisure towns.[53] There are problems in precisely identifying the number and range of such facilities: their absence from the records does not necessarily mean that they were not present in a town. As a result, Table 6.4 no doubt under-represents the range of leisure and cultural infrastructure especially in the smaller towns. Nonetheless, it is clear that promenades, theatres, assembly rooms and so on were widespread by the third quarter of the eighteenth century. Moreover, their development was paralleled by the 'improvement' of the urban environment as building styles and materials shifted from the vernacular to an increasingly national neo-classical standard of brick terraces, squares and columns.[54] This section details the localisation of such infrastructure within the towns of north-west England and discusses the role of leisure, sociability and luxury shopping in structuring the urban hierarchy.

Table 6.4 *Leisure and improvement in eighteenth-century north-west England*

	Theatre	Races	Assembly	Library	Quarter session[a]	Walks / gardens	Music	Squares	Total facilities
Chester	1	1	1	1	1	1	1	1	8
Liverpool	1	1	1	1	1	1	1	1	8
Manchester	1	1	1	1	1	1	1	1	8
Preston	1	1	1	1	1	1			6
Warrington	1	1	1	1		1			5
Ormskirk	1	1	1		1	[b]			4
Nantwich	1	1	1		1				4
Stockport	1	1	1				1		4
Wigan	1		1	1	1				4
Knutsford		1	1		1				3
Macclesfield	1		1	1					3
Rochdale	1	1		1					3
Blackburn	1			1			1		3
Bury	1		1	1					3
Newton		1	1						2
Northwich		1			1				2
Bolton	1			1					2
Colne			1	1					2
Chorley						1			1
Clitheroe		1							1
Congleton			1						1
Middlewich					1				1
Prescot		1							1
Altrincham	1								1
Burnley		1							1
Leigh							1		1
Frodsham									0
Haslingden									0
Malpas									0
Sandbach									0
Total towns	15	15	15	12	10	7	6	3	

Source: Baines, *County of Lancashire, passim*; Borsay, *Urban Renaissance*, pp. 323–67; Stobart, 'In search of a leisure hierarchy', pp. 37–8; Corry, *Macclesfield*, pp. 75 and 228–30; Aikin, *Country round Manchester, passim*; Duggan, *Ormskirk*, pp. 143–83.
Notes: [a] Middlewich until 1723; Nantwich until 1759; Northwich until 1759.
[b] The walks at Lathom Spa have not been included here as they lay well outside Ormskirk itself.

The presence of courts was often instrumental in drawing in gentry either to serve as Justices of the Peace or enjoy the social activities which frequently occurred around these legal processes.[55] All of the gentry towns identified in Figure 3.2 had quarter sessions, and the assizes formed the focus of major social seasons at Chester and Preston. The highlight of these social gatherings were undoubtedly the assemblies: 'smart evening gatherings given over to dancing, tea-drinking and card games'.[56] Here, Chester led the way in the north west. The first assemblies took place in the newly built Exchange at the end of the seventeenth century, and their evident popularity prompted the creation of two further eighteenth-century assembly rooms in Booth Mansion on Watergate Street (1740s) and in the Talbot Inn, Eastgate Street (1777), which subsequently became the centre of Chester society.[57] From 1682, there were large and prestigious assemblies linked to the meeting of the guild at Preston. The town hall was used for a range of social activities, the town itself having a 'great deal of good company' according to Defoe, whilst Aikin noted that it took 'the lead in point of gentility' amongst Lancashire towns. Nantwich had an assembly room from 1729, although the town faced increasing competition as a social centre from Chester, and rooms were also found in several smaller towns, including Ormskirk, Knutsford and Congleton, by the late eighteenth century. Such leisure activities spread beyond the leisure towns, however: assembly rooms were opened in Manchester and Liverpool by the 1730s and later in Stockport and Wigan.[58]

Entertainment could also be found at the theatre, from the late seventeenth century in Chester, initially at the old Wool Hall on Northgate Street, but after 1773 in the New Theatre. They appeared later in Liverpool (where the Drury Lane theatre opened in 1749), Manchester (King Street, 1753), Preston (Old Theatre, before 1762) and Nantwich (1729).[59] Facilities were variable in quality and the season often quite short. For example, the theatre in Beam Street, Nantwich was 'a plain piece of architecture, without internal or external ornaments' and suffered from 'an obscure and ineligible situation'.[60] Lesser towns also had theatres, or at least rooms regularly given over to companies of actors, but these appeared only in the last quarter of the century. This was true for Rochdale, Stockport, Blackburn, Wigan, Ormskirk and Bolton, whilst inns were used for plays in several others.[61] There was a music festival in Chester cathedral from the 1720s and regular concerts in Manchester from 1744 and Liverpool (1765), both towns having dedicated concert halls by the 1780s.[62] By the middle of the century, there were periodic concerts in Stockport's assembly rooms, whilst Blackburn had a Handel Society as early as 1754. Elsewhere, music undoubtedly played an important part in the cultural life of towns, but appears to have been less formalised (at least, it has left no formal records) or took place within the church or home.[63] Less formal gatherings also took place in the larger inns, which housed a range of visiting entertainers from magicians to freak shows and often formed the meeting place for the growing number of societies. In Chester these ranged from the Freemasons to the Free Conversation Society. In Liverpool, the more esoteric Academy of the Fine Arts had folded by 1775, but the Literary and Philosophical Society founded four years later in Manchester continued to flourish.[64] Libraries were also becoming more common, appearing in Manchester in 1757, Liverpool and Warrington by 1760, and Chester and Rochdale during the 1760s and 1770s.[65]

A growing number of outdoor activities could be enjoyed. Horseracing took place in thirteen towns and thirteen other places in the region; many towns also contained bowling greens and cockpits, and Chester at least possessed a tennis and a fives court as well.[66] Promenades and gardens also proliferated through the eighteenth century. In Chester, the city walls formed perhaps the most distinctive of the walks, but alternatives were to be found in The Groves (laid out in 1732 as a riverside walk) and the Cherry Gardens on Boughton, 'whose pleasant Walks and Arbours entice a great Number of People in Summer Time'. Elsewhere, the walk in Avenham Garden in Preston had gravelled paths and was planted with trees in the late 1690s, seats being added in the early eighteenth century.[67] Manchester had only an informal riverside walk, but Liverpool boasted three separate walks and its Ranelagh Gardens in the 1760s. All but St James' Walk had gone by 1800, however, swallowed up by housing development, canal cuttings and brickworks: a fate which appears typical of the marginal existence of many such facilities in the growing commercial towns.[68] In smaller centres, promenading often took place in church grounds, but in Chorley there was a Ladies Walk linked to nearby Gillibrand Hall, whilst the residents of Ormskirk could repair to the walks at nearby Lathom Spa, laid out as early as the 1660s.[69]

It is easy to overplay these developments: in many smaller towns cultural life often remained 'stuffy, shallow and sparse'.[70] However, there was a notable increase in the range and quality of cultural and leisure facilities in towns across the region which undoubtedly served to make urban life distinctive and certainly more varied than that in the surrounding countryside. This shared urbane culture, and the traffic in people, fashions and capital it involved, helped to draw together towns and their hinterlands and linked neighbouring centres. The distinctiveness and cohesiveness of town life and urban identity was further accentuated by improvements to the urban environment.[71] At one level this involved enhanced provision for street cleaning, paving and lighting. Town authorities began to take on such duties, traditionally seen as the responsibility of individual householders, from the late seventeenth century onwards. Naturally, corporate towns held the advantage here and Borsay highlights many county towns (York, Salisbury and Bristol amongst others) as prominent amongst the innovators in these improvements.[72] In the north west, Preston, Liverpool and Chester saw most progress in the eighteenth century, not least because they had active corporations to organise and fund such projects. The principal streets of Preston were largely paved by the 1730s; an official scavenger was active from at least 1656; and a modest street-lighting scheme introduced in 1699. In Liverpool, paving appears to have been less widespread, perhaps because of the speed of the town's growth, but scavengers were appointed in 1719 and an impressive array of forty-five lamps erected in 1718.[73] The main streets and several of the lanes in Chester were paved by the late seventeenth century, an official pavior having been appointed in 1584; cleaning was in the hands of three scavengers after 1670; and street lamps were installed by the corporation in 1725.[74] Problems remained, of course: Preston's first scavenger was also town beadle, swineherd and sexton, making his effectiveness uncertain to say the least. Similarly, whilst Liverpool had dozens of lamps by the late eighteenth century, away from the docks and main streets 'they are seldom seen to burn' and often went out early in the night.[75] Notwithstanding such imperfections, the general environment of such places and other towns in the north west was improving steadily. It was also being enhanced by the modernising influence of neo-classical and palladian architectural 'make-overs'. Initially, this seems to have been largely restricted to prominent public buildings and the town houses of the wealthy. By the middle of the eighteenth century, new town halls had been built in Chester (1698), Wigan (1723), Preston (rebuilt and improved in 1728) and Liverpool (rebuilt, 1754); an exchange constructed in Manchester (1729); a customs house erected in Liverpool (1722); and large mansions built in many towns, but especially Chester and Preston.[76] By the middle of the century improvement had spread onto the residential and shopping streets. This was epitomised by the construction of fashionable residential squares in Liverpool (1709), Manchester (1720 and 1739) and Chester (1750s), but was also seen in the refacing of old black and white buildings with more modern lath and plaster or brick, as was seen in many of the rows and streets in Chester.[77]

Leisure, the improved urban environment and the service functions of towns came together in the activity of viewing, choosing and purchasing goods. Shopping, always a social process, was increasingly part of sociability and shops provided arenas in which the (potential) consumer could interact with and broaden their experience of both goods and people. It was also a form of entertainment in itself, providing 'an exciting glimpse of ... consumer goods from around the world'.[78] As Glennie and Thrift argue, shops were therefore 'an active context rather than a passive backdrop' for consumption and were closely associated with leisure and leisure facilities. At Tunbridge Wells and Bath, high quality shops were constructed along some of the principal walks

Figure 6.1 *Retailing and leisure infrastructure in Chester, c.1780*

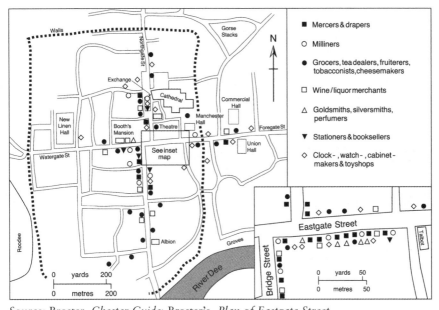

Source: Broster, *Chester Guide*; Broster's *Plan of Eastgate Street*.

and around the assembly rooms. Similarly, in Chester high status retailers were concentrated at the very centre of the city close to the social infrastructure: the rows on the east side of Bridge Street and especially the south side of Eastgate Street were favoured locations (Figure 6.1).[79] Moreover, with the emergence of shopping as leisure (at least for the wealthy), shops and shopping streets were seen and used as leisure spaces so that 'in major towns, especially resorts, the association of redefined shop spaces and leisure activities was extensive and axiomatic'. Eastgate Street and Bridge Street Rows certainly formed a 'fashionable promenade' where parading and shopping could combine as status-acquiring activities.[80] The shopping streets of Chester plus those of Preston, Liverpool and Manchester and possibly smaller towns such as Nantwich, like those of Bath and the resorts, provided opportunities for 'learning what was mostly worn, and buying clothes of the latest fashion'.[81]

Perhaps more significant, however, is the fact that shops were not the preserve of larger centres or gentry towns – they were found in all urban centres and, in many ways, formed the defining characteristic of the eighteenth-century town. Changes in the nature of consumer goods, the processes of shopping, and the structure and meaning of shops and shopping streets permeated the entire urban system, to a greater or lesser extent. Luxury as well as general tradesmen were found throughout the network of towns in the north west.

Table 6.5 *'Luxury' tradesmen in north-west England, 1701–60*
(selected trades and services)

	Clock-maker	Tobacco	Book-seller	Gold-smith	Lawyer	Cabinet maker	Peruke-maker	Musician etc.	Wine merchant
Manchester	1	9	6	1	3	11	2	5	6
Liverpool	2	7	3	4	2	14	3	3	4
Chester	2	3	4	6	4	8	1	2	4
Preston	2	1	1	1	2	2			
Nantwich		5	4	3		2	1		
Warrington	2	1	2		1		2		
Stockport				1	1	1		1	1
Ormskirk	1		2			1			
Rochdale	2		1					1	
Chorley	2	1							
Sandbach	2	1							
Wigan			1					1	
Macclesfield		1		1					
Altrincham				1	1				
Northwich	1						1		
Frodsham	1						1		
Middlewich	1	1							
Congleton		3							
Colne					1				
Knutsford			1						
Blackburn		1							
Bolton	1								
Bury	1								
Prescot	1								
Total (tradesmen / places)	22 / 15	34 / 12	25 / 10	18 / 8	15 / 8	39 / 7	11 / 7	13 / 6	15 / 4

Source: Probate records, 1701–60.

Towards the bottom end of the 'luxury tradesmen' scale, there were mercers or drapers in twenty-six of the region's thirty towns and grocers in twenty-three towns. Those in smaller towns probably operated at a smaller scale than their colleagues in the major centres. For example, the £20 1s 4d of shop goods recorded in the probate inventory of William Jordan of Malpas, equates more with the stock of rural mercers than with those in larger towns. However, their presence reflects the geographical and hierarchical dispersal of shops in the first half of the eighteenth century. The distribution of the higher status service functions was not so broad, but was still remarkably widespread (Table 6.5). These 'luxury' trades were spread between a total of twenty-four towns, and they were to be found in surprisingly diverse places. Thus, we find tobacconists in Chorley, Macclesfield and Middlewich; booksellers in Knutsford and Rochdale, and goldsmiths in Altrincham, Nantwich and Stockport. Even the rarer peruke-makers and wine merchants found their way into Stockport, Northwich and Frodsham as well as the larger towns. As with the leisure facilities discussed above, these shops drew in people from the surrounding countryside and from neighbouring or smaller towns. They therefore served to integrate local economies and societies, and structured spatial interaction within the wider urban system.

The well-developed service sector of north-west England gave relatively easy access to specialist goods and services so that consumers were able to acquire the luxuries, decencies and necessities of a leisured lifestyle without travelling too far afield. That said, provision was focused onto particular towns. Liverpool and Manchester, the two principal trading towns, were prominent – reinforcing the idea raised by Ellis that functional categories of towns are neither neat nor exclusive.[82] More generally, there was a concentration of these functions into the gentry or leisure towns, especially Chester, Preston and Nantwich. Together, these towns formed the main conduits through which new consumption patterns penetrated the north west, stimulating demand for manufactured goods from within and beyond the region and drawing it more closely into national cultural, social and economic systems. This extra-regional integration was strengthened still further in Chester by the presence of large numbers of officers and men in the town's garrison, and the lawyers and clergy clustered around Chester's functions as a diocesan, administrative and legal centre.[83] Such men formed a large and wealthy consumer population, stimulating production by the town's artisans and the region's manufacturers. Moreover, the salaries paid to the clergy were based on the revenues from church lands spread throughout the country and those paid to the garrison were based on national taxes. Wealth created elsewhere was thus drawn into the north west. The gentry towns formed a specialised and important aspect of the urban service economy of the region. Significantly, leisure-related trades were most prominent in precisely those towns which were more marginal to the region's increasingly rapid industrial development. Whilst the trading towns of eastern Lancashire were growing demographically and economically on the basis of burgeoning textiles manufacturing industries, Chester, Nantwich, Preston and the like remained economically vibrant places despite limited industrial growth during this period. The reasons for this inverse relationship are not difficult to find. At Chester, it was held to be 'the absence of manufactories, and the crowds of the lowest rabble they engender' that made it 'a desirable residence for the higher classes'.[84] Likewise, Preston's 'freedom from the bustle of traffic and manufacture' made it more attractive to the gentry. Its subsequent decline as a resort of the county society coincided with its rise as a cotton town in the late eighteenth century. Conversely, and despite its heavy industrial base, Wigan served as an important social centre for Lancashire Catholics, having 'the usual ornaments of a spa, opulent new houses and wealthy pseudo-gentry (many of them sons of the local Catholic landed gentry)'.[85]

Significantly, leisure-related economic activity may have served to stabilise an urban system undergoing profound reconfiguration around newly emergent activities and centres. Just as the nature of the urban hierarchy did much to determine access to leisure facilities and luxury-oriented services, so the presence of those activities impacted on the structure of that hierarchy. The multiple service functions of many towns underline the problems in achieving discrete functional categorisations of towns.[86] More importantly, they resulted in a series of overlapping roles so that several different urban service systems can be identified. One based on trading, another on the emergent leisure and cultural economy, and a third on locally-oriented 'central-place' services and goods. Nonetheless, a single hierarchy of towns, distinguished by the size and complexity of their service economies, served to structure the service economy of the region. Within this, some towns helped to stimulate demand both from their own population and from the surrounding countryside by making accessible new consumption and leisure practices. Here, information on fashion, prices and availability of goods as well as social behaviour and cultural mores moved principally down the hierarchy. In manufacturing areas, the fundamental central place hierarchy was overlain by a system of trading links which served to co-ordinate and stimulate local production and tie it to the wider economy. Hierarchical interaction again dominated, but was structured around specialist production locations and their links to key 'gateway' towns. These last places (epitomised by Manchester and Liverpool) were involved in links with other major trading towns: the merchant function emphasised by Vance. Services were important in providing links between production and consumption, but also structured the spatial aspects of these linkages through their location within the spatial and hierarchical framework of the urban system. In order to tease out the threads of the space economy of the north west, it is therefore necessary to uncover more about the structure of the central place hierarchy.

The central place hierarchy

In essence, all settlements are central places, but only the upper reaches of the system are considered here. In short, this means towns. There is a considerable body of work on historical central place systems, from Patten's relatively simplistic analysis of the East Anglian urban system, through more quantitative studies by Davies, Lewis and Carter on central places in Wales, and Barker on hierarchies in south-west England, to Noble's systematic survey of towns in east Yorkshire.[87] The present analysis differs from many of these studies since the objective is to uncover the structure of the central place system, not explore how it changed through time. To do this, use is made of Davies's functional index.[88] In this, each town (t) has a functional index (F) given by the formula:

$$F_t = \sum \frac{n.100}{N}$$

where N is the number of outlets of the function in the whole system and n is the number of outlets of the function in the given town. Using this measure to calculate indexes for each town on the basis of dealing and public and professional services, it is possible to assess the relative importance of each town within the central place system (Figure 6.2). This can be laid alongside the analysis of leisure and cultural infrastructure (Table 6.4) to give a wide-ranging picture of service centrality in the region.

The system was dominated by Chester, Manchester and Liverpool which, between them, accounted for more than half of regional centrality; in contrast, no other centre made up more than one-twentieth. These were the core centres in the regional urban system, dominating economic activity in north-west England. In terms of cultural infrastructure, these same three towns were again pre-eminent, although Preston and to a lesser extent Nantwich were also significant centres. Such primacy was not unusual in seventeenth- and eighteenth-century regional urban systems, although the degree to which functions and facilities were concentrated into the leading towns was particularly marked in north-west England. In east Yorkshire, Bridlington and Scarborough were pre-eminent, but Beverley, Driffield, Market Weighton and Howden were also significant service centres. Similarly, there were five major centres in East Anglia: Norwich, King's Lynn, Great Yarmouth, Ipswich and Bury St Edmunds.[89] Importantly, this dominance was a persistent feature of service provision in the north west from the early eighteenth century onwards. Path-dependence was a notable feature of the service sector as well as of manufacturing. In the shop tax of 1785, Manchester, Chester and especially Liverpool were again dominant, between them accounting for around three-quarters of the assessed tax in the region. Manchester traders paid over six times as much as those in the neighbouring textile towns of Bolton, Bury,

Figure 6.2 *Urban centrality in north-west England, 1701–60*

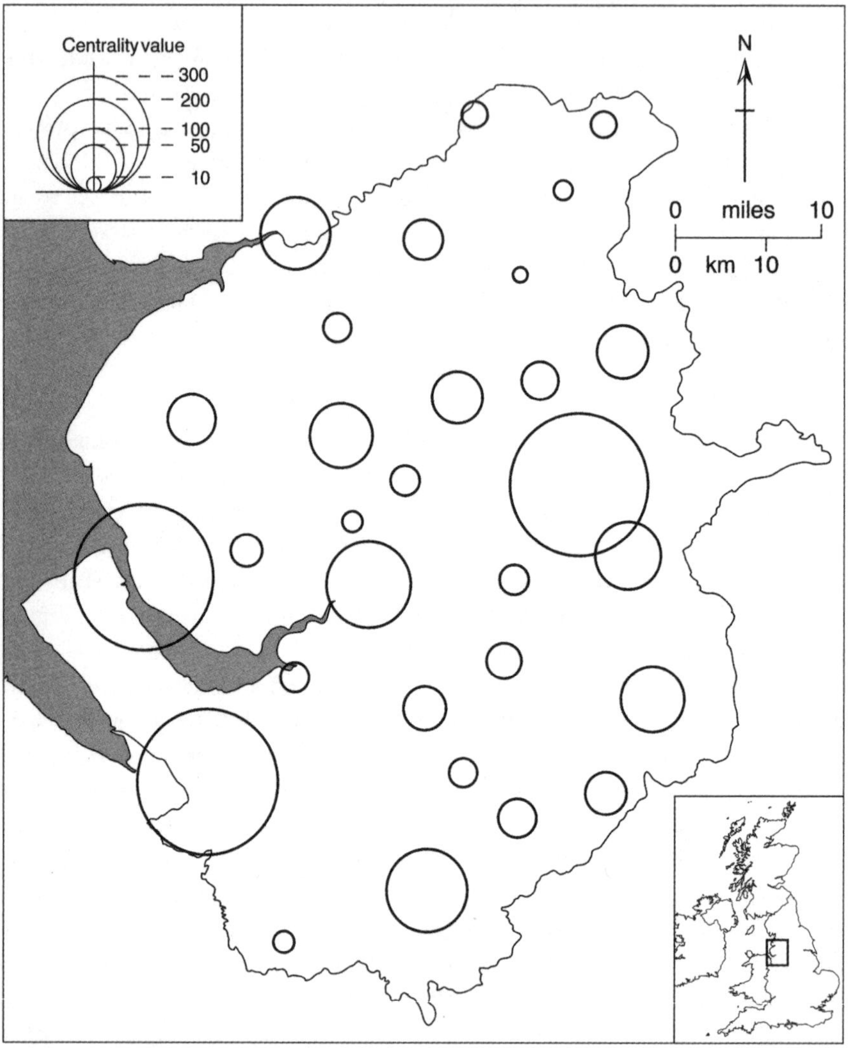

Source: Probate records, 1701–60.

Rochdale, Ashton-under-Lyne and Oldham combined. Similarly, the returns for Liverpool were four times greater than in the adjacent gentry and trading towns (Preston, Ormskirk, Wigan, Warrington and Prescot). In Cheshire, Chester traders paid £164 17s 5¼d – some 63 per cent of the county total and over five times that of Stockport, its nearest rival.[90] All three towns formed important financial centres in the late eighteenth century: the *Universal British Directory* lists seven banks, accountants and insurance agents in Liverpool,

Table 6.6 *Central place functions and order of settlement in north-west England, 1701–60*

Order of town	1st	2nd	3rd	4th	5th	No. of towns	No. of orders
Inns and alehouses	3	6	6	7	8	30	5
Chapmen	3	6	6	6	7	28	5
Medicine	3	6	6	7	4	26	5
Mercers and drapers	3	6	5	7	5	26	5
Butchers	3	6	5	6	5	25	5
Clergy	3	5	6	7	3	24	5
Clerks, etc.	3	6	5	5	4	23	5
Grocers	3	6	6	4	3	22	5
Hairdressers	3	6	5	4	1	19	5
Merchants	3	5	5	4	2	19	5
Hardware dealers	3	6	3	3	1	16	5
Schoolmasters	3	5	2	2	3	15	5
Law and commercial services	3	4	2	1	3	13	5
Horse racing	3	3	3	2	2	13	5
Assemblies and balls	3	6	2	1	1	13	5
Tobacconists	3	4	2	2	1	12	5
Wool dealers	3	3	4	1	1	12	5
Forces	3	5	1	1	1	11	5
Linen dealers	3	6	3	3		15	4
Theatres	3	6	4	1		14	4
Haberdashers	3	5	2	2		12	4
Booksellers	3	4	2	1		10	4
Quarter sessions	3	3	2	2		10	4
Cheese or corn dealers	3	3		2	1	9	4
Customs and excise	2	3	1	1		7	4
Raw materials	3	4	1			8	3
Arts	3	4			1	8	3
Goldsmiths, etc.	3	4			1	8	3
Libraries	3	2	1			6	3
Music concerts	3	1	1			5	3
Promenades and gardens	3	2				5	2
Vintners	3	1				4	2

Sources: Probate records, 1701–60; Baines, *County of Lancashire, passim*; Borsay, *Urban Renaissance*, pp. 323–67; Stobart, 'In search of a leisure hierarchy', pp. 37–8; Corry, *Macclesfield*, pp. 75 and 228–30; Aikin, *Country round Manchester, passim*; Duggan, *Ormskirk*, pp. 143–83.
Note: For order of towns, see Figure 6.6.

nine in Manchester and five in Chester, compared with one or two in places like Macclesfield, Wigan or Warrington.[91] Later still, Manchester (Kendle Milne, 1836) and Liverpool (Lewis's, 1856) were at the forefront of development of department stores in the mid-nineteenth century and as headquarters locations for late nineteenth-century multiple-retailers.[92]

The hierarchical structure of the early eighteenth-century system is revealed in Figure 6.3. From this, orders of settlement can be identified as groups of towns with similar centrality indexes. Although the first two orders are fairly distinct, other groupings are less coherent and the number of orders identified depends quite heavily on how many are 'required'. At their centre, they correspond to different magnitudes of central place provision, but this is far from being the discrete stratification which Marshall suggests is characteristic of a Christallerian central place hierarchy.[93] Towns of a given order thus had a range of functional indexes, indicating various different levels of service provision. This internal variation was in part a result of the specialist nature of the service functions of towns so that similar centrality indexes were based on a wide variety of functions. For example, Bolton (forty-eight) and Congleton (forty-five) had similar centrality scores but very different service economies: 17 per cent of Bolton's score was made up of chapmen and a further 18 per cent comprised food retailers; that of Congleton included 21 per cent aldermen, 20 per cent luxury retailers, and around 11 per cent each for hairdressing and medicine. Similarly, Middlewich's score of nineteen was largely comprised of food retailers, whereas Leigh (twenty-one) was dominated by cloth dealers and Altrincham (twenty) by luxury and specialist retailers.

Quite clearly, the hierarchical distribution of functions in the north west was very far removed from the Christallerian model. In this each order of town can be distinguished by characteristic assemblages of goods and services, with higher order goods only becoming available in higher order centres. It was noted earlier that high status functions were present in small towns. More formal analysis is now possible which cross-tabulates individual functions with orders of settlement (Table 6.6). There were very few functions which were exclusive to the higher order settlements: of the thirty-two functions identified, eighteen were found in all orders of central place and twenty-five were present in at least four orders. This was less true of leisure facilities than dealing or service functions, but even theatres were found in all but the smallest towns by the late eighteenth century. This distribution of high order functions throughout the central place hierarchy seems to have extended further in the north west than elsewhere. In East Anglia, there were several trades (including furrier and surgical instrument maker) which were only found in Norwich, and several others (for example, bookseller, ironmonger and scrivener) which were exclusive to the higher orders. In part this reflects the fact that Patten considered

Figure 6.3 *The central place hierarchy of north-west England, 1701–60*

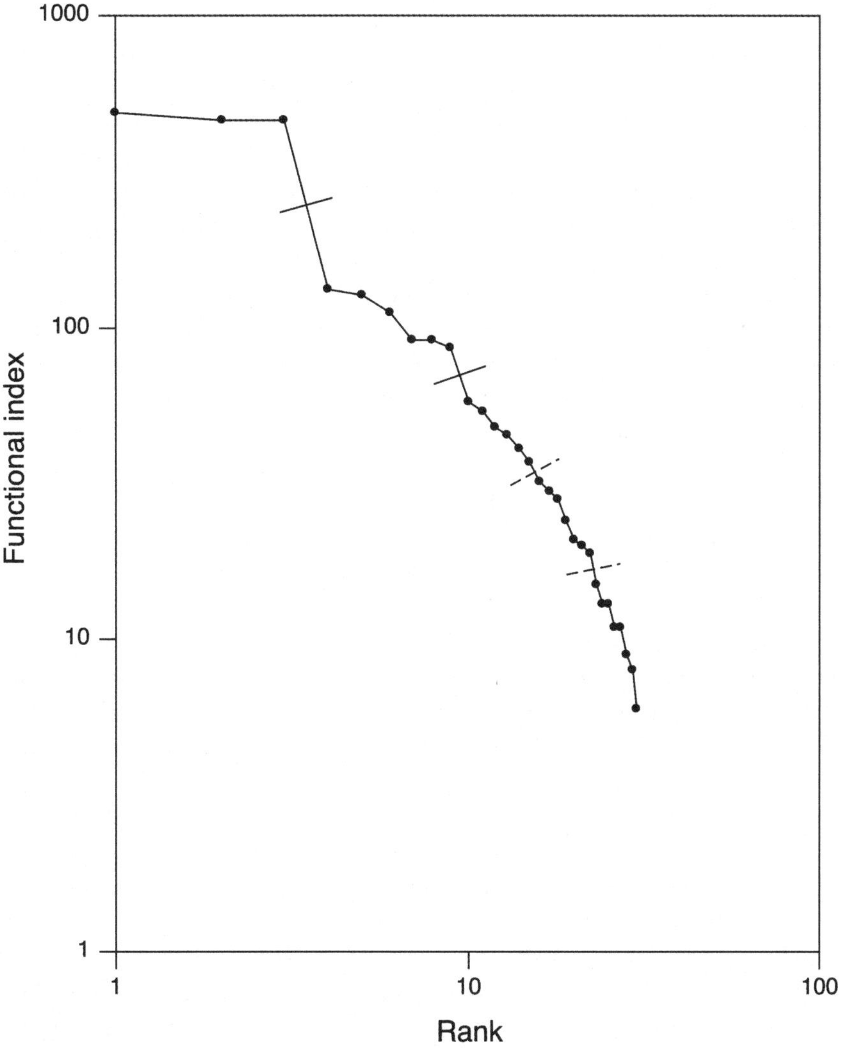

Source: Probate records, 1701–60.

individual trades rather than the broader functions studied here, but it seems clear that the distribution of service functions was structured more rigidly in East Anglia than in north-west England.[94] This is not to deny the importance of the hierarchical structuring of both the service economy and urban system. Certain goods and services were ubiquitous. Others, whilst present in some smaller towns, were predominantly located in larger centres. For example, inns were found in all orders and in all towns; merchants were present in all orders but only two-thirds of towns; and tobacconists were in all orders, but barely one-third of towns. This uneven distribution was most significant when it involved functions which were critical in the internal and external integration of the urban system. Through their involvement in capital investment, the organisation of production systems and long-distance trade, merchants and chapmen were critical to economic growth in the north west. Their concentration in Liverpool and Manchester respectively made these two towns the foci of trading patterns and the spatial inter-linkages which drew together the regional economy. In a similar way, the concentration of administrative, social and leisure functions drew the gentry into Preston and Chester, and made the latter in particular the centre of a parallel set of integrating social, cultural and economic linkages. The dominant position of these four towns, and especially Chester, Liverpool and Manchester, was reinforced by their position as the principal locations for the attorneys and scrivenors who did much to co-ordinate flows of capital between people, places and economic sectors in the early eighteenth century.[95] It is no accident that these towns were also the initial and always the principal centres of banking in north-west England.

The position of Chester, Liverpool and Manchester as core centres in the regional service economy is underlined in Figure 6.4. These three towns dominated the provision of high status goods and services. In the smaller towns, the situation was more complex. Of the second order centres, Preston was conspicuous, having eight high order functions, whereas Macclesfield contained just three: only one more than fourth order Altrincham. Of the third order centres, Rochdale and Ormskirk possessed four high order functions, whereas Bolton had none. Clearly, some towns (Congleton and Altrincham for instance) attained their status by offering a few high order goods and services, whereas others (including Bolton and Bury) reached a similar level through the possession of larger numbers of more common functions. For the north west as a whole, the dependence on larger towns to provide the high order or luxury goods and services was overlain by sporadic local availability of certain of these functions. This has important implications for the structure and operation of the regional urban system and underlines the marked specialisation and localisation of urban service economies already apparent in the early eighteenth century. Some of the less common high order functions were linked to local production. This can be seen in the appearance of woollen dealers in the smaller towns of eastern Lancashire as well as larger towns throughout the region.[96] It is also apparent in the location of customs and excise in the ports and salt-producing areas, and in the presence of cheese or corn dealers in many small towns in Cheshire, including Frodsham, Middlewich and Sandbach. The nature of the town was also influential. For example, leisure facilities and luxury dealing were often concentrated into areas with significant numbers of

Figure 6.4 *High order functions in the central place system, 1701–60*

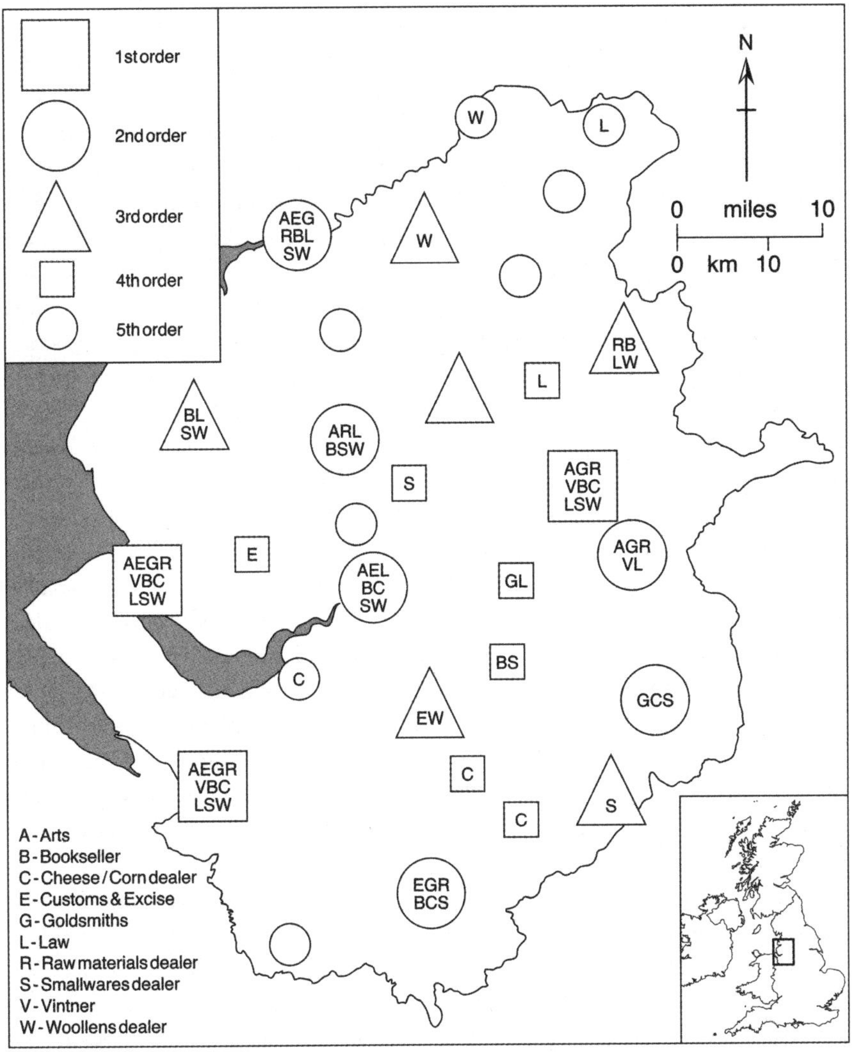

Source: Probate records, 1701–60.

gentry. This favoured towns in prosperous agricultural areas and/or with assizes or quarter sessions which the rural magistracy or gentry would periodically attend. Ormskirk had the additional benefit of nearby Lathom Spa, at least whilst it remained an attraction to local gentry in the early decades of the eighteenth century.[97] More specifically, towns such as Altrincham, Knutsford and Ormskirk were strongly influenced by the close proximity of large land-owners at Dunham Massey, Tatton Park and Tabley Hall, and Lathom House respectively. Much of the custom of these great houses went direct to London or the large towns, but the local towns were also important in supplying goods and services. Ormskirk was heavily influenced by the activities of the Earls of Derby, whilst Knutsford was said to obtain 'much of its support from the public spirit and liberality of the opulent gentry who reside in its neighbourhood'.[98]

This links to the more general observation that towns were different not just in their economic structure, but also in their orientation: some looked out to their hinterlands whilst others focused more on providing for the needs of their own growing populations. This has significance for the character of individual towns and for the structure of the urban system and hence the regional econ-omy as a whole. The outward-looking towns had, in this sense at least, strong externalities and might be expected to have a greater influence on the structure of interaction within the network of towns.[99] This idea can be explored through analysis of a simple 'externality rating' for each town calculated by dividing its functional index by its population (Figure 6.5).[100] Unsurprisingly, the ratings were higher for larger towns: they were providing goods and services for their own population, that of their hinterland and those of smaller towns. More revealing, perhaps, are the spatial and typological differences. Of the twelve towns which had ratings above the average for their order, only Stockport might be classed as a trading town, there being a marked absence of high ratings in the Lancashire textile districts. Instead, the servicing and gentry towns of Cheshire and west Lancashire stand out. This may relate, in part, to the larger market areas enjoyed by these towns – there being no towns in the centre-west of Cheshire and relatively few in west Lancashire – but the notion of competition, either with other towns or with rural provision, was less important than the nature of the urban economy itself.[101] The servicing and gentry towns by necessity looked outwards for their prosperity: they were defined by their service economies and their links to their hinterlands, whether narrowly or more broadly delimited. Whilst they were far from being parasitic on the body of rural wealth as Wrigley suggests, the fact that they drew on rural demand meant that these towns contained functions over and above those needed by the resident population.[102] Towns such as Chester, Preston and Ormskirk could prosper economically and considerably expand their influence without necessarily experiencing rapid population growth. Trading towns also looked outwards, but to co-ordinate and integrate local (rural) production or link that production to distant markets rather than primarily to provide goods and services. Although they all possessed local marketing functions, service activities in these towns were directed principally towards commerce and providing for the growing needs of their own populations which swelled as economic growth drew more workers into textile and metalworking trades or the docks.

Figure 6.5 *Externality ratings within the central place system, 1701–60*

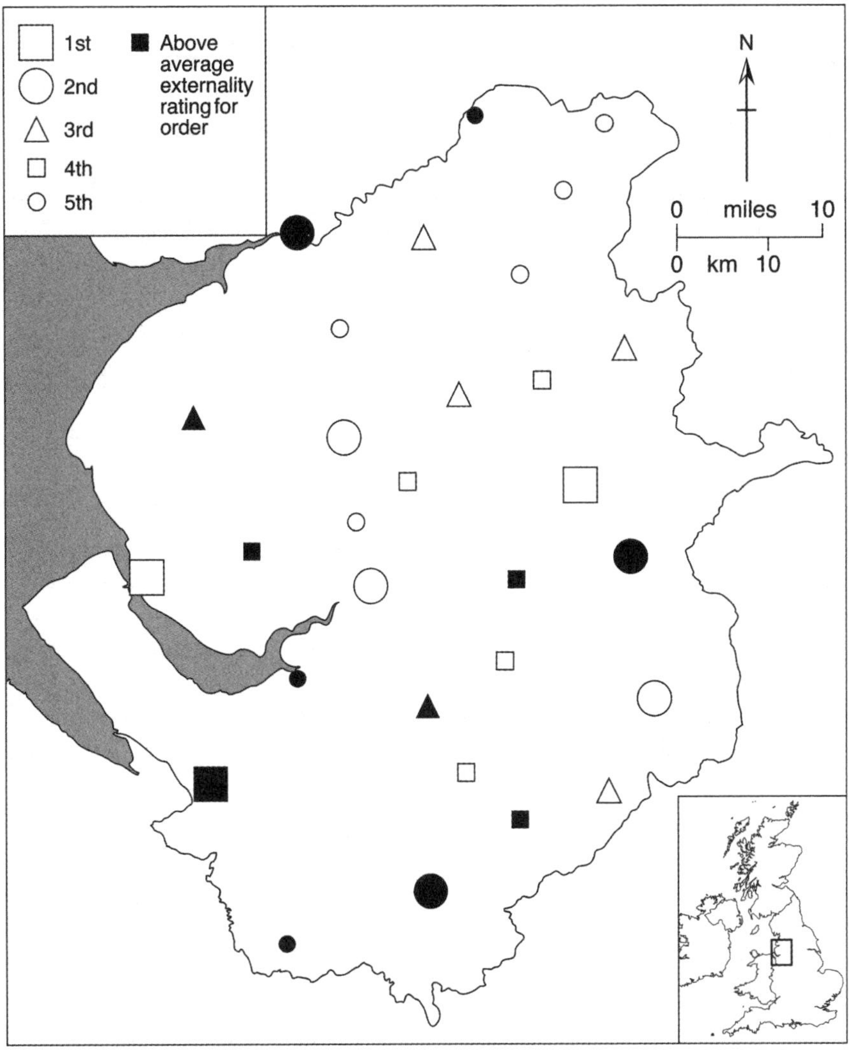

Source: Probate records, 1701–60.

Specialisation was not merely important in terms of the internal economy of towns; it was also fundamental to the relationship between town and hinterland, and in the structure of the urban system as a whole. The territorial relationships which characterised the servicing and gentry towns were the result of positive interaction between rural demand for, and urban supplies of, goods and services. Whilst it was demand that formed the ultimate engine for growth, new and essentially urban economic, cultural and social values provided the fuel and ultimately a new higher capacity design for that engine in the form of consumerism.[103] The textile trading towns were also characterised by close interaction with their hinterlands, but here the impetus for growth came from outside demand channelled through urban markets and capitalists. The spatial structure of interaction was thus far less rigid, with accessibility and local production specialities playing a significant role in shaping links between commercially-oriented towns. Overarching both these service systems was the hierarchical structuring of the regional urban system. This did much to shape intra- and extra-regional flows of goods, information and capital, thus integrating and generating growth in the economy of the north west. This hierarchy focused principally onto Liverpool, Manchester and Chester. The activities within and the links to these three centres were therefore crucial in integrating the spatial divisions of labour that characterised production and consumption – or manufacturing and services – in north-west England.

Conclusions: the service sector and the structure of the urban system

The service sector was an important part of the economy of north-west England in the early industrial period, employing thousands of men and women, generating significant local prosperity and provising vital intra- and inter-regional linkages. As Berg and Hudson suggest, in seeking to understand the processes and geography of industrialisation, we should not ignore changes in the wider economy.[104] Unsurprisingly, towns dominated service provision, although rural service activity was widespread and growing, especially in terms of dealing activities in the east of the region. Whilst this can be seen as part of a general commercialisation of the countryside, it is clear that towns were both the beneficiaries of the growing market orientation of household and local economies. They were also active agents in bringing about this change, linking local urban and rural demand to national and international supplies.[105] Marked specialisation arose from spatial divisions of labour within the service economy so that different towns played very different roles in this transformation and in the wider integrative function of the service sector. Trading towns were vital in linking local production to distant markets and in the intra-regional organisation of manufacturing. They were spatially concentrated into the textile districts in the east of the region and were characterised by intense interaction with the local countryside and with other textile towns in the district. These links were hierarchically structured, but were strongly influenced by inter-urban commercial webs focused onto Colne, Rochdale, Bolton and especially Manchester. Liverpool was an outlier from this system, but was the most important trading centre in the region: its extra-regional links with Ireland, Europe and the New World were matched by growing commercial and communication links with the rest of the north west and particularly south-west Lancashire and central Cheshire. Liverpool and Manchester thus formed what Vance terms 'gateway cities' for the two main manufacturing districts in the region. As Vance argues, it was the trading activities of urban merchants, financiers and professionals that drew together production within these districts. The spatial concentration of these activities especially into Liverpool and Manchester was both a cause and a reflection of their pivotal role in the regional space economy; the persistence of these concentrations meant that these two towns remained the spatial growth poles of the regional economy throughout eighteenth- and nineteenth-century industrialisation.

If growing trade was one aspect of the commercialisation and integration of the regional economy, then the growing dependence on the market place and the emergence of new forms of leisure and consumption was the other. This was characterised by the servicing and gentry towns, which were strongly oriented towards providing for what were increasingly prosperous and sometimes very extensive hinterlands. Whilst this function rarely generated strong demographic growth, the range and sophistication of goods, services and infrastructure that was provided in such places betokened and enhanced local prosperity. The fact that Chester was still the equivalent of Liverpool and Manchester in terms of service provision despite being only half their size by the middle of the eighteenth century is a testament to the importance of the leisure function in service towns.[106] A service/leisure economy overlay the agricultural economy of Cheshire and west Lancashire and prospered in parallel with the growing industrial economies of southern Lancashire. This spatial concentration formed another important division of labour within the regional economy, but changes in the nature of consumer goods and leisure and consumption practices permeated, to a greater or lesser extent, the entire urban system.

All towns were characterised by complex service economies, trading and leisure activities being overlain onto the basic servicing functions that maintained the populations of the town and its hinterland. Concentrations of leisure, professional, administrative or commercial services might result from local specialisation, but could also reflect a town's position within the urban hierarchy – larger or, in Christallerian terms, higher order centres, contained greater numbers, a wider range and higher order functions. Moreover, the multitude of specialist production and service locations, and the various economic sub-systems that were emerging the early eighteenth century, were drawn together through the central place system via the commercial, transport and personal linkages between individuals and towns. The (spatial) structure of the urban system thus becomes central to understanding the nature and development of the regional space economy. Unsurprisingly, Christaller's rigid hierarchical and spatial structuring is not an appropriate way of understanding the complex and varied nature of the central place system of early industrial north-west England. Production systems and specialities varied across the region and so did the demands made on and by the urban system. To an extent, the hierarchical and spatial structuring of the central place system and the existence of several production systems in the region argue for a Löschian system of overlapping central place networks. However, it is the specialisation and inter-dependence of towns which holds the key to the structuring of the urban system. Tertiary specialities cut across the hierarchical structuring of service provision and were often tied to particular production systems or sub-regions. Such patterns correspond more with Vance's ideas of specialising service centres tied together by non-hierarchical linkages: a sort of industrial specialisation based on service functions. Such ideas can only be tested by examining some of the real patterns of contact and interaction which tied together the urban system and served to integrate the detailed spatial divisions of labour within the regional economy. The final chapter attempts such an examination.

Notes

1 Chalmers, *Strength of Great Britain*, p. xiii.
2 Berg and Hudson, 'Rehabilitating', especially p. 29.
3 These texts are Floud and McCloskey, *Economic History of Britain*, and O'Brien and Quinault, *Industrial Revolution*.
4 Mathias, *First Industrial Nation*, pp. 223–4.
5 For a summary of these ideas, see Hudson, *Industrial Revolution*, pp. 173–92. The emergence of consumerism is considered in detail in McCracken, *Consumer Goods and Activities*, pp. 11–26; Glennie, 'Consumption in historical studies'; Pennell, 'Consumption and consumerism'.
6 See, for example, Fine and Leopold, *World of Consumption*, pp. 63–72; Engerman, 'Overseas trade'.
7 Hudson, *Industrial Revolution*, pp. 180–1; Engerman, 'Overseas trade', pp. 184–5; King and Timmins, *Industrial Revolution*, pp. 134–62.
8 Mitchell, 'Urban retailing', p. 259; Cox, *Complete Tradesman*, pp. 38–75.
9 Krugman, *Geography and Trade*, pp. 65–6.
10 Simmons, 'Urban system', p. 63; Vance, *Merchant's World*, p. 8; Corfield, *English Towns*, pp. 34–42.
11 Langton, 'Urban growth', pp. 470 and 474; Borsay, 'Health and leisure resorts', pp. 777–9. For discussion of the relationship between leisure and consumption, see Stobart, 'Shopping streets' and Beckett and Smith, 'Urban renaissance'.
12 Daunton, 'Towns and economic growth', pp. 250–1; King and Timmins, *Industrial Revolution*, pp. 150–9.
13 Vance, *Merchant's World*, p. 9.
14 Mui and Mui, *Shops and Shopkeeping*, p. 45. For discussion of the 'world of goods', see the various contributions to Brewer and Porter, *World of Goods*.

15 The service sector is better represented than manufacturing in the probate records. See Appendix 2.

16 Estabrook, *Urbane and Rustic England*, pp. 42–66.

17 See Shaw, 'Large-scale retailing'; Fine and Leopold, *World of Consumption*, especially pp. 219–26.

18 See Glennie, 'Consumption in historical studies'; Stobart, 'Shopping streets', Cox, *Complete Tradesman*; Fowler, 'Provincial retail practice, pp. 40–51; Larson, *Rise of Professionalism*, pp. 80–103.

19 Patten, *English Towns*, pp. 223–4; Shammas, *Pre-industrial Consumer*, pp. 225–65; Mitchell, 'Urban retailing', pp. 267–78; Borsay, *Urban Renaissance*, pp. 117–49 and 212–24; Cox, *Complete Tradesman*, pp. 38–75 and 197–222.

20 Weatherill, *Consumer Behaviour and Material Culture*, pp. 43–69; Cox, *Complete Tradesman*, pp. 38–75; Shammas, *Pre-industrial Consumer*, pp. 225–65; Mitchell, 'Urban retailing', pp. 267–70 and 275–8; Patten, *English Towns*, pp. 221–2.

21 Glennie and Thrift, 'Urbanism and modern consumption', pp. 429–30; Daunton, 'Towns and economic growth', pp. 250–1.

22 See Borsay, *Urban Renaissance*, pp. 199–212; Stobart, 'Shopping streets', pp. 10–15.

23 *Gore's Liverpool Directory*; Broster, *Chester Guide*.

24 See Cox, 'Distribution of retailing tradesmen', pp. 7–8.

25 *Adams Weekly Courant*, 6/17 December 1746.

26 *Chester Courant*, 1 July 1794.

27 *Adams Weekly Courant*, 17/28 April 1750.

28 Lysons and Lysons, *Magna Britannia*; Mitchell, 'Urban retailing', pp. 270–1; Shammas, *Pre-industrial Consumer*, pp. 226–9 and 248–60.

29 Langton, 'Urban growth', pp. 479–80.

30 Estabrook, *Urbane and Rustic England*. For the role of shops in shaping consumption practices, see Glennie and Thrift 'Urbanism and modern consumption', pp. 429–30; Glennie and Thrift, 'Consumption spaces', pp. 26 and 31–6.

31 Hudson, *Industrial Capital*, pp. 211–17; Anderson, 'Early capital market'; Neal, 'Finance of business', pp. 165–70.

32 Hudson, *Industrial Revolution*, pp. 182 and 187–90.

33 Cox, *Magna Britannia*; Broster, *Chester Guide*.

34 Public Record Office (PRO), E182/96.

35 Crosby, *Cheshire*, pp. 90–1, 95–7 and 112–13.

36 Krugman, *Geography and Trade*, p. 66.

37 Lepetit, *Urban System*, p. 134.

38 Power, 'Councillors and commerce', pp. 307 and 314; Hyde, *Liverpool*, p. 3.

39 Parkinson, *Port of Liverpool*, pp. 86–101; Hyde, *Liverpool*, pp. 30–4; Langton, 'Liverpool', p. 2.

40 Weatherill, *Pottery Trade*, pp. 81–95; Mountford, 'Thomas Wedgwood'; Keele University, Wedgwood Accumulation, for example E9–30248–30291; L52–30705; L120–23237. For a more general discussion of the trade in pottery, see Weatherill, 'Middlemen in the English pottery trade'.

41 CCA, CR 352/1 Letter Book of Daniel Peck; CR 656/1–35 Merchant's Papers; Craig, 'Trade and shipping', pp. 108–15.

42 The number of mariners appearing in the probate records is disproportionately high because all seamen had probate granted on their estate regardless of whether

they owned goods valued at over £5. Nonetheless, the striking increase in Liverpool mariners reflects genuine growth which dwarfed that in Chester.

43 Corfield, *English Towns*, p. 40.

44 Defoe, *Tour through Britain*, p. 542.

45 Clemens, 'Rise of Liverpool', p. 218.

46 Power, 'Councillors and commerce', p. 307.

47 Power argues that this had much to do with the growing commercial and political power of the merchant body in Liverpool. They constituted the largest single interest group and dominated the Corporation in the early eighteenth century: Power,'Councillors and commerce', p. 322.

48 Power,'Councillors and commerce', p. 302; Hyde, *Liverpool*, pp. 14 and 73–5. Such innovation undermines the often-repeated assumption that old-established corporations restricted development. See Chalklin, *Rise of the English Town*, pp. 59–65.

49 McGrath, *Bristol in the Eighteenth Century*, pp. 139–57. Chester's improvement schemes also faltered: Stobart, 'County, town and country', p. 174.

50 This is not to suggest that Bristol did not benefit from improvements to the Severn and Avon and increased links with Wales, but Liverpool's transport infrastructure developed far more rapidly in the mid-eighteenth century: Langton, 'Liverpool', pp. 3–7.

51 Langton, 'Liverpool', p. 1.

52 Beckett and Smith, 'Urban renaissance', pp. 33–6 and 40–8.

53 McInnes, 'Shrewsbury'; Borsay, 'The London connection'; Glennie and Thrift, 'Urbanism and modern consumption', pp. 429–30. See also, Sweet, *English Town*, pp. 257–66; Ellis, *Georgian Town*, pp. 106–28.

54 Jones and Falkus, 'Urban improvement', pp. 128–33; Borsay, *Urban Renaissance*, pp. 39–113; Borsay, 'Rise of the Promenade'. Sweet, *English Town*, pp. 75–114, notes that such improvements generally took place later in smaller provincial towns.

55 Borsay, *Urban Renaissance*, pp. 143–4 and 155–6.

56 McInnes, 'Shrewsbury, p. 65.

57 Carrington, *Chester*, p. 99; Willshaw, 'Inns of Chester', p. 13.

58 Defoe, *Tour through Britain*, p. 548; Aikin, *Country round Manchester*, p. 283; McInnes, 'Shrewsbury', p. 83; Corry, *Macclesfield*, p. 230; Stephens, *Congleton*, p. 123; Borsay, *Urban Renaissance*, pp. 336–49; Astle, *Stockport*, p. 124.

59 Borsay, *Urban Renaissance*, p. 118; Kennett, *Georgian Chester*, p. 36; Phillips and Smith, *Lancashire and Cheshire*, p. 114.

60 Platt, *Nantwich*, p. 76.

61 Hall, *Nantwich*, p. 218; Borsay, *Urban Renaissance*, p. 331; Aikin, *Country round Manchester*, p. 248; Duggan, *Ormskirk*, p. 154.

62 Kennett, *Georgian Chester*, p. 39; Troughton, *Liverpool*, p. 326; Aston, *Manchester Guide*, pp. 240–1.

63 Astle, *Stockport*, p. 125; Beattie, *Blackburn*, p. 115; Duggan, *Ormskirk*, pp. 156–61.

64 Willshaw, 'Inns of Chester', pp. 43–51; Stobart, 'Culture versus commerce'; Wilson, 'Cultural identity of Liverpool'.

65 Phillips and Smith, *Lancashire and Cheshire*, p. 115. Chester possessed circulating libraries based in booksellers' shops from the early eighteenth century, but only gained a subscription library in 1773: Kennet, *Georgian Chester*, p. 39.

66 Borsay, *Urban Renaissance*, pp. 356–7 and 360; Hemingway, *Chester*, volume 2,

p. 340; Chester City Library (CCL), de Lavaux 'Plan of Chester'; CCL, Stockdale, 'Plan of Chester'.

67 Broster, *Chester Guide*, p. 24; Borsay, *Urban Renaissance*, pp. 350–4.
68 Picton, *Liverpool Archives*, pp. 137 and 245–5; Muir, *Liverpool*, pp. 281–2; Wallace, *Liverpool*, p. 85. For a fuller discussion, see Stobart, 'Culture versus commerce'.
69 *UBD*, volume 2, p. 672; Duggan, *Ormskirk*, p. 163.
70 Ellis, *Georgian Town*, p. 82.
71 See Jones and Falkus, 'Urban improvement'; Ellis, *Georgian Town*, pp. 87–105.
72 Borsay, *Urban Renaissance*, pp. 68–74.
73 Hewitson, *Preston*, pp. 57–7; Picton, *Liverpool Archives*, pp. 64–5.
74 CCA, A/A/2/156v; A/B/2/169v; A/B/1/111v; A/B/1/193v; A/B/3/163v; A/B/3/264v; A/B/4/5v – Chester Assembly Records.
75 Wallace, *Liverpool*, p. 275; Borsay, *Urban Renaissance*, p. 69.
76 Borsay, *Urban Renaissance*, pp. 325–8; Carrington, *Chester*, pp. 92–4; Enfield, *Liverpool*, p. 59; Morris, *Journeys of Celia Fiennes*, p. 163.
77 Stobart, 'Shopping streets', pp. 18–20.
78 Perkins, 'The consumer frontier', p. 503; Glennie and Thrift, 'Consumption spaces', p. 35; Cox, *Complete Tradesman*, pp. 116–46.
79 Glennie and Thrift, 'Consumption spaces', p. 26; Borsay, *Urban Renaissance*, pp. 168–70; Towner, *Recreation and Tourism*, pp. 82–3; CCA, CR 63/2/133/17, Broster's *Plan of Eastgate Street* (c. 1754).
80 Glennie and Thrift, 'Consumption spaces', p. 33; Fletcher, *Stranger in Chester*, p. 32.
81 Austen, *Northanger Abbey*, quoted in Towner, *Recreation and Tourism*, p. 83.
82 Ellis, *Georgian Town*, p. 54.
83 Stobart, 'Shopping streets', p. 7; Stobart, 'County, town and country', pp. 174 and 179.
84 Hemingway, *Chester*, volume 2, p. 341.
85 Aikin, *County around Manchester*, p. 283; Langton, 'Lancashire Catholicism', p. 91.
86 Lepetit, *Urban system*, pp. 134 and 153–7; Ellis, *Georgian Town*, p. 54.
87 See Patten, *English Towns*, pp. 244–96; Davies, 'Centrality'; Lewis, 'Central place patterns'; Barker, 'Conceptual approach'; Noble, 'Regional urban system'.
88 Davies, 'Centrality', p. 63
89 Noble, 'Regional urban system', pp. 11–13; Patten, *English Towns*, pp. 282–90.
90 PRO, E182/96; E182/491.
91 See also Pressnell, *Country Banking*, pp. 49, 177 and 379; Black, 'Money, information and space'; Phillips and Smith, *Lancashire and Cheshire*, pp. 344–8.
92 Shaw, 'Large-scale retailing', pp. 140 and 154.
93 Marshall, *Location of Service Towns*, p. 66.
94 Patten, *English Towns*, p. 283.
95 Anderson, 'Early capital market'.
96 There were also woollen merchants in Colne and Haslingden, but these do not appear in the probate records: Swain, *Industry*, pp. 123 and 146; Tupling, *Rossendale*, pp. 183–8.
97 Duggan, *Ormskirk*, pp. 162–9.
98 Corry, *Macclesfield*, p. 229.

99 The idea of externalities is explored by Noble, 'Regional urban system', but under-emphasised in Lepetit, *Urban System*.

100 The populations taken are averages of the 1664 and 1775 figures (making them rather crude estimates of early eighteenth-century totals); the 'rating' is multiplied by 100 to make the numbers easier to describe.

101 Competition is discussed by Noble, 'Regional urban system', p. 19.

102 Wrigley, 'Parasite or stimulus', pp. 300–3.

103 See Glennie and Thrift 'Urbanism and modern consumption', pp. 431–4.

104 Berg and Hudson, 'Rehabilitating', pp. 24–50.

105 Langton, 'Urban growth', pp. 479–81; Borsay, *Urban Renaissance*, pp. 199–224; Ellis, *Georgian Town*, pp. 47–65.

106 See McInnes, 'Shrewsbury'; Ellis, 'Regional and county centres', pp. 673–84.

7

Spatial integration and the urban system

Manchester, like an industrious spider, is placed in the centre of the web ... An order sent from Liverpool in the morning is discussed by the merchants in the Manchester exchange at noon, and in the evening is distributed among the manufacturers in the environs.[1]

As Lepetit argues, it was the inter-relations between towns that made a loose framework of centres into a functioning urban system.[2] Much the same was true of the wider economy: growth based on specialisation and inter-dependence was only possible because the activities of individuals, localities and regions were integrated through real spatial interaction. In this way, the north west again forms a microcosm of processes occurring at the national level and across Europe, where economic diversity and spatial integration combined to encourage growth.[3] These were, in effect, two aspects of the same underlying processes. The people, functions and places which were central to the integration of the urban system were also critical in shaping and generating local, regional and national development.

Despite their undoubted significance, integration and interaction are often difficult to define and measure in real historical contexts. The most basic approach is to study the market areas of individual towns, exploring the interaction between a central place and its hinterland.[4] This splits the system into its component parts and offers what Lepetit calls bi-polar analysis. Whilst revealing of local inter-dependencies, this does not disclose much about the inter-urban linkages which served to tie together the urban system and the space economy, and link them to wider national and international processes. This can be achieved, at least implicitly, by assessing the complementarity of urban centres in terms of production and service specialities, the timing of markets, and so on. Such an approach has been widely adopted to throw welcome light on the ways in which the separate market areas or hinterlands of individual towns interacted in spatial, operational and developmental terms.[5] This type of study demonstrates the necessity and possibly the existence and structure of inter-*relationship* between centres; it does not reveal or explore the actual inter-*action* patterns which tied together diverse places and economies. The difficulty is finding useful measures that reveal these real spatial interactions. Lepetit follows Robson, Pred and others in privileging the role of innovation diffusion both as a means of examining the structure of the urban system and as a key determinant of the location of growth within that system.[6] But this still involves 'reading-off' linkages from the pattern of diffusion rather than revealing real tangible links between places.

This chapter explores a number of alternative measures of spatial interaction, first and foremost to analyse the structure and integration of the regional space economy, but also to offer an exemplar for studies of other regions. The analysis begins with the basic building blocks of spatial integration: local market areas. These are examined in terms of both their spatial and hierarchical arrangement, and some of the processes which served to tie together town and country. The latter comprised principally the periodic visits made to markets and shops, but also included more permanent migration to serve apprenticeships or following marriage and the sporadic journeys to attend elections or assizes, or to visit friends and business partners. How did such interaction serve to link town and country, and how did variations in the size and nature of the hinterland relate to the town's specialist functions and/or position in the urban hierarchy? Wider spatial integration is then examined through transport systems and services which can be seen as key indicators and initiators of economic growth and integration. It was transport and communication which brought together separate towns and local economic specialisations; improvements to systems and services are thus seen as opening up new areas for development and providing lubrication for the commerce which did much to generate economic and urban growth.[7] More specifically, the volume and type of traffic between centres directly demonstrates the nature and strength of interaction.[8] To what extent did the developing transport network mould itself around or serve to transform the urban system of north-west England? Which centres were privileged in the flows of goods, people, information and capital that moved around this network? Finally, attention focuses on the ways in which personal networks drew together the wider regional space. Studied at an individual level, the activities of attorneys, merchants and manufacturers can tell us much about the mechanisms by which the spatial divisions of labour were articulated and integrated. In aggregate, the socio-economic webs of contact revealed in the testator-executor links outlined in probate records can provide real insight into the structure of the urban system and the regional economy. There can be problems here of equating what were often, in essence, social ties with broader economic interaction. That said, towns are all too frequently reified: the interaction between places was, in reality, the summation of linkages between individual people. Any information which can reveal who was known to whom can show an enormous amount about the everyday ties that bound together regional and national economies in the eighteenth century.

Market areas and local integration

Everitt has suggested that the 'ideal distribution of markets in England would have been at a distance of eight to ten miles apart', allowing country dwellers to walk to and from market in a single day.[9] He recognised that this ideal was often not realised: the market areas of towns varied with local levels of population and economic development; with their own economic and social importance; and with the competition of adjacent centres.[10] But they could also vary for different goods and services and for different people. In the north west, the average distance between market towns was about seven miles, suggesting quite a dense coverage, especially given the presence of several rural markets, particularly in the area south of Preston.[11] However, uneven spacing of the towns meant that the Wirral, western Lancashire and the Woodhead area in eastern Cheshire were poorly served by towns, the market areas of Chester, Ormskirk, Manchester and others being enlarged accordingly. Whilst the lack of competition generally led to economic benefits and greater spheres of influence for these towns, a closer packing of towns did not necessarily mean smaller market areas for all centres. It has already been seen that Manchester dominated much of south-east Lancashire in terms of textile production and marketing, and it incorporated several smaller towns within its sphere of influence. Further north, the influence of Preston also extended beyond its immediate hinterland to encompass market areas of smaller towns, especially those of the Fylde. These were often by-passed by villagers who preferred to buy or sell at Preston. Indeed, as early as 1655, villagers petitioned for the improvement of the road through Markham so that they would not be 'debarred from the benefit of the Marquette at Preston'.[12]

The nesting of smaller market areas within larger spheres of influence is a familiar idea in geography and a key tenet of central place theory.[13] Larger towns had bigger market areas because they contained the high order functions unavailable or present in much smaller numbers in the lesser towns. As at Preston, there was a general and growing preference shown for larger market centres, both by consumers because of the greater choice and by sellers due to the larger number of buyers present in the bigger towns. That said, different individuals were willing and able to obtain goods and services over different distances. Wealthy consumers could afford the time and money for longer journeys or had sufficient buying power to have goods delivered to them from local or even metropolitan traders. For example, in the 1720s and 1730s the Leghs of Lyme bought corn, groceries, ironmongery, cloth, shoes and paper in Stockport, but had wine and books sent from Manchester or London. A decade later the Ardernes regularly shopped in Stockport, but bought cloth in Manchester and plate in London.[14] Further west Nicholas Blundell records numerous visits to Liverpool, Preston and Chester to acquire a range of goods and had regular orders with London tradesmen, but he also bought goods locally at Ormskirk and from itinerants who called at the door.[15] Itinerant salesmen were important links between town and country. They carried a range of goods – including surprisingly high value items such as the silver cutlery purchased by Blundell – and a good supply of information and gossip. Moreover, they travelled over wide areas, improving access to non-local products and effectively integrating local economies.[16] Not all men of substance chose to range so widely in their consumption patterns: Henry Prescott (not a part of the landed gentry, but an avid consumer of goods, food and drink and leisure) was able to satisfy his needs and wants within Chester itself.[17] For the middling sorts and the average working household, such modest horizons were probably more typical. Nonetheless, longer journeys would undoubtedly have been necessary for goods or functions not locally available.[18]

The hierarchical arrangement of the market areas of individual towns was mirrored by the diversity of distances over which a particular type of tradesman would operate. The market areas of small towns and their retailers are exemplified by John England, an apothecary whose probate inventory contained a long list of book debts which included 149 separate entries. Most were for small amounts (only twelve were for more than £1) and the majority were from local people: 116 were owed by people of an unspecified location – most were probably from Northwich where England spent most of his active life – and a further 8 were from Knutsford whence he had latterly moved. Of the other 25, only 5 were from places further than six miles from Northwich (Figure 7.1). In all, John England had a dense network of local customers who probably visited his shop on a fairly regular basis: he was a small-scale retailer in a market town. A step up the urban and service hierarchy were men such as Edward Twambrooks, a mercer from Warrington. He had a larger market area reflecting a more expansive business network and Warrington's greater sphere of influence. Twambrooks was owed a total of £147 16s 0½d by 66 individuals, most debts being for amounts less than £2, although £25 15s 6d was due from a man in neighbouring Fearnhead. Again, the greatest number were from Warrington itself or the immediate area, but there were also 14 from places more than six miles distant (Figure 7.1). If cloth could be sold over longer distances than apothecary's remedies, then furniture appears to have had an even larger range. Similarly, Chester commanded a much bigger market area than either Northwich or Warrington.[19] Thus, the business activities of Abner Scholes, a Chester upholsterer, covered a large area and involved considerable amounts of money. His probate inventory lists book debts of £1,134 19s 6d owed by 151 individuals, including some very large individual amounts. Sums of £38 12s 8d, £27 11s, £27 and £13 10s were owing from upholsterers, suggesting that Scholes may have supplied other craftsmen with materials, but there were also debts of £89 14s 10d, £18 0s 1d, £80, £54 7s 6d and £44 4s from wealthy customers. Clearly he had a substantial business which could supply large orders from customers who spread over a wide part of west Cheshire and north Wales, and included two baronets, five ladies and thirteen esquires. Such people, and many others, were obviously willing to overlook the service available at smaller towns such as Ruthin, Denbigh, Wrexham and Frodsham (whose market areas effectively nested within that of Chester) to acquire furniture from what was clearly a high quality craftsman.

England, Twambrooks and Scholes were essentially locally-oriented tradesmen, the size of their market area being determined by the nature of their trade and the town in which they operated. They were vital in integrating town and country at a local or sub-regional level. So too were various cultural facilities. The spa at Lathom drew people (especially the gentry) to neighbouring Ormskirk from a ten-mile radius and the races at Knutsford were attracting much of the east Cheshire gentry by the late eighteenth century.[20] This pull was particularly strong when a social season could be established around the sittings of the quarter sessions or assizes – as at Preston and especially Chester. In the latter, the gentry and middling sorts came not only from the whole of Cheshire, but also from large parts of north Wales. This wider hinterland incorporated a number of smaller towns including Denbigh and Wrexham, Frodsham, Northwich, Middlewich, Nantwich and Malpas, and even Whitchurch. In spatial terms this echoed the market area of tradesmen such as Scholes and also the residence of freemen eligible to vote in elections for the town's Members of Parliament. Around one-third of these lived outside Chester itself, mostly in Cheshire, but spread across eight counties in all.[21]

In addition to these periodic movements, towns also attracted more permanent migrants from their hinterlands, sometimes prompted by marriage but most often by economic opportunities. Whilst rural industrial development encouraged strong population growth in many parts of east and south Lancashire, rural–urban migration was common across the region.[22] For these moves to occur, there had to be some awareness of the opportunities that existed in town and most probably some specific contact already established. Such links might be based on previous personal experience (skilled workers especially could be highly mobile in the eighteenth century); on the presence in town of family or friends, or on formal contractual arrangements. The last of these most commonly involved the apprenticing of sons to urban tradesmen – a practice which allows the reconstruction of at least one aspect of the geography

Figure 7.1 *Debt patterns of selected tradesmen*

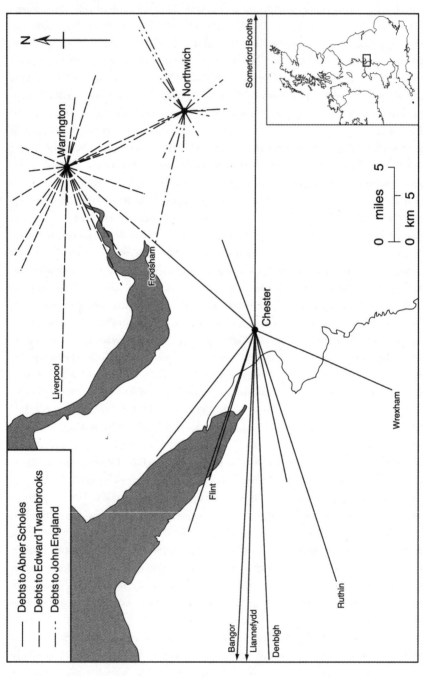

Source: CCA, WS 1756, Abner Scholes of Chester; CCA, WS 1711, John England of Knutsford; LRO, WCW 1732, Edward Twambrooks of Warrington.

Figure 7.2 *Origins of apprentices to Chester tradesmen, 1700–53*

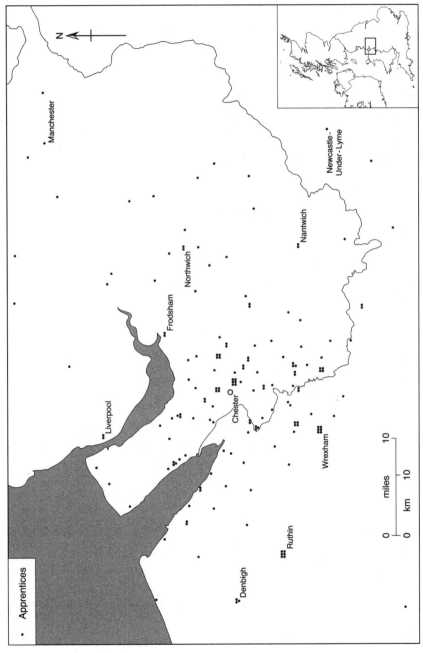

Source: CCA, MAB/2, Apprenticeship Registers.

Figure 7.3 *Buyers and sellers at the Chester horse markets, 1660–1723*

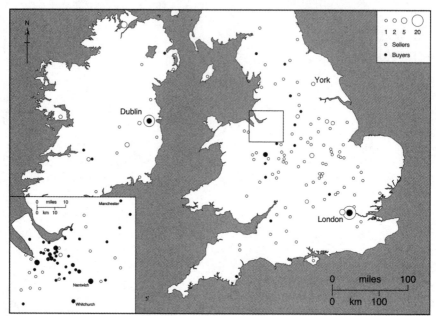

Source: CCA, SBT/2, Chester Horse Market.

of migration. Mapping the origin of apprentices in Chester shows close interaction between the town and a hinterland of villages and small towns up to
twelve miles distant (Figure 7.2). These linkages indicate that parents in such
settlements looked to Chester as a possible place of employment and that they
were aware of specific opportunities in the town's trades. It is possible that
they could even draw on personal contacts in the city. However, whilst they
drew on existing urban-rural links, the migration of their sons strengthened
these ties, offering clear lines of information and capital transfer, and potential
attractions to future migration along similar pathways.

   Migration to Chester also took place over considerably longer distances.
Numbers were comparatively small, but apprentices came from Manchester,
Newcastle-under-Lyme and Beaumaris, and from Warwickshire, Cambridge,
Essex, London and even Ireland. This reflected a less intense, but significantly
larger area of influence for the town which was paralleled by other functions
linking the north west into the national and international economy. For instance,
Warrington ironmongers supplied local nailers and hinge- and locksmiths with
iron from Cheshire and north Wales from the late seventeenth century and
dispatched their products throughout the country. Later Peter Stubbs drew on
suppliers throughout Lancashire and Yorkshire and sold his files and tools to

Figure 7.4 *Overseas debts of Richard Houghton*

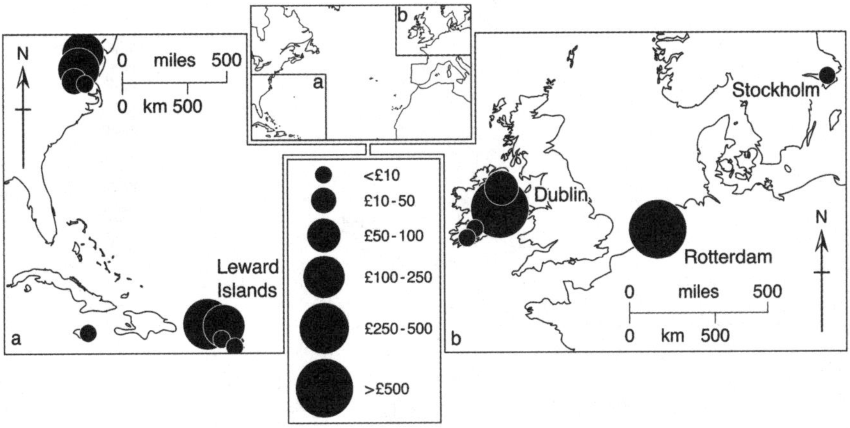

Source: LRO, WCW 1712, Richard Houghton of Liverpool.

hardware dealers across the country (see Figure 5.6). At an even bigger scale, the horse market at Chester drew dozens of buyers and sellers from Ireland as well as all parts of England (Figure 7.3). The buyers were predominantly from the north west (152 were from Chester itself, 44 from elsewhere in Cheshire and Lancashire, and only 43 from other parts of the country), but most sellers came from a great distance, including 45 from Ireland, 172 from England and Wales and just 37 from within the north west. Many of the sales were of one or two horses, suggesting that the vendors were selling surplus animals whilst in Chester on other business rather than being specialist dealers. Nonetheless, the market helped to supply the needs of the town and region for horses needed for transport and agriculture. More generally, it reflected the links between the city's economy and that of the country as a whole. This integrating function and the corresponding sphere of influence reached their peak in the business networks controlled by individuals engaged in long-distance trade. From Chester, Daniel Peck had dealings with suppliers and merchants in mid Wales, Milford, Bristol, Plymouth and London as well as overseas. Richard Houghton, the Liverpool merchant, had business links to North America, the Caribbean, northern Europe and Ireland – represented in his probate inventory by debts and assets worth a total of £4,017 0s 10½d (Figure 7.4).[23] Yet he was far from being isolated from his own region and was owed £375 10s 10d by fellow residents of Liverpool and £2,009 10s 10½d from thirteen other places in the north west, including £1,533 0s 9¼d from Manchester alone (Figure 7.5). Moreover, he was part of national trading networks and was owed £1,866 11s 11d from individuals spread throughout England and Wales: £411 12s 7d from two men in Gainsborough, £381 14s

Figure 7.5 *National and regional debts of Richard Houghton*

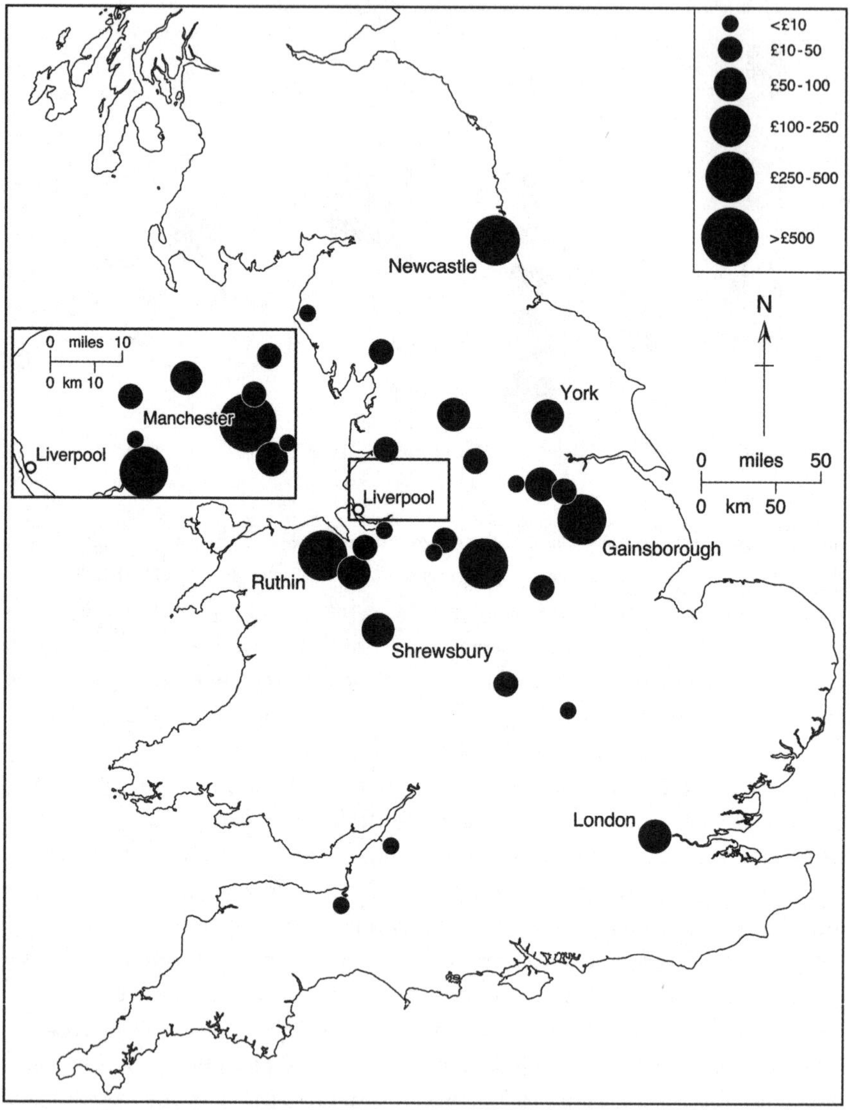

Source: LRO, WCW 1712, Richard Houghton of Liverpool.

10d from a single merchant in Ruthin, £300 9s 9d from Newcastle-upon-Tyne and £294 1s from Ashbourne. Commercial webs like Houghton's, which involved at least 162 people, encompassed numerous smaller networks in north-west England and tied the local nexus of market linkages into national and global business networks. We thus have a picture of market areas and contact patterns which varied according to the size of the centre and the type of trade in which individuals and towns were engaged. Smaller market areas were nested within larger ones in a manner resembling that modelled by Christaller (see Chapter 2). Consideration of Houghton has already taken us beyond bipolar (town / country) analysis. To move to multi-polar analysis and thus accommodate all towns and system-wide inter-relations requires a broader focus and different sources.

Transport systems and spatial integration

Transport is widely recognised as being critical in the integration and organisation of the space economy: interaction takes place via transport networks and services which shape and are shaped by that interaction.[24] There are notable examples of transport innovation stimulating rapid economic development or urban growth in the north west (see below). However, the primary purpose of most transport systems (roads, canals or railways) was to link together markets, entrepôts or centres of production, consumption or population. In short, towns. This relationship is apparent from analysis of transport hierarchies in the region. The first of these is based on the nodality of towns within the network of turnpikes and navigations (Figure 3.3) and shows a broad correlation between functional order and nodality.[25] Some small towns were quite well-positioned in the transport network (Middlewich, Newton and Knutsford, for instance, all lay on important north–south routes through the region), but the overall tendency was for larger centres to be the best connected (Table 7.1). In itself, this is unsurprising: infrastructure, even turnpike roads, is only a partial reflection of the traffic passing along particular routes. The roads and navigations provided the potential for interaction: it was the services which carried the goods, people and information that were the essence of spatial integration.

Table 7.1 *Central place order and the network nodality of towns in eighteenth-century north-west England*

Central place rank	Multiple junction	Complex cross-road	Simple cross-road	Through-road	Isolated or cul-de-sac
1st	3	0	0	0	0
2nd	0	3	3	0	0
3rd	0	1	2	2	1
4th	0	0	3	2	2
5th	0	0	2	3	3

Sources: Probate records, 1701–60; Albert, *Turnpike Road System*; Pawson, *Transport and Economy*; Hadfield and Biddle, *Canals of North West England*.
Note: For rank orders, see Figure 6.4.

Table 7.2 *Central place order and the 'transport service centrality' of towns in eighteenth-century north-west England*

Central place rank	>500	200–300	90–130	30–65	0–12
1st	3	0	0	0	0
2nd	0	1	4	1	0
3rd	0	2	0	3	1
4th	0	0	0	3	4
5th	0	0	0	4	4

Source: *Universal British Directory*, volumes 2, 3, 4 and 5.
Note: For rank orders, see Figure 6.4.

There are problems in assessing the amount of traffic on navigations and roads before the late eighteenth century as sources tend to be sporadic in time and space. Toll books are a useful source for certain navigations and canals, but their incomplete nature and the limited number of places linked to such water transport makes them of limited value in a region-wide study. Useful information on local and national road services is contained in the *Universal British Directory*, but even here services to and from some towns are covered incompletely. On top of this, it is often difficult to determine the precise route taken by a particular coach or carrier, and therefore the places linked together by that service. Notwithstanding this, the present analysis is based on data from the *Universal British Directory*. Two measures are taken: the 'service nodality' of each centre (that is, the number of towns to which it was immediately linked) and the number of coaches and wagons for which it was the origin or destination.[26] Multiplying these two figures gives a crude, but probably fairly true picture of the transport service hierarchy in the north west (Figure 7.6). Again, it was the larger centres which generally enjoyed the best transport links (Table 7.2). No small towns enjoyed exceptionally good transport services and, although certain places (for example Nantwich and Congleton) appear to have been under-provisioned for their size, their lowly position is probably somewhat illusory. Nantwich, in particular, was served by many more coaches and carriers, but lay on a main route to London and so had relatively few which terminated in the town.

Despite analytical difficulties of this nature, it seems clear that the transport network was, as Lepetit argues for pre-industrial France, largely 'fashioned to the contours of the existing urban hierarchy'. Transport infrastructure and services would thus tend to reinforce hierarchical and centre-periphery relations within the region.[27] This was true of the eighteenth century and beyond: the railways too were constructed to connect towns and served to strengthen the existing system. This is not to say that transport had no impact on urban and

Figure 7.6 *Inter-urban coach and carrier network in north-west England, c.1790*

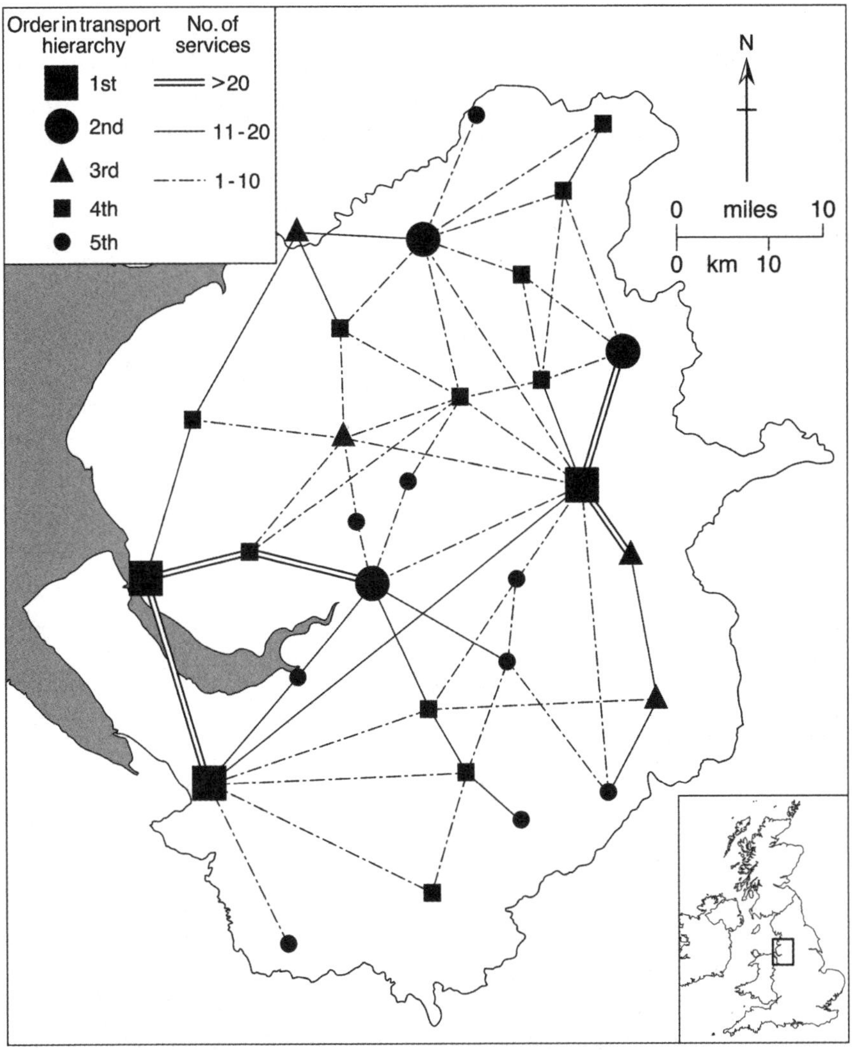

Source: *Universal British Directory*, volumes 2, 3, 4 and 5

economic development. Canal building helped to promote an upsurge in production and urban development in advantaged areas, as with the emergence of St Helens from the nexus of industries at the head of the Sankey Brook. It also led to the growth of Runcorn as a port and later a chemicals town. Crewe was entirely a product of the railways.[28] Indeed, Corfield notes that 'everywhere, urban growth levels ... were intimately connected with the sustenance of a transportation network'.[29] In general, though, there appears to be no consistent link between either network nodality or service centrality and urban growth (Table 7.3). Chester, Wigan and Macclesfield were all well linked but grew relatively slowly; Leigh, Ormskirk and Haslingden were comparatively poorly served by transport facilities, but all grew faster than the regional average, and, if St Helens owed its existence to the Sankey navigation, Ashton-under-Lyne and Oldham were created by forces which had little to do with transport advantages. As Ellis suggests, then, 'access to the busy transport networks of Georgian Britain … was just as likely to be the consequence as the cause of urban prosperity'.[30]

Table 7.3 *Transport and urban growth in eighteenth-century north-west England*

Growth rate	Network nodality					Service centrality				
	Multiple junction	Complex cross-road	Simple cross-road	Through-road	Isolated or cul-de-sac	>500	200–300	90–130	30–65	0–12
>urban mean	2	1	1	3	0	2	3	0	1	1
>regional mean	0	1	4	1	1	0	0	2	5	0
>rural mean	0	1	2	0	0	0	0	2	1	0
<rural mean	1	1	3	3	5	1	0	0	4	8

Sources: Stobart 'Eighteenth-century revolution?', p. 36 and p. 40; probate records, 1701–60; Albert, *Turnpike Road System*; Pawson, *Transport and Economy*; Hadfield and Biddle, *Canals of North West England; Universal British Directory*, volumes 2, 3, 4 and 5.

The fact that transport innovations were not revolutionising the urban system of north-west England does nothing to undermine the importance of networks and services in the integration of the regional space economy. As such, the patterning of the transport system has much to tell us about the structure and functioning of the urban hierarchy. Transport networks and services confirm its essentially hierarchical nature. Instead of preferentially connecting specialist production or trading centres, communication lines fed into larger centres from smaller towns and were focused onto the three pre-eminent towns in the region: Chester, Liverpool and Manchester. These dominated both intra- and extra-regional linkages and constituted the 'gateway' towns of the region. Liverpool, of course, had extensive links with south-west Lancashire and central Cheshire and, through its port, with a growing world economy; but it was also tied into regional and national space

Figure 7.7 *Coach and carrier links from north-west England, c.1790*

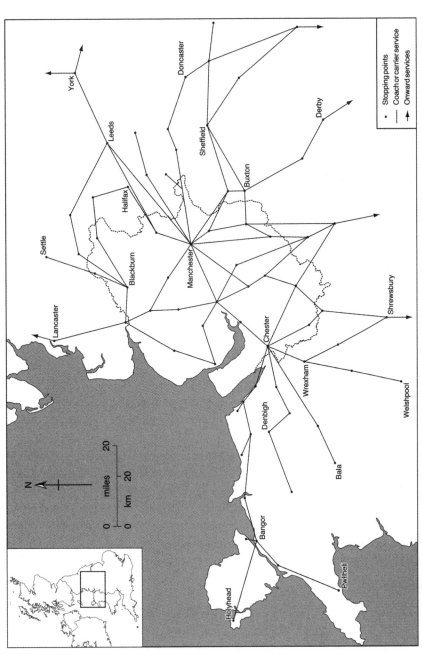

York
Leeds
Doncaster
Halifax
Sheffield
Settle
Buxton
Blackburn
Derby
Manchester
Lancaster
Shrewsbury
Chester
Wrexham
Denbigh
Welshpool
Bala
Bangor
Holyhead
Pwllheli

N
miles
0   20
0   20
km

Stopping points
Coach or carrier service
Onward services

Source: *Universal British Directory*, volumes 2, 3, 4 and 5.

economies. By the late eighteenth century, there were over thirty coaches and many more wagons each day connecting Liverpool with London, the Midlands, the West Country, Yorkshire and the north. Chester also maintained overseas links especially to Ireland, and there were coaches leaving the town daily to meet the regular crossing from both Parkgate and Holyhead. Its more extensive links were with north Wales, however, and by the 1790s there were thirty-three coaches and about twenty-six wagons each week connecting Chester to at least twenty-three Welsh towns and villages including places as far afield as Welsh-pool, Bala, Pwllheli and Beaumaris (Figure 7.7).[31] Similarly, Manchester was served by a multitude of coaches and carriers. Many travelled to local destinations and thus tied the town very firmly to its immediate hinterland, but others headed for London, Norwich, Hull, the Midlands, Newcastle and Scotland. Links to Yorkshire towns were especially strong and it is clear that Manchester was acting as an entrepôt for much of east Lancashire and north-east Cheshire, if not beyond. In all, the *Universal British Directory* lists 112 coaches and 331 wagons leaving these towns each week for sixty-six different end-destinations. Across the country there were similar transport and interaction foci playing a vital role in the generation of an integrated national economic space which incorporated leisure and culture as well as manufacturing and trade.[32]

The linkages offered by towns such as Liverpool, Manchester and Chester allowed regions to specialise in particular economic activities. They were also instrumental in developing the commercial, industrial and cultural roles of the towns themselves, and therefore served to reinforce the position of these places as centres of control within the regional economy. The towns' individual specialisms made them important players on a national scale and gave them complementary roles in regional integration. Local integration was also focused on these three towns (Figure 7.6) and both services and routes were concentrated onto them in a manner which underlined the spatial and functional focusing of specialist sub-regional economies in the north west. Their distinctiveness is evidenced by the different modes of transport which dominated in each. Chester's transport services were characterised by a high proportion of coach services: over half of the services recorded in the *Universal British Directory* were mail or ordinary coaches.[33] This reflected its importance as a social and administrative rather than production centre. In complete contrast, wagons outnumbered coaches by about three to one in Manchester, with many serving the surrounding towns and villages. No doubt many were loaded with textiles for finishing in and/or export from Manchester. Although it had a large number of coach and carrier services, Liverpool was linked to production locations in the mineral-based economy by a system of navigations and canals far more developed than those serving the textiles economy to the east.[34] Over and above these sub-regional systems and interactions, Liverpool, Manchester and Chester were vital to wider regional integration. Most coaches, and certainly the mail services, focused on these three towns which therefore dominated the flow of information into the region and structured its subsequent diffusion to other centres. Notwithstanding the gentry's direct links with London, news, prices, fashions and innovations reached these towns and their merchant bodies first, giving them additional power and influence in the region.[35] From there, information travelled through the north west via newspapers, advertisements, correspondence, personal contacts and so on.

The big three centres by no means monopolised external linkages or supplies of information. Various others, often those near to the boundaries of the region, were the origin or destination of extra-regional transport services. Thus, Macclesfield had carriers to Buxton; Rochdale was linked to Halifax and Leeds; Blackburn to Settle, Keighley and Leeds; and Preston to Lancaster, Kendal and the Fylde. These links provided invaluable information from the rest of the country and gave such towns independence from their larger neighbours, but the frequency and distances involved were less than those of the services running to the three main centres. No region, the north west included, was isolated from surrounding districts and these coach and wagon services represented important links to neighbouring areas, signalling considerable, if variable, interaction in terms of manufacturing, trade and servicing activities. Indeed, it could be argued that neighbouring regions and urban systems effectively shared key 'border' settlements. Thus, whilst being an integral part of the north west, Rochdale was an active outlier of the west Yorkshire wool industry. Similarly, Preston's position as *de facto* county town and an important social centre reinforced its local marketing ties to the towns and villages of the Fylde. Combined, these drew the town into the national urban system and that of north Lancashire.[36] If inter-regional linkages were offered by these towns, other places stand out as important to intra-regional integration (Figure 7.6). Blackburn was an important gateway to the textile towns of north-east Lancashire, linking them to the north-south axis of the Preston–Warrington road as well as to Manchester. Further south, Rochdale and Bolton appear to have operated in a similar way for the surrounding parishes.[37] Warrington was prominent as a crucial locus of the regional road and canal networks. Although relatively few services terminated in the town, it stood at the cross-roads of important north-south and east-west routes, including those followed by London- and cross-post mail coaches. In the 1790s, something over sixty coaches and many more wagons were passing through Warrington each week heading for London, Liverpool, Manchester and York, and the North. There were also 239 flats based in the town and trading between Liverpool, Northwich and Winsford via the Weaver navigation and Trent and Mersey Canal.[38]

This brief analysis of transport in the north west indicates that a relatively small number of towns formed clear foci of transport systems in the region. The fact that these were often the larger rather than the most dynamic centres supports Lepetit's suggestion that transport networks followed the spatial and hierarchical patterning of the existing urban system.[39] It also emphasises the fact that Richardson's locational constants of towns and transport nodes were almost always spatially coincident. Other than in exceptional cases such as St Helens and Runcorn, this meant that agglomeration and other economies accruing from urban and transport advantages were mapped onto the same places.[40] Transport was thus one element of the broader 'layers of investment' which structured the location of activity within the regional space economy.[41] That said, the relatively poor match between transport nodality and urban growth suggests that other forces were also important in determining the geography of regional and national development. Lepetit has argued that local and regional industrial growth cut across expected transport/economic growth relationships.[42] However, it is important to remember that transport is just one aspect and measure of a much broader set of integrating processes which included inter- and intra-firm commercial linkages, credit systems, kin and friendship relations, information networks and religious or social fraternities. All of these helped to tie together places and more importantly people within the north west, and link their local and regional economic and social worlds to national and international arenas. The problem, of course, is how to measure these types of interaction and assess their impact on shaping the urban system and its operation – an issue explored in the next section.

Personal networks and patterns of spatial interaction

Outside analyses of transport networks, attempts to systematically investigate the linkages between towns are far from common. When it is incorporated more centrally into analysis, interaction and especially its spatial structure is often implied from the spread of key innovations such as savings banks, building societies and telephone exchanges.[43] Although these provide important clues about the operation and dynamics of national urban hierarchies, they rely on the ability to read-off processes of spatial interaction from the diffusion patterns of the chosen innovation. At best, this approach gives a partial picture of the inter-relationships between places. By emphasising nationally significant innovations and counting their first appearance in a particular town, it privileges links to key centres within and beyond the locality, and especially those with the metropolis. Larger centres, which dominated transport and communication systems and (therefore) flows of information, almost inevitably received news of and adopted innovations earlier than smaller, more specialist or transport poor centres. It follows almost inevitably that such places benefited most from those innovations and experienced preferential growth.[44] Such analysis is fine up to a point, but under-emphasises the importance of the volume or strength of interaction and ignores the significance of other forms of inter-linkage. In particular, it plays down local and regional interactions, for instance those between specialist production locations or between production points and their market which, as we have already seen, did much to tie together the regional space economy. These spatial relationships must be approached through more direct analysis of real linkages between people and places.

There is no ideal source for analysing the patterning of these real contacts, partly because most tend to represent particular forms of interaction instead of the full range of economic, social and cultural ties that linked towns with their hinterlands and their neighbours, and partly because few are available across an entire region. Credit or supply networks can show how individuals or certain towns or industries were linked with wider webs of interaction, but they are extremely difficult to recreate across an entire region.[45] The analysis attempted here follows Wrightson and Levine and others in drawing on information on the location of executors to wills and signatories to administration bonds.[46] However, it develops a new, more systematic approach to both the data and the networks being examined. Data on the identity of executors can be obtained for the whole of the north west, but are problematical in terms of what they can tell us about general inter-place linkages.[47] In essence, there are two levels of difficulty. The first is understanding the precise nature of the inter-personal linkages recorded in wills and administration bonds, and the second is defining the relationship between these personal and social contact patterns and the wider nexus of inter-settlement linkages and economic interaction discussed earlier.

It is reasonable to assume that both executors and signatories to administration bonds would have known the deceased person quite well. After all, the executor was trusted to carry out the instructions of the will, a task which was often time-consuming and only infrequently repaid by monetary reward. Equally, people taking out administration bonds had enough interest in the estate of the deceased to make this legal process worthwhile. They would generally be the next of kin or the principal creditor, with one or two other interested parties acting as co-signatories. The obvious candidates for both jobs were family and friends or business associates, and practical considerations such as trustworthiness, proximity or literacy must have focused attention onto a small section of an individual's social network.[48] Indeed, Joseph Hudson –

a prominent lawyer and pamphleteer from the early nineteenth century – urged any testator to 'look around among his kindred and friends, for a man of intelligence, activity and honour, to become his executor'.[49] Thus, being asked to act as an executor was, at least in part, a mark of status: it sent out a very public signal of trust and confidence in an individual's ability to perform what were often complex duties.[50] It also implied and, *post mortem*, almost required quite close contact between the executor on the one hand, and the testator and/or his family on the other. Levine and Wrightson have argued that the appearance of individuals as beneficiaries of a will does not imply frequent interaction,[51] but both administrators and especially executors probably enjoyed far more regular, although by no means constant, intercourse with the testator. For any particular individual, wills and administration bonds probably record close friends and family who comprised a small proportion of much wider networks of personal contacts. As such, they could reflect a range of socio-economic relationships: marriage patterns, migration of the deceased or the executor (perhaps as apprentices, but also as traders or professionals), business networks, religious or social fraternities, or social links between neighbours or more distant friends.[52] Certainly, probate records should not be thought of as showing any single type of contact. Moreover, as each of these bases for contact would generate mutual interaction, the link existed between the two places rather than being uni-directional. For example, a person dying in Manchester and naming a friend in Bolton as an executor does not indicate a contact from Manchester to Bolton, but rather a link between the two towns.

Taken together, these individual contacts constitute a comprehensive dataset of inter-personal links within and beyond north-west England. They therefore paint a picture of 'local country' – the occupational, religious, kinship and neighbourhood networks through which people lived their daily lives – and illustrate the spatial ties which bound together this nexus.[53] Of course, even when combined these individual contact patterns are not perfect representations of the inter-linkages in a region since they do not equate directly with actual flows of goods, capital, services or information between centres. That said, there must have been some correspondence between these two sets of linkages. Indeed, personal friendship or family ties were frequently the cause or outcome of economic interaction, so that social and economic networks were inter-related, intertwined and mutually reinforcing. To divorce social from economic interaction and assume that the one was spatially or functionally unrelated to the other is to ignore both the deeply personal nature of much economic activity, and the reliance on kin, religious and other social groupings in the organisation of business and industry in the eighteenth century. For example, Everitt has observed of the seventeenth century that trade was significantly shaped by the 'channels of family influence and local connexion' that are reflected in the probate records. Moreover, his argument that 'there was little that was strictly impersonal about the inland commerce' of early modern England holds true for the eighteenth century as well.[54] Apprentices and journeymen were personally contracted to the craftsmen or retailer; supplies of raw materials and consignments of goods were sent by and to individual manufacturers and merchants; agents in distant towns (including London) were frequently family members; money was often raised from fellow non-conformists or Catholics; family businesses were often dispersed across several towns, but shared common financial support networks; and the emergence of a consumer society made shopping a social as much as economic activity.[55] Almost everywhere in manufacturing, trade and retailing, economic and social contacts overlapped and inter-linked: eating business lunches, entertaining clients and using 'contacts' are certainly not twentieth-century innovations. As Muldrew states, eighteenth-century tradesmen 'were able to use chains of association based on kinship or the trading connections established by friends or ... their former masters'.[56] The socio-economic links revealed in probate records may not represent the full range of ties which drew together the regional space economy, but the intense and multi-faceted relationships which they do reflect mean that the place of residence of executors provides an invaluable insight into which places were linked by broader economic ties. Furthermore, the number of such contacts should be broadly representative of the strength of links between centres. Naturally, great caution is needed and the data should not be over-interpreted, but they have the potential to illuminate the otherwise murky area of region-wide contact patterns. More importantly, not only do the patterns which they reveal match what little we know about regional integration at this time, they also tell us much about the processes underlying this geographical patterning.

From a sample of 2,606 probate records, a total of 5,091 place-specific contacts were found referring to 450 different places in the north west and throughout the country. These show a remarkable degree of closure in the region: three-quarters of the recorded contacts were with people living in the same town as the deceased (a consequence of wives, children and neighbours acting as executors and administrators) and just 4 per cent involved places outside north-west England. This underlines the integrity of Cheshire and southern Lancashire as a region, but tells us little about its spatial structure. More revealing in this regard are the range and destination of the 1,255 contacts with people living outside the home town of the deceased. Overall, inter-personal contacts were local: numbers remained roughly constant up to distances of about twenty miles after which they fell off rapidly. However, as Table 7.4 indicates, the spatial characteristics of rural and urban contacts differed considerably.

Table 7.4 *Contact patterns of the towns of north-west England,*
1701–60

	Urban		Rural	
	Number	Per cent	Number	Per cent
All contacts	589	47.0	666	53.0
< 5 miles	2	0.6	312	99.4
5–10 miles	117	43.7	151	56.3
11–20 miles	213	62.5	128	37.5
21–50 miles	158	71.8	62	28.2
> 50 miles	99	88.4	13	11.6
Extra-regional contacts	149	71.0	61	29.0
Bordering	61	54.0	52	46.0
London	56	100.0	0	0.0
Other	32	78.0	9	22.0

Source: Probate records, 1701–60.

Almost half of the links with rural locations were over distances of less than five miles, strong distance decay reducing contacts to a barely significant number over distances of fifty miles or more. Urban contacts took place over a markedly greater distance: almost three-quarters were with places over 10–50 miles distant. From this, it appears that town dwellers were strongly linked to their own hinterland, a variety of urban centres within the region and a smaller number of others some distance from the north west. This pattern was especially evident in extra-regional linkages where the importance of urban contacts rose with distance from the region. The areas immediately bordering the region embraced more than half of these contacts (links with north Lancashire, Yorkshire and Staffordshire being most numerous) but only 54 per cent were with towns. Further afield, over three-quarters of non-metropolitan contacts were with towns, including major centres such as Dublin (three contacts), Oxford (four), Nottingham (two), Bristol (two) and Norwich (two), and various lesser towns such as Darlington (two), Huntingdon (one), Buckingham (one). London itself accounted for one-quarter of the extra-regional contacts. The people and economy of north-west England were intimately and personally tied to the national urban system in which London appears especially influential, as Wrigley and Borsay have argued.[57] Despite the density of intra-regional linkages and the enormous friction of distance – London was still two days journey away in the 1750s[58] – these long-distance links were clearly important to the vitality of regional economy, society and culture as they provided links to new ideas, markets and value systems.

This dichotomy of personal contacts – local rural and distant urban – implies a dense heartland of linkages coupled with fewer distant contacts, comparable with both a Christallerian service economy and a proto-industrial urban network. Such structuration is confirmed by the number of towns and villages linked to centres in the urban system: the 589 urban contacts were concentrated into 82 towns (including those in the region) at an average of 7.2 contacts per settlement; 666 rural contacts were spread between 368 places – 1.8 per settlement. The concentration of longer-distance contacts onto relatively few urban centres is unsurprising. Towns were generally more widely spaced than villages and hamlets (causing concentration); they usually possessed larger populations (producing greater numbers); and they also housed the higher order functions which, according to Christaller, engendered journeys and hence contacts over longer distances.[59] Although the contact patterns of individual towns followed this general pattern, the regional web of linkages was dense and complex. 'Local' countryside was often on the opposite side of another town and 'distant' towns could lie on the far side of the region, with several other centres intervening between the two points of contact. The result was a tangle of linkages which reaffirms high levels of interaction, but apparently had little structure. However, some order can be discerned, first by categorising towns according to the nature of their individual contact patterns, and second by examining the inter-town linkages of the urban system.

Groupings within a detailed classification system can become somewhat artificial and are less helpful than broader differentiations based on the status and range of contacts. A distinction can be drawn here between those towns where the majority of contacts were with rural settlements and those where inter-urban links were more important (see Figure 7.8). The former was the larger group comprising towns, like Stockport, Burnley and Prescot, with strong links to their immediate hinterlands and to neighbouring larger towns, and those whose local rural contacts were paired with others to a broader range of urban centres, for example, Manchester, Rochdale and Wigan. These towns were located in the east and centre of the region, rural links being especially strong in eastern and southern-central Lancashire – a distribution which strongly reflects the concentration of rural industry. Indeed, it is notable that rural-urban contact was strongest in the small towns of north-east Lancashire which formed an important interface between rural production and urban marketing of textiles (see Chapter 4). For example, a Blackburn chapman called Alexander Mercer had executors in nearby Accrington and Walton-le-Dale; Richard Rothwell, a clothier from Haslingden, had ties with a dyer, a butcher and a yeoman in neighbouring Newchurch, and James Townsend, a Burnley draper, had links with a merchant in Spotland and a cloth-maker in Whalley as well as a kinsmen in Bury. These predominantly local links reflect

Figure 7.8 *Executorial contact patterns in north-west England, 1701–60: a simple typology*

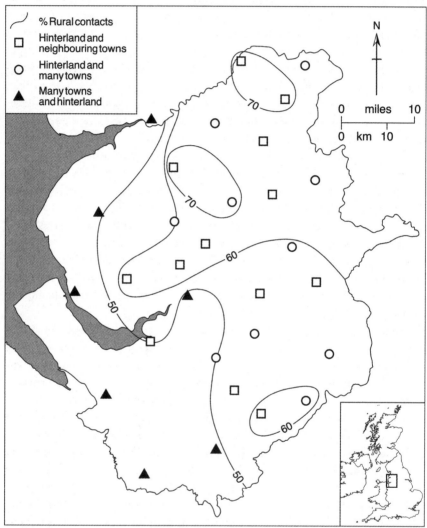

Source: Probate records, 1701–60.

the activities of such individuals in organising local (rural) production. James Anderton, for example, gave out wool to be carded, spun and woven in the villages and hamlets around Haslingden,[60] whilst Thomas Smalley employed a number of spinners around Blackburn. Such production relationships are reiterated in greater geographical detail by the pattern of loans, secured by personal bonds, made by Edward Davenport, a Stockport gentleman. These varied from

£5 to £200 and, typically of personal loans, appear to have been made as 'part of the reciprocal obligations of neighbourliness'.[61] Loans to three people in Manchester reflect the close links between the two towns, but the vast majority of bonds were with inhabitants of surrounding villages, chiefly in north-east Cheshire (Figure 7.9). The median distance over which Davenport made loans was just 2.7 miles. This underlines the importance of personal knowledge and trust in these financial arrangements and reaffirms both the significance of local country in framing such familiarity and, contra Estabrook, the strength of real interaction between town and country.[62] Equally significant is the greater range and geographical spread of urban links found in the larger textile centres: Rochdale, Macclesfield and especially Manchester. The inhabitants of these towns had links with the surrounding textile districts, but also with towns in west and central Lancashire, Yorkshire and the Midlands, and with London. Between them, the inhabitants of these three towns named forty-six such contacts. These contact patterns reflect the role of these towns as important gateways linking local manufacturing with wider supplies and markets. Manchester's particularly extensive web of linkages underlines the town's role in integrating local and regional space economies. As well as acting to spread growth stimuli to surrounding districts, it also helped to concentrate resources, capital and economic power into the town. This reinforced Manchester's position as a key centre of control in eighteenth-century north-west England and presaged its rise to national prominence in the nineteenth century.[63]

Those towns where urban links were more important in structuring contact patterns were principally found in the west of the region, away from the heartlands of manufacturing (Figure 7.8). Some, like Warrington, had important links to local industry and this was reflected in intense clustering of contacts around the town. Isaac Hall, a draper from the town, was typical of many, having contacts with nearby Lachford and Keckwick and in Warrington itself. All these towns, though, were linked to a range of urban centres. In the medium-sized centres, such as Nantwich and Warrington, contacts were largely restricted to the north west or neighbouring districts, with only a handful of individuals naming executors more than 50 miles distant. In Liverpool and Chester these longer-distance linkages were dominant. The inhabitants of the former had extensive contacts with west Yorkshire and London, and those in the latter enjoyed links with some 84 places in the north west, north Wales, the Midlands, Scotland, Ireland and, of course, London.[64] As with Manchester, these wide-ranging links helped to make both Liverpool and Chester centres of social, economic and cultural change, and at the same time concentrated development within the towns themselves.

Such variations in the contact patterns of individual towns related to differences in the economic function of the town and its relationship with local

Figure 7.9 *Bonds owing to Edward Davenport of Stockport*

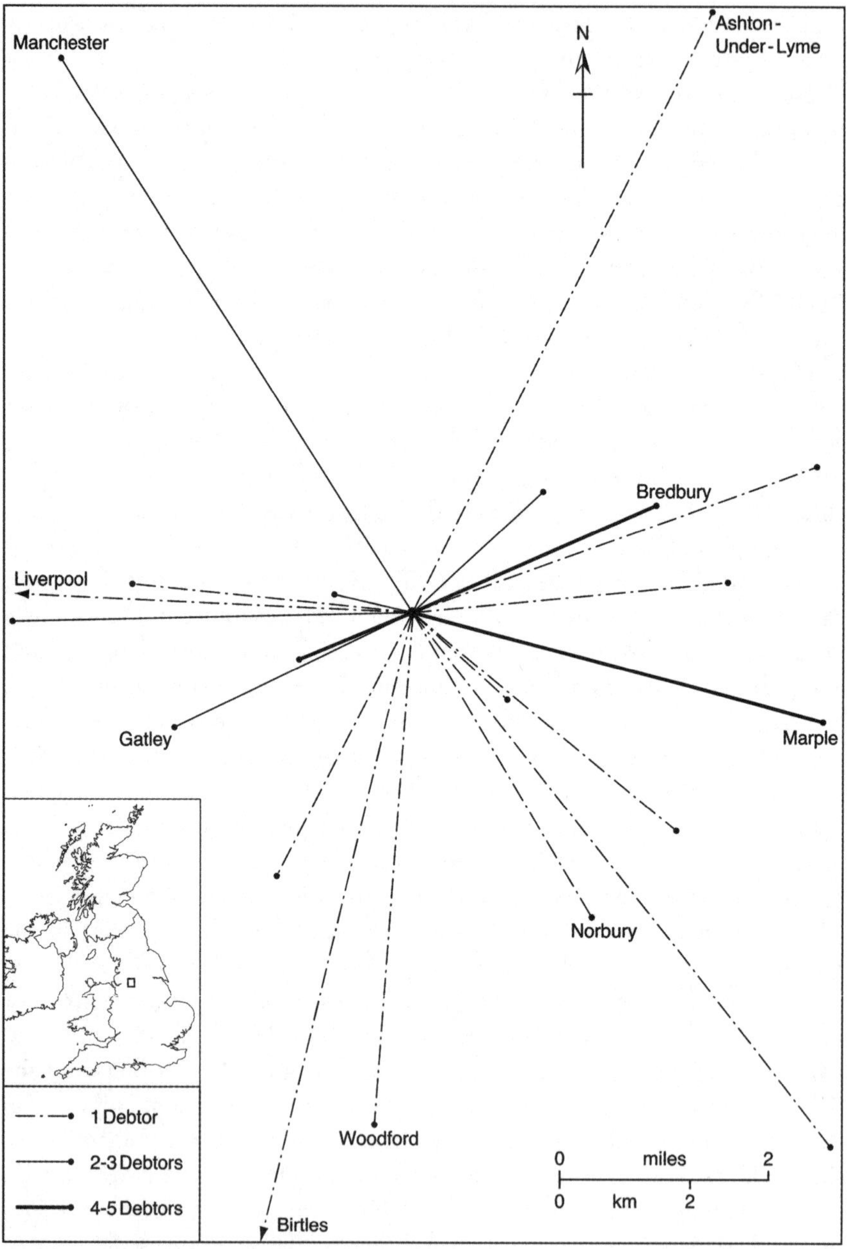

Source: CCA, WS 1717, Edward Davenport of Stockport.

Figure 7.10 *Interaction within the urban system of north-west England, 1701–60*

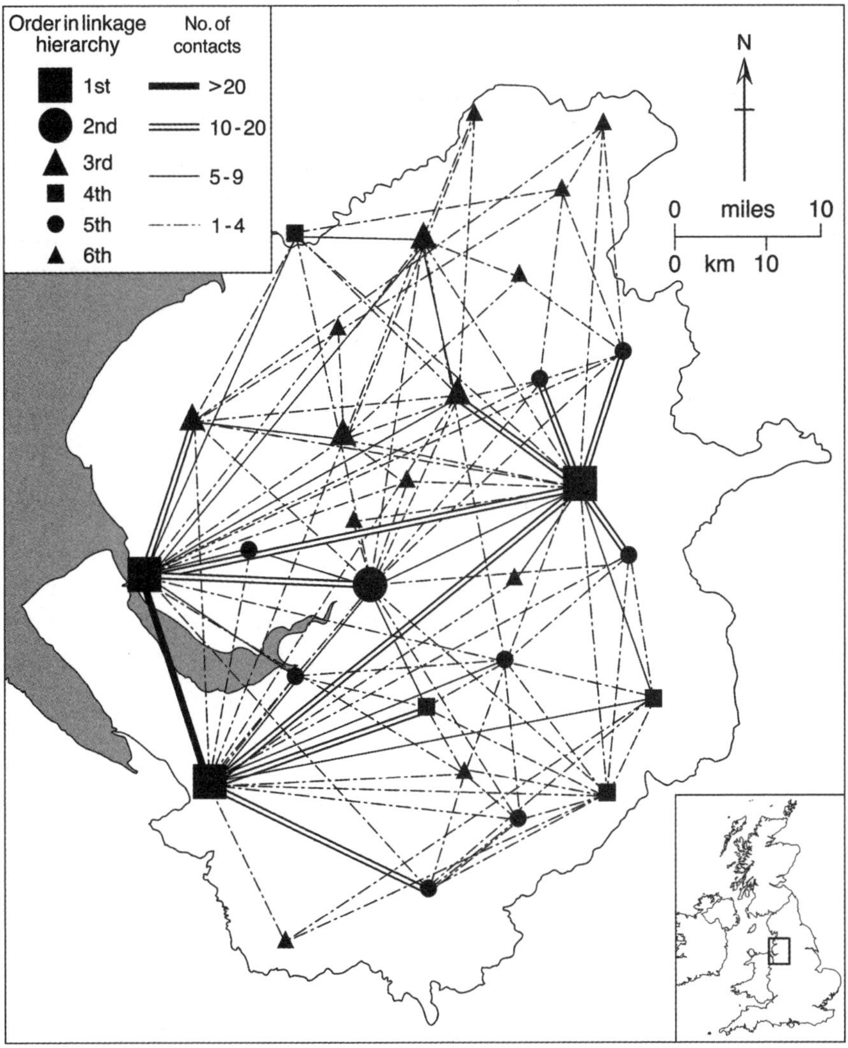

Source: Probate records, 1701–60.

rural activity. For example, manufacturing, particularly of textiles, appears to have engendered more urban-rural links than agriculture or a social/cultural urban function – a reflection of the numbers involved in each form of activity and the intensity and frequency of contact. However, different linkage patterns were also related to the position of the town within the urban system. Inter-action between towns was vital in the integration of the space economy:

without inter-linkaging, there would be limited diffusion of innovations or fashions; fragmented information and credit networks; and little trade. Local specialised economies could only exist as part of regionally and nationally integrated economic systems. As part of this broader process of spatial integration, interaction between centres was also important in shaping and structuring the urban system and (hence) the geography of local and regional development.[65] It helped to define local and regional centres and peripheries. Figure 7.10 shows the network of probate contacts between towns in the north west. There was a high level of interaction within the urban system and certainly a denser web of connections than that indicated by the coach and carrier services (Figure 7.6). This reflects the fact that transport services formed only one conduit of interaction, and tended to emphasise the major routes rather than highlighting the web of individual links. What is also apparent from Figure 7.10 is the different intensity of contact between different towns. For instance, there were seventy-one contacts between Liverpool, Manchester and Chester; forty-six between Manchester and its immediate neighbours; thirty-one between Liverpool and Wigan and Ormskirk; and a similar number linking Chester to Northwich and Nantwich. When viewed as a whole, these variations produced what was effectively a 'linkage hierarchy' in the north west.[66] This was dominated by the larger centres and especially Liverpool, Manchester and Chester but, unlike the transport system, it was not mapped onto the urban system as it stood in the early eighteenth century (Table 7.5).

Table 7.5 *Central place order and the 'linkage centrality' of towns in north-west England, 1701–60*

Central place rank	>2000	>1000	300–400	175–200	75–150	<50
1st	3	0	0	0	0	0
2nd	0	1	1	2	2	0
3rd	0	0	3	2	1	0
4th	0	0	0	0	4	3
5th	0	0	0	0	1	7

Source: Probate records, 1701–60.

The smaller towns generally had the weakest linkages, but Ormskirk and Blackburn possessed an unusually good range of contacts for their size, whereas several larger places (notably Nantwich, Stockport, Rochdale and Macclesfield) seem to have been relatively poorly linked despite their importance in the central place system. In reality, the strength of linkages was the product of a complex amalgam of factors, including transport nodality and geographical location; town size and function appear to have been secondary factors. Exceptionally strong and widespread probate contacts were found in Blackburn, Northwich and particularly Warrington, all of which were well placed in the region's transport networks. Conversely, apparently poor links were sometimes due to a town lying in the 'shadow' of a larger neighbour or having a large proportion of extra-regional contacts. Stockport and Bury, for example, were dominated by contacts to Manchester: they had many links, but with relatively few places, thus suppressing their 'linkage centrality'. Equally, places such as Nantwich, Macclesfield and Preston had strong links with places lying within their hinterlands, but outside the region, again reflecting the fact that certain towns were drawn into neighbouring urban systems as well as that of the north west.

In general, the strength and diversity of inter-town linkages was quite closely associated with urban dynamism. The best-linked towns grew at more than three times the rate of those with the poorest links and increased their share of the urban population of the region from one third to one half. Moreover, some of the towns growing unexpectedly slowly given their economic structure (Bury and Burnley in particular) appear quite low down the linkage hierarchy, whereas those with rapid growth (Ormskirk and perhaps Warrington) were especially well linked within the urban system. Interaction with other (economically specialised) places clearly formed an important growth stimulus in the eighteenth century. It constituted the basis of Pred's and Robson's arguments for the preferential growth of larger centres through their domination of the information, ideas and innovations flowing through the urban system.[67] Importantly, though, it was not necessarily large towns, but those which were best connected which enjoyed these advantages. Rather than inevitably leading to stability, interaction could produce differential growth, at least in the early eighteenth century. Interaction levels did not enjoy a straightforward relationship with urban growth, however. In the county, leisure and ecclesiastical town of Chester, residents possessed extensive links both inside and beyond the region, but the town grew relatively slowly. In contrast, Blackburn, Rochdale and especially Leigh grew very rapidly for their lowly position in the linkage hierarchy. That said, places like Chester were prosperous and economically vibrant at this time; relatively slow demographic growth reflected the absence of an activity offering large-scale employment (textiles, mining or a growing port) not a lack of dynamism in the urban economy.

It would be foolish to suggest that levels of interaction alone can explain the rate and pattern of urban growth. Much would depend on which centres a town was linked to – were they fast or slow growing, trading or servicing, specialist manufacturing or general craft-production centres? Much would also depend on the links enjoyed with dynamic rural areas. Towns could be closely tied to local rural production (Blackburn, Bolton or Manchester, for instance) or might be set within an area of rural manufacturing and have little to do with that production (Clitheroe or Wigan). Of course, close linkages could also bring heightened competition, so that not just proximity to but also interaction with more dynamic centres could drain the economic lifeblood from a town. Noble has highlighted competition as a growth-inhibiting factor for some towns in east Yorkshire, most notably Market Weighton and Pocklington, but there is limited evidence of this in the north west.[68] Although Bolton lost a large portion of its textile trading activity to Manchester merchants in the later eighteenth century, the town continued to prosper and grow. In general, links with the major dynamic centres appear to have engendered growth rather than crisis. These towns were all part of the same dynamic system. Growth stimuli passed up the urban hierarchy from a productive countryside and down from national demand channelled via the larger regional centres. In effect, there was both spread and backwash from the region's core centres. The strong expansion of the Lancashire towns with their close links to Liverpool and/or Manchester contrasts sharply with the more modest growth seen in the Cheshire towns which possessed fewer links with these geographical 'growth poles'. At the same time, though, Cheshire towns still enjoyed growth generally equal to or above that of the country as a whole. Their proximity to the dynamic centres of south Lancashire had a beneficial if muted effect on growth rates.[69]

Spatial integration was critical to both the pace and geography of regional and national development. The webs of interaction that integrated the spatial divisions of labour within north-west England were structured by and also served to (re-)structure the regional urban system. However, whilst the system as a whole was important in shaping patterns of interaction, the integrative processes were focused onto certain centres and functions which promoted growth and prosperity in local economies and effectively tied together the regional space. It is these key centres and functions that form the focus of the final section in this chapter.

Spatial integration: key centres and key functions

All models of urban systems highlight the role of certain centres in processes of spatial integration. In central place theory and Simmons's staple-export model, those at the top of the hierarchy are the most important; for Vance, it is the so-called gateway cities; in Lepetit's analysis, it is those places that dominate diffusion networks; and in industrial specialisation models, the focus is on major production locations.[70] In north-west England, the key centres were Liverpool, Manchester, Chester and, perhaps, Warrington. Without the links to and from these towns the urban system effectively split into two distinct sub-systems of interaction centred on south-east Cheshire and central Lancashire. Warrington was especially well linked with towns on the principal north–south road through the region and those involved in the mineral economy of south-west Lancashire and central Cheshire; its poorer contacts with the towns of north-east Lancashire are unsurprising as these were part of a different economic system. Liverpool had fewer apparent contacts with Cheshire towns (although its close ties with the salt industry at Northwich and Middlewich are not highlighted here[71]), but had links with towns throughout southern and central Lancashire, including several textile towns. As Langton argues, the port was not isolated in economic or interaction terms from the rest of the region.[72] Unsurprisingly, Manchester enjoyed the best links with the textile districts, although no direct contacts are recorded with Burnley or Haslingden. As was argued previously (see Chapter 4) these towns were principally linked with Manchester and the national economy through intermediate centres such as Colne, Blackburn and Rochdale. Significantly, these are places with which the smaller towns did have probate contacts. Manchester also had links with towns in east and central Cheshire, most notably Stockport, Macclesfield and Altrincham. Chester, though, possessed links with all Cheshire towns, making it central to the integration of the county. Its contacts in Lancashire were less extensive, being limited to the south of the county, but ranged from Bury in the east to Ormskirk in the west.

Of course, regional integration was more than simply joining Cheshire and Lancashire. It involved bringing together towns and their hinterlands (through production systems and central place services); linking a variety of local economies within the north-west, and binding the regional into the national and international economies. One way of assessing the wider integrative role of all towns in the north west is to identify those with a high proportion or number of contacts with settlements more than twenty miles distant. In broad terms, 'integrating' contacts (those over distances of 20–50 miles) would serve to draw together the north west and/or link it to neighbouring districts and economies; long-distance contacts (those more than 50 miles) are more indicative of links to national economy and society. In staple-export and Vancian mercantile systems internal integration would be dominated by hierarchical interaction over relatively short distances (i.e. comparatively few integrating contacts) whilst long-distance links were more numerous, but concentrated into large gateway cities (see Chapter 2). With greater industrial or service specialisation, increased interaction within the urban system – with large and small specialist centres having many integrating linkages – would be paired with relatively high external closure and few long-distance contacts.

As might be expected, Liverpool, Manchester and Chester accounted for nearly 60 per cent of the so-called integrating contacts. Of the smaller towns, Preston and Blackburn both had a very high proportion, if only a modest number, of contacts with settlements 20–50 miles away (Table 7.6). Blackburn was strongly linked to towns and villages in south-east Lancashire and north-east Cheshire, and thus played a significant part in linking the activities of north-east Lancashire with the core area of textile production. In contrast, Preston was characterised by contacts with towns north of the region, particularly Lancaster, and was correspondingly less involved in regional integration. The apparent lack of integrating links from Warrington can best be explained by its location in the centre of the region which meant that it, and other centrally located towns such as Northwich and Bolton, had a much higher proportion of contacts in the 10–20 miles range. These places were involved in the same integrating processes as Blackburn, Congleton and Macclesfield, but over shorter distances.

Table 7.6 *Towns in north-west England with a high proportion of executorial linkages over distances greater than 20 miles, 1701–60*

	Integrating contacts (20–50 miles)		Long-distance contacts (> 50 miles)	
	Number	% town's contacts	Number	% town's contacts
Chester	35	28.0	31	24.8
Liverpool	50	23.3	21	12.9
Manchester	46	25.0	15	8.2
Macclesfield	9	17.3	8	15.4
Preston	13	33.3	3	7.7
Nantwich	7	10.8	9	14.8
Blackburn	11	33.3	1	3.0
Warrington	7	10.5	5	7.5
Wigan	4	8.6	6	12.8
Others	37	7.8	13	2.7
Total	219		112	

Source: Probate records, 1701–60.

In general, the domination by Chester, Liverpool and Manchester of the integrating links seems to have pushed most other towns into a more locally-oriented integrative role, re-confirming a hierarchical structuring of the urban system. However, three things contradict this simple interpretation. The first problem is that these integrating contacts formed a much higher proportion of the total in all three towns than would be expected in centres which were at the top of integrated and hierarchical urban systems. Such links would generally be broken into stages, being passed between spatially and hierarchically intermediate centres on their way to these large towns. The second is that twenty-four towns possessed some links with settlements 20–50 miles distant; large towns by no means held a monopoly. This argues for Vancian point–point links between specialist centres. Third, it would be wrong to bracket Liverpool,

Chester and Manchester too closely together in distinguishing them from the lower order centres. As discussed in the previous section, they were characterised by very different contact patterns themselves: Liverpool and Chester were dominated by inter-urban contacts, whereas Manchester was more directly engaged in territorial interaction with its immediate and broader hinterland – it lacked the broad range of long-distance links seen in its neighbours to the west.

These same three towns dominated long-distance contacts, again accounting for around 60 per cent of such links (Table 7.6). They had contacts with a wide range of places throughout the British Isles, and effectively tied the north west into the national economy. London was the centre of this system and links with the metropolis were important in connecting the region to national economic, social and cultural processes. However, it did not dominate the extra-regional links of major integrating centres such as Liverpool, Manchester and Chester as they enjoyed extensive interaction with equivalent towns in other regions. This stands in contrast with the smaller centres where two-thirds of long-distance contacts were with London, reflecting their more limited role in broader spatial integration. This was largely mediated through regional centres or the capital, underlining the hierarchical structuring of interaction within the regional urban system. Contacts fed up through the hierarchy and hence out of the region, as well as coming in the opposite direction. Once more, though, it would be mistaken to look upon Chester, Liverpool and Manchester as identical in their role of extra-regional integration. Around one-half of Manchester's links were with London, reflecting the importance of the capital in the marketing of textiles.[73] Liverpool, in contrast, had little contact with London, and eleven of its twenty-one long-distance links were with manufacturing and commercial centres in Yorkshire, indicating the growing importance of the port to the industries of the West Riding.[74] Chester, however, had the most widespread and varied network of contacts; a great number were with London (reflecting the social and political importance of Chester), but links existed with centres throughout the country. If the network of towns in the north west was, indeed, drawn into a single functional system, then Chester appears to have been the principal gateway city. It was by no means overshadowed by its more commercially- or industrially-oriented neighbours, and was particularly important in integrating the region into the social and political life of the country.[75]

Although processes of spatial integration were largely focused onto the larger towns, this was due to the accumulation therein of a critical mass of manufacturing, commercial, social, cultural and political activities, rather than the possession of particular high order functions.[76] Of course, Liverpool's port was critical in its growing importance in internal and external spatial integration.

Much the same could be argued for the textile markets and trades of Manchester, and the cathedral, courts and social infrastructure in Chester. However, analysis of the individual occupations involved in integrating and long-distance links indicates a predominance of fairly common functions: the middling sort of merchants, professions and shopkeepers (Table 7.7).

Table 7.7 *Tertiary functions involved in integrating and long-distance links in north-west England, 1701–60*

	Integrating contacts (20–50 miles)		Long-distance contacts (> 50 miles)	
	Number	*Percentage*	*Number*	*Percentage*
General and textile dealing	103	47.0	57	50.9
Professionals	36	16.4	22	19.6
Food and drink dealing	48	21.9	9	8.0
Public service	22	10.0	12	10.7
Luxury dealing	5	2.3	8	7.1
Other	5	2.3	4	3.6
Total	219		112	

Source: Probate records, 1701–60.

The majority of medium-distance integrating links revealed in the probate records were made by general and textile dealers. These were the tradesmen who were most actively involved in industrial production, and in the buying and selling of the output of industry. Moreover, they often needed business associates in a number of different locations to allow them to feed into and draw out of what was often rural production. This arrangement is exemplified by the linen drapers and fustian manufacturers of Manchester and Bolton, and by Liverpool merchants. Henry Escricke of Bolton was a dealer in raw cotton, linen yarns and fustians.[77] His correspondence from the mid-eighteenth century details close interaction with outworkers and small-scale manufacturers in Manchester, Oldham, Middleton, Blackburn and Rochdale, to whom he put out cotton and yarn. In this manner he drew together the spatial divisions of labour within the fustian-producing districts, but his business activities also integrated these local specialisms with the wider regional economy. He made frequent visits to Liverpool and Lancaster to acquire supplies of raw cotton. Thus he wrote on 11 April 1738 that 'the yarn is safely arrived at Liverpool and I have a wagon promised to go the next week for it'. In the same letter he mentioned buying 'Jamacco Cotton' whilst at the Lancaster assizes. Similarly, Liverpool merchants did much to integrate specialist production locations in the north west and across the country. In addition to their vital role in enhancing the sophistication and importance of financial and credit systems, and in modernising transport infrastructure, they were central to the spatial integration of the regional economy.[78] Significantly, this was achieved predominantly through the urban system. Excluding overseas links, 93 per cent of Richard Houghton's debts outside Liverpool were with town dwellers. This was Vancian mercantile trade between commercial towns which were both the subject and object of regional and national integration. They formed the nodes on the nervous system of the national body.[79] Such trade did not generate a spatially contiguous market area linking town and country, but rather a larger and looser system of inter-urban contacts in which towns were gateways between specialised local and regional economies.

Of less importance than these merchants, but still significant to regional integration, were innkeepers, grocers and the like who might receive customers from a relatively wide area (particularly if it were a coaching inn), or supply country houses with wines, spirits and foodstuffs.[80] Such trades might draw on customers from a very large area. For example, John Bradshaw, a Chester innkeeper, had debts owed from as far afield as Dewsbury, Anglesey and Kilkenny, and numbered an earl, two lords and ladies, five baronets and eight esquires amongst his patrons. Unlike merchants, however, their businesses did not rely on having a range of distant contacts to articulate their trade and commerce. Both they and professional services are best conceptualised as central place functions, relying on visits from the surrounding area, rather than having agents spread throughout the region. These two groups, then, might build up a clientele from quite a wide area, but they had less impact on drawing the economy of the region together. One notable exception to this was provincial attorneys, who played an important role in integrating local and regional money markets. As Anderson argues, the nature of their legal work enabled them to 'delve deep into the private business affairs of a large number of people' giving valuable insights into their financial position 'while at the same time cultivating those personal contacts so essential, for instance, when raising a mortgage loan' or investing deposits.[81] Many attorneys in the north west were engaged in these areas, and two aspects of their activities will serve to illustrate the ways in which they facilitated spatial interaction in the region. The first is the broad geographical web of people making deposits and seeking loans. From his base in Liverpool, John Plumbe developed an extensive money-lending business which incorporated individuals across south-west Lancashire, including merchants, widows, gentlemen and manufacturers in Liverpool, an ironmaster in Birkacre, gentlemen in Prescot and Aughton, and a vicar in Walton. He not only effected interaction between these people and places, but also helped to stimulate local economic activity by providing investment capital for trade, industry and agriculture. The second aspect is less tangible, but no less important. In both their legal and money-lending activities, attorneys interacted closely with one another, thus bringing together their respective localities. John Plumbe had dealings with other attorneys in Liverpool, Prescot and Warrington. From Daniel Lawton, his contact in Prescot, the network stretched further to encompass attorneys in Wigan, Manchester and Ormskirk. This professional networking drew together the regional space and created lines of communication and flows of information.[82]

Turning to the longer-distance linkages, trading activities were again predominant. Many chapmen and merchants like Richard Bolton of Bury, John Lane of Chester and Richard Holland of Macclesfield possessed a range of long-distance links, sometimes with relations in similar trades in distant towns. This not only underlines the importance of long-distance trade to the economy of the north west and the integration of the national space economy, but also re-emphasises the close relationship between business and family networks.[83] For example, Henry Escricke, the Bolton merchant, had dealings with merchants in Leeds and Bristol, but enjoyed an especially close relationship with Messrs Wilson and Harrop in London, from whom he purchased raw materials and through whom he sold finished cloth.[84] Their correspondence was regular and often personal in nature, and Escricke's son lived with the London merchants whilst at school in the capital. On occasions, this son was called in to assist in his father's business dealings as when Escricke was seeking to settle his accounts with another London merchant, Mr Pearson. He wrote that 'I have a son goes to school in London. I'll order him to call upon you when I have your answer.'[85] Richard Houghton also had business partners throughout the country which tied Liverpool's port with national demand for New World goods such as sugar and tobacco (see Figure 7.5). Similarly, Daniel Peck was in regular correspondence with at least thirty-three individuals in ten different locations, but had especially close dealings with fellow merchants in Bristol, Dublin and London. Through these contacts he found markets for much of the coal, salt, lead and cheese that formed his staple exports from Chester.[86]

Professionals, with their fraternities and contacts, and luxury dealers with their London suppliers, were also significant in linking north-west England with the wider economy, society and culture. Attorneys such as John Plumbe and Daniel Lawton were tied to the London Inns of Court, both for their training and ongoing legal advice and a number named London attorneys or barristers as executors. Their money-lending activities also encouraged links with the metropolis and other major centres. In securing a mortgage for a local gentleman, Isaac Greene – another Liverpool-based attorney – dealt with a London goldsmith who was, in turn, acting for clients in the capital. John Plumbe, meanwhile, had a 'business rendezvous at the Exchange tavern in Dublin where he made payments for Liverpool merchants trading to that port'.[87] In a similar manner, mercers, drapers, furniture dealers and silversmiths were all keen to emphasise their metropolitan links, often effected through long-standing dealings with London shops and merchants. For example, Robert Wadds, a Nantwich linen draper, clearly enjoyed close business links with several linen drapers and mercers in the capital, three of whom acted as administrators to his estate. Later in the eighteenth century, Susannah Brown made frequent trips to London, visiting regular suppliers to supply her mercer's shop on Chester's Eastgate Street.[88] At a similar date, George Lowe, the Chester goldsmith and jeweller, advertised 'an extensive assortment of the most fashionable items' brought from London, Birmingham and Sheffield.[89] Viewed from the London end of such linkages, the law and especially trade were again important. Of the forty-seven Londoners appearing as executors or adminis-trators for whom occupations are known, eleven were gentry, five were professionals and twenty-two were engaged in trade.

In general, it was dealers and men of business with contacts, agents and business partners throughout the region and the country who linked one town to another in a web of interactions. That this type of integration was occurring across the country in the early eighteenth century seems very likely: certainly there was nothing in the functions effecting this spatial integration which was peculiar to the north west or even to large towns. Integration and development appear to have been less influenced by the indigenous qualities of the individual centres and more by the structure and functioning of the urban system as a whole. Economic, social and cultural activity throughout the region was fo-cused into key sites, which helped to induce growth in those places, as Pred, Robson and Krugman argue. As Rozman suggests, though, it also shaped the geography and pace of subsequent regional and national development.[90]

Conclusions: spatial integration and the urban system

Interaction between towns and the countryside, and between different towns and regions was central to the structure and growth of the English economy in the eighteenth century.[91] The three perspectives on spatial integration taken here have each emphasised the strong interaction taking place within north-west England and with the country as a whole. In the first perspective, it was seen that the market areas of particular towns comprised the principal forums for urban-rural interaction. The countryside drew on goods and services, capital and information in the central town; the towns tapped into the productive capacity of their hinterlands and attracted large numbers of temporary visitors and permanent migrants. That smaller market areas were nested within larger ones is a commonplace, but similar processes and patterns occurred for different goods and services. Certain functions had essentially local markets whilst others, especially merchants, traded over larger areas and were important in wider processes of regional and national integration. The second approach underlined the importance of transport to trade: it formed the key vector for spatial interaction. Goods, people, information and capital were all moved through space along physical transport routes: a reality to which Defoe and his contemporaries were very much alive, but which can often escape us in an age of mass telecommunication. As Lepetit argues, transport networks in the north west, as those elsewhere, were largely moulded on the pre-existing urban hierarchy, but they still had an important bearing on the integration of the regional space economy.[92] Transport nodes and urban centres were generally one and the same so that interaction and economic development were closely structured around the urban system and, within the north west, particularly around Liverpool, Manchester and Chester. These were the principal towns of the region and the heads of three contrasting economic regimes. As the third perspective demonstrated, they were also the major foci of contact patterns and interaction, and were instrumental in the effective integration of the regional urban and economic systems. They were not only pre-eminent in contacts with more distant places both within the north west and in the wider national economy, but also dominated the trading functions which did much to integrate the regional space.

The position of these three towns at the head of an integrated system does not preclude the fact that the contact patterns of these towns and the sub-regional economies in which they were situated were very different from one another. Links with rural areas dominated the contact patterns of the east Lancashire textile towns, but there also appears to have been a distinctly hierarchical structuring to these linkages. The strong links which Haslingden, Leigh, Bury, Burnley and Bolton possessed with their hinterlands and with larger towns nearby fits well with a role as the basic interfaces between rural and urban textiles production, as described by Wadsworth and Mann.[93] Colne, Blackburn and Rochdale had contacts with towns both up and down the hierarchy which again matches their intermediate position between the smaller centres and Manchester – the focus of and principal gateway for this textiles economy. Although direct comparisons with models of interaction are rather simplistic, these contact patterns resemble the interaction network of a staple-export or proto-industrial system: local contacts between town and country were complemented by links up the hierarchy to the principal town which formed the focus for extra-regional contacts.[94] This neat interpretation of an apparently hierarchical urban system quickly runs into a number of problems. Several towns possessed links with distant as well as local rural areas: Rochdale and Blackburn had links with villages more than 20 miles distant, whilst 'the Manchester fustian manufacturers cast their net wider ... in the country around Bolton and Blackburn, where they competed for labour with the local manufacturers'.[95] Moreover, Colne and Rochdale had direct links with places outside the region (including London)[96] and many other towns had contacts with Chester or Liverpool, again reflecting wider economic connections and undermining the hierarchical structure.

Despite the importance of salt, silk, hat-making and so on, agriculture remained the principal economic activity in much of eighteenth-century Cheshire and many towns were essentially social centres or service towns (see Chapter 6). To an extent, the linkage patterns reflect this in a simplified hierarchical system in which all centres had direct contacts with Chester as the county town and main market centre.[97] However, Chester also had direct links with a number villages up to 20 miles away, whilst Nantwich and Macclesfield possessed long-distance urban contacts (mostly with London), short-circuiting the putative hierarchical system from either end.[98] Similarly, several towns in east Cheshire were linked to Manchester whilst those in the north of the county had ties with Warrington and Liverpool, again breaking the monopoly of Chester on links out of this agricultural area. More significant, given the long-term trend away from Chester in both the urban system and regional economy, there was a large amount of contact between the smaller towns; in part a response to the emerging and complex pattern of local specialisation in east and central Cheshire.

Detailed local specialisation also characterised the mineral economy of south-west and central Lancashire and central Cheshire, suggesting a greater proportion of direct contact between specialist centres. Despite the strong influence of Liverpool in the area, there were relatively high levels of interaction between Wigan, Warrington, Prescot and Frodsham. This intensity is underlined by the strong extra-regional ties held by Liverpool, Warrington, Preston and Wigan, offering several points of exit and entry from the system and reducing the domination by a single 'gateway city' seen in the other two systems. That said, areal contacts were of overwhelming importance in several towns (including Wigan), making it difficult to conceptualise the system as being entirely comprised of a series of point–point linkages. Furthermore, both Warrington and Wigan were increasingly drawn into the textiles economy of eastern Lancashire as well as the more traditional metalworking, so that two potentially very different economic and urban systems were superimposed on one another.[99]

Spatial divisions of labour were, of necessity, integrated into wider economic structures. Local specialisms in north-west England interacted positively and increasingly closely: the textile economy spread west and north in Lancashire; Liverpool was ever more involved in salt production in central Cheshire and became increasingly important in supplying raw materials to and exporting products from the textile districts; many settlements in east Cheshire developed

Figure 7.11 *Spatial structure of the economy of north-west England*

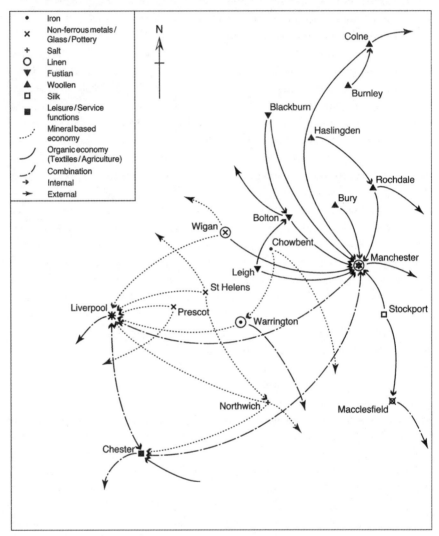

textile industries in the late eighteenth century (most obviously in the parishes around Stockport, but also in Altrincham and Knutsford); and agricultural produce from Cheshire was sold on Liverpool and Manchester markets. By the early nineteenth century, many towns and districts were characterised by strong and mutually reinforcing specialisations. The spatial integration of these divisions of labour was realised through interaction structured around the regional urban system. Significantly, later development generally took place within the geographical framework established by the urban system in the early eighteenth century. Although several new towns emerged in the region, only the growth of Ellesmere Port and Birkenhead caused any fundamental shift in the geography and structure of the regional space economy.

In the eighteenth century, spatial interaction was locally differentiated – it varied in accordance with resource base, product type, manufacturing system and cultural norms – but it was effective at a region-wide and indeed nation-wide scale, principally through the activities of individuals in the larger towns. These places frequently stood at the head of hierarchically structured sub-regional systems: a point emphasised by the analysis offered in Chapters 4 and 5. Yet regional integration was much more than a series of semi-independent hierarchical structures linked through gateway cities. As Figure 7.11 illustrates, the regional economy was integrated by a complex series of linkages that ran between as well as within local specialist systems. Small and large towns were inter-connected and local production and consumption was linked into wider economies. The interaction that articulated specialisation was structured around the regional urban system as a whole so that local town–country links were complemented by regional and extra-regional links between towns.

Notes

1 Faucher, Manchester in 1844, p. 15.
2 Lepetit, *Urban System*, pp. 97 and 349–50.
3 See Pollard, *European Economic Integration*; Berend and Ranki, *European Periphery and Industrialization*.
4 See, for example, Rodgers, 'Market areas of Preston'; Estabrook, *Urbane and Rustic England*.
5 Particularly good examples of this approach are: Noble, 'Regional urban System'; Lepetit, *Urban system*, pp. 350–75.
6 Lepetit, *Urban System*, pp. 375–94; Robson, *Urban Growth*, pp. 217–24; Pred, *City Systems*, pp. 20–2 and 33–71.
7 Gregory, 'Geographies of industrialization', pp. 381; Lepetit, *Urban System*, pp. 299–347; Pawson, *Transport and Economy*, pp. 3–14.
8 Noble, 'Regional urban system', pp. 13–14; Langton, 'Liverpool', pp. 3–15.
9 Everitt, 'Agricultural produce', p. 498.
10 Patten, *English Towns*, p. 217; Noble, 'Regional urban system', pp. 18–19.
11 Rodgers, 'Market areas of Preston', pp. 51–3.
12 Quoted in Sharpe-Francis, 'Highway from Preston into the Fylde', p. 33; Rodgers, 'Market areas of Preston', p. 51.
13 Patten, *English Towns*, pp. 217–20; Beavon, *Central Place Theory*, pp. 25–6.
14 Mitchell, 'Urban retailing', pp. 262–3.
15 Blundell, 'The Great Diurnal of Nicholas Blundell', *passim*.
16 Cox, *Compete Tradesman*, pp. 122, 136 and 208.
17 See Addy, 'Diary of Henry Prescott'.
18 Cox, *Complete Tradesman*, pp. 38–76.
19 Mitchell, 'Urban retailing', pp. 261–3.

20 Duggan, *Ormskirk*, p. 163; *UBD*, volume 3, p. 592.

21 Kennett, *Georgian Chester*, pp. 20–1.

22 See Schwarz, 'North-east Lancashire'; King, 'Rossendale'; Wyatt, 'Nantwich and Wybunbury'.

23 CCA, CR 352/1 Letter Book of Daniel Peck.

24 Lepetit, *Urban System*, p. 299; Noble, 'Regional urban system', p. 18; Gregory, 'Geographies of industrialization', p. 381; Turnbull, 'Provincial road carrying', p. 17.

25 The approach taken and relationships revealed reflect those of Lepetit, *Urban System*, pp. 308–13.

26 Nodality scores ranged from one (Malpas) to fourteen (Manchester). There is clearly a problem here of under-emphasising the nodality of Liverpool, for example, since its many services were channelled along just three routes, through Ormskirk, Prescot and (via ferry) Chester. However, including the number of services as well as the number of routes to give an overall 'service centrality' for each town, does much to compensate for this problem.

27 Lepetit, *Urban System*, p. 347. For a sustained argument for the positive impact of transport on industrial and urban development see: Berend and Ranki, *European Periphery and Industrialization*, pp. 91–100.

28 Langton, *Geographical Change*, pp. 93 and 154.

29 Corfield, 'Small towns', p. 125.

30 Ellis, *Georgian Town*, p. 38.

31 *UBD*, volume 3, pp. 635–730; *UBD*, volume 2, pp. 692–727.

32 Gregory, 'Geographies of industrialization', p. 379; Borsay, *Urban Renaissance*, pp. 180 and 293–4.

33 There were undoubtedly more carrier services visiting Chester than those appearing in the *UBD*, but the importance of coach services relative to that seen in other towns is clear and unequivocal.

34 Langton, 'Liverpool', p. 7. Canals in east Lancashire developed rapidly from the 1780s: see Hadfield and Biddle, *Canals of North-west England*, pp. 243–335.

35 Pred, *City Systems*, pp. 33–78; Ogborn, *Spaces of Modernity*, pp. 7–8 and 203–11.

36 Wadsworth, 'Rochdale woollen trade'; Rodgers, 'Market areas of Preston', pp. 51–3.

37 Schwarz, 'North-east Lancashire', pp. 64–5; Wadsworth and Mann, *Cotton Trade*, pp. 43–5 and 78–87.

38 *UBD*, volume 4, pp. 755–61.

39 Lepetit, *Urban System*, pp. 317 and 347; Noble, 'Regional urban system', p. 18.

40 Richardson, *Regional Growth Theory*, pp. 175–96; Pred, *City Systems*, pp. 78–92; Lepetit, *Urban System*, pp. 337 and 347; Krugman, *Geography and Trade*, pp. 24 and 49–54.

41 Massey, *Spatial Divisions of Labour*, pp. 117–19; Krugman, *Development*, pp. 46–52.

42 Lepetit, *Urban System*, pp. 346–7.

43 Lepetit, *Urban System*, pp. 375–89; Robson, *Urban Growth*, pp. 143–84.

44 See Robson, *Urban Growth*, pp. 214–28; Pred, *City Systems*, pp. 33–78.

45 Zell, 'Credit in the woollen industry', pp. 667–9; Holderness, 'Credit in English rural society'; Muldrew, *Economy of Obligation*, especially pp. 186–94.

46 Wrightson and Levine, *Poverty and Piety*, pp. 99–103; Lane, 'An industrialising town'.

47 For a detailed discussion of these problems, see Stobart, 'Social and geographical contexts of property transmission', pp. 110–12.

48 Cox and Cox, 'Probate 1500–1800', pp. 15–34.

49 Hudson, *Plain Directions*, p. 70. See also, Owens, 'Duty and obligation'.

50 Owens 'Duty and obligation', p. 98–104; D'Cruze, 'The middling sort', pp. 181–2.

51 Levine and Wrightson, *Making of an Industrial Society*, p. 330.

52 These various causes of social interaction are discussed in Stone, *Family, Sex and Marriage*, pp. 411–16; Wrightson, 'Kinship in an English village'; Stobart, 'Social and geographical contexts of property transmission', pp. 117–23.

53 For a critical review of the concept of local country see King, 'Migrants at the margin?', pp. 285–6.

54 Everitt, *Change in the Provinces*, p. 29.

55 Corfield, *English Towns*, pp. 88–9 and 126–8; Wadsworth and Mann, *Cotton Trade*, pp. 29–36; Langton, 'Lancashire Catholicism', p. 91; Walton, *Lancashire*, pp. 91–5; D'Cruze, 'The middling sort', p. 187; Glennie and Thrift, 'Consumption spaces', pp. 26–31; Cox, *Complete Tradesman*, pp. 146–63.

56 Muldrew, *Economy of Obligation*, p. 191.

57 See Wrigley 'London's importance'; Borsay, 'The London connection'.

58 Bagwell, *Transport Revolution*, p. 42.

59 Marshall, *Location of Service Towns*, pp. 7–8.

60 Tupling, *Rossendale*, p. 188.

61 Muldrew, *Economy of Obligation*, p. 129.

62 See Muldrew, *Economy of Obligation*, pp. 153–86; Wrightson and Levine, *Poverty and Piety*, pp. 73–82.

63 See Baines, *Liverpool*, p. 302; Faucher, *Manchester in 1844*, p. 15.

64 For more detailed analysis of Chester's extra-regional links, see Stobart, 'County, town and country', pp. 178–86.

65 These ideas are central to the arguments of Pred, *City Systems*; Robson, *Urban Growth*; de Vries, *European Urbanization*.

66 The position of town within the hierarchy was given by multiplying its total number of contacts by the number of places within the urban system to which it was linked.

67 Pred, *City Systems*, pp. 33–78; Robson, *Urban Growth*, pp. 186–213.

68 Noble, 'Regional urban system', p. 19.

69 Langton, 'Urban growth', figures 14.2 and 14.3.

70 See Simmons, 'Urban system'; Vance, *Merchant's World*, Lepetit, *Urban System*. These models are discussed more fully in Chapter 2.

71 See Barker, 'Lancashire coal'.

72 Langton, 'Liverpool', pp. 1 and 7.

73 Despite the significance of fairs and travellers in the distribution of Manchester-wares, links to partners in London were vital to the success of much textiles manufacturing in the Manchester area; Wadsworth and Mann, *Cotton Trade*, pp. 236–40.

74 The need for improved links to Liverpool lay behind several canal schemes in the late eighteenth and early nineteenth centuries: Langton, 'Liverpool', pp. 3–7; Hadfield and Biddle, *Canals of North-west England*, pp. 85–181.

75 Stobart, 'County, town and country', pp. 187–93.

76 For a fuller discussion of these processes of accumulation and agglomeration, see Krugman, *Geography and Trade*, pp. 28–35 and 49–52.

77 Escricke's activities are described in detail in Wadsworth and Mann, *Cotton Trade*, pp. 263–72.

78 Wadsworth and Mann, *Cotton Trade*, p. 268; Price, 'What did merchants do?', pp. 278–84.

79 See, for example, Vance, *Merchant's World*, pp. 1–12; Lepetit, *Urban System*, pp. 308–13; Amin and Graham, 'Cities of connection', pp. 8–10.

80 Mitchell, 'Urban retailing', pp. 262–3.

81 Anderson, 'Early capital market', p. 67.

82 See Anderson, 'Early capital market', pp. 59–69.

83 Muldrew, *Economy of Obligation*, pp. 188–91.

84 See Wadsworth and Mann, *Cotton Trade*, pp. 263–72.

85 Wadsworth and Mann, *Cotton Trade*, p. 271.

86 CCA, CR 352/1 Letter Book of Daniel Peck.

87 Anderson, 'Early capital market', pp. 54–5 and 58.

88 Mass Observation, *Browns and Chester*, pp. 18–37. See also, Stobart, 'Shopping streets', pp. 10–15; Cox, *Complete Tradesman*, pp. 180–9.

89 *Chester Courant*, 1 July 1794.

90 Rozman, 'Urban networks'.

91 Gregory, 'Geographies of industrialization', pp. 377–84; Stobart, 'Geography and industrialization', pp. 691–2.

92 Lepetit, *Urban System*, p. 347.

93 Wadsworth and Mann, *Cotton Trade*, pp. 170–83, 261–73 and 314–24.

94 Simmons, 'Urban system', pp. 62–8.

95 Wadsworth and Mann, *Cotton Trade*, p. 251.

96 Swain, *Industry*, p. 146; Tupling, *Rossendale*, pp. 185–6; Wadsworth and Mann, *Cotton Trade*, pp. 261–70.

97 Mitchell, 'Urban retailing', pp. 270–3.

98 The long-distance trading of the wealthy Macclesfield chapmen is charted in Spufford, *Great Reclothing*, especially p. 43.

99 Walton, 'Proto-industrialisation', p. 51.

8

Conclusions: the integration of local, regional, national and international economies

It is impossible to contemplate the progress of manufactures in Great Britain within the last thirty years without wonder and astonishment'.[1]

Many of the processes of modernisation occurring in Britain during the eighteenth century had both their causes and consequences at the regional level. Regional growth was not simply a reflection of spatially and sectorally specific development, it was crucial to Britain's emergence as the first industrial nation.[2] For Pollard, it was the existence of 'relatively limited regions' which spawned contained economies wherein 'new ideas could reverberate and gain reinforcing strength'.[3] In other words, the early industrial regions were hothouses of development, nurturing growth which subsequently spread elsewhere in Britain, Europe and throughout the world. Furthermore, Dunford argues, the industrial revolution was not only a regionally variable phenomenon across Europe, the regional and local patterns of industry and commerce were instrumental in structuring that revolution. They both reflected and shaped Massey's 'layers of investment' – accretions of labour skills, credit and marketing networks, entrepreneurial dynamism and so on.[4] Notwithstanding the national and international impacts of industrialisation, then, the heartlands of the industrial revolution remained relatively fixed in space and often highly specialised at the local and regional level. Indeed, it was growing internal integration of specialised regions such as the west Midlands, west Yorkshire and north-west England that created the critical mass of manufacturing, service and transport activities upon which sustained development was dependent.[5] As Langton puts it: 'the initiating regions derive stimulus from some particular concatenation of economic circumstances existing within them and from linkages with other growing regions'.[6] These same linkages also tied local, regional, national and international economies into increasingly inter-dependent systems of production, distribution and consumption.

The early development of these kinds of relationships in the north west and elsewhere meant that the industrial region was vital to national economic development not only in the late eighteenth and nineteenth centuries, as Hudson and others have argued, but also in the early eighteenth century. During this period, many industrial regions were still emerging and their manufacturing and service industries as well as their spatial structures, inter-dependencies and integration were in a state of flux.[7] Analysis of north-west England during the early industrial period has thus allowed us to explore the crucial formative processes and geographies of regional economic growth. It has also provided insights into national development and, in particular, the relationship between specialisation and integration. In many ways, this region formed a microcosm of Britain as a whole: the juxtapositioning of industrial regions and the mutual interaction between them which did much to stimulate wider industrialisation in the nineteenth century was evident within the north west a century earlier.[8] The emergence of a coherent regional identity and consciousness was perhaps only beginning in the middle decades of the eighteenth century, but, as an economic region, north-west England was already an integrated and dynamic unit.[9] The region was characterised by a range of localised but dynamic manufacturing industries, several of which were intimately tied to global supplies and demands. Its service sector was strong and expanding, stimulating new patterns of demand, integrating regional production and linking it to the national and international economy. As a consequence, the growth of its constituent parts was strong and mutual, benefiting from 'complementary relationships of co-operative activity'.[10] In short, the spatial and functional integration of local and regional specialisations which characterised early industrialisation did much to structure the geography and pace of subsequent development.

Towns were central to both specialisation and integration, and were instrumental in the structure and dynamic of the regional economy, not so much as individual places, but rather as nodes on networks of interaction. Wrigley has long argued that they were not parasites on a productive countryside as simplistic readings of proto-industrialisation theory suggest,[11] and it is clear that manufacturing and a range of other wealth-generating activities remained strong in towns: urban centres grew at twice the rate of their hinterlands. This growth was not restricted to 'new' towns or to non-corporate towns. Indeed, many such places were by-passed by this general expansion, at least until the late eighteenth century. Chorley and Bury, for example grew strongly only from the 1770s, whilst Sandbach and Middlewich amongst others remained small market towns. Similarly, the development of the old borough towns, which, according to conventional wisdom, suffered badly as a result of the restrictive practices of their guilds and corporations, was very mixed. Liverpool and Preston grew rapidly; Chester and Congleton relatively slowly;

Macclesfield and Wigan expanded steadily during the early eighteenth century and then experienced strong growth in the last few decades of the century. This paralleled the highly variable growth rates of corporate towns across the country: York and Exeter, for example, grew very slowly in the eighteenth century; Bristol, Newcastle and Nottingham more strongly. If the rate of growth was variable, then so too was the role of the corporations in encouraging local economic development. In Liverpool the corporation was very active in making the extensive improvements to the docks which were vital to the emergence of the town as the second port of the country.[12] Chester's assembly was enthusiastic, if sporadic, in its attempts to promote industrial and commercial development in the town, but success, as with the Chester Canal, was often limited. Most frequently, corporate status was largely neutral. We have seen, for example, that the decline of Wigan's traditional industries had more to do with fashion than restrictive practices; its subsequent re-emergence as a coal, iron and cotton town came through the accretion of these industries around the edge of the town rather than through strong centralised activity.

Overall, economic functions and fortunes varied greatly across the region, so that different places were characterised by very different sets of activities and very different growth rates. Manufacturing industry was located in certain favoured locations, congregating around local resource sites, including coalpits and saltworks, rivers and fast-flowing streams, agricultural supplies, and sources of skilled labour. These are the principal factors in classic models of industrial location and regional development from Weber to Richardson to Massey.[13] Whilst a wide variety of resources led to a diverse set of spatial patterns of industrial organisation, the importance of these natural and human resources was evident in all. That said, several of the more significant industries depended upon supplies of raw materials from outside the region as much as locally available resources. For example, wool came from Ireland and the Midlands; flax from Ireland and the Baltic; silk from the Orient; cotton from the Levant and the West Indies; iron from Wales, Shropshire and Cheshire; and copper and tin from Cornwall.[14] These were generally channelled into the north west through towns, often either Liverpool or Manchester, but also Warrington, Chester, Rochdale, Bolton, Macclesfield and Wigan. Indeed, almost all towns with significant commercial and manufacturing sectors were involved in linking local demand with distant supplies of raw materials, their merchants and manufacturers frequently operating via agents in London. In many cases, and particularly in the textile industries of eastern and central Lancashire, these same individuals also controlled supplies of capital and credit to rural or small-town workers, thus reinforcing the centrality of towns to much of the region's manufacturing.

The pivotal role of towns in the functioning of many industries in the north west often led to the agglomeration of manufacturing and service activities – the localisation of industry theorised by Marshall and, more recently, Krugman.[15] This generated a critical mass of interacting and mutually reinforcing functions at the local, district and regional level. It was seen most clearly in the clustering of textile manufacturing, finishing and dealing, and the subsequent emergence of metalworking, engineering and chemicals production and financial and professional services in Manchester. Despite its isolation from the principal raw materials, the town became the world centre for cotton production in the nineteenth century.[16] Similar agglomerations were seen elsewhere in the region, including Liverpool, at least up to the 1790s, and subsequently around Wigan, Warrington, Northwich and what became St Helens. Such congregation of economic activity mirrored the broader clustering of development into industrial regions during the eighteenth and nineteenth centuries. In this way, Langton argues, 'the industrial revolution can disappear from national statistical series, but still be dazzlingly bright in widely scattered regional patches of massive urban growth' and economic development.[17] We therefore need to fundamentally rethink our conceptualisation of economic development. The methodologies of macro-economics can be deployed to measure the degree of economic change spatially – say region by region – and thus demonstrate relative rates of growth in different places. But such an approach fails to capture the dynamism, the inter-connectedness and the webs that constituted and structured urban and regional economic systems. In order to appreciate the magnitude and impact of socio-economic change, we need to be attentive and sensitive to its geographies: its location and scale; the processes of relative growth and decline; but most importantly the evolving networks of relationship, inter-dependency and linkage which it reflected and recreated.

The industrial revolution was a time of complex changes in the urban system and economic structure of Great Britain, but the transformation of the national economy was clearly presaged and shaped by processes under way in the early eighteenth century within key regions. In places like north-west England, as this study has demonstrated, the economy and society were changing in ways that were truly revolutionary in the half century up to 1760. How can we best understand these changes? What factors lay behind the rapid demographic and economic growth of certain regions and certain towns during this period? Central to the development seen in north-west England and other industrial regions was the presence of several industries with expanding regional, national and world markets for their produce. These were typified by the nascent cotton industry, but woollen textiles, coal, salt, ferrous and non-ferrous metalworking, agricultural produce and the processing of tropical goods (and later engineering and chemicals industries) were also important. Indeed, it was in the diversity of the regional economy that much of its dynamism was to be found: in regions with a more limited range of industries – south Wales, Shropshire or Cornwall, for example – there was no critical mass of inter-related industries and growth often proved more difficult to sustain over the long term.[18] However, the marked de-industrialisation of the Weald in the seventeenth century demonstrates that economic diversity was not, in itself, sufficient to project a regional or, by extension, a national economy into sustained growth.[19] In addition to important sociocultural limitations, what was critical in the decline of the Weald, significant in the nineteenth-century de-industrialisation of Shropshire and Cornwall, and vital to strong industrial growth in the north west was effective economic and spatial integration and, ultimately, the presence of a dynamic and interactive urban system. If, as Wrigley argues, functional specialisation was the 'gateway to economic improvement' in early industrial Britain, then integration through developing communication and urban systems held the key to that gate. In the absence of a dynamic and interacting network of towns, there could be no critical mass of industries, no sustained economic development and ultimately, Deacon argues, little cohesive identity as an industrial region.[20]

Towns were important and often very specialised production locations, but were also centres of trade, consumption and integration. They linked local manufactures to distant markets and supplied their own workforces and those of their hinterlands with a range of goods and services. As de Vries argues, the growing commercialisation of the household and local economies which this entailed was vital in stimulating domestic demand for industrial products. In this way, towns were the principal agents of social and cultural change in the region, helping to spread new patterns of consumption which acted to stimulate trade and manufacturing alike.[21] In all these functions, we need to view towns not simply as isolated specialised economies, but as part of a system which included hinterlands and neighbouring urban centres, and other towns and cities across the country and the world.[22] The links which ran between these constituents were formed by urban service industries, particularly transport, finance and commercial activities. Their importance echoes Hudson's argument that 'the growth of specialised mercantile and financial services within the dominant regions served to increase the external economies and significantly to reduce both intra-regional and inter-regional transaction costs'.[23] Effective spatial integration was vital to regional and national economic development. Within north-west England, scattered and diverse production was integrated through and in towns, which were thus vital in articulating spatial divisions of labour and the operation of competitive advantage. In other words, 'growth of functional specialisation necessarily involves increased exchange of goods and services pulsing through a network which is also an urban hierarchy'.[24] Importantly, the ways in which local specialities were being drawn together in the early eighteenth century to form a coherent regional economy parallel the integration of Britain's industrial regions later in the century.

High levels of inter-dependence and interaction within the regional urban system indicate that the economy of north-west England was highly integrated. They also suggest that the geography and development of local, regional, national and even international economies were closely linked to the structure of the urban system. This structure, though, was neither uniform nor simple; nor was it unchanging. Just as the regional urban system affected economic growth, resource exploitation, communication networks and so on, it was itself influenced by these forces. Yet there is limited evidence of a fundamental transformation of the overall structure and functioning of the urban system. Rather, as Massey argues, we see an overlaying of different functional bases and patterns of interaction. Both territorial-hierarchical and inter-urban linkages were important in drawing together the regional space economy. The former was most common in the textile and agricultural districts where rural production was strongest. The latter characterised linkages between specialist production locations in the mineral-based economy. There was, however, widespread overlap between the two, not least because of the importance of rural metalworking and mining in south-west Lancashire and the strong localisation of specialisation seen within the textile industries. Liverpool, Manchester and Chester were the principal foci of both types of interaction and thus formed the lynchpins around which turned the urban system and regional economy. Lower down the hierarchy, though, there were some significant shifts in the relative importance of towns. Some old-established centres, such as Nantwich and Congleton, became marginal to the mainstream of economic activity (although they often remained important in social and cultural terms) and the system slowly reconfigured itself around growing industrial and commercial towns such as Stockport, Blackburn and Warrington. The changing nature of the hierarchy was related to changing patterns of interaction: although hierarchical interaction remained strong, it was increasingly cut across by direct interaction between these burgeoning and often specialised centres.

By the mid-eighteenth century at the latest, the north west was comprised of a series of internally integrated and externally inter-dependent and interacting local economies. Similar patterns of interaction also began to emerge between specialist regions and, for the next one hundred years or more, the country was characterised by a mosaic of inter-linked industrial, commercial and agricultural regions.[25] It was not until the railway age was well advanced that a single national economy became the dominant feature of British industrial and commercial development.[26] This national integration was also anticipated by the extra-regional influences and linkages which characterised the north west in the early eighteenth century. Indeed, integration with national and international economies was crucial to the development of key economic activities (the manufacturing of cotton, silk, iron, salt and cheese and the provision of commercial leisure facilities) and the regional economy as a whole. Again, these longer-distance links were dominated by the gateway cities: Liverpool, Manchester and Chester. However, many other towns enjoyed extensive extra-regional contacts (often with neighbouring regions and especially with west and south Yorkshire) and London's influence was widespread and pervasive. The metropolis was important as a market and an entrepôt for overseas trade. It was a major money market and credit centre for the north west and other regions, and, through the diffusion of innovation and fashions, shaped culture and consumption throughout the country.[27]

The relationship, though, was not one-way. London was influential in the provinces, but the vitality of the metropolis was ultimately based on a complex spatial division of labour – a regional economic and urban geography that linked it with all corners of Britain and with other parts of the world. Similarly, within the north west, it was the urban network as a whole which structured and articulated industrial and commercial development of the regional space economy. Rozman has argued that a fully integrated urban system was a 'necessary preparation for entry into the modern world',[28] but this interactive system was more than simply a precondition for 'modern' development: its structure was instrumental in determining the pace and geography of that modernisation. Demographic and economic growth was determined by a complex web of inter-related forces, including the presence of natural and human resources, and the local and regional sociocultural environment. Of critical importance, though, were the extrinsic relationships of localities and towns: their links to the economic, social and cultural development taking place in other places. The position of a town in the urban system (its external linkages to both town and country) did as much to determine its growth as the functions found within it. It was, therefore, the *system* of towns as well as the qualities of individual centres which drew the productive forces of the region together and stimulated local and regional growth. To fully understand early industrial development in Britain, then, we need to look to processes of specialisation and integration, and therefore to the local and inter-regional trading activities and the commercial and social linkages of the urban system. These tell us as much about the timing and geography of industrial development as traditional explanations of resources, technology and proto-industry. In doing so, we need to refocus attention onto the region, not simply as the product of uneven development during the industrial revolution, but as the fundamental geographical and functional unit of industrialisation.

Notes

1   Colquhoun, *Wealth, Power and Resources*, p. 68.
2   Hudson, *Regions and Industries*, p. 23.
3   Pollard, *Peaceful Conquest*, p. 19.
4   Dunford, *Regional Development*, especially pp. 11–47, 162–207 and 337–48; Massey, *Spatial Divisions of Labour*, pp. 117–19.
5   Krugman, *Geography and Trade*, p. 35; Pollard, *Peaceful Conquest*, p. 39.
6   Langton, *Geographical Change*, p. 1.
7   Langton, 'Industrial revolution', pp. 150–61.
8   Hudson, *Regions and Industries*, pp. 20–3. See also, Pollard, *Peaceful Conquest*, pp. 1–29.
9   Langton, 'Industrial revolution', pp. 150–63. See also, Paasi 'Institutionalization of regions'.
10 Capello, 'City network paradigm', p. 1925.
11 Wrigley, 'Parasite or stimulus', pp. 307–9.
12 Power, 'Councillors and commerce'.
13 See Hayter, *Industrial Location*, pp. 83–110.
14 Wadsworth and Mann, *Cotton Trade*, pp. 35–46, 183–92 and 235; Langton, *Geographical Change*, pp. 97–8 and 176–9.
15 See Krugman, *Geography and Trade*, pp. 36–54.
16 Farnie, *English Cotton Industry*, pp. 45–77.
17 Langton, 'Urban growth', p. 489.
18 See Evans, 'Two paths', pp. 215–20; Richards, 'Margins of the industrial revolution', pp. 205–10; Deacon, 'Proto-regionalisation', pp. 29–33.
19 Short, 'De-industrialisation of the Weald'.
20 Wrigley, 'Parasite or stimulus', p. 308. See also Thrift, 'Inhuman geographies', pp. 263–72; Deacon, 'Proto-regionalisation', p. 33.
21 De Vries, 'The industrious revolution'.
22 See Lepetit, *Urban System*, especially pp. 78–123 and 349–96; Amin and Graham, 'Cities of connection', pp. 11–14.
23 Hudson, *Regions and Industries*, p. 23.
24 Wrigley, 'Parasite or stimulus', p. 302.
25 It is this later development which is highlighted by Hudson, *Regions and Industries*; Pollard, *Peaceful Conquest*; Gregory 'Geographies of industrialization'; and theorised by Dunford, *Regional Development*, Krugman, *Geography and Trade*; Storper, *Regional World*.
26 Langton and Morris, *Atlas of Industrializing Britain*, pp. xxvii–xxx; Hudson, *Regions and Industries*, pp. 20–3; Gregory, 'Geographies of industrialization', pp. 377–84.
27 See Wrigley, 'London's importance'; Borsay, 'The London connection'; Ellis, *Georgian Town*, pp. 137–41.
28 De Vries, *European Urbanization*, p. 10.

APPENDIX I

Sources of urban population totals for north-west England in the 1770s

Town	Source	Notes
Altrincham	census, 1772 (Percival, p. 9)	
Blackburn	Walton, p. 65	Law's estimate of 6,000 seems too high
Bolton	census, 1772 (Percival, p. 8)	
Burnley	Bishop's Visitation, 1778	families; calculated from chapelry total (Burnley = 23%)
Bury	census, 1772 (Percival, p. 9)	
Chester	census, 1774 (Law, p. 24)	
Chorley	Bishop's Visitation, 1778	families
Clitheroe	Bishop's Visitation, 1778	families; calculated from chapelry total (Clitheroe = 61%)
Colne	Bishop's Visitation, 1778	families; calculated from chapelry total (Colne = 38%)
Congleton	Bishop's Visitation, 1778	households
Frodsham	Bishop's Visitation, 1778	households; calculated from chapelry total (Frodsham = 22%)
Haslingden	Moffit, p. 142	
Knutsford	Bishop's Visitation, 1778	households; calculated from chapelry total (Knutsford = 72%)
Leigh	Bishop's Visitation, 1778	households; calculated from chapelry total (Leigh = 21%). This gives a figure of 2,547 which, given the strong rural expansion in the parish, seems too high. A lower figure of c.2,000 seems more appropriate
Liverpool	census, 1773 (Enfield, p. 68),	
Macclesfield	Law, p. 23	
Malpas	Bishop's Visitation, 1778	households; calculated from chapelry total (Malpas = 17%)
Manchester	census, 1772 (Percival, p. 2)	
Middlewich	Bishop's Visitation, 1778	families; calculated from chapelry total (Middlewich = 31%)

Town	Source	Notes
Nantwich	Bishop's Visitation, 1778	households
Newton	Bishop's Visitation, 1778	households; calculated from chapelry total (Newton = 13%)
Northwich	Bishop's Visitation, 1778	households; Law's estimate of 3,000 probably includes Witton
Ormskirk	Bishop's Visitation, 1778	population total given (2,280) seems too high given Duggan's figure of 1,210 for 1754
Prescot	Bishop's Visitation, 1778	households; calculated from chapelry total (Prescot = 20%)
Preston	Law, p. 24	total from Bishop's Visitations seems too low; Walton's total seems too high
Rochdale	Law, p. 24; Walton, p. 65	
Sandbach	Bishop's Visitation, 1778	households; calculated from chapelry total (Sandbach = 44%)
Stockport	Law, p. 23; Walton, p. 77	
Warrington	Bishop's Visitation, 1778	households
Wigan	Walton, p. 77	Law's estimate seems too low

Sources: CCA, EDV/7 Bishop's Visitation; Enfield, *Liverpool*; Law, 'Urban population'; Moffit, *Eve of the Industrial Revolution*; Percival, 'Observations on the state of population'; Walton, *Lancashire*.

Notes: Responses to the letters of enquiry sent out prior to the Bishop's Visitation of 1778 sometimes referred to parishes or chapelries rather than townships, necessitating some disaggregation of the data. In such cases the proportion of the parish population made up by the urban township in 1664 was calculated and assumed to remain constant. The 1778 urban population was then calculated by taking the same percentage of the 1778 estimate for the whole parish. As urban growth rates were greater than those of rural areas during the period, this method results in approximate minimum population totals.

For households, a multiplier of 4.75 is applied; for families the multiplier is 4.5. See Stobart, 'Eighteenth-century revolution?', pp. 33–4.

APPENDIX 2

Probate records as sources of occupational information

Economies cannot be reduced to the sum of their parts; to a simple count of occupations. They also involve complex webs of supply and demand, credit and capital, and the intense inter-personal relationships of work and labour. That said, most studies of seventeenth- and eighteenth-century economic change at least start by recreating occupational structures. A variety of sources are available for such an undertaking including muster and freeman rolls, militia lists, apprentice indentures and frank-pledge lists, but all of these are spatially or temporally specific, precluding systematic analysis of regional trends.[1] Parish registers offer a more widely available source drawn on for several national surveys, most notably those by Lindert. However, whilst being widely available, these are by no means uniform in their content or characteristics: parochial autonomy means that the registers often differed greatly from one parish to the next, with occupational information being especially variable and often absent from early eighteenth-century records.[2] Parish registers, therefore, can provide occupational data only for a sample of a region's population and there must be some doubt about how representative such a sample might be. In her national survey of the rural economy, Kussmaul felt the need to supplement Lindert's nominally national, but in reality somewhat southern-biased, material with extra parishes from the 'industrial north'.[3]

For a systematic and comprehensive survey, probate records offer several advantages over parish registers. They contain a standardised form of occupational information, offer comprehensive spatial and temporal coverage and have produced relatively few and centralised bodies of records, so that a wide-ranging data-set can be gleaned from a small number of archives. Critically, for the majority of small towns and villages, they form the only consistently available source and, as a consequence, have been widely used in regional and comparative analyses.[4] Moreover, for north-west England many of the records are catalogued in published indexes: all the probates granted at the courts at Chester and Richmond, as well as the contested or transmitted cases dealt with by the Diocesan Court in Chester are listed in volumes 13, 20,

22, 23 and 25 of the *Transactions of the Records Society of Lancashire & Cheshire*. Records of probate granted at the Probate Courts of Canterbury and York are listed in manuscript indexes in the Public Record Office, London and Borthwick Institute, York respectively. Drawing on these various indexes gives comprehensive coverage of the probate-leaving population of the region for the period 1701–60. Indeed, there are only two notable gaps: the lack of 'infra' wills (those worth less than £40) in Cheshire before 1730 and for either Lancashire or Cheshire for 1758–60. In all, the probate records form a reliable and consistent source for creating a large data-base for north-west England containing the occupation and precise location for 28,757 individuals.[5]

Despite these advantages as sources of occupational information, probate records are not without their problems. Some of these are common to all eighteenth-century occupational sources, but remain problematical nonetheless. First is the existence of dual occupations and the lack of occupational specialisation in the early modern period so that an individual labelled with one occupational title might be undertaking a variety of different forms of work, perhaps at different times of the year.[6] Multiple occupations appear less frequently in the probate records than in other sources. Early trade directories, for instance, are littered with what can seem very unlikely combinations: clockmaker and grocer, linen draper and barber, and silversmith, hosier and hat-maker all feature in Gore's first Liverpool Directory.[7] In contrast, combined occupations appearing in the probate records are the more usual plumber and glaziers or barber and peruke-makers. However, this simplicity may be illusory and could reflect a second difficulty with occupational information: that multiple sources of income are hidden under a single occupational title. This was especially common in rural areas of north-west England where industrial employment was frequently used as a supplement to agricultural incomes.[8] Spinning and weaving form perhaps the classic example, but it was also a common feature of both mining and metalworking.[9] Related to this is the third problem area: self-aggrandisement and the use of ostensibly occupational titles as signifiers of status. 'Yeoman' was still being used as an honorific as well as descriptive title in the early eighteenth century and, although its use was declining, was clearly preferred to manufacturing titles in many situations. As Walton notes, around 70 per cent of probate inventories in late seventeenth-century Rossendale contained cloth-making equipment when only 40 per cent of occupations were textiles related.[10] Similarly, 'gentlemen' could be of genuinely independent means, but also included an indeterminate number of sometimes 'retired' tradesmen.[11] This is a particular problem with probate records. Not only were the titles often self-assigned, the very nature of the records means that they include a large proportion of older tradesmen. A fourth problem is that a particular sector may have had relatively few 'dedicated' traders, especially in terms of employers. For instance, most coal mines in south-west Lancashire were owned and run by the gentry at this time. In contrast, textile production throughout the region was controlled by men within the industry (drapers, clothiers, and so on).[12] This can lead to one sector being seen as disproportionately important within the regional or local economies.

The principal problem specific to probate records is the social coverage which they afforded. Probate records represent only a limited section of society: that with sufficient wealth to make probate a legal requirement or a worthwhile expenditure of time and money. It was unnecessary, although not uncommon, to seek probate for any estate worth less than £5 and so there are very few wills or inventories for the indeterminate but undoubtedly large number of 'poor' within the region. Camp suggests that around 6 per cent of the population left wills in the late eighteenth century.[13] Adding another 2–3 per cent for whom letters of administration were granted gives a figure which closely matches the 8.6 per cent of the population leaving a probate record in early eighteenth-century Lancashire and Cheshire.[14] Such figures are somewhat misleading, however: around half the population were children and they probably accounted for more than half the recorded deaths. Given this, it would seem that about 40 per cent of the adult population left some form of probate record, be it a will, inventory or letter of administration.[15]

Of the majority of the population who did not leave records, many were poor wage earners. With their low incomes, such workers generally owned fewer of the personal and household goods that comprised a substantial part of any estate. They also owned less trade-related stock and equipment than their counterparts in higher status crafts and trades. Significantly, these people would have been concentrated into certain occupational groups. Under-representation was probably most marked amongst labourers (of whom only around 8 per cent left wills) and the proletarianised workforce within capitalist industries like mining; but it was also true of some artisanal trades such as tailoring.[16] The other major section of the population under-represented in the probate records were women, who would generally make wills only if they were unmarried.[17] Only about one in five of the probates in the north west were for women and, with a handful of exceptions, marital status (i.e. widow or spinster) appeared in place of occupations.[18] This has implications for the overall occupation structure. Baigent notes that women's work was sectorally distinctive and highlights the food and drink and clothing industries. In the north west, Wadsworth and Mann suggest that women weavers were numerous by the mid-eighteenth century, but perhaps the largest body of female labour to go unrecognised in the region is spinning – often a part-time activity carried out by women in their own homes.[19]

To what extent is it possible to compensate for these omissions? The location of coal and salt mines is well established and so their geography can be reconstructed relatively easily without listings of individual mine owners. Other groups are less straightforwardly dealt with, especially when the activity of workers effectively defined the structure of that industry, as is the case with textile manufacturing. That said, it is possible to roughly estimate the number of spinners from the number of weavers leaving probate records. Wadsworth and Mann describe the activities of weavers who had to visit five or six spinners in order to collect enough weft to last the day, and it is commonly suggested that, with the introduction of the flying shuttle in the middle decades of the eighteenth century, a ratio of eight spinners to each weaver was more usual.[20] Taking a conservative figure and applying a ratio of five spinners for every weaver to the cloth-working districts of north-east Lancashire, we can see that around 40–60 per cent of the adult population was engaged in textile manufacture. This proportion accords well with the parish register evidence for southern Rossendale and Haslingden, which suggests that between one-half and two-thirds of males were cloth workers.[21] Including a multiplier for spinners whilst not attempting similar 'corrections' for miners, labourers, and so on, is somewhat hazardous, not least because the textiles industries may thus be inflated in relation to other forms of manufacture. The difficulty, though, is that these other sectors have no 'known' body of workers (such as the weavers) to act as a basis for any multiplier. However, whilst it risks introducing a new bias into the data set, the multiplier for spinners is warranted because it provides a truer picture of both regional and local economies than would otherwise be possible. Furthermore, it allows some account to be taken of the enormous contribution made by women and children to economic activity in the north west.[22]

Notes

1 Pound, 'Validity of the freemen's lists'; Glennie, 'Distinguishing men's trades', pp. 46–65; McInnes, 'Shrewsbury', pp. 59–65; Goose and Evans, 'Wills as an historical source', pp. 58–9.
2 Glennie, 'Distinguishing men's trades', pp. 30–2. See Lindert, 'English occupations'.
3 Kussmaul, *Rural Economy of England*.
4 See, for example, Patten, *English Towns*; Evans, 'Male testators in Cambridgeshire'; Trinder and Cox, *Yeomen and Colliers*.
5 The data-base contains 40,057 records, 30,948 of which have a specified occupation. Of these, 2191 cannot be allocated to a specific township giving 28,757 (72 per cent) records with both spatial and occupational data.
6 Arkell, 'Interpreting probate inventories', p. 79; Hey, *Rural Metalworkers*, pp. 16–41; Langton, *Geographical Change*, pp. 67–78.

7 *Gore's Liverpool Directory.*

8 Berg, *Age of Manufactures,* pp. 66–72 and 89–91.

9 Langton, *Geographical Change,* pp. 67–8. See also Large, 'Urban growth and agricultural change'; Rowlands, *Masters and Men,* pp. 41–3; Hey, *Rural Metalworkers,* pp. 16–41.

10 Walton, 'Proto-industrialisation', pp. 54–5.

11 Evans, 'Male testators in Cambridgeshire', pp. 180–4; Patten, 'Urban occupations'.

12 Langton, *Geographical Change,* pp. 120–8; Wadsworth and Mann, *Cotton Trade,* pp. 29–53.

13 Camp, *Wills and their Whereabouts,* p. xxxviii.

14 Given a 1664 population of about 200,000 for the region and a death rate of 28/1,000, around 5,600 deaths would have occurred each year, rates which probably held good for the early eighteenth century. In 1701–10, there were about 480 probates proved per annum; that is 8.6 per cent of those dying.

15 The adult population would have been 90–100,000 in 1664 and the *adult* death rate about 11–14/1,000, giving between 990 and 1,400 adult deaths per annum (figures from private communication with E. A. Wrigley). Removing minors from the count of probate records leaves about 460 per annum, meaning that 33–46 per cent of adults died leaving a probate record.

16 Glennie, 'Distinguishing men's trades', p. 34; Langton, *Geographical Change,* pp. 194–212.

17 Until the second half of the nineteenth century, married women had no possessions of their own and could only make wills with the express permission of their husbands. Such instances are marked the indexes with F C (*Fidei Commissum*).

18 The total of 19.51 per cent tallies well with the 19.15 per cent found in Staffordshire inventories by Trinder and Cox, *Yeomen and Colliers,* p. 90.

19 Baigent, 'Economy and society', p. 117; Wadsworth and Mann, *Cotton Trade,* pp. 332–6.

20 Wadsworth and Mann, *Cotton Trade,* p. 276.

21 Walton, 'Proto-industrialisation', pp. 54–6.

22 Berg and Hudson, 'Rehabilitating', pp. 35–8. This multiplier has also been used in the analysis offered in Stobart 'Geography and industrialization' and Stobart 'Textile industries'.

Bibliography

Primary sources

Cheshire and Chester Archives

Newspapers
Adams Weekly Courant
Chester Courant

Probate records
WS 1707, John Bradshaw of Chester
WS 1728, Thomas Booth of Werneth
WS 1717, Edward Davenport of Stockport
WS 1711, John England of Knutsford
WS 1712, Samuel Garnett of Nantwich
WS 1703, Thomas Gilbody of Stockport
WS 1713, Thomas Gyles of Nantwich
WI 1750, Joseph Heald of Ashton-upon-Mersey
WS 1732, Richard Holland of Macclesfield
WS 1709, William Jordan of Malpas
WS 1752, Thomas Kent of Church Hulme
WS 1724, Thomas Moreton of Chester
WS 1734, John Lane of Chester
WS 1717, James Parratt of Middlewich
WS 1702, James Rathbone of Macclesfield
WS 1728, Zacariah Shelley of Congleton
WS 1756, Abner Scholes of Chester
WS 1702, John Sherwin of Macclesfield
WS 1716, Richard Smith of Bunbury
WS 1710, Samuel Thornicroft of Macclesfield
WS 1716, Richard Upton of Stockport
WS 1730, Robert Wadds of Nantwich
WS 1721, Robert Wilkinson of Nantwich
WS 1729, Richard Worthington of Macclesfield

Other records
A/A/2/156v; A/B/2/169v; A/B/1/111v; A/B/1/193v; A/B/3/163v; A/B/3/264v; A/B/4/5v,
  Chester Assembly Records

CR 63/2/133/17, Peter Broster's *Sketch Plan of Eastgate Street* (c. 1754)
CR 352/1, Letter Book of Daniel Peck
CR 656/1–35, Merchant's Papers
EDV/7, Bishop's Visitation
MAB/2, Apprenticeship Registers
SBT/2, Chester Horse Market

Chester City Library

MF5/3, Plan of City and Castle of Chester by Alexander de Lavaux (1745)
MF 1/12A, Plan of Chester by I. Stockdale (1796)

Keele University

Keele University Wedgwood Accumulation
E9–30248–30291; L52–30705; L120–23237

Lancashire Record Office

Probate records
WCW 1731, John Antrobus of Manchester
WCW 1692, Robert Banks of Wigan
WCW 1720, James Beck of Manchester
WCW 1747, Richard Bolton of Bury
WCW 1669, John Bulling of Warrington
WCW 1728, Richard Chow of Chowbent
WCW 1724, Isaac Hall of Warrington
WCW 1727, Joseph Hampson of Leigh
WCW 1708, John Hatton of Chowbent
WCW 1748, James Heyworth of Haslingden
WCW 1712, Richard Houghton of Liverpool
WCW 1740, David Jackson of Manchester
WCW 1735, Joseph Jolley of Manchester
WCW 1715 (infra), Roger Key of Bolton
WCW 1730, Peter Latham of Wigan
WCW 1753, Richard Lathom of Wigan
WCW 1708, Christopher Mann of Tyldesley
WCW 1725, Laurence Marsden of Wigan
WCW 1756, Alexander Mercer of Blackburn
WCW 1720, Samuel Morris of Tyldesley
WCW 1728, Francis Roby of Billinge
WCW 1753, Richard Rothwell of Haslingden
WCW 1721, Thomas Smalley of Blackburn
WCW 1727, Henry Tarbocke of Parr
WCW 1721, George Taylor of Atherton
WCW 1731, Joseph Titley of Warrington
WCW 1742, James Townsend of Burnley
WCW 1732, Edward Twambrooks of Warrington
WCW 1715, John Wareing of Bury

WCW 1679, Nicholas Withington of Atherton

Public Record Office, London
E182/96 Shop Tax 1785, Cheshire
E182/491 Shop Tax 1785, Lancashire

Stoke-on-Trent Archives
D4842/14/3/25, Crate Book of J. B. Wood

Secondary sources

Adams, J. *Index Villaris* (London: T. Sawbridge and M. Gillyflower, 1690).

Addy, J. (ed.). 'The diary of Henry Prescott, LLB', *Record Society of Lancashire and Cheshire*, 127 (1987).

Aikin, J. *A Description of the Country from Thirty to Forty Miles round Manchester* (London: J. Stockdale, 1795).

Albert, W. *The Turnpike Road System in England 1663–1840* (Cambridge: Cambridge University Press, 1972).

Aldcroft, D. and M. Freeman (eds). *Transport in the Industrial Revolution* (Manchester: Manchester University Press, 1983).

Allen, J., D. Massey and A. Cochrane. *Rethinking the Region* (London: Routledge, 1998).

Allen, J., D. Massey and M. Pryke (eds). *Unsettling Cities: Movement/Settlement* (London: Routledge, 1999).

Allen, R. 'Agriculture during the industrial revolution', in R. Floud and D. McCloskey (eds) *The Economic History of Britain since 1700, Volume 1: 1700–1860* (Cambridge: Cambridge University Press, second edition, 1994), pp. 96–122.

Amin, A. and S. Graham. 'Cities of connection and disconnection', in J. Allen, D. Massey and M. Pryke (eds) *Unsettling Cities: Movement/Settlement* (London: Routledge, 1999), pp. 7–48.

Anderson, B. L. 'The attorney and the early capital market in Lancashire', in J. R. Harris (ed.) *Liverpool and Merseyside* (London: Frank Cass, 1969), pp. 50–77.

Arkell, T. 'Interpreting probate inventories', in T. Arkell, N, Evans and N. Goose (eds) *When Death Do Us Part: Understanding and Interpreting the Probate Records of Early Modern England* (Oxford: Local Population Studies, 2000), pp. 72–102.

Arthur, W. B. 'Competing technologies, increasing returns, and lock-in by historical events', *Economic Journal*, 99 (1989), 116–31.

Ashton, T. *An Eighteenth-Century Industrialist: Peter Stubbs of Warrington* (Manchester: Manchester University Press, 1939).

Astle, W. *History of Stockport* (Stockport: Swain, 1922).

Aston, J. *The Manchester Guide* (Manchester: J. Aston, 1804).

Austen, J. *Northanger Abbey* (1818; London: Virago, 1989).

Awty, B. 'Charcoal ironmasters of Cheshire and Lancashire 1600–1785', *Transactions, Historic Society of Lancashire and Cheshire*, 109 (1958), 71–119.

Bagwell, P. *The Transport Revolution from 1770* (London: Batsford, 1974).

Baigent, E. 'Economy and society in eighteenth century English towns: Bristol in the 1770s', in D. Denecke and G. Shaw (eds) *Urban Historical Geography – Recent*

Progress in Britain and Germany (Cambridge: Cambridge University Press, 1988), pp. 109–24.

Bailey, F. and T. Barker. 'The seventeenth-century origins of watchmaking in south-west Lancashire', in J. R. Harris (ed.) *Liverpool and Merseyside* (London: Frank Cass, 1969), pp. 1–15.

Baines, E. *History of the Commerce and Town of Liverpool* (London, 1852).

Baines, E. *History, Directory and Gazetteer of the County Palatine of Lancaster*, 2 volumes (1824–5; reproduced Newton Abbot: David and Charles, 1968).

Barker, D. 'A conceptual approach to the description and analysis of an historical urban system', *Regional Studies*, 12:1 (1978), 1–10.

Barker, T. 'Lancashire coal, Cheshire salt and the rise of Liverpool', *Transactions, Historic Society of Lancashire and Cheshire*, 103 (1951), 83–101.

Barker, T. and J. Harris. *A Merseyside Town in the Industrial Revolution: St Helens, 1750–1900* (Liverpool: Liverpool University Press, 1954).

Beavon, K. S. O. *Central Place Theory: A Re-interpretation* (London: Longman, 1977).

Beattie, D. *Blackburn: The Development of a Lancashire Cotton Town* (Halifax: Ryburn Publishing, 1992).

Beckett, J. and C. Smith. 'Urban renaissance and consumer revolution in Nottingham, 1688–1750', *Urban History*, 27:1 (2000), 31–50.

Bennett, A. *Old Wives' Tale* (London, 1908; Everyman edition 1935).

Berend, I. and G. Ranki. *The European Periphery and Industrialization 1780–1914* (Cambridge: Cambridge University Press, 1982).

Berg, M. 'Women's work, mechanisation and the early phases of industrialisation in England', in P. Joyce (ed.) *The Historical Meanings of Work* (Cambridge: Cambridge University Press, 1987), pp. 64–98.

Berg, M. 'Commerce and creativity in eighteenth-century Birmingham', in M. Berg (ed.) *Markets and Manufacture in Early Industrial Europe* (London: Routledge, 1991), pp. 173–205.

Berg, M. *The Age of Manufactures 1700–1820* (London: Routledge, second edition, 1994).

Berg, M. 'Factories, workshops and industrial organisation', in R. Floud and D. McCloskey (eds) *The Economic History of Britain since 1700, Volume 1: 1700–1860* (Cambridge: Cambridge University Press, second edition, 1994), pp. 123–50.

Berg, M. and P. Hudson. 'Rehabilitating the industrial revolution', *Economic History Review*, 45:1 (1992), 4–50.

Berg, M., P. Hudson and M. Sonenscher. *Manufacture in Town and Country before the Factory* (Cambridge: Cambridge University Press, 1983).

Berry, B. J. and W. Garrison. 'Functional bases of the central place hierarchy', *Economic Geography*, 34:2 (1958), 145–54.

Berry, B. J. and F. Horton. *Geographic Perspectives on Urban Systems* (Englewood Cliffs: Prentice Hall, 1970).

Betty, J. *Wessex from AD 1000* (London: Longman, 1986).

Black, I. 'Money, information and space: banking in early-nineteenth century England and Wales', *Journal of Historical Geography*, 21:4 (1995), 371–97.

Blake, G. 'Mr Wedgwood and the Porcelain trade', *English Ceramic Circle, Transactions*, 12:2 (1985), 93–108.

Blome, R. *Britannia* (London: T. Rycroft, 1673).

Blundell, N. 'The Great Diurnal of Nicholas Blundell of Little Crosby, Lancashire', edited by F. Tyrer, *Record Society of Lancashire and Cheshire*, 3 volumes (1968–72).

Boney, K. *Liverpool Porcelain of the Eighteenth Century and its Makers* (London: Batsford, 1957).

Borsay, P. 'The rise of the promenade, c.1660–1800', *British Journal of Eighteenth-Century Studies*, 9 (1986), 125–40.

Borsay, P. *The English Urban Renaissance: Culture and Society in the Provincial Town, 1660–1770* (Oxford: Clarendon Press, 1989).

Borsay, P. 'The London connection: cultural diffusion and the eighteenth-century provincial town', *London Journal*, 19 (1994), 21–35.

Borsay, P. 'Health and Leisure resorts 1700–1840', in P. Clark (ed.) *The Cambridge Urban History of Britain, volume II 1540–1840* (Cambridge: Cambridge University Press, 2000), pp. 775–803.

Borsay, P. (ed.). *The Eighteenth Century Town, 1688–1820: A Reader in English Urban History* (London: Longman, 1990).

Bourne, L. S. and J. W. Simmons (eds). *Systems of Cities: Readings on Structure, Growth, and Policy* (New York: Oxford University Press, 1978).

Boyer, G. 'The old poor law and the agricultural labour market in southern England: an empirical analysis', *Journal of Economic History*, 46:1 (1986), 113–35.

Brayshay, M., P. Harrison and B. Chalkley. 'Knowledge, nationhood and governance: the speed of the Royal post in early-modern England', *Journal of Historical Geography*, 24:3 (1998), 265–88.

Brewer, J. and R. Porter (eds). *Consumption and the World of Goods* (London: Routledge, 1993).

Broster, P. *The Chester Guide* (Chester: P. Broster, 1782).

Bruton, F. *A Short History of Manchester and Salford* (Manchester: Sherratt and Hughes, 1924).

Bryson J. and N. Henry. 'The global production system: from Fordism to post-Fordism', in P. Daniels, M. Bradshaw, D. Shaw and J. Sidaway (eds) *Human Geography: Issues for the 21st Century* (Harlow: Prentice Hall, 2001), pp. 342–73.

Buckatzch, E. 'The geographical distribution of wealth in England 1086–1843', *Economic History Review*, 3:2 (1950–51), 180–202.

Burdett, P. *Survey of the County Palatine of Chester ... 1777* (ed. J. B. Harley and P. Laxton – London: Historic Society of Lancashire and Cheshire, 1974).

Burt, R. 'Proto-industrialisation and "stages of growth" in the metal mining industries', *Journal of European Economic History*, 27:1 (1998), 85–104.

Calvert, A. *Salt in Cheshire* (London: E. and F. N. Spon, 1915).

Camagni, R. 'From city hierarchy to city networks: reflections about an emerging paradigm', in T. Lakshmanan and P. Nijkamp (eds) *Structure and Change in the Space Economy: Festschrift in Honour of Martin Beckmann* (Berlin: Springer Verlag, 1993), pp. 66–87.

Camp, A. J. *Wills and their Whereabouts* (London: The Author, fourth edition, 1974).

Cannadine, D. 'British history: past, present and future?', *Past and Present*, 116 (1987), 169–91.

Capello, R. 'The city network paradigm: measuring urban network externalities', *Urban Studies*, 37:11 (2000), 1,925–45.

Carrington, P. *English Heritage Book of Chester* (London: Batsford, 1994).

Carter, H. 'Towns and urban systems 1730–1914', in R. A. Dodgshon and R. A. Butlin (eds) *An Historical Geography of England and Wales* (London: Academic Press, second edition, 1990), pp. 401–28.

Carter, H. *The Study of Urban Geography* (London: Arnold, fourth edition, 1995).

Carus-Wilson, E. M. 'An industrial revolution in the thirteenth century', *Economic History Review*, 2:1 (1940/41), 39–60.

Caunce, S. 'Complexity, community structure and competitive advantage within the Yorkshire woollen industry c.1700–1850', *Business History*, 39:4 (1997), 26–43.

Chalklin, C. *The Provincial Towns of Georgian England: A Study of the Building Process, 1740–1820* (London: Arnold, 1974).

Chalklin, C. *The Rise of the English Town 1650–1850* (Cambridge: Cambridge University Press, 2001).

Chalmers, G. *An Estimate of the Comparative Strength of Great Britain* (London: John Stockdale, 1794 edition).

Chaloner, W. 'Salt in Cheshire, 1600–1870', *Transactions, Lancashire and Cheshire Antiquarian Society*, 71 (1961), 58–74.

Chapman, S. *The Lancashire Cotton Industry* (Manchester: Manchester University Press, 1904).

Chartres, J. 'The marketing of agricultural produce', in J. Thirsk (ed.) *The Agrarian History of England and Wales, VII, 1640–1750* (Cambridge: Cambridge University Press, 1985), pp. 406–502.

Chartres, J. and G. Turnbull. 'Road transport', in D. Aldcroft and M. Freeman (eds) *Transport in the Industrial Revolution* (Manchester: Manchester University Press, 1983), pp. 64–99.

Christaller, W. (translated by C. Baskin) *Central Places in Southern Germany* (Englewood Cliffs: Prentice Hall, 1966).

Clapham, J. *An Economic History of Modern Britain*, 3 volumes (Cambridge: Cambridge University Press, 1926–38).

Clark, P. 'Small towns in England 1550–1850: national and regional population trends', in Clark, P. (ed.) *Small Towns in Early Modern Europe* (Cambridge: Cambridge University Press, 1995).

Clark, P. (ed.): *The Early Modern Town* (London: Longman, 1976).

Clarkson, L. 'The environment and dynamic of pre-factory industry in Northern Ireland', in P. Hudson (ed.) *Regions and Industries* (Cambridge: Cambridge University Press, 1989), pp. 252–70.

Clemens, P. 'The rise of Liverpool, 1650–1750', *Economic History Review*, 29:2 (1976), 211–25.

Coleman, D. 'Growth and decay during the Industrial Revolution: the case of East Anglia', *Scandanavian Economic History Review*, 10 (1962), 115–27.

Coleman, D. 'Proto-industrialization: a concept too many', *Economic History Review*, 36:3 (1983), 435–48.

Colquhoun, P. *A Treatise on the Wealth, Power and Resources of the British Empire* (1814; London: Cass, 1969 reprint).

Corfield, P. J. 'A provincial capital in the late seventeenth century: the case of Norwich', in P. Clark and P. Slack (eds) *Crisis and Order in English Towns, 1500–1700* (Oxford: Oxford University Press, 1972), pp. 263–310.

Corfield, P. J. 'Urban development in England and Wales in the sixteenth and seventeenth centuries', in D. Coleman and A. John (eds) *Trade, Government and Economy in Pre-industrial England* (London: Weidenfeld & Nicolson, 1976), pp. 214–47.

Corfield, P. J. *The Impact of English Towns, 1700–1800* (Oxford, Oxford University Press, 1982).

Corfield, P. J. 'Small towns, large implications: social and cultural roles of small towns in eighteenth-century England and Wales', *British Journal of Eighteenth-Century Studies*, 10 (1987), 125–38.

Corry, J. *The History of Macclesfield* (London: Ferguson, 1817).

Cox, J. and N. Cox. 'Probate 1500–1800: a system in transition', in T. Arkell, N. Evans and N. Goose (eds) *When Death Do Us Part: Understanding and Interpreting the Probate Records of Early Modern England* (Oxford: Local Population Studies, 2000), pp. 14–37.

Cox, N. 'The distribution of retailing tradesmen in north Shropshire, 1660–1750', *Journal of Regional and Local Studies*, 13:1 (1993), 4–22.

Cox, N. *The Complete Tradesman. A Study of Retailing, 1550–1850* (Aldershot: Ashgate, 2000).

Cox, T. *Magna Britainnia et Hibernia* (London: C. Ward and R. Chandler, 1731).

Crafts, N. F. R. *British Economic Growth during the Industrial Revolution* (Oxford: Oxford University Press, 1985).

Crafts, N. F. R. 'The Industrial Revolution', in R. Floud and D. McCloskey (eds) *The Economic History of Britain since 1700, Volume 1: 1700–1860* (Cambridge: Cambridge University Press, second edition, 1994), pp. 44–59.

Crafts, N. F. R. and C. Harley. 'Output growth and the British industrial revolution: a restatement of the Crafts/Harley view', *Economic History Review*, 45:4 (1992), 703–30.

Craig, R. 'Some aspects of the trade and shipping of the river Dee in the eighteenth century', *Transactions, Historic Society of Lancashire and Cheshire*, 114 (1963), 99–128.

Crang, P. 'Cultural turns and the (re)constitution of economic geography', in R. Lee and J. Wills (eds) *Geographies of Economies* (London: Arnold, 1997), pp. 3–15.

Cromar, P. 'The coal industry on Tyneside, 1715–1750', *Northern History*, 14 (1978), 193–207.

Crosby, A. *A History of Cheshire* (Chichester: Phillimore, 1996).

Crump, W. 'Saltways from the Cheshire Wiches', *Transactions, Lancashire and Cheshire Antiquarian Society*, 54 (1939), 84–142.

D'Cruze, S. 'The middling sort in eighteenth-century Colchester: independence, social relations and the community broker', in J. Barry and C. Brooks (eds) *The Middling Sort of People: Culture, Society and Politics in England, 1550–1800* (Basingstoke: Macmillan, 1994), pp. 181–207.

Daniels, G. 'Samuel Crompton's census of the cotton industry in 1811', *Economic History*, 2 (1930–33), 107–10.

Daniels, P. 'Geography of the economy', in P. Daniels, M. Bradshaw, D. Shaw and J. Sidaway (eds) *Human Geography: Issues for the 21st Century* (Harlow: Prentice Hall, 2001), pp. 305–41.

Darity, W. 'British industry and the West Indies plantations', *Social Science History*, 14 (1990), 117–49.

Daunton, M. 'Towns and economic growth in eighteenth century England', in P. Abrams and E. A. Wrigley (eds) *Towns in Societies: Essays in Economic History and Historical Sociology* (Cambridge: Cambridge University Press, 1978), pp. 245–77.

Daunton, M. *Progress and Poverty* (Oxford: Oxford University Press, 1995).

David, P. 'Historical economics in the long-run: some implications of path-dependence', in G. Snooks (ed.) *Historical Analysis in Economics* (London: Routledge, 1993), pp. 29–40.

Davies, C. S. *A History of Macclesfield* (Manchester: Manchester University Press, 1961).

Davies, W. K. D. 'Centrality and the central place hierarchy', *Urban Studies*, 4:1 (1967), 61–79.

Davies, W. K. D. and C. R. Lewis. 'Regional structures in Wales: two studies of connectivity', in H. Carter and W. K. D. Davies (eds) *Urban Essays: Studies in the Geography of Wales* (London: Longman, 1970), pp. 22–48.

de Vries, J. *European Urbanization, 1500–1800* (London: Methuen, 1984).

de Vries, J. 'The industrial revolution and the industrious revolution', *Journal of Economic History*, 54:2 (1994), 249–71.

Deacon, B. 'Proto-regionalisation: the case of Cornwall', *Journal of Regional and Local Studies*, 18:1 (1998), 27–41.

Deane, P. and W. Cole. *British Economic Growth 1688–1959: Trends and Structures* (Cambridge: Cambridge University Press, 1967).

Defoe, D. *A Tour through the Whole Island of Great Britain* (1724–26; London: Penguin edition, 1971).

Dicken, P. *Global Shift: Transforming the World Economy* (London: Paul Chapman, third edition, 1998).

Dicken, P. and P. Lloyd. *Location in Space: Theoretical Perspectives in Economic Geography* (New York: HarperCollins, third edition, 1990).

Duggan, M. *Ormskirk: The Making of a Modern Town* (Stroud: Sutton, 1998).

Dunford, M. *Capital, the State, and Regional Development* (London: Pion, 1988).

Edwards, M. *The Growth of the British Cotton Trade, 1780–1815* (Manchester, Manchester University Press, 1967).

Ellis, J. 'Regional and county centres, 1700–1840', in P. Clark (ed.) *The Cambridge Urban History of Britain, volume II 1540–1840* (Cambridge: Cambridge University Press, 2000), pp. 673–704.

Ellis, J. '"The stocking country": industrial and urban growth in Nottingham 1680–1840', in J. Stobart and P. Lane (eds) *Urban and Industrial Change in the Midlands, 1700–1840* (Leicester: Centre for Urban History, University of Leicester, 2000), pp. 93–117.

Ellis, J. *The Georgian Town, 1680–1840* (Basingstoke: Palgrave, 2001).

Enfield, W. *An Essay Towards the History of Leverpool* (London: Johnson, 1774).

Engerman, S. 'Mercantilism and overseas trade, 1700–1800', in R. Floud and D. McCloskey (eds) *The Economic History of Britain since 1700, Volume 1: 1700–1860* (Cambridge: Cambridge University Press, second edition, 1994), pp. 182–204.

Estabrook, C. *Urbane and Rustic England: Cultural Ties and Social Spheres in the Provinces, 1660–1780* (Manchester: Manchester University Press, 1998).

Evans, N. 'Two paths to economic development: Wales and the north-east of England', in P. Hudson (ed.) *Regions and Industries* (Cambridge: Cambridge University Press, 1989), pp. 201–27.

Evans, N. 'Male testators in Cambridgeshire', in T. Arkell, N. Evans and N. Goose (eds) *When Death Do Us Part: Understanding and Interpreting the Probate Records of Early Modern England* (Oxford: Local Population Studies, 2000), pp. 176–88.

Everitt, A. 'The marketing of agricultural produce', in J. Thirsk (ed.) *The Agrarian History of England and Wales, IV, 1500–1640* (Cambridge: Cambridge University Press, 1967), pp. 466–592.

Everitt, A. *Change in the Provinces: The Seventeenth Century* (Leicester: Department of English Local History, University of Leicester, 1972).

Everitt, A. 'Country, county and town: patterns of regional evolution in England', *Transactions, Royal Historical Society*, 5th series, 29 (1979), 79–108.

Farnie, D. *The English Cotton Industry and the World Market, 1815–96* (Oxford: Clarendon Press, 1979).

Faucher, L. *Manchester in 1844: Its Present Condition and Future Prospects* (London: Simpkin and Marshall, 1844).

Feinstein, C. and S. Pollard (eds). *Studies in Capital Formation in the United Kingdom 1750–1920* (Oxford: Clarendon Press, 1988).

Fine, B. and E. Leopold. *The World of Consumption* (London: Routledge, 1993).

Finer, A. and G. Savage. *The Selected Letters of Josiah Wedgwood* (London: Cory, Adams and Mackay, 1965).

Fletcher, J. *The Stranger in Chester* (Chester: Fletcher, 1816).

Flinn, M. W. *The History of the British Coal Industry, Volume 2, 1700–1830: The Industrial Revolution* (Oxford: Clarendon Press, 1984).

Floud, R. and D. McCloskey (eds). *The Economic History of Britain Since 1750, Volume 1 1700–1860* (Cambridge: Cambridge University Press, second edition, 1994).

Fowler, C. 'Changes in provincial retail practice during the eighteenth century, with particular reference to central-southern England', *Business History*, 40:1 (1998), 37–54.

Freeman, M. 'The industrial revolution and the regional geography of England: a comment', *Transactions, Institute of British Geographers*, 9:4 (1984), 507–12.

Freeman, M. 'Transport', in J. Langton and R. J. Morris (eds) *Atlas of Industrializing Britain, 1780–1914* (London: Methuen, 1986), pp. 86–8.

Freudenberger, H. *Industrialization of a Central European City: Brno and the Fine Woollen Industry in the 18th Century* (Wiltshire: Pasold Research Fund, 1977).

Giddens, A. *The Consequences of Modernity* (Cambridge: Cambridge University Press, 1990).

Glennie, P. 'Distinguishing men's trades: occupational sources and debates for pre-census England', *Historical Geography Research Series*, 25 (1990).

Glennie, P. 'Consumption within historical studies', in D. Miller (ed.) *Acknowledging Consumption: A Review of New Studies* (London: Routledge, 1995), pp. 164–203.

Glennie, P. and N. Thrift, 'Modernity, urbanism and modern consumption', *Environment and Planning D*, 10 (1992), 423–43.

Glennie, P. and N. Thrift, 'Consumer identities and consumption spaces in early-modern England', *Environment and Planning A*, 28 (1996), 25–45.

Goose, N. and N. Evans. 'Wills as an historical source', in T. Arkell, N. Evans and N. Goose (eds) *When Death Do Us Part: Understanding and Interpreting the Probate Records of Early Modern England* (Oxford: Local Population Studies, 2000), pp. 38–71.

Gore, J. *Gore's Liverpool Directory* (Liverpool: J. Gore, 1766).

Gray, M. *The History of Bury, Lancashire, 1660–1876* (Bury: Bury Times, 1970).

Greasley, D. and L. Oxley. 'Rehabilitation sustained: the industrial revolution as a macroeconomic epoch', *Economic History Review*, 47:4 (1994), 760–8.

Green, D. *From Artisans to Paupers: Economic Change and Poverty in London, 1790–1870* (Aldershot: Ashgate, 1995).

Gregory, D. *Regional Transformation and Industrial Revolution* (Basingstoke: Macmillan, 1982).

Gregory, D. 'Areal differentiation and post-modern geography', in D. Gregory and

R. Walford (eds) *Horizons in Human Geography* (Basingstoke: Macmillan, 1989), pp. 67–96.

Gregory, D. ' "A new and differing face in many places": three geographies of industrialization', in R. A. Dodgshon, and R. A. Butlin (eds) *An Historical Geography of England and Wales* (London: Academic Press, second edition, 1990) pp. 351–99.

Gregory, D. 'The friction of distance? Information circulation and the mails in early nineteenth-century England', *Journal of Historical Geography*, 13:2 (1987), 130–54.

Gregory, D. 'The production of regions in England's industrial revolution', *Journal of Historical Geography*, 14:1 (1988), 50–8.

Gurr, D. and J. Hunt. *The Cotton Mills of Oldham* (Oldham: Oldham Leisure Services, 1985).

Hadfield, C. and G. Biddle. *The Canals of North-west England* (Newton Abbot: David and Charles, 1970).

Haggett, P. *Geography: A Modern Synthesis* (London: Harper and Row, 1972).

Hall, J. *A History of the Town and Parish of Nantwich* (Nantwich: printed for the author, 1883).

Harley, C. K. 'British industrialisation before 1841: evidence of slower growth during the industrial revolution', *Journal of Economic History*, 42:2 (1982), 267–89.

Harley, C. K. and N. F. R. Crafts. 'Simulating the two views of the British industrial revolution', *Journal of Economic History*, 60:4 (2000), 819–41.

Hatcher J. and T. Barker. *A History of British Pewter* (London: Longman, 1974).

Hawke, G. 'Reinterpretations of the industrial revolution', in P. O'Brien and R. Quinault (eds) *Industrial Revolution and British Society* (Cambridge: Cambridge University Press, 1993), pp. 54–78.

Hayter, R. *The Dynamics of Industrial Location: The Factory, the Firm and the Production System* (Chichester: Wiley, 1998).

Heaton, H. *The Yorkshire Woollen and Worsted Industries from Earliest Times up to the Industrial Revolution* (Oxford: Clarendon Press, 1920).

Heaton, H. 'Industrial Revolution', in *Encyclopaedia of the Social Sciences, VIII* (New York: Macmillan, 1933).

Hemingway, J. *History of the City of Chester*, 2 volumes (Chester: J. Fletcher, 1831).

Hewitson, A. *History of Preston* (1883; reprinted Wakefield: SR Publishers, 1969).

Hey, D. *The Rural Metalworkers of the Sheffield Region* (Leicester: Department of English Local History, University of Leicester, 1972).

Hodson, J. H. *Cheshire 1660–1780: Restoration to the Industrial Revolution* (Chester: Cheshire Community Council, 1978).

Holderness, B. A. 'Credit in English rural society before the nineteenth century', *Agricultural History Review*, 24:1 (1976), 97–109.

Hudson, J. *Plain Directions for Making Wills in Conformity with the Law* (London: Longman, 1838).

Hudson, P. *The Genesis of Industrial Capital: A Study of the West Riding Wool Textiles Industry* (Cambridge: Cambridge University Press, 1982).

Hudson, P. 'The regional perspective', in P. Hudson (ed.) *Regions and Industries* (Cambridge: Cambridge University Press, 1989), pp. 5–38.

Hudson, P. 'Capital and credit in the West Riding wool textile industry c.1750–1850', in P. Hudson (ed.) *Regions and Industries* (Cambridge: Cambridge University Press, 1989), pp. 69–99.

Hudson, P. *The Industrial Revolution* (London: Arnold, 1992).

Hudson, P. 'Proto-industrialization in England', in S. Ogilvie and M. Cerman (eds) *European Proto-industrialization* (Cambridge: Cambridge University Press, 1996), pp. 49–66.

Hudson, P. 'Regional and local history: globalisation, postmoderism and the future', *Journal of Regional and Local Studies*, 20:1 (1999), 5–24.

Hudson, P. (ed.) *Regions and Industries* (Cambridge: Cambridge University Press, 1989).

Hudson, P. and S. King. 'Rural industrializing townships and urban links in eighteenth-century Yorkshire', in P. Clark and P. Corfield (eds) *Industry and Urbanization in Eighteenth-century England* (Leicester: Centre for Urban History, University of Leicester, 1994), pp. 41–79.

Hudson, P. and S. King. 'Two textile townships, c.1660–1820: a comparative demographic analysis', *Economic History Review*, 53:4 (2000), 706–41.

Hyde, C. *Technological Change in the British Iron Industry* (Princeton: Guilford, 1977).

Hyde, F. *Liverpool and the Mersey: An Economic History of a Port 1700–1970* (Newton Abbot: David and Charles, 1971).

Jackson, G. 'What was the rate of economic growth during the industrial revolution?', in G. Snooks (ed.) *Was the Industrial Revolution Necessary?* (London: Routledge, 1994), pp. 79–95.

Jackson, G. 'Ports 1700–1840', in P. Clark (ed.) *The Cambridge Urban History of Britain, volume II 1540–1840* (Cambridge: Cambridge University Press, 2000), pp. 705–31.

Jefferson, M. 'The law of the primate city' *Geographical Review*, 29 (1939), 226–32.

Johnson, B. 'The Foley partnerships', *Economic History Review*, 4:3 (1951), 322–40.

Johnson, G. 'Rank-size convexity and system integration: a view from archaeology', *Economic Geography*, 56:3 (1980), 234–47.

Jones, E. 'Environment, agriculture and industry', *Agricultural History*, 51 (1977), 491–502.

Jones, E. and M. Falkus, 'Urban improvement and the English economy in the seventeenth and eighteenth centuries', reproduced in P. Borsay (ed.) *The Eighteenth Century Town, 1688–1820: A Reader in English Urban History* (London: Longman, 1990), pp. 116–58.

Jones, G. *Modern Wales: A Concise History* (Cambridge: Cambridge University Press, 1984).

Kellet, J. The *Impact of Railways on Victorian Cities* (London: Routledge and Keegan Paul, 1969).

Kennett, A. (ed.) *Georgian Chester* (Chester: Chester City Record Office, 1987).

Kenny, S. 'The location and organisation of the early Lancashire cotton industry: a systems approach', *Manchester Geographer*, 3 (1982), 5–27.

King, P. 'The Vale Royal Company and its rivals', *Transactions, Historic Society of Lancashire and Cheshire*, 142 (1992), 1–18.

King, S. 'Migrants at the margin? Mobility, integration and occupations in the West Riding, 1650–1820', *Journal of Historical Geography*, 23:3 (1997), 284–303.

King S. and G. Timmins. *Making Sense of the Industrial Revolution: English Economy and Society 1700–1850* (Manchester: Manchester University Press, 2001).

King, W. 'The economic and demographic development of Rossendale, c.1650–1795', unpublished PhD thesis, University of Leicester, 1979.

Knox P. and J. Agnew. *The Geography of the World Economy* (London: Arnold, third edition, 1998).

Kowalewski, S. 'The evolution of primate regional systems', *Comparative Urban Research*, 11 (1982), 60–78.

Kriedte, P., H. Medick and J. Schlumbohm, *Industrialization before Industrialization: Rural Industry in the Genesis of Capitalism* (Cambridge: Cambridge University Press, 1981).

Krugman, P. *Geography and Trade* (Cambridge, MA: MIT Press, 1991).

Krugman, P. *Development, Geography and Economic Theory* (Cambridge, MA: MIT Press, 1995).

Kussmaul, A. *A General View of the Rural Economy of England, 1538–1840* (Cambridge: Cambridge University Press, 1990).

Lane, P. 'An industrialising town: social and business networks in Hinckley, Leicestershire c.1750–1839', in J. Stobart and P. Lane (eds) *Urban and Industrial Change in the Midlands, 1700–1840* (Leicester: Centre for Urban History, University of Leicester, 2000), pp. 139–66.

Langford, P. *A Polite and Commerical People: England 1727–1783* (Oxford: Clarendon Press, 1992).

Langton, J. 'Industry and towns 1500–1730', in R. A. Dodgshon and R. A. Butlin (eds) *An Historical Geography of England and Wales* (London: Academic Press, 1978), pp. 173–98.

Langton, J. *Geographical Change and Industrial Revolution: Coalmining in South-West Lancashire, 1590–1799* (Cambridge: Cambridge University Press, 1979).

Langton, J. 'Liverpool and its hinterland in the late eighteenth century', in B. L. Anderson and P. Stoney (eds) *Commerce, Industry and Transport: Studies in Economic Change on Merseyside* (Liverpool: Liverpool University Press, 1983), pp. 1–25.

Langton, J. 'The industrial revolution and the regional geography of England', *Transactions, Institute of British Geographers*, 9:2 (1984), 145–67.

Langton, J. 'The continuity of regional culture: Lancashire Catholicism from the late sixteenth to the early nineteenth century', in E. Royle (ed.) *Issues of Regional Identity* (Manchester: Manchester University Press, 1997), pp. 82–101.

Langton, J. 'Proletarianization in the industrial revolution: regionalism and kinship in the labour markets of the British coal industry from the seventeenth to the nineteenth centuries', *Transactions, Institute of British Geographers*, 25:1 (2000), 31–50.

Langton, J. 'Town growth and urbanisation in the Midlands', in J. Stobart and P. Lane (eds) *Urban and Industrial Change in the Midlands, 1700–1840* (Leicester: Centre for Urban History, University of Leicester, 2000), pp. 7–48.

Langton, J. 'Urban growth and economic change from the seventeenth century to 1841', in P. Clark (ed.) *The Cambridge Urban History of Britain, volume II 1540–1840* (Cambridge: Cambridge University Press, 2000), pp. 453–90.

Langton, J. 'John Mackay', in C. Matthew, *The New Dictionary of National Biography* (Oxford: Oxford University Press, forthcoming).

Langton, J. 'Sir Roger Bradshaigh', in C. Matthew, *The New Dictionary of National Biography* (Oxford: Oxford University Press, forthcoming).

Langton, J. and R. J. Morris (eds). *Atlas of Industrializing Britain, 1780–1914* (London: Methuen, 1986).

Large, P. 'Urban growth and agricultural change in the West Midlands during the seventeenth and eighteenth centuries', in P. Clark (ed.) *The Transformation of English Provincial Towns 1600–1800* (London: Hutchinson, 1984), pp. 169–89.

Larson, S. *The Rise of Professionalism: A Sociological Analysis* (Berkeley: University of California Press, 1977).

Law, C. M. 'Some notes on the urban population of eighteenth-century England', *Local Historian*, 10 (1972), 13–26.

Lawton, R. and C. Pooley. *Britain 1740–1950: An Historical Geography* (London: Arnold, 1992).

Laxton, P. 'Textiles', in J. Langton and R. J. Morris (eds) *Atlas of Industrializing Britain, 1780–1914* (London: Methuen, 1986), pp. 106–23.

Lee, R. 'Making Europe: towards a geography of European integration', in M. Chisholm and D. Smith (eds) *Shared Space: Divided Space* (London: Unwin Hyman, 1990), pp. 325–59.

Leibowitz, S. and S. Margolis. 'Path dependence, lock-in, and history', *Journal of Law, Economics and Organization*, 11:1 (1995), 205–26.

Lemire, B. *Fashion's Favourite: The Cotton Trade and the Consumer in Britain, 1660–1800* (Oxford: Oxford University Press, 1991).

Lepetit, B. *The Pre-industrial Urban System: France, 1740–1840* (Cambridge: Cambridge University Press, 1994).

Levine, D. and K. Wrightson. *The Making of an Industrial Society: Whickham, 1560–1765* (Oxford: Oxford University Press, second edition, 1991).

Lewis, C. R. 'The central place patterns of mid-Wales and the middle Welsh borderland', in H. Carter and W. K. D. Davies (eds) *Urban Essays: Studies in the Geography of Wales* (London: Longman, 1970), pp. 228–68.

Lindert, P. 'English occupations, 1670–1811', *Journal of Economic History*, 40:4 (1980), 695–712.

Lloyd-Jones, R. and M. Lewis, 'The economic structure of "Cottonopolis": Manchester in 1815', *Textile History*, 17:1 (1986), 71–89.

Lloyd-Prichard, M. 'The decline of Norwich', *Economic History Review*, 3:3 (1950), 371–7.

Lösch, A. (translated by W. Woglom and W. Stopler), *The Economics of Location* (New Haven: Yale University Press, 1954).

Lysons, D. and S. Lysons. *Magna Britannia, A Concise Topographical Account of the Several Counties of Great Britain* (London: T. Cadell and W. Davies, 1806–22).

Mager, W. 'Proto-industrialization and proto-industry: the uses and drawbacks of two concepts', *Continuity and Change*, 8:2 (1993), 181–215.

Malet, H. *Bridgewater, the Canal Duke* (Manchester: Manchester University Press, 1977).

Mallet, J. 'John Baddeley of Shelton', *English Ceramic Circle, Transactions*, 6:2 (1966), 124–66.

Mann, J. de L. *The Cloth Industry in the West of England* (Oxford: Oxford University Press, 1971).

Marshall, J. *The Location of Service Towns: An Approach to the Analysis of Central Place Systems* (Toronto: University of Toronto Press, 1969).

Mass Observation, *Browns and Chester: Portrait of a Shop, 1780–1946* (London: L. Drummond, 1947).

Massey, D. *Spatial Divisions of Labour: Social Structures and the Geography of Production* (Basingstoke: Macmillan, second edition, 1995).

Mathias, P. *The First Industrial Nation: An Economic History of Britain, 1700–1914* (London: Routledge, second edition, 1983).

McCracken, G. *Culture and Consumption: New Approaches to the Symbolic Character of Consumer Goods and Activities* (Bloomington: Indiana University Press, 1988).

McGrath, P. *Bristol in the Eighteenth Century* (Newton Abbot: David and Charles, 1972).

McInnes, A. 'The emergence of a leisure town: Shrewsbury 1660–1760', *Past and Present*, 120:1 (1988), 53–87.

McKendrick, N. 'The consumer revolution of eighteenth-century England', in N. McKendrick, J. Brewer and J. Plumb (eds) *The Birth of a Consumer Society: The Commercialisation of Eighteenth-Century England* (London: Methuen, 1982), pp. 9–33.

McKendrick, N. 'Josiah Wedgwood and the commercialisation of the Potteries', in N. McKendrick, J. Brewer and J. Plumb (eds) *The Birth of a Consumer Society: The Commercialisation of Eighteenth-Century England* (London: Methuen, 1982), pp. 100–45.

McKendrick, N. 'George Packwood and the commercialisation of shaving: the art of eighteenth-century advertising', in N. McKendrick, J. Brewer and J. Plumb (eds) *The Birth of a Consumer Society: The Commercialisation of Eighteenth-Century England* (London: Methuen, 1982), pp. 146–94.

Mendels, F. 'Proto-industrialization: the first phase of the industrialization process', *Journal of Economic History*, 32:3 (1972), 241–61.

Mendels, F. 'Proto-industrialization: theory and reality. General report', Eighth International Economic History Congress, Budapest (1982), pp. 69–107.

Minchinton, W. 'Bristol – metropolis of the west in the eighteenth century', *Transactions, Royal Historical Society*, 5th series, 4 (1954), 69–89.

Mitchell, I. 'The development of urban retailing 1700–1815', in P. Clark (ed.) *The Transformation of English Provincial Towns 1600–1800* (London: Hutchinson, 1984), pp. 259–83.

Moffit, L. *England on the Eve of the Industrial Revolution* (London: P. S. King and Son, 1925).

Mokyr, J. 'Has the industrial revolution been crowded out?', *Explorations in Economic History*, 24:3 (1987), 293–319.

Mokyr, J. 'Technological change, 1700–1830', in R. Floud and D. McCloskey (eds) *The Economic History of Britain since 1700, Volume 1: 1700–1860* (Cambridge: Cambridge University Press, second edition, 1994), pp. 12–43.

Moran, D. 'Pewtermaking in Wigan 1650–1750: urban industry before the Industrial Revolution', *Journal of Regional and Local Studies*, 19:1 (1997), 1–22.

Morris, C. (ed.). *The Journeys of Celia Fiennes* (London: Cresset Press, 1947).

Mountford, A. R. 'Thomas Wedgwood, John Wedgwood and Jonah Malkin, potters of Burslem' unpublished MA thesis, Keele University (1972).

Mui, H. and L. Mui. *Shops and Shopkeeping in Eighteenth Century England* (London: Routledge, 1989).

Muir, R. *A History of Liverpool* (London: Liverpool University Press, 1907).

Muldrew, C. *The Economy of Obligation: The Culture of Credit and Social Relations in Early-Modern England* (Basingstoke: Macmillan, 1998).

Musson, A. *The Growth of British Industry* (London: Batsford, 1978).

Myrdal, G. *Economic Theory and Under-developed Regions* (London: Duckworth, 1957).

Neal, L. 'The finance of business during the industrial revolution', in R. Floud and D. McCloskey (eds) *The Economic History of Britain since 1700, Volume 1: 1700–1860* (Cambridge: Cambridge University Press, second edition, 1994), pp. 151–81.

Nef, J. *The Rise of the British Coal Industry*, 2 volumes (London: Routledge and Sons, 1932).

Nef, J. 'The progress of technology and the growth of large-scale industry in Great Britain 1540–1640', *Economic History Review*, 5:1 (1934), 3–24.

Nef, J. 'The Industrial Revolution reconsidered', *Journal of Economic History*, 3:1 (1943), pp. 1–31.

Noble, M. 'Growth and development in a regional urban system', *Urban History Yearbook* (1987), 1–19.

O'Brien, P. and R. Quinault (eds). *The Industrial Revolution and British Society* (Cambridge: Cambridge University Press, 1993).

Ogborn, M. *Spaces of Modernity: London's Geographies, 1660–1780* (New York: Guilford Press, 1998).

Ogborn, M. 'Historical geographies of modernisation', in B. Graham and C. Nash (eds) *Modern Historical Geographies* (Harlow: Prentice Hall, 2000), pp. 43–69.

Ogilvie, S. 'Social institutions and proto-industrialization', in S. Ogilvie and M. Cerman (eds) *European Proto-industrialization* (Cambridge: Cambridge University Press, 1996), pp. 23–37.

Owens, A. '"The duty and paramount obligation of every considerate and rational man": property, will-making and estate disposal in an industrial town, 1800–1857', in J. Stobart and A. Owens (eds) *Urban Fortunes: Property and Inheritance in the Town c.1700–1900* (Aldershot: Ashgate, 2000), pp. 79–107.

Owens, W. *Owen's Book of Fairs in England and Wales* (London: no publisher given, new edition, 1756).

Paasi, A. 'The institutionalization of regions: a theoretical framework for understanding the emergence of regions and the constitution of regional identity', *Fennia*, 164 (1986), 105–46.

Paasi, A. 'Deconstructing regions: notes on the scales of spatial life', *Environment and Planning A*, 23 (1991), 239–56.

Parkinson, C. *The Rise of the Port of Liverpool* (Liverpool: Liverpool University Press, 1952).

Patten, J. 'Urban occupations in pre-industrial England', *Transactions, Institute of British Geographers*, 2:3 (1977), 296–313.

Patten, J. *English Towns, 1500–1700* (Folkestone: Dawson, 1978).

Pawson, E. *Transport and Economy: The Turnpike Roads of Eighteenth Century Britain* (London: Academic Press, 1977).

Peet, R. 'The cultural production of economic forms', in R. Lee and J. Wills (eds) *Geographies of Economies* (London: Arnold, 1997), pp. 37–46.

Pennell, S. 'Consumption and consumerism in early modern England', *The Historical Journal*, 42:2 (1999), 549–64.

Percival, T. 'Observations on the state of population in Manchester', reproduced in B. Benjamin (ed.) *Population and Disease in Early-Industrial England* (London: Gregg International, 1973), pp. 1–67.

Perkins, E. 'The consumer frontier: household consumption in early Kentucky', *Journal of American History*, 78:2 (1991), 486–510.

Phillips, C. B. and J. H. Smith. *Lancashire and Cheshire from AD1540* (London: Arnold, 1994).

Picton, J. *Memorials of Liverpool*, 2 volumes (London: Longmans Green, 1873).

Picton, J. *City of Liverpool: Municipal Archives and Records, 1700–1835* (Liverpool: Walmsley, 1886).

Pigot, J. and R. Dean. *Pigot and Dean's Manchester and Salford Directory for 1815* (Manchester: R. and W. Dean, 1815).

Platt, J. *The History and Antiquities of Nantwich* (London: Longman et al., 1818).

Pollard, S. *European Economic Integration, 1815–1970* (London: Thames and Hudson, 1974).

Pollard, S. *Peaceful Conquest: The Industrialization of Europe 1760–1970* (Oxford: Oxford University Press, 1981).

Pollard, S. 'Economic development: national or regional?', *ReFRESH*, 18 (1994).

Porteous, J. *Canal Ports: The Urban Achievement of the Canal Age* (London: Academic Press, 1977).

Pound, J. F. 'The validity of the freemen's lists: some Norwich evidence', *Economic History Review*, 34:1 (1981), 48–59.

Power, M. 'Councillors and commerce in Liverpool, 1650–1750', *Urban History*, 24:3 (1997), 301–23.

Pred, A. *City Systems in Advanced Economies* (London: Hutchinson, 1977).

Pressnell, L. *Country Banking in the Industrial Revolution* (Oxford: Clarendon Press, 1956).

Price, J. 'What did merchants do? Reflection on British overseas trade, 1660–1790', *Journal of Economic History*, 49:2 (1989), 267–84.

Raffald, E. *Directory of Manchester and Salford* (1773; reprinted Manchester: Manchester Press Co., 1889).

Randall, A. 'Work, culture and resistance to machinery in the West of England woollen industry', in P. Hudson (ed.) *Regions and Industries* (Cambridge: Cambridge University Press, 1989), pp. 175–98.

Richards, E. 'Margins of the industrial revolution', in P. O'Brien and R. Quinault *Industrial Revolution and British Society* (Cambridge: Cambridge University Press, 1993), pp. 203–28.

Richardson, H. W. *Regional Growth Theory* (London: Macmillan, 1973).

Richardson, H. W. *Regional and Urban Economics* (Harmondsworth: Penguin, 1978).

Riden, P. 'Iron and steel', in J. Langton and R. J. Morris (eds) *Atlas of Industrializing Britain, 1780–1914* (London: Methuen, 1986), pp. 127–31.

Robson, B. *Urban Growth: An Approach* (London: Methuen, 1973).

Rodgers, H. 'The market areas of Preston in the sixteenth and seventeenth centuries', *Geographical Studies*, 3 (1956), pp. 46–93.

Rowlands, M. *Masters and Men in the West Midland Metalware Trades before the Industrial Revolution* (Manchester: Manchester University Press, 1975).

Rozman, G. 'Urban networks and historical stages', *Journal of Interdisciplinary History*, 9 (1978), 65–91.

Schwarz, S. 'Economic change in north-east Lancashire, c.1660–1760', *Transactions, Historic Society of Lancashire and Cheshire*, 144 (1995), 47–94.

Scola, R. *Feeding the Victorian City: The Food Supply of Manchester 1770–1870* (Manchester: Manchester University Press, 1992).

Scott, A. *Regions and the World Economy: The Coming Shape of Global Production, Competition and Political Order* (Oxford: Oxford University Press, 1998).

Scott, A. 'Capitalism, cities and the production of symbolic forms', *Transactions, Institute of British Geographers*, 26:1 (2001), 11–23.

Scott, A. and M. Storper. *Production, Work, Territory: The Geographical Anatomy of Industrial Capitalism* (London: Allen and Unwin, 1986).

Scrivenor, H. *History of the Iron Trade* (London, 1854; reprinted Bath: C. Chivers, 1968).

Sellar, W. and R. Yeatman. *1066 and All That* (London, 1930; Harlow: Penguin edition, 1960).

Shammas, C. *The Pre-industrial Consumer in England and America* (Oxford: Clarendon Press, 1990).

Sharpe, P. 'De-industrialization and re-industrialization: women's employment and the changing character of Colchester, 1700–1850', *Urban History*, 21:1 (1994), 77–96.

Sharpe-Francis, R. 'The highway from Preston into the Fylde', *Transactions, Historic Society of Lancashire and Cheshire*, 97 (1945), 27–58.

Shaw, G. 'The evolution and impact of large-scale retailing in Britain', in J. Benson and G. Shaw (eds) *The Evolution of Retailing Systems* (Leicester: Leicester University Press, 1992), pp. 135–65.

Shelley, R. 'Wigan and Liverpool pewterers', *Transactions, Historic Society of Lancashire and Cheshire*, 97 (1945), 3–15.

Short, B. 'The de-industrialisation process: a case study of the Weald, 1600–1850', in P. Hudson (ed.) *Regions and Industries* (Cambridge: Cambridge University Press, 1989), pp. 156–74.

Simmons, J. W. 'The organization of the urban system', in L. S. Bourne and J. W. Simmons (eds) *Systems of Cities: Readings on Structure, Growth, and Policy* (New York: Oxford University Press, 1978), pp. 61–9.

Smith, A. *An Enquiry into the Nature and Causes of the Wealth of Nations* (1776; reprinted in two volumes, Oxford: Oxford University Press, 1976).

Smith, C. 'Modern and pre-modern urban primacy', *Comparative Urban Research*, 11 (1982), 79–96.

Smith, J. H. 'The development of the English felt and silk hat trades, 1500–1912', unpublished PhD thesis, University of Manchester, 1980.

Smith, S. D. 'Market for manufactures in the thirteen continental colonies', *Economic History Review*, 51:4 (1998), 676–708.

Soja, E. *Postmodern Geographies: The Reassertion of Space in Critical Social Theory* (London: Verso, 1989).

Sprunt, W. 'Old Warrington trades and occupations', *Transactions, Lancashire and Cheshire Antiquarian Society*, 61 (1949), 167–9.

Spufford, M. *The Great Reclothing of Rural England: Petty Chapmen and their Wares in the Seventeenth Century* (London: Hambledon Press, 1984).

Stephens, W. *History of Congleton* (Manchester: Manchester University Press, 1970).

Stobart, J. 'An eighteenth-century revolution? Investigating urban growth in north-west England, 1664–1801', *Urban History*, 23:1 (1996), 26–47.

Stobart, J. 'Geography and industrialization: the space economy of northwest England, 1701–1760', *Transactions, Institute of British Geographers*, 21:4 (1996), 681–96.

Stobart, J. 'Shopping streets as social space: leisure, consumerism and improvement in an eighteenth-century county town', *Urban History*, 25:1 (1998), 3–21.

Stobart, J. 'Textile industries in north-west England in the early eighteenth century: a geographical approach', *Textiles History*, 29:1 (1998), 3–18.

Stobart, J. 'In search of causality: a regional approach to urban growth in eighteenth-century England', *Geografiska Annaler*, 82B:3 (2000), 149–63.

Stobart, J. 'Social and geographical contexts of property transmission in the eighteenth century', in J. Stobart and A. Owens (eds) *Urban Fortunes: Property and Inheritance in the Town c.1700–1900* (Aldershot: Ashgate, 2000), pp. 108–30.

Stobart, J. 'In search of a leisure hierarchy: English spa towns in the urban system', in P. Borsay, G. Hirschfelder and R. Mohrmann (eds) *New Directions in Urban History. Aspects of European Urban Cultural Life: In the Mirror of Art, Health and Tourism* (New York: Waxmann, 2000), pp. 19–40.

Stobart, J. 'Regions, localities and industrialisation: evidence from the east midlands circa 1780–1840', *Environment and Planning A*, 33 (2001), 1305–25.

Stobart, J. 'County, town and country: three histories of urban development in eighteenth-century Chester', in P. Borsay and L. Proudfoot (eds) *Provincial Towns in Early Modern England and Ireland: Change, Convergence and Divergence* (Proceedings of the British Academy, volume 108, 2002), pp. 171–94.

Stobart, J. 'Culture versus commerce: societies and spaces for elites in eighteenth-century Liverpool', *Journal of Historical Geography*, 28:4 (2002), pp. 471–85.

Stobart, J. and P. Lane (eds). *Urban and Industrial Change in the Midlands, 1700–1840* (Leicester: Centre for Urban History, University of Leicester, 2000).

Stone, L. *The Family, Sex and Marriage in England, 1500–1800* (Harmondsworth: Penguin, 1979).

Storper, M. *The Regional World: Territorial Development in a Global Economy* (New York: Guilford, 1997).

Styles, J. 'Clothing the North: the supply of non-elite clothing in the eighteenth-century north of England', *Textile History*, 25:2 (1994), 139–66.

Swain, J. *Industry before the Industrial Revolution* (Manchester: Chetham Society, 1986).

Sweet, R. *The Writing of Urban Histories in Eighteenth-Century England* (Oxford: Clarendon Press, 1997).

Sweet, R. *The English Town 1680–1840: Government, Society and Culture* (London: Longman, 1999).

Tann, J. 'Fuel saving in the process industries during the industrial revolution: a study in technical diffusion', *Business History*, 25:2 (1973), 149–59.

Thirsk, J. 'Industries in the countryside', in F. J. Fisher (ed.) *Essays in the Economic and Social History of Tudor and Stuart England* (Cambridge: Cambridge University Press, 1961), pp. 70–88.

Thrift, N. 'Transport and communication, 1730–1914', in R. A. Dodgshon and R. A. Butlin (eds) *An Historical Geography of England and Wales* (London: Academic Press, second edition, 1990), pp. 453–86.

Thrift, N. 'Inhuman geographies: landscapes of speed, light and power', in N. Thrift (ed.) *Spatial Formations* (London: Sage, 1996), pp. 256–310.

Timmins, G. *Made in Lancashire: A History of Regional Industrialisation* (Manchester: Manchester University Press, 1998).

Towner, J. *An Historical Geography of Recreation and Tourism in the Western World, 1540–1940* (Chichester: Wiley, 1996).

Trinder, B. *The Industrial Revolution in Shropshire* (Chichester: Phillimore, 1973).

Trinder, B. 'Industrialising towns', in P. Clark (ed.) *The Cambridge Urban History of Britain, volume II 1540–1840* (Cambridge: Cambridge University Press, 2000), pp. 805–30.

Trinder, B. and J. Cox. *Yeomen and Colliers in Telford* (London: Phillimore, 1980).

Troughton, T. *The History of Liverpool* (Liverpool: W. Robinson, 1810).

Tupling, G. *The Economic History of Rossendale* (Manchester: Manchester University Press, 1927).

Tupling, G. 'The early metal trades and the beginnings of engineering in Lancashire', *Transactions, Lancashire and Cheshire Antiquarian Society*, 61 (1949), 1–35.

Turnbull, G. 'Provincial road carrying in England in the eighteenth century', *Journal of Transport History*, 4:1 (1977), 17–39.

Turnbull, G. 'Canals, coal and regional growth during the industrial revolution', *Economic History Review*, 40:4 (1987), 537–60.

Universal British Dictionary (UBD), P. Barfoot and J. Wilkes, 5 volumes (London: Barfoot and Wilkes, 1793–98).

Unwin, G. *Industrial Organisation in the Sixteenth and Seventeenth Centuries* (Oxford: Clarendon Press, 1904).

Unwin, G. *Samuel Oldknow and the Arkwrights* (Manchester: Manchester University Press, 1924).

Vance, J. E. *The Merchant's World: The Geography of Wholesaling* (Englewood Cliffs: Prentice Hall, 1970).

Vardi, L. *The Land and the Loom: Peasants and Profit in Northern France 1680–1800* (London: Duke University Press, 1993).

Vidal de la Blache, P. (translated by M. Todd) *Principles of Human Geography* (London: Constable, 1926).

Von Tunzelman, G. 'Technological and organizational change in industry during the Industrial Revolution', in P. O'Brien and R. Quinault (eds) *The Industrial Revolution and British Society* (Cambridge: Cambridge University Press, 1993), pp. 254–82.

Wadsworth, A. 'The history of the Rochdale woollen trade', *Transactions of the Rochdale Literary and Sicentific Society*, 15 (1923–25), 90–110.

Wadsworth, A. and J. de L. Mann. *The Cotton Trade and Industrial Lancashire, 1600–1780* (Manchester: Manchester University Press, 1931).

Wallace, J. *A General and Descriptive History of Liverpool* (Liverpool: Phillips 1795).

Wallwork, K. 'The mid-Cheshire salt industry', *Geography*, 44 (1959), 171–86.

Walsh, C. 'Shop design and the display of goods in eighteenth-century London', *Journal of Design History*, 8 (1995), 157–76.

Walton, J. K. *Lancashire: A Social History* (Manchester: Manchester University Press, 1987).

Walton, J. K. 'Proto-industrialisation and the first industrial revolution: the case of Lancashire', in P. Hudson (ed.) *Regions and Industries* (Cambridge: Cambridge University Press, 1989), pp. 41–68.

Warren, K. 'Chemicals', in J. Langton and R. J. Morris (eds), *Atlas of Industrializing Britain, 1780–1914* (London: Methuen, 1986), pp. 114–18.

Weatherill, L. *The Pottery Trade and North Staffordshire, 1660–1760* (Manchester: Manchester University Press, 1971).

Weatherill, L. 'The business of middlemen in the English pottery trade before 1780', in R. Davenport-Hines and J. Liebenau (eds) *Business in the Age of Reason* (London: Frank Cass, 1987), pp. 51–76.

Weatherill, L. *Consumer Behaviour and Material Culture in Britain, 1660–1760* (London: Routledge, second edition, 1996).

Whyte, I. 'Proto-industrialisation in Scotland', in P. Hudson (ed.) *Regions and Industries* (Cambridge: Cambridge University Press, 1989), pp. 228–51.

Willan, T. *The Navigation of the River Weaver in the Eighteenth-Century* (Manchester: Cheetham Society, 1951).

Williamson, J. 'Coping with city growth', in R. Floud and D. McCloskey (eds) *The*

Economic History of Britain since 1700, Volume 1: 1700–1860 (Cambridge: Cambridge University Press, second edition, 1994), pp. 332–56.

Willshaw, E. 'The inns of Chester, 1775–1832', unpublished MA thesis, University of Leicester, 1979.

Wilson, A. 'The cultural identity of Liverpool, 1790–1850: the early learned societies', *Transactions, Historic Society of Lancashire and Cheshire*, 147 (1997), 55–80.

Wilson, R. 'The supremacy of the Yorkshire cloth industry in the eighteenth century', in N. Harte and K. Ponting (eds), *Textile History and Economic History* (Manchester: Manchester University Press, 1973), pp. 225–46.

Wrightson, K. 'Kinship in an English village: Terling, Essex 1550–1700', in R. Smith (ed.) *Land, Kinship and Life-Cycle* (Cambridge: Cambridge University Press, 1984), pp. 313–32.

Wrighson, K. and D. Levine. *Poverty and Piety in an English Village: Terling 1525–1700* (Oxford: Oxford University Press, second edition, 1995).

Wrigley, E. A. 'The supply of raw materials in the industrial revolution', *Economic History Review*, 15:1 (1962), 1–16.

Wrigley, E. A. 'Parasite or stimulus: the town in a pre-industrial economy', in P. Abrams and E. A. Wrigley (eds) *Towns in Societies: Essays in Economic History and Historical Sociology* (Cambridge: Cambridge University Press, 1978), pp. 295–309.

Wrigley, E. A. 'A simple model of London's importance in changing english society and economy 1650–1750', reproduced in E. A. Wrigley (ed.), *People, Cities and Wealth* (Cambridge: Cambridge University Press, 1987), pp. 133–56.

Wrigley, E. A. *Continuity, Chance and Change* (Cambridge: Cambridge University Press, 1988).

Wrigley, E. A. 'Urban growth and agricultural change: England and the Continent in the early-modern period', reproduced in P. Borsay (ed.) *The Eighteenth Century Town, 1688–1820: A Reader in English Urban History* (London: Longman, 1990), pp. 39–82.

Wrigley, E. A. 'The classical economists, the stationary state and the industrial revolution', in G. Snooks (ed.) *Was the Industrial Revolution Necessary?* (London: Routledge, 1994), pp. 27–42.

Wyatt, G. 'Nantwich and Wybunbury, 1680–1819: a demographic study of two Cheshire parishes', *Transactions, Historic Society of Lancashire and Cheshire*, 139 (1990), pp. 1–30.

Young, A. *A Six Months Tour through the North of England*, 3 volumes (London: Strahan, second edition, 1771).

Zell, M. *Industry in the Countryside: Wealden Society in the Sixteenth Century* (Cambridge: Cambridge University Press, 1994).

Zell, M. 'Credit in the pre-industrial English woollen industry', *Economic History Review*, 49:4 (1996), 667–91.

Zipf, G. K. *National Unity and Disunity* (Bloomington: Principia Press, 1941).

Index